Lonely Planet Publications
Melbourne | Oakland | London

Christmas 2006
Love from
Elaine and Harry

Andrew Bender

Amsterdam

D0973413

The Top Five

1 Red Light District
Walk around one of the prettiest districts in Amsterdam (p66-8)

2 Eastern Docklands
See the future of architecture today (p46)

3 Museumplein
Dose up on culture at the museums surrounding this park (p95)

4 Canals
Explore the city on a boat tour (p60-1)

5 Albert Cuypmarkt
Shop for anything at Amsterdam's biggest street market (p107)

Contents

Published by Lonely Planet Publications Pty Ltd
ABN 36 005 607 983

Australia Head Office, Locked Bag 1, Footscray,
Victoria 3011, ☎ 03 8379 8000, fax 03 8379 8111,
talk2us@lonelyplanet.com.au

USA 150 Linden St, Oakland, CA 94607,
☎ 510 893 8555, toll free 800 275 8555,
fax 510 893 8572, info@lonelyplanet.com

UK 72–82 Rosebery Ave, Clerkenwell, London,
EC1R 4RW, ☎ 020 7841 9000, fax 020 7841 9001,
go@lonelyplanet.co.uk

The Author

Andrew Bender

Born in New England and schooled in Philadelphia, Andy has lived in France, Tokyo and now Los Angeles, but he's considered Amsterdam his spiritual home since he first swapped biking at the beach for biking the canals. That bond has only grown since he wrote the previous edition of this book. Yet another Lonely Planet author with an MBA, he did what every MBA secretly dreams of – get out of the business world and see the real world. His writing has since appeared in the *Los Angeles Times*, *Travel + Leisure*, *Departures*, *Men's Journal*, in-flight magazines and several Lonely Planet guides. When not on the road, he still bikes at the beach, consults on cross-cultural communication, makes valiant efforts to keep up with friends and family, obsesses over Korean and Japanese food and schemes over ways to spoil his nieces and nephews. You can see more of his work at www.andrewbender.com.

PHOTOGRAPHER
Richard Nebeský

Richard was not born with a camera in his hand; but, not long after, his father, an avid photo enthusiast, gave him his first happy snap unit. Ever since then, a camera was always by his side while skiing, cycling or researching Lonely Planet travel guidebooks around the globe. Work for various magazines and travel-guidebook publishers and plenty of social photography followed.

ANDY'S TOP AMSTERDAM DAY

It's a gorgeous blue sky above the rooftops of the Old South. I unlock both chains on the junky but trusty bike and ride through the stately Spiegel Quarter to a late breakfast in the Jordaan with a friend. We browse the Noordermarkt and swing down to the Negen Straatjes to window-shop. The bells of the Westerkerk remind us to break for coffee or a *biertje*, with its two perfect fingers of foam, in one of the nearby cafes.

The afternoon is for stretching out, and there's nowhere better than a grassy stretch in the Vondelpark, or people-watching at the Round Blue Teahouse.

Dinner is in Chinatown before the show at the Muziekgebouw aan 't IJ, which is also a good time to admire the architecture. Afterwards, we'll club, or at least chill, at 11, the rooftops of the whole city spread out at our feet and twilight's last orange glow over the harbour.

Introducing Amsterdam

Balloon animal, bandanna, boa, body paint, brassiere, cardigan, carrot, chador, crown, garland, grass skirt, hair dye, hat (innumerable permutations), jeans, lei, parka, pashmina, soccer scarf, tennis-racquet cover, tulip.

Visit Amsterdam on Queen's Day, the city-wide street party when spring is officially in the air and it never seems to rain, and this is just some of what you'll see people wearing. As wide-ranging as these adornments are, they all have one thing in common: they're orange, the national colour of the Netherlands.

It's a poignant yet subtle metaphor for this city's prevailing ethic: we're all individuals, yet we're in this together. Want to smoke dope? Do as you please. Hookers? We've got 'em. Same-sex marriage? Sure – what do you want as a wedding gift? Amsterdam has long been the most tolerant and, by many measures, the freest city in the world.

Recent events, however, have made Amsterdammers question whether there is such a thing as too much tolerance and whether freedom is always beneficial. Yet even this concern is in character: Amsterdam recognises that freedom's fraternal twin is responsibility – the responsibility not to harm or inconvenience others, and to afford others the same freedoms you have.

Being on the water – indeed being *of* the water – Amsterdam has always looked outwards. Its traders brought silks from Japan, porcelain from China, tea from Ceylon, coffee and cocoa; objects once foreign are now commonplace. With new goods came new people – Huguenots, Jews, Indonesians, Turks – and new words, ways and foods.

Since there was no royalty or church calling the shots for much of Amsterdam's history, trade, industry and populism came to rule. What's more, a can-do spirit led to a breezy confidence. Need more land? Go make some!

Amsterdam's also a place of clever beauty. Without a single internationally known building, it has looks that make Paris, London and even Venice jealous. A stroll along the western canals, through the lanes of the Jordaan or beneath the greenery of the Plantage can lead straight into a trance. The interplay of water and steeple, window and tree, brick and bridge, and roofline and sky can mesmerise.

One other element completes the picture, though it's as hard to define as it is to pronounce. It's called *gezelligheid*, translating somewhere between conviviality,

AMSTERDAM

NETHERLANDS

GERMANY

BELGIUM

LOWDOWN

Population 743,000 (plus an estimated 20,000 unregistered)
Bicycles 600,000 (estimated)
Time Zone Western European (GMT+1hr)
Windmills 6
Houseboats 2500
Three-star double hotel room around €125
Cup of coffee €1.75
Glass of Heineken €2
Tram ticket €1.60
Bicycle rental (day) €7
Van Gogh Museum admission €10
'Oral favours' in the Red Light District €30
No-no Walking on the bike path. What are you, suicidal?

friendliness, snugness, taking an interest, and wanting-to-be-around-others-but-not-so-much-that-you-make-a-pain-out-of-yourself.

But Amsterdam is about more than an attitude or a building or an object. It's about a moment: sipping a perfectly poured beer in a centuries-old 'brown café', biking with the wind against your skin and the cobblestones beneath your feet, losing yourself within Rembrandt's brushstrokes, cosying in a park, meditating on a bell gable, savouring the *gehakt* at a sandwich shop or a tomato-basil-chocolate bonbon, laughing at a drag queen or, better, laughing with her.

We love Amsterdam because it sweats the big stuff and doesn't worry about the small stuff. We love it because we've never had a bad time there. We love it because we don't know of a more relaxing city in northern Europe. And we're betting that in the long run tolerance, Amsterdam's greatest gift to the world, will triumph over adversity.

City Life

City Life

AMSTERDAM TODAY

Spokes.

It's hard to imagine Amsterdam without them.

We *could* talk about the spokes on bicycles, unavoidable on the city's streets – as you'll see from the moment you set foot. We could even say that, from the air, the city resembles a wheel, with its lovely semicircular canals around the centre and the radial canals forming its spokes.

Of course, all spokes lead to a hub, and that's the way this city has long thought of itself: the world's original melting pot. Immigration of Jews and Huguenots from the middle of the last millennium gave way to more recent immigration of Indonesians, Surinamese, Moroccans and Turks, just to name a few.

That fundamental self-concept was challenged on 2 November 2004, when the Dutch film-maker Theo van Gogh (see boxed text, p13) was assassinated on an Amsterdam street. It's not an exaggeration to say that it impacted the life of every Amsterdammer. Even though, on the surface, Amsterdam continues to go its merry way, you don't have to wait too long before the subject comes up and people become contemplative.

HOT CONVERSATION TOPICS

You're enjoying a beer with friends at a café overlooking a canal. What are you likely to hear?

- 'It took me forever to park my bike!'
- 'What are you getting Jakob and Pieter as a wedding gift?'
- 'I wish I could afford to live in the Canal Belt, but I bought a great flat in Bos en Lommer.'
- 'Let's go for a ride on my boat on Saturday.'
- 'Where's the after-party?'
- 'They're saying the new metro line will open in 2011. I wonder what they'll be saying in 2013!'
- 'I wonder if the smoking ban will ever take effect…'
- 'I hope my bike is still there.'

CITY CALENDAR

There's no bad time to visit Amsterdam. In any given month, there are festivals and celebrations. Queen's Day on 30 April is the biggest street party in the Netherlands, an unforgettable experience. Later in the year, when the weather warms up, Amsterdammers take to the streets and canalsides, and even restaurants with drop-dead interiors might move their seating outdoors. Summer abounds with open-air concerts, theatre and festivals, often free.

Noteworthy cultural events include the Holland Festival in June, Julidans in July and the quirky Parade and the Uitmarkt in August. Outdoors enthusiasts will want to take in National Cycling Day or one of the road races throughout the year.

A few of the events listed here are out of town but are worth the trip. Amsterdam RAI convention centre (www.rai.nl) also hosts trade shows throughout the year: arts, boats, film and horse-jumping events among them. Where no contact information is given, inquire at tourist offices (p259).

See p255 for a list of public holidays – when the city has a tendency to shut down.

TOP FIVE QUIRKY HOLIDAYS & EVENTS

- **Koninginnedag** (opposite) April
- **Luliak** (opposite) May
- **Gay Pride Canal Parade** (p10) August
- **Arrival of Sinterklaas** (p11) November
- **Cannabis Cup** (p11) November

JANUARY

ELFSTEDENTOCHT (ELEVEN CITIES' JOURNEY)

If it has been cold enough for long enough, this gruelling skating marathon through the countryside of Friesland attracts thousands of participants. They emerge from all over, since years may pass before conditions are right. When they are, it provides great relief from January's cold, dull, dark days.

FEBRUARY

CARNAVAL

A Catholic tradition, best enjoyed in the cities of southern Holland (especially Maastricht), that shows Amsterdammers also know how to don silly costumes and party for Carnaval.

COMMEMORATION OF THE FEBRUARY STRIKE

Held on 25 February, wreaths are laid at the Dockworker monument, in the former Jewish quarter, in memory of the anti-Nazi general strike in 1941.

MARCH

STILLE OMGANG (SILENT PROCESSION)

Held on the Sunday closest to 15 March, Catholics walk along the Holy Way (the current Heiligeweg is a remnant) to commemorate the 1345 Miracle of Amsterdam (see boxed text, p71).

APRIL

NATIONAL MUSEUM WEEKEND

Usually held on the second weekend of April, there is free entry to all museums (it's extremely crowded).

KONINGINNEDAG (QUEEN'S DAY)

Held on 30 April (actually the birthday of Queen Juliana, mother of the current Queen Beatrix), Queen's Day is a crazy, wonderful madhouse. There's a free market throughout the city (anyone can sell anything they like – kids love it), street parties, live music, dense crowds and lots of beer. People from all over the country come to join the fun. Wear something orange.

MAY

REMEMBRANCE DAY

Held on 4 May for the victims of WWII. Queen Beatrix lays a wreath at the Nationaal Monument on the Dam and the city observes two minutes' silence at 8pm; making noise at this time is thoughtless in the extreme.

LIBERATION DAY

The end of German occupation in 1945 is commemorated with street parties, a free market and live music on 5 May. The Vondelpark is a good place to be.

LUILAK ('LAZY-BONES')

In the early hours on the Saturday before Whit Sunday, children go around ringing door bells, making noise and waking people up. Luilak is a remnant of a pre-Christian festival celebrating the awakening of spring.

NATIONAL WINDMILL DAY

Held on the second Saturday of May, windmills unfurl their sails and are open to the public.

NATIONAL CYCLING DAY

Held in mid- to late May, and includes family cycling trips along special routes.

OPEN GARDEN DAYS

www.opentuinendagen.nl
Running over for a weekend in mid-May, this is a unique opportunity to see some of the private gardens behind the canal museums.

ESSENTIAL AMSTERDAM

- **Albert Cuypmarkt** (p107) Where the diversity of the city comes together
- **Eastern Docklands** (p115) Up-and-coming neighbourhood, with architecture that's setting world standards
- **Negen Straatjes** (p84) Nine canal-laced alleys brimming with chic boutiques and bubbling cafés
- **Red Light District** (p66) At once blissfully tawdry and achingly beautiful, especially at night
- **Reguliersgracht** (p90) The city's prettiest canal

PINKPOP
www.pinkpop.nl
This three-day outdoor rock festival, held around Pentecost (May/June), takes place near Landgraaf in the southeast (about 135km from Amsterdam). Past festivals have featured performers such as Moby and the Chemical Brothers.

JUNE
OVER HET IJ FESTIVAL
www.overhetij.nl in Dutch
From June or July, big performing-arts events (dance, theatre, music) take place for a week and a half around the former NDSM shipyards (Nederlandsche Doken Scheepsbouwmaatschappij) north of the IJ. It's often exciting and always interesting.

HOLLAND FESTIVAL
www.holndfstvl.nl
For all of June the country's biggest music, drama and dance extravaganza centres on Amsterdam. Highbrow and pretentious meet lowbrow and silly.

ROOTS MUSIC FESTIVAL
www.amsterdamroots.nl
A week-long festival of world music and culture held in late June at various locations throughout the city.

PARKPOP
www.parkpop.nl
On the last Sunday of the month, Europe's largest, free rock festival is held in the Zuiderpark in Den Haag. Some 350,000 people attend annually. It's been going strong for a quarter century.

INTERNATIONAL THEATRE SCHOOL FESTIVAL
For 10 days around the end of the month, Dutch and international theatre students strut their stuff.

JULY
NORTH SEA JAZZ FESTIVAL
www.northseajazz.nl
The world's largest indoor jazz festival is held mid-month in the Netherlands Congress Centre in Den Haag. Pretty much any name you've heard of has performed here. Many of the musicians visit Amsterdam as well.

5 DAYS OFF
www.5daysoff.nl
Features indoor electronica dance parties at venues around town, including Paradiso and the Heineken Music Hall. Other events take place at the Netherlands Media Arts Institute.

JULIDANS
www.julidans.nl
Dance festival at venues city-wide. It gets some 20,000 visitors, all the more remarkable given that it takes place in small venues.

AUGUST
GAY PRIDE FESTIVAL
www.amsterdampride.nl
Pretty much every large venue in town goes gay the first weekend of the month, with parties and special events. A highlight is the world's only waterborne gay-pride parade.

PARADE
www.mobilearts.nl
For the first two weeks of the month, this carnivalesque outdoor theatre festival, held in the Martin Luther King Park, provides unforgettable ambience.

DANCE VALLEY
www.dancevalley.nl
Held mid-month, tens of thousands fill a valley outside of town to groove to loads of DJs.

GRACHTENFESTIVAL (CANAL FESTIVAL)
www.grachtenfestival.nl
Held in the second half of the month, this is a five-day music festival (mainly classical), around the Canal Belt. It features the Prinsengracht Concert from barges in front of the Hotel Pulitzer.

HARTJESDAGEN ZEEDIJK
Held on the third Monday and the weekend leading up to it, this festival, dating back to medieval times, showcases street theatre, a parade and all kinds of music along the Zeedijk and Nieuwmarkt Square.

UITMARKT
For the last weekend of the month, local troupes and orchestras present their forth coming repertoires free of charge throughout the city. A bit like Koninginnedag in April but much more easy-going.

SEPTEMBER

BLOEMENCORSO (FLOWER PARADE)
www.bloemencorso.com/aalsmeer
On the first Saturday of the month, a spectacular procession of floats wends its way from Aalsmeer (home of the world's largest flower market, p245) to the Dam.

JORDAAN FESTIVAL
☎ 624 69 08; www.jordaanfestival.nl
Held during the second week of the month, this street festival promotes merriment and entertainment in a 'typically Amsterdam' neighbourhood. It celebrated its 30th year in 2005. Hundreds of small boats take to the canals.

MONUMENTENDAG
☎ 552 48 88; www.bmz.amsterdam.nl
Registered historical buildings have open days on the second weekend of the month.

CHINESE FESTIVAL
www.zeedijk.nl/chineesfestival-eng.html
Along the Zeedijk, the city's Chinatown, you'll find food, cultural performances and, of course, the lion dance.

Glitter and canal boats at the Gay Pride Festival (opposite)

DAM TOT DAM LOOP
www.damloop.nl
This is a 16km foot-race between the Dam in Amsterdam and the Dam in Zaandam. Expect around 30,000 runners and up to 200,000 spectators.

OCTOBER

AMSTERDAM MARATHON
www.amsterdammarathon.nl
Held mid-month, thousands of runners loop through the city, starting and finishing at the Olympic Stadium. A variety of races take place.

NOVEMBER

CANNABIS CUP
www.hightimes.com
This marijuana festival, held during the last half of the month, is hosted by *High Times* magazine. Awards given out are for the best grass, biggest spliff (cannabis cigarette) etc; there is also a hemp expo and a fashion show.

SINTERKLAAS ARRIVES
St Nicholas arrives by boat from Spain (see boxed text, p12) in mid- to late November.

ZEEDIJK JAZZ & BLUES FESTIVAL
www.zeedijk.nl/jazzfestival-eng.html
Amsterdam's biggest jazz festival, held on the last weekend of the month, sees hundreds of jazz and blues acts out on the street and in the pubs along Zeedijk, all free of charge.

DECEMBER

SINTERKLAAS FESTIVAL
Officially 6 December but the main focus is gift-giving on the evening of 5 December, in honour of St Nicholas (see boxed text, p12).

CHRISTMAS
Celebrated on 25 and 26 December, but religious families mark Christmas Eve on 24 December with Bible readings and carols.

NEW YEAR'S EVE
You'll see wild parties everywhere; the drunken revelry includes fireworks and often injuries.

SINTERKLAAS

Every year on 6 December, the Dutch celebrate Sinterklaas in honour of St Nicholas (Klaas is a nickname for Nicholas, or Nicolaas in Dutch). Historically the bishop of Myra in western Turkey around AD 345, St Nicholas is the patron saint of children, sailors, merchants, pawnbrokers – and Amsterdam.

In mid- to late November, the white-bearded saint, dressed as a bishop with mitre and staff, arrives in Amsterdam by ship from 'Spain' and enters the city on a horse to receive the city keys from the mayor. He is accompanied by a host of mischievous servants called *Zwarte Pieten* (Black Peters), Dutch helpers in blackface (or politically correct blue- or greenface) who throw sweets around and carry sacks in which to take naughty children away. Well-behaved children get presents in a shoe that they've placed by the fireplace with a carrot for the saint's horse (he stays on the roof while a Black Peter climbs down the chimney).

On the evening of 5 December people give one another anonymous and creatively wrapped gifts accompanied by funny or perceptive poems about the recipient written by Sinterklaas. The gift itself matters less than the wrapping (the greater the surprise the better) and poetry (the more the receiver is put on the spot the better).

The North American Santa Claus evolved from the Sinterklaas celebrations at the Dutch settlement of New Amsterdam (which eventually evolved into New York).

CULTURE
IDENTITY

Amsterdam sits below sea level, on a mixture of spongy peat and clay above a stable layer of sand more than 12m down. The first wooden houses were simply placed on top of the peat, and occasionally they sank.

When heavier brick and stone replaced wood, engineers perfected the art of driving wooden piles down to the sand layer, sawing off the protruding ends to equal height and erecting buildings on top of the stable foundation – there are 13,659 piles under the palace on the Dam alone! As long as the wooden pile remained free of contaminants, it would hold up indefinitely.

Sociologists have long drawn parallels between the structure of buildings and Dutch society, and even if it's no longer entirely correct there are lessons to be learned. In the traditional social order, called *verzuiling* (pillarisation), it's as if each persuasion (religious, business interest, political etc) has its own identity (the pillar), but ultimately works with the others to support the overall structure. It's often referred to as the polder model. Many Dutch cities are actual polders: lowlands reclaimed from the sea and protected by dykes.

The result was a legacy of tolerance. Through recent memory, the prevailing ethic in Amsterdam has been that people should be free to do as they please as long as it doesn't inconvenience others. Eccentric conduct in public might go without comment; hence the Dutch saying: 'Act normal, that's crazy enough.'

Two recent high-profile murders (see boxed text, opposite) have upset this notion. When we were researching this book, we heard people talking daily about how it's not as easy to be tolerant anymore. 'People are getting killed', we were told more than once.

Yes, Amsterdammers have taken it very hard, and they're coming to grips, yet thankfully some parts of the local character seem ingrained and may even help them through. One of those is *gezelligheid* (see boxed text, p14), a deeply social nature that comes out at the drop of a hat. Flight attendants leaving Amsterdam are prepared for hours of drinking and chatting with Dutchmen congregating in the back of the plane. Expect chummy moments at the supermarket.

Somewhat contradictory is the Amsterdammer's moralistic streak (coming from the Calvinist tradition) and a tendency to wag the finger in disapproval. Nonsmokers who wince at people smoking nearby might well be told they're making the smokers feel uncomfortable. And raising a criticism over job professionalism or the calculation of a bill will probably result in a very frosty reception. This manner may seem blunt or even arrogant to foreigners, but the impulse comes from the desire to be direct and honest, all in the service of upholding the polder.

Yet even criticism often comes with a sense of humour. Amsterdammers love to complain about their little city and their 'irrelevant' country, but always with a smile. One of our earliest Amsterdam memories is of a grandmother and her young grandson in a shop, doubled-up with laughter over a postcard showing a pile of dog mess on an Amsterdam sidewalk (an ever-present problem) topped with a little Dutch flag as on a cupcake.

Sex & Drugs

These are another reason we love this city, even if we don't necessarily partake. The ever-practical Dutch world-view seems to be that vice is not going to go away so you might as well have some control over it. When you don't have to sneak, there is no mystique.

Sex is discussed openly (such as a newspaper article on puberty, with full-on photos of the development of male and female genitalia). In a pub, you might well overhear Jan telling all the details of making whoopee. The Dutch parliament once held a debate on whether to ban a TV show called *How to Screw* (but decided not to ban it). And even though prostitution is famously legal, promiscuity is the furthest thing from (most) Dutch minds.

Marijuana and hashish are also legal, of course, yet none of this means that every Amsterdammer tokes up or that local males routinely pay for their jollies. On the contrary, only about 5% of business in the Red Light District comes from Dutch customers (Brits comprise about 40%). And only about 6% of the Dutch population are pot users, compared to 8% in Britain and the US and 9% in France, where drug policies are much stricter. Locals

---

THE LEGACY OF THEO & PIM

If the 2004 assassination of Theo van Gogh rocked Amsterdam, it was the assassination of Pim Fortuyn 2½ years earlier that gave the initial push.

The political career of the charismatic Fortuyn (fore-*town*) lasted a mere five months, yet his impact on the Netherlands has proved indelible. His campaign for parliament in 2002 is best remembered for his speeches on immigration: particularly that the Netherlands was 'full' and that immigrants should not be allowed to stay without learning the language or integrating.

Thousands of white, low-income earners in Fortuyn's home base of Rotterdam and other cities rallied round the gay, dandyish former university professor. Fortuyn was feted as the next prime minister, even as his opponents accused him of pursuing right-wing, racist policies.

Just days before the general election in May 2002, Fortuyn was assassinated by an animal-rights activist in Hilversum, some 20km from Amsterdam. Riots erupted outside parliament, and for a brief instant the threat of anarchy hung in the air.

His political party, the Lijst Pim Fortuyn (LPF), had a number of members elected to parliament and was included in the next coalition, but without the dynamic Fortuyn it sputtered in search of a leader; in the 2003 election, voters all but deserted the LPF.

Enter Theo van Gogh (p36), a film-maker whose 11-minute documentary *Submission Part 1* featured four short stories centred on Quranic verses that could be interpreted as justifying violence against women. The film was a collaboration with Ayaan Hirsi Ali, a Muslim-born woman who had emigrated from Somalia to escape an arranged marriage and eventually became a member of parliament. Hirsi Ali had become an outspoken critic of Islamic law and declared herself an atheist.

The documentary aired on Dutch television in 2004, and Van Gogh was shot and his throat slashed as he was biking down an Amsterdam street in rush hour. A letter threatening the nation, politicians and Hirsi Ali in particular, was impaled on a knife stuck in Van Gogh's chest. Hirsi Ali went into hiding. The killing was all the more shocking to locals because the 27-year-old killer, while of Moroccan descent, was born and raised in Amsterdam. He proclaimed that he was acting in the defence of Islam and would do the same thing again if given the chance, and he was sentenced to life imprisonment (one of only a few dozen life sentences in the Netherlands since WWII).

If Fortuyn and his assassination set minds thinking in this city, Van Gogh's murder was a blow to the heart. It also galvanised politicians to require immigrants to know something about Dutch culture. In 2005 the national government imposed an exam for prospective immigrants before their departure from their home countries, covering Dutch language and culture; an accompanying video includes such customs as women sunbathing topless and gay marriage.

Locals hope it's not too little, too late.

leave these vices to slackers and tourists. Harder drugs (heroin, LSD, cocaine and ecstasy, for example) are outlawed, and dealers are prosecuted.

This world-view also applies to diseases like AIDS. Amsterdam has an active education program for at-risk groups, and it was one of the pioneers of a needle-exchange program for drug addicts.

Gays & Lesbians

Partisan estimates put the proportion of gay and lesbian people in Amsterdam at 20% to 30%. This is probably an exaggeration, but Amsterdam is certainly one of the gay capitals of Europe.

The Netherlands has long led the way in gay rights. Discrimination on the basis of sexual orientation is both legally and morally taboo, the police advertise in the gay media for applicants, and homosexuals are admitted to the armed forces on an equal footing. Most significantly, in 2001 the Netherlands became the first country to legalise same-sex marriages (Belgium, the US state of Massachusetts, Spain and Canada have followed suit). Amsterdam was one of the first cities to court lesbian and gay travellers, hosting the Gay Games (the Olympics of the lesbian and gay world) way back in 1988.

Not that the welcome is universal. The last few years have seen a rise in gay-bashing, including one high-profile incident in which a crowd of ethnically Moroccan youths beat up an American magazine editor who was walking hand-in-hand with his boyfriend. Locals gripe that this sort of thing happens more than is reported (and that it would not have received so much attention if the victim had been local); some homosexuals have begun to move out of the city, citing concerns over safety.

The vast majority have stayed, however, and the venues they frequent are generally open and welcoming. Throughout the city there are more than 100 bars and nightclubs (p170), hotels (p212), bookshops, sport clubs, choirs, archives etc, and a wide range of support organisations (p254) that cater especially to gay clientele. However, Amsterdam's well-developed scene isn't typical of the country as a whole. Rotterdam is also an exception, as are the university towns.

The centrepiece of Amsterdam's Gay Pride Festival is the Canal Parade, which takes place on the first Saturday in August. Dozens of floats make their way around the Prinsengracht as hundreds of thousands of spectators of all stripes look on. The days around the parade are marked by sport and culture programs and lots of parties.

Another big party is **Koninginnedag** (Queen's Day; p9) on 30 April. Queen Beatrix is very popular among the gay community (and the Netherlands in general) and many gays agree that Princess Máxima, the Argentine-born wife of Crown Prince Willem-Alexander, is *maximaaaal* (ultra cool).

Dutch Obsessions

Dutch people have a great love of detail. Statistics on the most trivial subjects make the paper (eg the number of applications for dog licences, incidence of rubbish being put

---

THAT'S *GEZELLIG*

This particularly Dutch personality trait is one of the best reasons to visit Amsterdam. It's variously translated as snug, friendly, cosy, informal, companionable and convivial, but *gezelligheid* (the state of being *gezellig*) is something more easily experienced than defined. To wit (with apologies to fans of *That's Amore* and the late, great Dean Martin):

When you hang out all day
in an old brown café, that's *gezellig*.
Sit and gab with your friends
and the fun never ends, that's *gezellig*.

You can sing (ting-a-ling-a-ling, ting-a-ling-a-ling)
riding on your canal boat,
While you sway (tippy-tippy-tay, tippy-tippy-tay)
from the beer someone else bought.

Take your grill to the street,
bring your couch for a seat, that's *gezellig*.
Or go chat on the porch
in your old undershorts. Suits us fine.

When you live at close range
but are never heard screaming or yelling,
It's no scam, sir or ma'am,
back in old Amsterdam that's *gezellig*.

out early), and somewhere down the line it feeds mountains of bureaucracy. That said, when the system breaks down the Dutch are happy to improvise solutions; perhaps this comes from the strong legacy of juggling diverse interests.

There's also a keen interest in all things foreign. The Dutch are inveterate travellers and the media is full of English phrases.

Last but not least, the Dutch are famously thrifty with their money – and they often don't know what to think of this. In one breath they might joke about how copper wire was invented by two Dutchmen (they were fighting over a penny, neither one would let go, and they stretched it), and in the next tell you that they don't like being called cheap.

Ethnic Makeup

Amsterdam has a long history of welcoming immigrants and integrating them into society; records show 174 nationalities among the city's registered residents. However, there's a sense of concern over the latest wave of immigration, particularly from the Middle East and North Africa.

The past few years have witnessed a significant political shift to the right throughout the Netherlands. It's no police state (this is Holland), but the assassinations of politician Pim Fortuyn and film-maker Theo van Gogh (see boxed text; p13) made many Dutch consider whether immigrants were upholding the polder model or trying to force the traditions of their home countries onto the Netherlands. A poll in 2005 found that a majority of Dutch citizens favoured the banning of Islamic head scarves for public servants.

Controls on immigration have tightened in recent years, yet more than 5% of the national population is still without Dutch nationality. Admission of immigrants is now restricted to a few narrow categories – eg people whose presence serves the 'national interest' or who have compelling humanitarian reasons for getting a residence permit.

Out of approximately 740,000 people in Amsterdam (plus an estimated 20,000 unregistered residents), about 47% are ethnic minorities. The most recent wave of immigration goes back to the 1960s, when 'guest labourers' from Morocco and Turkey performed jobs spurned by the Dutch. In the mid-1970s, the granting of independence to the Dutch colony of Suriname in South America saw a large influx of Surinamese, who now compose the majority of the city's 10% Black population.

The vast majority of these immigrants live in the city's outskirts where housing is less expensive, such as the communities of Bijlmer and the Old West. There's also a presence in De Pijp, but as that neighbourhood gentrifies and becomes more expensive there's likely to be a shift.

Foreign residents from Western countries include some 19,000 Germans, 7500 Britons, 3700 Americans and 1000 Australians. Thousands of (temporary) expatriates are not included in these figures.

LIFESTYLE

It's hard to say that there's such a thing as a typical Amsterdammer, but Joop is a good start. Joop (pronounced yohp), 39, lives in De Pijp, south of the central city, and pretty happily. Like Joop, De Pijp is a little scruffy and very cool. To reach his flat, you have to walk up two typically narrow flights of stairs – uneven steps that force you to look down as you tread. Technically it's a one-bedroom flat with a living room, dining room (bonus!), bedroom, decent-sized kitchen and back balcony (another bonus!), but Joop has turned the flat's large closet into a bedroom and uses the windowed bedroom as an office. Although the building is prewar, inside the flat is clean and comfortable. Sleekly modern furnishings offset the antique timber flooring (he has excellent taste).

Even though Joop can be out of work for long periods (he's in the performing arts), he can afford this place because it's social housing for which he pays €495 per month. Whereas in other countries social housing carries a stigma, in Amsterdam some 56% of the population lives in it – the waiting list can be five years.

Joop likes to go out – for lunch in a café in the neighbourhood, a performance night with his 'husband' (they haven't married, though technically they could – they've only been together a couple of years, so why rush into things?). He loves the city, he says, because there's something cultural to do any night of the week, especially in summer.

Women

Dutch women attained the right to vote in 1919, and by the 1970s abortion-on-demand was paid for by the national health service. Dutch women are remarkably confident; on a social level, equality is taken for granted and women are almost as likely as men to initiate social and romantic contact. It's still a different story in the workplace – relatively few women are employed full-time and fewer still hold positions in senior management.

The feminist movement is less politicised than elsewhere and certainly more laid-back. Efforts focus on practical solutions such as cultural centres, bicycle-repair shops run by and for women, or support systems to help women set up businesses.

FOOD

If you're invited to a home for dinner, bring something for the host: a bunch of flowers or a plant, a bottle of wine, or some good cake or pastries. It's polite to arrive five to 15 minutes late (never early). The proper toast is *prost*, or the Italian *cin-cin*.

Cuisines

The most prominent cuisines in Amsterdam are Dutch, Indonesian and Surinamese, but many others are well represented too: Turkish, Greek, Chinese (particularly in the little Chinatown near the Zeedijk), Italian, Thai and Argentine (especially steaks). Spanish-style tapas and other international 'small plates' menus are the current rage. There are some lovely fish restaurants and, if you must, fast food. See the Eating chapter for places to eat in Amsterdam.

DUTCH

Traditional Dutch cuisine concentrates on filling the stomach rather than titillating the taste buds, based on large portions of rudimentary meat, potato and vegetables. That said, contemporary Dutch chefs have made some great strides, and what's now called 'Dutch' often has echoes of far-off, mystical lands.

Traditional Dutch dishes include *stamppot* (mashed pot) – potatoes mashed with vegetables (usually kale or endive) and served with smoked sausage or strips of pork. *Hutspot*, similar to *stamppot* but with carrots, onions and braised meat, is a popular winter dish. *Erwtensoep* is a thick pea soup (a spoon stuck upright in the pot should fall over slowly) with smoked sausage and bacon.

White *asperges* (asparagus), served with ham and butter, is very popular in the spring. *Mosselen* (mussels) are best eaten from September to April; the classic preparation is to cook with white wine, chopped leeks and onions, and serve with a side of *frites* or *patat* (French fries). Use an empty shell to pluck out the bodies, and don't eat mussels that haven't opened properly as they can be poisonous.

Year-round favourites include *broodjes*, for which the translation of 'sandwiches' doesn't begin to tell the story. Quality *broodjeswinkels* or *broodjeszaken* (sandwich shops) are small

Try this sandwich for size

but elaborate delis. Pile hot or cold ingredients onto a choice of breads and rolls, from roast beef or fish salads to cheeses and *osseworst* (raw beef sausage, a Dutch delicacy). Wash it down with a beer or a cool glass of *melk* (milk).

Kroketten (croquettes) are a Dutch classic: a dough-ragout with meat (sometimes fish or shrimp) that's crumbed and deep-fried. They are also served as small balls called *bitterballen*, with mustard – a popular pub snack. *Pannenkoeken* translates as 'pancakes', although North Americans will be in for a surprise – the Dutch variety is huge and a little stretchy, served flat, one to a plate and topped with wide combination of ingredients, both sweet and savoury.

There's plenty of seafood at stalls in strategic locations around the city. *Haring* (herring) is a national institution, eaten lightly salted or occasionally pickled but never cooked; a Dutch herring is decapitated, split, filleted, and served pretty much as is, with diced onion and sometimes sweet-pickle chips as a garnish. *Paling* (eel) is another favourite, usually smoked. Don't dismiss these until you've tried them!

Other popular fish include *schol* (plaice), *tong* (sole), *kabeljauw* (cod) and freshwater *forel* (trout). *Garnalen* (shrimps, prawns) are also found on many menus, large species are often called by their Italian name of *scampi*. On Mondays, fish tends to be old and the locals avoid it.

Some typically Dutch desserts are fruit pie (apple, cherry, banana cream or other fruit), *vla* (custard) and pancakes. Many snack bars and pubs serve *appeltaart* (apple pie) and coffee throughout the day – there's a reason Dutch apple pie is so admired.

INDONESIAN

A tasty legacy of Dutch colonial history. Some dishes are colonial concoctions rather than traditional Indonesian, but that doesn't make them less appealing. If it isn't stamped in passports that visitors to Amsterdam are required to try Indonesian *rijsttafel* (a dozen or more Indonesian dishes, with rice), it should be. Smaller *nasi rames* (boiled rice) is similar in concept and served on one plate. *Bami rames* is the same dish with thick noodles.

Gado-gado (lightly steamed vegetables with peanut sauce and hard-boiled egg) feels good in all respects. *Saté* or *sateh* (satay) is marinated barbecued beef, chicken or pork on small skewers; the best versions are coated lightly (not smothered) in peanut sauce. Other stand-bys are *nasi goreng* (fried rice with onions, pork, shrimp and spices, often topped with a fried egg or shredded omelette) and *bami goreng* (the same thing but with noodles instead of rice).

Indonesian food is usually served mild for Western palates. If you want it hot (*pedis*, pronounced p-*dis*), say so but be prepared for the ride of a lifetime. You can play it safe by asking for *sambal* (chilli paste – it may already be on the table) and helping yourself. *Sambal*

17

oelek is red and hot; the dark-brown *sambal badjak* is based on onions and is mild and sweet. If you overdo it, a spoonful of plain rice will quench the flames; drinking distributes the *sambal* and only makes things worse.

Indonesian food should be eaten with a spoon and fork. The drink of choice is beer or water.

Note: many places serving Indonesian food call themselves Chinese-Indonesian and usually end up serving bland dishes to suit Dutch palates. The food is OK and can be great value, but if you want the real thing, go to a place without *Chinees* in its name.

TRADITIONAL DUTCH DISHES

Dutch Pea Soup

This thick soup tastes even better the next day. Serve with hot, crusty bread.

    3 cups split green peas
    1 pig's trotter
    1 pig's ear
    1 cup diced bacon
    1kg/2.2lbs potatoes
    2 leeks
    2 onions
    1 celeriac
    4 frankfurters
    salt and pepper to taste

- Wash peas, cover with water and soak overnight.
- Boil softened peas in 3L of water for one hour.
- Add pig's trotter, ear and bacon and continue to cook for two hours.
- Add sliced potatoes, diced leeks, diced onions and diced celeriac and simmer for a further one hour.
- Add sliced frankfurters to soup for the last five minutes. Season with salt and pepper.

Dutch Appeltaart

    1 packet shortcrust pastry
    1½ tsp gelatine
    1kg/2.2lbs apples
    1 tbsp lemon juice
    2 tbsp sugar
    2 tsp cinnamon
    150g/5¼ ounces of dried fruit soaked in 3 tbsp rum
    ¼ cup butter
    1 tbsp milk
    1 tsp caster sugar (cane sugar)
    ½ cup whipped cream

- Preheat oven to 175ºC/350ºF.
- Use three-quarters of the shortcrust pastry dough to line base and sides of a 24cm/9in greased round cake tin; sprinkle with the gelatine.
- Peel and core apples, slice thinly, sprinkle with lemon juice and mix in sugar and 1 tsp of cinnamon.
- Place alternate layers of apple slices and dried fruit in tin, sprinkling each layer with some cinnamon and sugar. Use apples for the top layer and dot with butter.
- Roll the remaining dough into a rectangle, cut into 1cm-wide strips and lay in a lattice over fruit, sealing at ends; brush with milk, and sprinkle caster sugar mixed with remaining cinnamon on top.
- Bake for 45 minutes or till golden.
- Cool and serve with a generous amount of whipped cream.

SURINAMESE

Food from this former South American colony is similar to Caribbean food – an African/Indian hybrid – with Indonesian influences contributed by indentured labourers from Java. Confusingly, many Surinamese places also have *Chinees* in their names. Chicken features strongly, along with curries (chicken, lamb or beef), potatoes and rice, and *roti* (unleavened pancakes). The food can be hot and spicy, but it's always wholesome and good value.

WE DARE YOU

Amsterdammers love raw fish. Herring season is announced with all the fanfare of the new Beaujolais elsewhere: look for 'Hollandse Nieuw' signs throughout town. The proper way to eat a herring is to dangle it above the mouth and bite bit by bit (don't worry, it's already been filleted for you).

And only the Dutch can stomach the intense, salty black liquorice known as *drop*.

Drinks

Amsterdam tap water is fine but it does have a slight chemical taste, so mineral and soda waters are popular. Dairy drinks include chocolate milk, Fristi (a yogurt drink), *karnemelk* (buttermilk) and of course milk itself. A wide selection of fruit juices and soft drinks are available too. See p155 for a roundup of alcoholic drinks.

The hot drink of choice is coffee – after all, it was the merchants of Amsterdam who introduced coffee to Europe. It should be strong and can be excellent if it's freshly made. If you simply order *koffie* you'll get a sizeable cup of the black stuff with a small container of *koffiemelk,* similar to unsweetened condensed milk. *Koffie verkeerd* (coffee 'wrong') comes in a bigger cup with plenty of real milk. *Espresso* and *cappuccino* are also available, and most places can arrange decaf. The Coffee Company chain has locations throughout town.

Remember, there's a *big* difference between a *koffiehuis* (coffee house) and a 'coffeeshop'; the latter may have nothing to do with coffee (and a lot to do with cannabis), while lighting up in the former will get you a tongue-lashing at best.

Tea is usually served as a cup of hot water with a tea bag; many places offer a choice of bags. If you want milk, ask *'met melk, graag'* (with milk, please); many locals add a slice of lemon instead.

FASHION

Although Amsterdam has some interesting designers, we'll admit that it's not the first city you think of when you think fashion. Probably some of that has to do with the traditional Dutch aversion to showiness (although it's wise to dress up for a nice dinner out). We also suspect that it's because it's hard to ride a bicycle (the city's principal mode of transportation) while wearing one's finest, especially if it's likely to rain.

That said, office workers, particularly in banking and finance, do dress smartly for work. International designers can be found at the higher-end department stores and on the PC Hooftstraat (p95), the city's fanciest shopping street, and the Negen Straatjes (Nine Alleys, p84), a wonder of tiny boutiques.

For years the club world was pretty much styleless, but nowadays club doormen are beginning to be more selective. There are quite a number of shops around town catering to club-goers, some of them as fun as the clubs themselves.

SPORT

Football (Soccer)

The Dutch are pretty low-key when it comes to national pride, except when it comes to football. It's the Dutch national game, which is no surprise in the land of past masters Johan Cruyff and Ruud Gullit. Passions for football run so high it's almost scary. The National Football Association counts a million members.

The national football team competes in virtually every World Cup. The Eindhoven-based PSV (Philips Sport Vereniging) coach Guus Hiddink led the South Korean team to the quarter-finals in the 2002 World Cup, and still enjoys a status akin to sainthood in that country.

Amsterdam's team, Ajax (pronounced *ah*-yahks), plays in the Amsterdam ArenA. Hooliganism is not unheard of, but the ArenA has a modern, hi-tech police force, and you're unlikely to notice crowd trouble.

Korfball

This sport epitomises Dutch values of equality, teamwork and cooperation. Invented by an Amsterdam schoolteacher in 1903, korfball looks like the child of a *ménage à trois* between basketball, volleyball and netball. A team of four men and four women tries to sink a ball into a basket, but unlike in

Tours of the city often take place on distinct yellow bicycles

basketball there's no running with the ball, and it's impossible for the team to feed the ball again and again to one player to shoot. Players may not hinder members of the opposite sex. If you'd like to learn more, visit www.korfballnet.com.

Skating

Ice-skating is as Dutch as croquettes, and thousands hit the ice when the country's lakes and ditches freeze over. The Netherlands has dozens of ice rinks with Olympic-sized tracks, and areas for hockey and figure skating. Amsterdam's main ice rink was named for Jaap Eden, a legend around 1900. The hero of the hour is Jochem Uytdehaage, celebrated for netting two Olympic gold medals in Salt Lake City in 2002. A perennially popular event, when the weather cooperates, is the Friday Night Skate (p181), on in-line skates, not ice.

Cycling

To say that Amsterdammers are avid cyclists is a bit of an understatement. There are some 400km of bike paths in the city alone, and even if these are not used competitively, virtually every Amsterdammer can relate to the sport. The five-day Tour de Nederland speeds through the city at the end of August. See the Walking & Cycling Tours chapter for suggested cycling routes and safety tips.

THE FLYING HOUSEWIFE

Quick: who was the greatest women's track-and-field star of the 20th century?

Francisca ('Fanny') Koen was born in Amsterdam in 1918 and showed early prowess in a number of sports. She finally settled on running, and by 1935, at age 17, she had set a national record as a sprinter. The next year she competed in the Olympics in Berlin, though with only middling results.

WWII got in the way of further international track meets, and in the interim Fanny married Jan Blankers (a star of the 1928 Amsterdam Olympics), gave birth and turned 30, any of which would normally be a career-ender in those days. But a drive to win spurred her to compete. Despite food shortages and the German occupation, she continued to train in Amsterdam through the war years and set world records in the hurdles, the long jump and the 100-yard dash.

At the 1948 Olympics in London, Fanny Blankers-Koen won four gold medals, a record that has been matched but never surpassed in track-and-field, and became world-famous as 'the flying housewife'. Through her career, she set an astounding 58 Dutch records in events from sprinting to shot-put; later she was an outspoken booster of sports worldwide.

Blankers-Koen was named Female Athlete of the 20th Century by the International Association of Athletics Federations – the male winner was American Carl Lewis, who tied her Olympic record. Blankers-Koen died in 2004, but her legacy lives on through legend and the annual Thales FBK Games, held in the town of Hengelo, east of Amsterdam, where up-and-coming athletes continue to set world records.

Other Sports

Sports tend to rise and fall with the fate of Dutch athletes. Tennis has been popular since Richard Krajicek fell to his knees after clinching the 1996 Wimbledon final. The national tennis club is the country's second-largest sporting club, after football, and many people book time on courts in all-weather sports halls. Krajicek has hung up his racket, but there's fresh talent on the circuit, including the likes of Sjeng Schalken.

Darts is another example, gaining an enthusiastic following after the victories of Raymond van Barneveld, a frequent champion. (Despite this you're not likely to find too many bars with *dartbanen* in the city. If you wander into a place with a 'tandarts' sign out front, you'll find yourself in a dentist's office!)

Johan Kenkhuis, a silver medallist on the 2004 Olympic swim team, has a following in two constituencies of which he's a member: Dutch and gay. The Netherlands has long had the world's foremost water-polo league.

See p183 for places where you can play sports.

MEDIA

It makes sense that the world's first museum devoted to news photography, News Photo (p69), just opened here. Amsterdammers are media savvy and voracious media consumers. All you need to do is go to a café with a reading table to see. Whether it's the free *Metro* magazine picked up on their commute or the flagship newspapers published here, people are, above all else, aware. It makes this small city seem even smaller. If you want an Amsterdammer to think you're in the know, tell him or her that the restaurant you've chosen for dinner was rated nine out of 10 by Johannes van Dam (food critic for *Het Parool*).

Of the 32 daily newspapers published in the Netherlands, some of the most important (*Telegraaf, Het Parool, NRC Handelsblad*) are based or have bureaus here. And, like most places, there's a huge selection of gossip rags and mags. Visitors will have little trouble finding English-language publications such as *Time, Newsweek,* the *International Herald Tribune* and many UK-based dailies. Many are also popular among Dutch readers. See p257 for further info.

Dutch TV tends not to travel well overseas, mostly due to the language. However, foreign-language remakes of Dutch shows are both popular and enormously profitable. The current reality-TV craze began here with *Big Brother,* produced by Endemol (based in Hilversum, about 20km out of town). *Big Brother* was swiftly copied in the UK, Germany and the USA – and has now spread to territories as diverse as Brazil, Mexico and Africa. Endemol is also behind such international hits as *Fear Factor, Extreme Makeover: Home Edition* and *Ready, Steady, Cook.* With its close observation of human foibles, could reality TV be the Netherlands' way of spreading worldwide *gezelligheid*?

While there are local TV stations (AT5 is probably the leader) and national networks, Amsterdam also looks outward for its media coverage and you can find channels from other nations and other continents on many cable systems.

LANGUAGE

When you come from a tiny country with a long history of trade, you learn to adapt or wither.

Amsterdam has always looked outward, and as a result most people you will encounter in the city speak English very well. Foreign films and TV are shown with subtitles, and the Dutch have long used other languages in their dealings overseas. Many websites (especially tourist publications) are published in English, with the occasional German, French, Italian and, increasingly, Turkish and Arabic publication.

Part of the reason for this outward focus may be that the Dutch language is confounding. Many linguists believe that Dutch is the closest relative to English, but it won't be apparent to the uninitiated. If you've studied German, Dutch will make sense grammatically, and once you get past some spelling differences you'll probably be able to get the gist of it, especially written. Spoken Dutch is another matter entirely – its pronunciation is chock full of odd vowels, throat-clearing *g*'s and *ch*'s, roiling, rolling *r*'s and *v*'s that sound like *f*'s.

The Dutch speak English so well that visitors will rarely have the opportunity to practise Dutch. When they do, the most valiant attempts at pronunciation will probably be met with quizzical looks.

Nevertheless, a few words in Dutch are always appreciated, especially the phrase *Spreekt u Engels?* (Do you speak English?) with elderly people. Foreigners who have settled in the Netherlands report that speaking Dutch, while hardly compulsory, warms their Dutch friends and colleagues.

For a brief guide to Dutch and some useful words and phrases, see the Language chapter, and check language courses on p253. For more extensive coverage of the language, pick up Lonely Planet's *Western Europe phrasebook*.

ECONOMY & COSTS

Visitors will find Amsterdam less expensive than other European capitals like London or Paris. If you're coming from the UK, prices may look the same numerically but the exchange rate on the pound usually makes Amsterdam a bargain. Although inexpensive lodging is available (though often dingy), you'll pay dearly for anything of quality. Transport and meals, on the other hand, are relatively cheap.

Locals don't exactly see it that way. The Netherlands dropped its beloved guilder in favour of the euro in 2002, which many people view as the beginning of a period of inflation. Proprietors took advantage of the changeover to raise prices, and the trend hasn't really stopped since. (This is a complaint we've heard in other euro-zone countries as well.)

Through the 1990s and the beginning of this century, the Dutch economy was the miracle of Europe, with consistent growth while other European economies flagged, and it was all the more remarkable considering the Netherlands' generous welfare benefits. However, the last few years have been tough, with rising unemployment and stagnant wages; in other words, the nation is becoming more like its neighbours.

Still, Amsterdam has fared comparatively well. Many multinationals have their European headquarters and distribution centres in office complexes west, south and southeast of the city centre, drawn by a highly skilled, multilingual workforce and easy-going tax laws.

Important industries include logistics and distribution (particularly in the automotive and technology industries). Amsterdam's harbour is Europe's fifth busiest (Rotterdam's is first) and Schiphol airport is the continent's third largest in terms of freight (fourth for passengers). Finance also thrives, as does technology (in some 15 regional science parks), and the life sciences (fed by several important universities). The Dutch control about 45% of European road freight; many of these trucking companies are based in Amsterdam. And although Amsterdam is home to about 4.5% of the overall Dutch population, it accounts for some 25% of the country's creative industries (advertising, design, fashion etc).

Amsterdam is one of Europe's top 10 tourist destinations and top five for conventions and congresses; the latter alone generate some €4 billion in annual revenue and employ about 38,000 people.

Visitors typically find costs in Amsterdam in the middle range of northern European cities. Figure that a typical lunch will set you back between €5 and €10, with dinner about double that. Hostel rates start at around €20 per person, and the average midrange hotel room goes for around €125 for a double.

This means that a couple staying in midrange hotels and eating in midrange restaurants can expect to spend €75 to €100 per person per day in peak season. Budget

HOW MUCH?

- Tip in a public toilet: €0.50
- Loaf of packaged *boerenbrood* (farmer bread) at Albert Heijn supermarket: €0.74
- *Kroket* sandwich at van Dobben: €2
- One hour of parking: €3
- *Strippenkaart* (strip-card for public transit): €6.50
- Cinema ticket (varies by time and location): €7.50
- Dutch-English dictionary: €7.50
- *Dagschotel* (dish of the day) at de Blaffende Vis: €8.50
- Bicycle lock: €10
- Train ticket to Rotterdam: €12.60
- *Rijsttafel* dinner at Tujuh Maret Indonesian restaurant: €23.50

travellers staying in hostels, eating in modest restaurants and visiting a museum or two should be able to get by on around €40 a person per day. See the Sleeping and Eating chapters for further details.

Discounts on things like museum admission are not as plentiful as elsewhere but still available. See p254 for discount cards, special passes and packages. If you're looking to save money, avoid taxis! Fares vary but are generally €3.20 at the drop and another €1.90 per kilometre, and fares mount quickly.

GOVERNMENT & POLITICS

Although Amsterdam is the nation's 'capital', the functions of government are actually 60km away in Den Haag (The Hague). That's not the only complicated relationship Amsterdammers have with their compatriots. Much of the country sees Amsterdam as too 'anything-goes' for its taste; many Amsterdammers, for their part, have traditionally seen the rest of the nation as too conservative.

It's further complicated because much of Europe views the Netherlands as a *bête noir* whose lax policies on drugs, prostitution etc are corrupting the youth of other nations. (Many Dutch retort that the Netherlands' own drug-abuse rates are among Europe's lowest and it's the other nations that should get their own houses in order!) Some Amsterdammers see their city in particular being used as a scapegoat. No doubt this mindset and related fears over immigration helped contribute to the resounding 'no' vote that the Netherlands gave the European Constitution in 2005.

Amsterdam is run by a mayor (Job Cohen), appointed by the monarchy, and a 45-member city council elected to four-year terms by the city's 15 boroughs. At last count, the council was one-third Social Democrats, another third Liberals and Greens and the rest a variety of parties. Looked at another way, the council includes 18 women and 11 residents of non-Dutch citizenship. Council members receive an allowance for their work and not a salary, as it is performed on a volunteer basis. The council meets every second Wednesday in public session.

Amsterdam is further divided into boroughs, each with its own 'neighbourhood council' responsible for the day-to-day running of the district. In these councils, Amsterdam is as participatory as the polder model would suggest. Neighbourhood councils hear local concerns and are responsible for implementing block-to-block changes: installing new bike racks, cleaning up dog mess etc.

Amsterdam is also the sort of place where locals create informal councils to solve problems of mutual concern even without any government input, such as the Night Mayors (see boxed text, p168).

ENVIRONMENT

Much of the land around Amsterdam is polder, land that used to be at the bottom of lakes or the sea. It was reclaimed by building dykes across sea inlets and rivers, and pumping the water out with windmills (later with steam and diesel pumps). While other nations were busy colonising other territories, the Dutch just went out and built them!

Polders were created on a massive scale: in the 20th century, huge portions of the former Zuiderzee (now the IJsselmeer, a lake closed off from the sea by a dyke) were surrounded by dykes and the water was pumped out to create vast swaths of flat and fertile agricultural land – the province of Flevoland, northeast of Amsterdam, was reclaimed from the sea.

GREEN AMSTERDAM

The city centre is both very green and very much not. The central streets of Damrak, Rokin and Spuistraat, for example, feel like brick jungles, but virtually any canal is a lush green belt. Another place to spot greenery is out the back window: many homes in the Canal Belt back onto gardens or courtyards.

To let loose, your best bet is the large open field of Museumplein (p95), or the lovely Vondelpark (p97) nearby, both just south of the city centre. A short ride away is the Amsterdamse Bos (p115). Don't neglect the large and lovely Artis Zoo (p108), the city's first park, in the Plantage district.

Recycling & Waste

The Netherlands is well known for being forward-thinking with recycling – it was one of the first nations in the world to ban the import of electronic equipment containing components that degrade and cause environmental harm – but if you're walking around looking for a place to recycle your half-litre water bottle you'll be looking for a long time. There are recycling bins for *papier* (paper) and *glas* (glass), but the rest goes into the bin conveniently marked 'rest'. Same goes for metal cans. Larger bottles are sold with a deposit of €0.25 (bottles don't need to be returned to the shop where you bought them). In an effort to cut down on waste, most supermarkets do not give away bags, though you're free to bring your own. Otherwise, bags can be purchased for about €0.10.

The Vondelpark (p97–8) is great for all kinds of games

In residential neighbourhoods, nifty new garbage receptacles are built right into the sidewalk – a truck comes along, the receptacles rise out of the ground and are replaced.

There's a similarly nifty system of *urinoirs*, whose numbers seem to multiply in warm weather and during festivals. These tall plastic stands look like the letter 'x' from the top, and in each of the four inner corners is a hole for your 'water' – face inward, not outward, please! When they get full a truck comes and replaces them (OK, most of the time). Simple, very practical and a lot cheaper than paying €0.50 to use a public toilet somewhere (although there's no place to wash one's hands). Major drawback? There's no women's equivalent.

URBAN PLANNING & DEVELOPMENT

'Finding rented accommodation in Amsterdam sometimes seems an impossible task', reads the city's own website. 'Generally speaking you should expect a waiting time of over five years.' Daunting, isn't it?

In a way, the history of Amsterdam's planning has always been about finding adequate space for housing, with solutions ranging from sinking piles into polders to carving out canals for houseboats to building high rises and housing blocks for immigrants. A mere 15% of city real estate is owner-occupied; the rest is rental property. Rents are strictly controlled, unless the property is so upmarket that it jumps the hurdle into a higher-end 'free-market' category. Other strict controls include the number of rooms a household may contain.

New construction in the Eastern Docklands district has begun to alleviate this and some of the other difficulties that arose from the large-scale apartment blocks in areas like Bijlmer, southeast of the city centre. Although the Eastern Docklands is a vestige of an industrial and shipping heritage long since gone, the hope is that this new construction, with adventurous, standard-setting designs, will create practical and indeed desirable housing solutions.

Arts ■

Arts

Isn't it strange that some of the world's best-known artists can get by on just one name? In Amsterdam, they go by Rembrandt and Vincent.

But for heaven's sake don't stop there. Dutch artists have been at the forefront of the art world since Rembrandt's time. Imagine how much poorer the world would be without the likes of Johannes Vermeer, Frans Hals, Piet Mondriaan and Karel Appel, just to name a few.

TOP FIVE ANNUAL CULTURAL EVENTS

- National Museum Weekend (p9) April
- Koninginnedag (p9) April
- Open Garden Days (p9) May
- Grachtenfestival (p10) August
- Monumentendag (p11) September

It's not just visual art either. Amsterdam's music scene – classical, jazz, world and contemporary – is second to none. Between music, theatre and dance, the city offers an astounding 40,000 performances a year. If you haven't caught the work of these modern masters, you've missed one of Amsterdam's great pleasures.

It confirms what we've long known in our hearts: more than just a cultural centre, Amsterdam is one of the world's great *creative* centres. In some cities, art is seen as optional or, worse, elitist, but in Amsterdam the arts are part of everyday life. In other cities, streets are named for political leaders or wealthy landowners, but Amsterdam has an entire section of town with streets named for artists and musicians. In other cities art is what other people did in the past, but just see the crowds at the concert halls, arts festivals, theatres and museums to see how much the arts matter to the everyday Amsterdammer.

PAINTING

With a line-up that includes Rembrandt, Frans Hals and Jan Vermeer, the Dutch Masters are arguably the best-known painters ever to come out of northern Europe. Follow that line further and you'll see artists who've made a splash in whatever field they chose.

To understand them, though, requires a bit of history. It starts at a time when Italy was the centre of the art world and painters would go there to study.

FLEMISH & DUTCH SCHOOLS

Prior to the late 16th century, art in the Low Countries centred on the southern provinces (present-day Belgium), particularly the Flemish cities of Ghent, Bruges and Antwerp. Paintings of the Flemish School featured biblical and allegorical subject matter popular with the Church, the court and to a lesser extent the nobility, who, after all, paid the bills and called the shots.

Among the most famous names of that time are Jan van Eyck (d 1441), the founder of the Flemish School who was the first to perfect the technique of oil painting; Rogier van der Weyden (1400–64), whose religious portraits showed the personalities of his subjects; and Hieronymus (also known as Jeroen) Bosch (1450–1516), with macabre allegorical paintings full of religious topics. Pieter Breugel the Elder (1525–69) used Flemish landscapes and peasant life in his allegorical scenes.

In the northern Low Countries (present-day Netherlands), artists began to develop

TOP FIVE ART MUSEUMS

- CoBrA Museum (p116)
- Museum Het Rembrandthuis (p76)
- Rijksmuseum (p96)
- Stedelijk Museum (p114)
- Van Gogh Museum (p97)

a style of their own. Although the artists of the day never achieved the level of recognition of their Flemish counterparts, the Dutch School, as it came to be called, was known for favouring realism over allegory. Haarlem was the centre of this movement, with artists like Jan Mostaert (1475–1555), Lucas van Leyden (1494–1533) and Jan van Scorel (1494–1562). Painters in the city of Utrecht were famous for using chiaroscuro (deep contrast of light and shade), a technique associated with the Italian master Caravaggio.

GOLDEN AGE (17TH CENTURY)

With the Spanish expelled from the Low Countries, the character of the art market changed. There was no longer the Church to buy artworks and no court to speak of, so art became a business, and artists were forced to survive in a free market. Very Dutch. In place of Church and court was a new, bourgeois society of merchants, artisans and shopkeepers who didn't mind spending 'reasonable' money to brighten up their houses and workplaces. The key: they had to be pictures the buyers could relate to.

PAINTING STYLES FROM THE GOLDEN AGE

Next time you're in an Amsterdam museum, see if you can spot the following:

- **Religious art** Unlike in the earlier Flemish School, which favoured allegory, Dutch School art had to be 'historically correct', in line with the Calvinist emphasis on 'true' events as described in the Bible. The same went for paintings of Greek and Roman historical scenes.
- **Portraiture** A smash hit in this society of middle-class upstarts – group portraits did exceedingly well. Group portraits also had the advantage of costing less per head.
- **Maritime scenes and cityscapes** Sold well to the government.
- **Landscapes** Winter scenes and still lifes (of priceless, exotic flowers and delicious meals), found in many living rooms.
- **Genre painting** Depicted domestic life or daily life outside.

Painters became entrepreneurs in their own right, churning out banal works, copies and masterpieces in factory-like studios. Paintings were mass-produced, sold at markets alongside furniture and chickens. Soon the wealthiest households were covered in paintings from top to bottom. Foreign visitors commented that even bakeries and butcher shops seemed to have a painting or two on the wall. Most painters specialised in one of the main genres of the day (see boxed text, above).

Sculpted figures along the walls of the Rijksmuseum (p96)

REMBRANDT: LAUDED, REVILED, GENIUS

The 17th-century's greatest artist, Rembrandt van Rijn (1606–69) grew up a miller's son in Leiden, but had become an accomplished painter by his early twenties.

In 1631 he came to Amsterdam to run the painting studio of the wealthy art dealer Hendrick van Uylenburgh. Portraits were the studio's cash cow, and Rembrandt and his staff (or 'pupils') churned out scores of them, including group portraits such as *The Anatomy Lesson of Dr Tulp* (1632). In 1634 he married Van Uylenburgh's niece Saskia, who often modelled for him.

Rembrandt fell out with his boss, but his wife's capital helped him buy the sumptuous house next door to Van Uylenburgh's studio (the current Museum Het Rembrandthuis p76). There Rembrandt set up his own studio, with staff who worked in a warehouse in the Jordaan. These were happy years: his paintings were a success and his studio became the largest in Holland, though his gruff manner and open agnosticism didn't win him dinner-party invitations from the elite.

Rembrandt became one of the city's main art collectors, and often sketched and painted for himself, urging his staff to do likewise. Residents of the surrounding Jewish quarter provided perfect material for his dramatic biblical scenes.

In 1642, a year after the birth of their son Titus, Saskia died and business went downhill. Although Rembrandt's majestic group portrait *The Nightwatch* (1642) was hailed by art critics (it's now the Rijksmuseum's prize exhibit), some of the influential people he depicted were not pleased. Each subject had paid 100 guilders, and some were unhappy at being shoved to the background. In response, Rembrandt told them where they could shove their complaints. Suddenly he received far fewer orders.

Rembrandt began an affair with his son's governess but kicked her out a few years later when he fell for the new maid, Hendrickje Stoffels, who bore him a daughter, Cornelia. The public didn't take kindly to the man's lifestyle and his spiralling debts, and in 1656 he went bankrupt. His house and rich art collection were sold and he moved to the Rozengracht in the Jordaan.

No longer the darling of the wealthy, Rembrandt continued to paint, draw and etch – his etchings on display in the Rembrandthuis are some of the finest ever produced. He also received the occasional commission, including the monumental *Conspiracy of Claudius Civilis* (1661) for the City Hall, although authorities disliked it and had it removed. In 1662 he completed the *Staalmeesters* (the 'Syndics') for the drapers' guild and ensured that everybody remained clearly visible, though it ended up being his last group portrait.

The works of his later period show that Rembrandt had lost none of his touch. No longer constrained by the wishes of clients, he enjoyed new-found freedom; his works became more unconventional yet showed an ever-stronger empathy with their subject matter, as for instance in *A Couple: The Jewish Bride* (1665). The many portraits of Titus and Hendrickje, and his ever-gloomier self-portraits, are among the most stirring in the history of art.

A plague epidemic in 1663–64 killed one in seven Amsterdammers, including Hendrickje. Titus died in 1668, aged 27 and just married, and Rembrandt died a year later, a broken man.

Then there was Rembrandt van Rijn (see boxed text, above), who defied easy classification. The greatest and most versatile of 17th-century artists, he excelled in all artistic categories. Sometimes he was centuries ahead of his time, particularly with the emotive brush strokes of his later works.

Another great painter of this period, Frans Hals (1581/85–1666), was born in Antwerp but lived in Haarlem, just west of Amsterdam. He devoted most of his career to portraits, dabbling in occasional genre scenes with dramatic chiaroscuro. His ability to render the expressions of his subjects was equal to Rembrandt's, though he didn't explore their characters as much. Both masters used the same expressive, unpolished brush strokes and their styles went from bright exuberance in their early careers to darker and more solemn later on. Hals' work was also admired by the 19th-century Impressionists. In fact, his *The Merry Drinker* (1630) in the Rijksmuseum's collection, with its bold brush strokes, could almost have been painted by an Impressionist.

Hals also specialised in beautiful group portraits in which the groups almost looked natural, unlike the rigid line-ups produced by lesser contemporaries – though he wasn't as cavalier as Rembrandt in subordinating faces to the composition. A good example is the pair of paintings known collectively as *The Regents & the Regentesses of the Old Men's Alms House* (1664) in the Frans Hals Museum (p232) in Haarlem. It was a space Hals knew intimately; he lived in that almshouse, and the almshouse is now the museum.

The grand trio of 17th-century masters is completed by Johannes (also known as Jan) Vermeer (1632–75) of Delft. He produced only 35 meticulously crafted paintings in his career and died poor with 10 children – his baker accepted two paintings from his wife as payment for a debt of more than 600 guilders. Yet Vermeer mastered genre painting like no other artist. His paintings include historical and biblical scenes from his earlier career, his famous *View of Delft* (1661) in the Mauritshuis (p235) in Den Haag, and some tender portraits of unknown women, such as the stunningly beautiful *Girl with a Pearl Earring* (1666), also in the Mauritshuis.

Vermeer's work is known for serene light pouring through tall windows. The calm, spiritual effect is enhanced by dark blues, deep reds, warm yellows and supremely balanced composition. Good examples include Rijksmuseum's *The Kitchen Maid* (also known as *The Milkmaid,* 1658) and *Woman in Blue Reading a Letter* (1664), or, for his use of perspective, *The Love Letter* (1670). *The Little Street* (1658) in the Rijksmuseum's collection is Vermeer's only street scene.

Around the middle of the century, the stern focus on mood and subtle play of light began to make way for the splendour of the baroque. Jacob van Ruysdael (c 1628–82) went for dramatic skies and Aelbert Cuyp (1620–91) for Italianate landscapes. Van Ruysdael's pupil Meindert Hobbema preferred less heroic and more playful bucolic scenes full of pretty detail. (Note that Cuyp, Hobbema and Ruysdael all have main streets named after them in the Old South and De Pijp sections of the city. Many other, smaller, streets in this area are also named for Dutch artists.)

The genre paintings of Jan Steen (1626–79) show the almost frivolous aspect of baroque. Steen was also a tavern-keeper, and his depictions of domestic chaos led to the Dutch expression 'a Jan Steen household'. A good example is the animated revelry of *The Merry Family* (1668) in the Rijksmuseum's collection: it shows adults having a good time around the dinner table, oblivious to the children in the foreground pouring themselves a drink.

18TH & 19TH CENTURIES

The Golden Age of Dutch painting ended almost as suddenly as it began, when the French invaded the Low Countries in 1672. The economy collapsed and took with it the market for paintings. Painters who stayed in business concentrated on 'safe' works that repeated earlier successes. In the 18th century they copied French styles, pandering to the awe for anything French.

The results were competent but not ground-breaking. Cornelis Troost (1697–1750) was one of the best genre painters, sometimes compared to the British artist William Hogarth (1697–1764) for his satirical as well as sensitive portraits of ordinary people; Troost, too, introduced scenes of domestic revelry into his pastels.

Gerard de Lairesse (1640–1711) and Jacob de Wit (1695–1754) specialised in decorating the walls and ceilings of buildings – de Wit's trompe l'oeil decorations (painted illusions that look real) in the Theater Instituut Nederland (p88) and Bijbels Museum (p86) are worth seeing.

The late 18th century and most of the 19th century produced little of note, save for the landscapes and seascapes of Johan Barthold Jongkind (1819–91) and the gritty, almost photographic Amsterdam scenes of George Hendrik Breitner (1857–1923). They appear to have inspired French Impressionists, many of whom visited Amsterdam.

Jongkind and Breitner reinvented 17th-century realism and influenced the Hague School of the last decades of the 19th century. Painters such as Hendrik Mesdag (1831–1915), Jozef Israels (1824–1911) and the three Maris brothers (Jacob, Matthijs and Willem) created landscapes, seascapes and genre works, including the impressive *Panorama Mesdag* (1881), a gigantic, 360-degree cylindrical painting of the seaside town of Scheveningen viewed from a dune.

Without a doubt, the greatest 19th-century Dutch painter was Vincent van Gogh (1853–90), whose convulsive patterns and furious colours were in a world of their own and still defy comfortable categorisation. A post-Impressionist? A forerunner of Expressionism? For more about his life and works, see the Van Gogh Museum (p97).

PAINTING

DE STIJL

In his early career, Piet Mondriaan (1872–1944) – he dropped the second 'a' in his name when he moved to Paris in 1910 – painted in the Hague School tradition, but after flirting with Cubism he began painting in bold rectangular patterns, using only the three primary colours (yellow, blue and red) set against the three neutrals (white, grey and black). He named this style 'neo-Plasticism' and viewed it as an undistorted expression of reality in pure form and pure colour. His *Composition in Red, Black, Blue, Yellow & Grey* (1920), in the Stedelijk Museum's collection, is an elaborate example. Mondriaan's later works were more stark (or 'pure') and became dynamic again when he moved to New York in 1940. The world's largest collection of his paintings resides in the Gemeentemuseum (Municipal Museum; p235) in his native Den Haag.

Mondriaan was one of the leading exponents of De Stijl (The Style), a Dutch design movement that aimed to harmonise all the arts by bringing artistic expressions back to their essence. Its advocate was the magazine of the same name, first published in 1917 by Theo van Doesburg (1883–1931). Van Doesburg produced works similar to Mondriaan's, though he dispensed with the thick, black lines and later tilted his rectangles at 45 degrees, departures serious enough for Mondriaan to call off the friendship.

Throughout the 1920s and 1930s, De Stijl also attracted sculptors, poets, architects and designers. One of these was Gerrit Rietveld (1888–1964), designer of the Van Gogh Museum and several other buildings, but best known internationally for his furniture, such as the Mondriaanesque *Red Blue Chair* (1918) and his range of uncomfortable zigzag chairs that, viewed side-on, are simply a 'Z' with a backrest.

One of the most remarkable graphic artists of the 20th century was Maurits Cornelis Escher (1902–72). His drawings, lithos and woodcuts of blatantly impossible images continue to fascinate mathematicians and hang on college dorm walls everywhere: a waterfall feeds itself; people go up and down a staircase that ends where it starts; a pair of hands draw each other. You can see his work at Escher in het Paleis (p235) in Den Haag.

COBRA MOVEMENT

After WWII, artists rebelled against artistic conventions and vented their rage in abstract expressionism. In Amsterdam, Karel Appel (1921–) and Constant (Constant Nieuwenhuis, 1920–2005) drew on styles pioneered by Paul Klee and Joan Miró, and exploited bright colours and 'uncorrupted' children's art to produce lively works that leapt off the canvas. In Paris in 1945 they met up with the Danish Asger Jorn (1914–73) and the Belgian Corneille (Cornelis van Beverloo, 1922–), and together with several other artists and writers formed a group known as CoBrA (COpenhagen, BRussels, Amsterdam). It's been called the last great avant-garde movement.

CURRENT DUTCH ART & DESIGN

Marlene Dumas (1953–), a native of South Africa and now resident of Amsterdam, achieved fame in the 1980s and is now best known for her drawings and paintings of the human figure – instead of using live models, she relies on images from the mass media for her subjects. Amsterdam-based painter Peter Klashorst (1957–) specialises in portraits and nudes in bright colours. He was imprisoned in Africa for painting nude women and was also the subject of a reality TV show.

In the world of sculpture, Rotterdam-based Joep van Lieshout (1963–), through his company, Atelier Van Lieshout, is known for furniture, mobile-home units, model farms, even a self-contained replica village. If you don't catch his work in an exhibition, you can view his Mediamatic Supermarket (see Map pp290–1), an aluminium clad, curved box of an addition to the Spar Market near the southern entrance to the IJ-Tunnel (it's modular so that it can be easily removed in case the road is ever widened). Hans van Houwelingen (1957–) is especially known for creating art in public spaces.

Contemporary Dutch designers who are finding an international following include Amsterdam's own Marcel Wanders (for chairs of knotted rope), and Rotterdam's Hella Jongerius (for hand-embroidered ceramics – yes, ceramics).

CoBrA Museum (p116)

Their first major exhibition, in the Stedelijk Museum in 1949, aroused a storm of protest ('My child paints like that too'). Still, the CoBrA artists exerted a strong influence in their respective countries even after they disbanded in 1951. The CoBrA Museum (p116) in Amstelveen displays a good range of their works, including colourful ceramics.

PHOTOGRAPHY

For obvious reasons photography does not have the history of painting in Amsterdam, but what it lacks in longitude it makes up for in latitude. The area of the Jordaan around the Elandsgracht brims with photography studios and small galleries, while the museums FOAM (p92) and Huis Marseille (p87) specialise in photography.

Portraiture is a major theme of contemporary Dutch photography. Rineke Dijkstra (1959–) creates unflinching head-on portraits, both analytical and empathetic, of common people like soldiers carrying rifles and folks in bathing suits on the beach. Hellen van Meene's (1972–) portraits are more intimate, such as a series commissioned by the *New York Times* featuring pubescent Japanese girls, innocent with a tinge of eroticism. Inez van Lamsweerde (1963–) and Vinoodh Matadin (1961–), both born and educated in Amsterdam, create shots for exhibitions and advertising campaigns, at turns grim and glamorous.

Amsterdam-based Aernout Mik (1962–) has exhibited in Europe and North America with film installations known for their combining studies in group dynamics with a sculptor's sense of space. Marijke van Warmerdam (1959–), based in Amsterdam and New York, creates absurdist loops of everyday life in repeating sequences – eg the Japanese technique of bowing.

MUSIC

The dour church elders who once dismissed music as frivolous began to allow organ music in churches in the 17th century – it kept people out of pubs. With the possible exception of Jan Pieterszoon Sweelinck (1562–1621), an organ player in the Oude Kerk with an international reputation as a composer and a strong following in Germany, Amsterdam contributed relatively little to the world's music scene of that era.

Today, however, the world's top acts appear regularly and local musicians excel in (modern) classical music, jazz and techno/dance. In summer, free jazz, classical and world-music performances are staged in the Vondelpark, and free lunch-time concerts are held at various venues throughout the year. The Uitmarkt festival at the end of August also provides lots of free music. For more about music venues, see the Entertainment chapter (p174), and check the free entertainment papers for details.

CLASSICAL

The Netherlands has orchestras in cities throughout the country, but Amsterdam's Concertgebouw Orkest (Royal Concertgebouw Orchestra, p176) towers over them all, not least because of its winning concert hall, the Concertgebouw (p95), which has virtually perfect acoustics. The orchestra's director, Mariss Jansons (whose long list of credentials includes the Pittsburgh Symphony), took over in 2004 from Riccardo Chailly; Chailly had been with the orchestra since the late 1980s. The orchestra also frequently performs abroad, matching works by famous composers with little-known gems of the modern era. If you're looking to catch one of the top-flight soloists in the world, head here first.

The Concertgebouw is only one of several venues in town for classical music. Chamber music plays in the Beurs van Berlage, and very often the city's extant or converted churches host concerts. Check listings.

If you're looking for Dutch home-grown talent, you can hardly do better than pianist Ronald Brautigam. He performs around Holland and all over the world and brings a perfect piano-player mop-top too. Violinist-violist Isabelle van Keulen also brings in the crowds – she has founded her own chamber music festival in Delft. Cellists of note (so to speak) are Quirine Viersen and fiery Pieter Wispelwey, known for challenging himself with difficult music and succeeding.

Young pianist Wibi Soerjadi (1970–) is one of the country's most successful classical musicians. He specialises in romantic works – and being handsome. Elderly ladies swoon over his Javanese-prince looks and his penchant for driving his Ferrari fast.

Soprano Charlotte Margiono is known for her interpretations of *Le Nozze de Figaro* and *The Magic Flute*. Mezzo-soprano Jard van Nes has a giant reputation for her solo parts in Mahler's symphonies.

For 'old music' you can't go past the Combattimento Consort Amsterdam, concentrating on the music of the 17th and 18th centuries (Bach, Vivaldi and Handel; venues vary). The Amsterdam Baroque Orchestra (ABO) and Choir, conducted by Ton Koopman, has just completed what the *Guardian* called 'the recording project of the '90s', all of the existing cantatas of JS Bach. The ABO tours internationally but, when home, can often be seen performing at the Concertgebouw. Koopman also conducts the Radio Chamber Orchestra and guest conducts with orchestras worldwide. Performances by the Radio Philharmonic Orchestra are often recorded for radio and TV. One of its former artistic directors, Frans Brüggen, also works with the Orchestra on 18th-century pieces.

The Nederlandse Opera is based in the Stopera (officially called the Muziektheater; p176), where it stages world-class performances, though occasionally experimental fare stirs up controversy.

TOP FIVE TRACKS

- **Geef mij maar Amsterdam** (Give me Amsterdam every time) Sure to get locals going.
- **Het is Stil in Amsterdam** (It's quiet in Amsterdam) Melancholy ballad.
- **Op de Amsterdamse Grachten** (On the canals of Amsterdam) Great singalong number in a café.
- **Tulips from Amsterdam** Yes, it's a cliché, but that doesn't mean it's not popular; listen for a street-organ version.
- **Amsterdam Amsterdam** Oompah ballad that seems to close every public festival.

MODERN CLASSICAL & EXPERIMENTAL

The new Muziekgebouw aan 't IJ (p113) is the venue for this sort of work, which seems to thrive in Amsterdam. What used to be called de IJsbreker has moved to this fabulous waterside building near the Passenger Ship Terminal. Dutch modern composers include Michel van der Aa, Louis Andriessen, Theo Loevendie, Merlijn Twaalfhoven, Klaas de Vries and the late Ton de Leeuw. Worthwhile performers include the Trio, Asko Ensemble, Ives Ensemble, Nederlands Kamerkoor, Nieuw Ensemble, the Mondriaan Kwartet and the Schönberg Quartet.

Noorderkerk (p82) is one of several churches in Amsterdam that hosts music concerts

JAZZ

The distinction between modern classical and improvised music can be vague. Jazz-band leaders such as Willem Breuker and Willem van Manen of the Contraband have a decades-long reputation for straddling the two genres.

Recently, the Dutch jazz scene has become more mainstream with gifted young chanteuses such as Fleurine and especially Suriname-born Denise Jannah, widely recognised as the country's best jazz singer. The latter is the first singer from Suriname to be signed to the legendary Blue Note label. Her repertoire consists of American standards but she adds elements of Surinamese music on stage.

Astrid Seriese and Carmen Gomez operate in the crossover field, where jazz verges on, or blends with, pop. Father and daughter Hans and Candy Dulfer, tenor and alto saxophonists respectively, are a bit more daring. Dad, in particular, constantly extends his musical boundaries by experimenting with sampling techniques drawn from the hip-hop genre. Candy is better known internationally, thanks to her performances with Prince, Van Morrison, Dave Stewart, Pink Floyd and Maceo Parker, among others, which have introduced her to a wide audience.

Trumpeter and Jordaan-native Saskia Laroo mixes jazz with dance but is also respected in more traditional circles. Other leading instrumental jazz players include pianist and Thelonius Monk Award–winning Michiel Borstlap and bass player Hein van de Geyn – the latter appeared recently at the Concertgebouw. Among Borstlap's other honours, he was commissioned to write the world's first opera in Arabic, by the Emir of Qatar. It was called *Ibn Sina*, and premiered in 2003.

An effervescent soloist on the flute is Peter Guidi, who set up the jazz program at the Muziekschool Amsterdam and leads its Jazzmania big band.

The city's most important jazz venue is Bimhuis (p175) in the Muziekgebouw aan 't IJ. There are a number of smaller clubs in the streets east of the Leidseplein. For the biggest party with the biggest names in jazz, check out the **North Sea Jazz Festival** (p10), near Den Haag, every summer.

POP & DANCE

Amsterdam is the pop capital of the Netherlands, and bands and DJs are attracted to the city like moths to a flame. If successful they usually jump on a plane to London or LA, as the Dutch themselves lament.

THEY DID IT THEIR WAY...

Some Dutch musicians led exciting lives, but their deaths ... spectacular.

Herman Brood was both musician and artist – you can see his works at the Herman Brood Galerie (p190) above Cafe Dante, just off Spui Square – and a famous junkie. Although he completed a detox programme, his liver was so badly damaged that he did not want to face a life of sobriety, and in 2001 he flung himself from the roof of the Amsterdam Hilton hotel (which he used to famously wander with a parrot on his shoulder). His funeral, at the club Paradiso, was broadcast on national TV. After his death, his version of 'My Way' became his only No 1 hit in the Netherlands.

Andre Hazes was one of the Netherlands' best-loved folk singers, for his dramatic and often melancholy music. In 2004 he died of a heart attack attributed to a lifelong overindulgence in beer. His funeral took place in the Amsterdam ArenA football stadium (p184), with Dutch stars covering his tunes and 40,000 in attendance, plus an estimated 7 million more via TV. His family is quoted as saying 'Andre always wanted to play the ArenA just one more time'.

In the 1960s, though, the country's pop centre was Den Haag. Even if the self- proclaimed 'Dutch invasion' seems a stretch, the band Shocking Blue hit No 1 in the USA with 'Venus', and Golden Earring (still going strong for over 40 years) had a string of hits and successful international tours; their album *Eight Miles High* went gold in the USA. Famous Amsterdam bands in the 1960s were the Outsiders – a wild band whose lead singer, Wally Tax, was reputed to be the man with the longest hair in the country – and the Hunters, an instrumental guitar group that included Jan Akkerman. Akkerman later achieved international fame in the progressive rock band Focus (featuring Thijs van Leer as chief yodeller) and was proclaimed the best guitarist in the world in 1973. Also in the '70s, Herman Brood burst onto the scene with *His Wild Romance* and became a real-life druggy rock star.

In the late 1970s the squatter movement spawned a lively punk-music scene, followed by New Wave. In the mid-1980s Amsterdam was a centre for guitar-driven rock bands like Claw Boys Claw. Most lyrics were in English, but the pop group Doe Maar broke through in Dutch, inspiring scores of bands such as Tröckener Kecks.

Around this time Amsterdam also evolved into a capital of club music. Music evolved from house to techno to R&B. Perhaps the best-known Dutch dance variant of house was 'gabber', a style that was popularised by acts like Charly Lownoise & Mental Theo in which the number of beats per minute and the noise of buzzing synthesizers went beyond belief.

The hip grooves of Candy Dulfer (and the hip-hoppy Urban Dance Squad) made America's Top 20 during the 1980s. Bettie Serveert (Betty serves), a nod to Dutch tennis player Betty Stöve, grew into one of the biggest bands on the club circuit. The last decade saw a growing and vital hip-hop scene, spearheaded by the Dutch-rapping Osdorp Posse and Brainpower. Following in their footsteps, the current power-player is the immensely popular Moroccan-Dutch rapper Ali B, who won a Mobo at the Royal Albert Hall in 2004 (and dissed the audience with his Dutch raps about them being rich, lazy and too commercial). Lange Frans and Bas B are also climbing the charts.

Amsterdam is a major centre for DJs – not just for the Netherlands but for the world; there are thousands of DJs in town. Top names on the international circuit include Tiesto, Armin van Buren and Marco V. You can find them at large and small venues in town, although the latter sell out quickly! Other locally known names include Bart Skils and his nu-techno beats, Joost van Bellen with his old-school club style, and the UNK team with underground gay-friendly electro parties.

Pop festivals come out of the woodwork in the warmer months: Pinkpop (p10) in Landgraaf and Parkpop (p10) in Den Haag. Dance Valley (p10) near Haarlem pulls more than 100 bands and a sleepless crowd of near-Woodstock proportions.

WORLD MUSIC

Cosmopolitan Amsterdam offers a wealth of world music. Suriname-born Ronald Snijders, a top jazz flautist, often participates in world-music projects. Another jazz flautist heading towards 'world' is the eternal Chris Hinze with his album *Tibet Impressions*, though most of his repertoire falls in the New Age category.

Fra-Fra-Sound plays 'paramaribop', a unique mixture of traditional Surinamese *kaseko* (fusion of African, European and American music styles) and jazz. The moniker is a contraction of Paramaribo (the capital of Suriname) and bebop. But the bulk of world repertoire from Amsterdam is Latin, ranging from Cuban salsa to Dominican merengue and Argentinian tango.

An interesting Amsterdam-Brazilian band is Zuco 103, that combine bossa nova and samba with DJ rubs on the turntable. It has strong ties with the equally eclectic New Cool Collective, a 22-member big band that blends jazz with drum 'n' bass. It has received raves for the soundtrack it performed with the live-action version of the film *The Jungle Book*. World-music clubs and events to check out while you are in Amsterdam include Marmoucha (for Moroccan live bands and DJs), Laziz (for Arabian dance music), Que Pasa (with an intriguing mix of dance music from Mexican to Russian) and Club Mahsen (Turkish dance music).

The Amsterdam Roots Festival of world music is organised at different locations every year in June, centred on the Oosterpark – check for details with the Uitburo, the VVV, or www.amsterdamroots.nl. The Tropeninstituut Theater (p176) often hosts non-Western music concerts.

LITERATURE

The following contemporary books are written by local and foreign authors and set in Amsterdam or nearby. Of the books among them originally written in Dutch, all are available in English thanks to the Dutch Literary Production and Translation Fund (www.nlpvf.nl), which propagates Dutch literature abroad. See the History chapter (boxed text, p48) for historical works of importance to the city.

Cees Nooteboom is one of the Netherlands' most prolific writers of fiction, non-fiction, book introductions, etc, etc. His novel, *The Following Story,* won the Aristeion European Prize for Literature in 1991, while his most recent work, 2004's *Paradise Lost,* is an allegorical tale of angels and humans told in two parts: Brazilians in Australia and a literary critic in Austria.

Love in Amsterdam by Nicholas Freeling was the inaugural book of the Van der Valk detective series, which later gained fame when it was made into a series on the BBC. *Girl with a Pearl Earring* by Tracy Chevalier was made into a Hollywood movie starring Colin Firth (as Jan Vermeer) and Scarlett Johansson (as a maid in his employ). The story explores the conflicts between duty and sexuality. It is set not in Amsterdam but Delft, yet it nonetheless offers real insights into life in the Golden Age of Dutch painting.

A Dutchman's Slight Adventures by Simon Carmiggelt is an amusing collection of vignettes about De Pijp from the author's column in the newspaper *Het Parool. Parents Worry* by Gerard Reve is a contemporary classic, a tragicomic novel about a day in the ravaged life of a singer and poet with one hell of a case of writer's block and an amusing fight to overcome it. Reve's *On my Way to the End* (1963) tells his story in letter form – homosexuality, conversion to Catholicism and more. Anyone wanting to learn the ins and outs of the sex trade will want to grab *The Happy Hooker* by Xaviera Hollander.

Turkish Delight by Jan Wolkers, an odd love story, about a man who loves too much, shocked Dutch readers in 1969. It's provocatively misogynistic but also powerful. It was later made into a (Dutch) film by Paul Verhoeven starring Rutger Hauer that put both of them on the map.

Tulip Fever by Deborah Moggach offers a feel for Amsterdam proper around the time when Rembrandt was at his peak and tulips were worth more than their weight in gold. A nice bonus is the reproductions of Dutch paintings in some editions.

TOP FIVE EARLY DUTCH AUTHORS

- Joost van den Vondel – dramatist, often called 'the Shakespeare of the Netherlands'
- Baruch de Spinoza – Jewish philosopher who rejected the notion of free will
- Pieter Cornelisz Hooft – poet and philosopher
- Erasmus – satirist and humanist
- Multatuli – wrote *Max Havelaar,* on groundbreaking themes of relations between the races

The *UnDutchables*, by Colin White and Laurie Boucke, is a point of reference for virtually anyone who goes to live in the Netherlands. Over two decades, these two Americans have discovered – and don't hesitate to point out – foibles that many Dutch themselves seem not to recognise, making it a point of reference even for Dutch people.

RED-LIGHT READS

American author John Irving (*The World According to Garp*, *The Cider House Rules*) set his novel *A Widow for One Year* in Amsterdam's Red Light District, and the British novelist Irvine Welsh (*Trainspotting*, *Porno*) wrote *The Acid House*, a short-story collection about Amsterdam's drug underworld.

CINEMA

Dutch films haven't exactly set the world on fire, though this has more to do with the language barrier and funding problems in a modest distribution area than with lack of talent. The Dutch film industry produces about 20 films annually, often in association with other countries. Private funding is increasing as government funding has been scaled back in recent years. Many of the leading directors swing back and forth between film and TV.

But what films have been produced tend to get attention. Ben Sombogaart's *Twin Sisters* (Dutch title: *de Tweeling*; 2002), a touching story of twins separated in the Netherlands and Germany during WWII, was nominated for an Academy Award for best foreign language film in 2004. In 2003, *Zus & So* directed by Paula van der Oest also was nominated for an Academy Award for best foreign language film.

Dutch film-makers who have made it big in Hollywood include Amsterdam-born Paul Verhoeven (*Total Recall*, *Basic Instinct*, *Starship Troopers*) and Jan de Bont who directed the box-office hits *Speed*, *Twister*, *Lara Croft: Tomb Raider* and the upcoming *Meg*, in addition to producing *Minority Report*. Cinematographer Rogier Stoffers shot *School of Rock* and the 2005 remake of *The Bad News Bears*.

Foreign movies screened in Amsterdam are rarely ever dubbed but instead subtitled – as any film purist will tell you they should be.

THEO VAN GOGH

Obituaries for Theo van Gogh, famously murdered on an Amsterdam street in November 2004, refer to him as a film-maker, but that's too simple. He was a provocateur, personality, gadabout and, above all, deeply charismatic.

Van Gogh was born in Den Haag in 1957 (a distant relative of that *other* Theo van Gogh – the painter's brother) but made his home in Amsterdam. When, as a young man, he applied for admission to the Dutch Film Academy, he was rejected and advised to see a psychologist. His first film, *Lüger* (1980), included images of a pistol being inserted into a woman's vagina and (faked) footage of kittens in a clothes dryer. After the premiere, one audience member spat in Van Gogh's face.

He made 25 films over the years, some of little distinction, although his greatest box-office success *06* (also called *1-900* in some territories; 1994), about a phone-sex relationship, was the top-grossing Dutch film of the year.

Van Gogh seemed to enjoy spending as much time in front of the camera as behind it, especially the act of tweaking others about the nose. He appeared on a 'VIP' version of *Big Brother*. In articles and speeches and on his website *The Happy Smoker* (he chain-smoked), he took positions at odds with most of the Netherlands' – in favour of cruise missiles, US President George W Bush, the War in Iraq – and predicted the assassination of Pim Fortuyn (p13). He enraged the local Jewish community by saying that they made too much of Auschwitz.

But his most famous diatribes – which ultimately did him in – were reserved for Muslim immigrants, regularly referring to Moroccans as 'goatf**kers'. His last book, the 2003 *Allah weet het beter* ('Allah knows best'; 2003), was as cynical as the title implies.

Submission: Part 1 was Van Gogh's last film, four stories in 11 unflinching minutes showing how verses from the Quran could be used to justify violence against women.

Yet for all Van Gogh's biting and bluster, the moments immediately before his death were telling. After he was knocked off his bike by the first bullet, he is quoted as saying to his attacker: 'We can still talk about it.' For details of the murder, see p13.

Kriterion (p178), cinema at Oosterpark

The Filmmuseum (p98) in the Vondelpark occasionally screens interesting films from its huge archive and elsewhere, and there are many art-house cinemas in town.

There are several film festivals held during the year throughout the country, including the Rotterdam International Film Festival in February, Utrecht's Netherlands Film Festival in September, and Amsterdam's International Documentary Film Festival in December.

THEATRE

The city has a rich theatrical tradition dating back to medieval times. In the Golden Age, when Dutch was the language of trade, local companies toured the theatres of Europe with the tragedies of Vondel, the comedies of Bredero and verses of PC Hooft. They're still performed locally, even if there's precious little in English translation.

Theatre was immensely popular with all levels of society for many reasons, not least of which was because plays were often performed outdoors. Towards the end of the 19th century, however, theatre had become snobbish, with little room for development.

This attitude persisted until the late 1960s, when disgruntled actors began to throw tomatoes at their older colleagues and engage the audience in discussions about the essence of theatre. Avant-garde theatre companies such as Mickery and Shaffy made Amsterdam a centre for experimental theatre, and many smaller companies sprang up in the 1970s and 1980s.

Most of these have now merged or disappeared, but survivors and newcomers still stage excellent productions – visual feasts with striking sets, lighting and creative costumes. The language barrier can be an issue, depending on the production.

When it's not touring abroad, De Dogtroep stages fancy and unpredictable 'happenings' in quirky venues like the Passenger Ship Terminal. Each show is supported by flashy multimedia effects and technical gadgetry, with every set specially developed by a team of designers and painters. A spin-off, Warner & Consorten, stages dialogue-free shows that inject humour into everyday situations and objects, while music is generated with weird materials.

Cosmic (p180) deserves special mention for productions reflecting the city's multicultural communities (Surinamese, Indonesian etc). The comedy scene is led by English-language outfits like Boom Chicago (p178).

37

English-language companies often visit Amsterdam, especially in summer – check the *Uitkrant* or ask at the Uitburo. Glitzy large-budget musicals have won over audiences in recent years – typically they play to full houses in the Koninklijk Theater Carré (p170) or other large venues.

The Dutch also produce some of the world's best youth theatre, and don't forget the Marionettentheater (p179), where marionettes perform opera.

The **Holland Festival** (p10), **Over Het IJ** (p10) and the **Uitmarkt** (p10) are big theatre events. Also worth catching is the **International Theatre School Festival** (p10) at the end of June, in the theatres around Nes (Frascati, Brakke Grond etc).

Those with a particular interest in theatre should be sure to visit the Theatre Museum in the Theater Instituut Nederland (p88).

DANCE

Amsterdam's National Ballet (www.het-nationale-ballet.nl) performs mainly classical ballets, but also presents 20th-century works by Dutch choreographers like Rudi van Dantzig and Toer van Schayk. The Ballet has helped launch careers of promising dancemasters such as John Wisman and Ted Brandsen (who is now the artistic director).

The Netherlands is also a world leader in modern dance. The troupe of the Nederlands Dans Theater in Den Haag leaps and pirouettes to international audiences. There are also many smaller modern-dance companies such as Introdans, which can truly be described as poetry in motion. Amsterdam's Julidans festival in July brings dancers together from all over the world.

Architecture ∎

Architecture

Amsterdam is an architectural marvel, with no fewer than 7000 registered historical buildings. Yet only a few buildings impress with size or scale. Rather, the city's beauty lies in the countless private dwellings, especially within the Canal Belt – each one, it seems, stands out in its own way. No other city in Europe has such a wealth of residential architecture.

Amsterdam was largely built by citizens and businesses, although the government has traditionally provided land, determined sizes for housing plots and enforced building standards. Even today, authorities tend to give architects more leeway than they're used to elsewhere, ensuring that Amsterdam remains at the architectural cutting edge. The newest constructions, especially in the Eastern Docklands, may prove to be the marvels of centuries to come.

Those with a serious interest in architecture should visit Arcam (Stichting Architectuur Centrum Amsterdam; p112), or at least its website www.arcam.nl.

MIDDLE AGES

Amsterdam was built on marsh, and the soft ground precluded the use of heavy materials in early construction.

The earliest houses were made of timber and clay with thatched roofs, but even these were occasionally too heavy and sank into the ground, needing to be pulled back up. That was not the only danger: fires in the 15th century burnt down much of the city centre, forcing the use of noncombustible material, and therein lay the problem. There was plenty of clay to be used for bricks, but brick was too heavy. Stone was out of the question.

Engineers got around this problem by bolstering the ground beneath the city, driving piles into the peat until it struck the sandy layer below, sometimes several metres down. The tops of the piles were then evened off, and the construction could go forward with the heavier materials. Thus timber side walls gave way to brick, and in the 16th century thatched roofs were replaced by tiles. Timber continued to be used for façades, floor beams, roof frames and gables into the 17th century, but eventually brick and sandstone triumphed here too.

WHAT TO SEE

Only two early houses with timber façades have survived to this day. The house at **Begijnhof 34** (Map pp286–7), in the Begijnhof, a lovely courtyard that is an escape unto itself near Spui Square, dates from 1465, making it the oldest preserved wooden house in the country. Another preserved wooden house from the mid-16th century is at **Zeedijk 1** (Map pp286–7).

The city's oldest surviving building is the Gothic **Oude Kerk** (Old Church, 1340; p65), considered a prime example of the Dutch brick Gothic style. The second-oldest is the late-Gothic **Nieuwe Kerk** (New Church; p69) from the early 15th century. If you're familiar with church architecture, you'll note how the interior focus has shifted from the (Catholic) choir and altar to the (Protestant) pulpit. In both churches, notice the wooden roof frames.

Another classic of the era is the **Montelbaanstoren** (Map pp290–1; cnr Oude Schans & Oude Waal). In the 1510s, after an attack by troops from Gelderland in the east, the area was fortified by means of a wide canal, the Oude Schans, and the Montelbaanstoren was constructed as a gun tower in 1516. Its octagonal steeple was added in 1606 to a design by Hendrick de Keyser (see opposite). In addition to being a signature building for the city, it was also a favourite subject of Rembrandt's. Today the tower is used by the city water works.

TOP FIVE NOTABLE BUILDINGS

- **Oude Kerk** (p65) & **Nieuwe Kerk** (p69)
- **Royal Palace** (p70)
- **Rijksmuseum** (p96)
- **Het Schip** (p81)
- **Muziekgebouw aan 't IJ** (p113)

GABLES, HOISTS & HOUSES THAT TIP

One of the hallmarks of Amsterdam is the gables (home-front façades at roof level) that adorn houses along the city's canals. They're cheery and fun, and when you get a bunch of them in a row the play of geometry can be dramatic.

The gables both hid the roof from public view and helped to identify the house, until the French-led government introduced house numbers in 1795 (though the current system dates from 1875). The more ornate the gable, the easier it was to recognise. Other distinguishing features included façade decorations, signs or wall tablets (see boxed text, p42).

There are four main types of gables. The simple spout gable, with diagonal outline and semicircular windows or shutters, mimicked the earliest wooden gables and was used mainly for warehouses from the 1580s to the early 1700s. The step gable was a late-Gothic design favoured by Dutch-Renaissance architects from 1580 to 1660. The neck gable, also known as the bottle gable because it resembled a bottle spout, was introduced in the 1640s and proved the most durable, featuring in designs through the early 19th century; some neck gables also incorporated a step. The bell gable first appeared in the 1660s and became popular in the 18th century.

From the 18th century onwards many newly constructed houses no longer had gables but straight, horizontal cornices, though often richly decorated.

Many canal houses look as if they're tipping forward. Rest assured, they're not about to collapse on you; rather, they were designed that way. Given the narrowness of the houses (and particularly their staircases, as anyone who's ever been inside one can attest) owners needed a way to move large goods and furniture to upper storeys directly from the outside. The solution: a hoist built into the gable or cornice, to lift objects up and in through (removable) windows. The houses tip so that the goods won't bump into them. Clever, elegant, still in use and very cool to watch (we hope you catch one in action). A few houses have huge hoist-wheels in the attic with a rope and hook that run through the hoist beam. Almost all others have a beam with a hook for a hoist block.

The forward lean is also said to make houses seem larger, which makes it easier to admire the façade and gable from the street – a fortunate coincidence for everyone.

DUTCH RENAISSANCE

From the middle of the 16th century, the Italian Renaissance began to filter to the Netherlands, and architects here developed a unique style with rich ornamentation that merged classical and traditional elements. In the façades they used mock columns (pilasters) and replaced the traditional spout gables with step gables (see boxed text, above) richly decorated with sculptures, columns and obelisks. The playful interaction of red (or sometimes orange) brick and horizontal bands of white or yellow sandstone was based on mathematical formulas and designed to please the eye.

The best known name of this time was Hendrick de Keyser (1565–1621), the city sculptor, with valuable cooperation from Hendrick Staets (who also planned the Canal Belt) and the city bricklayer Cornelis Danckerts.

WHAT TO SEE

Be sure to check out the **Bartolotti House**, now part of the **Theater Instituut Nederland** (p88), which was designed by De Keyser. He also designed the three 'directional churches' in town: the **Zuiderkerk** (Southern Church; p79) and **Westerkerk** (Western Church; p89), both in which he retained the usual Gothic elements, and the **Noorderkerk** (Northern Church;

Noorderkerk (p82), built in 1623 by Hendrick de Keyser

WALL TABLETS

Before the introduction of street numbers in 1795, many of Amsterdam's residences were identified by their wall tablets. These painted or carved stone plaques (dating from the mid-17th century) were practical decorations to identify not only the inhabitant's house but also their origin, religion or profession. Beautiful examples of these stones are still found on many of the buildings along the main canals. Occupations are the most frequently occurring theme: tobacconists, milliners, merchants, skippers, undertakers and even grass-mowers.

As well as being colourful reminders of the city's former citizens, these tablets also provide hints about the city's past. A stone depicting a mail wagon at Singel 74 commemorates the commencement of the postal service between Amsterdam and Den Haag in 1660. Further down the street, a tablet portraying the scene of Eve tempting Adam with an apple attests to the time when that part of the street operated as a fruit market (known as the 'apple market').

Many wall tablets dotted throughout the city celebrate the life of famous citizens like the maritime hero Michiel Adriaenszoon de Ruyter and biologist Jan Swammerdam, but the most appealing are memorials to domestic life and common vocations of the age.

Map pp286–7), in which he defined a new style for Dutch Protestant church architecture, with the church laid out like a Greek cross with the pulpit in the centre. An eastern church was contemplated but never built as grandly as the rest, on the site of the present-day Amstelkerk.

De Keyser was also something of a tower specialist. He created the steeple of the Montelbaanstoren (p40) and was responsible for another city landmark, the Munttoren (Mint Tower; Map pp292–3; cnr Rokin & Singel). On this site stood the 15th-century Regulierspoort, a city gate that burned down in 1619, and De Keyser built the tower on what was left of the gate. The tower received its current name in 1672–73, when the French occupied much of the republic and the national mint was transferred here for safekeeping (it had been in the city of Dordrecht).

Also attributed to De Keyser is the Rasphuis Gate (Map pp292–3). Halfway along Heiligeweg, on the southeastern side, it once gave access to the Rasphuis, a model penitentiary where beggars and delinquents were put to work to ease their return to society. One of their backbreaking jobs was to rasp (scrape roughly) Brazil wood for the dyeing industry. Now it's a gateway to the Kalvertoren Shopping Centre (Map pp292–3).

Important commercial buildings of the era include the step-gabled Greenland Warehouses (Map pp286–7; Keizersgracht 40-44). They belonged to the Greenland (or Nordic) Company, which dominated Arctic whaling in the early 17th century. Whale oil was much sought after for soap, lamp oil, paint etc, and wells in these warehouses held 100,000L of the precious stuff. The storage facilities were moved in the 1680s, but you can still see decorations related to whaling on many nearby houses.

Another wonderful example of this period is the Huis aan de Drie Grachten (House on the Three Canals, 1609; Map pp286–7; Oudezijds Achterburgwal 329), where the three *burgwallen* (fortified embankments) meet. Note the house's steep gables, leaded glass windows and handsome shutters.

DUTCH CLASSICISM

During the Golden Age of art in the 17th century (p27), architects such as Jacob van Campen (1595–1657), and Philips Vingboons (1607–78) and his brother Justus adhered more strictly to Greek and Roman classical design and dropped many of De Keyser's playful decorations. Influenced by Italian architects such as Palladio and Scamozzi, they made façades resemble temples, and pilasters look like columns. The idea was to impress. Van Campen was known for his public buildings, while the Vingboons brothers specialised in residential architecture in the Western Canal Belt.

To accentuate the vertical lines, they changed the step gable to a neck gable with decorative scrolls, topped to imitate a 'temple roof'. Soft red brick was made more durable with brown paint. Later in the 17th century, external decorations made way for sumptuous interiors, while exterior faux columns became less ornamental or disappeared altogether.

With the building of the Southern Canal Belt, wealthy Amsterdammers often bought two adjoining plots and built houses with five windows across instead of the usual three. Adriaan Dortsman (1625–82) was perhaps the most representative architect of this austere classicist style. A mathematician by training, he favoured a stark, geometrical simplicity – preferably with flat, sandstone façades – that enhanced the grandeur of his buildings.

WHAT TO SEE

The most impressive example of the Dutch Classicist style is Van Campen's city hall (now Royal Palace, p70).

Works by the Vingboons brothers include the current Bijbels Museum (p86), the White House (now also part of the Theater Instituut Nederland, p88) and the fine example at Keizersgracht 319.

Justus Vingboons' Trippenhuis (Map pp286–7; Kloveniersburgwal 29) is a good example of the later style with less external ornamentation. Just south of the Nieuwmarkt, the Trippenhuis was built in 1660–64 to house the wealthy Trip brothers, Lodewijk and Hendrik, who made their fortune in metals, artillery and ammunition. The greystone mansion with Corinthian pilasters consists of two separate houses with false middle windows, and the chimneys are shaped like mortars to indicate their owners' trade.

You can view the work of Dortsman in the Ronde Lutherse Kerk (Round Lutheran Church; p70) and the current Museum Van Loon (p94).

18TH-CENTURY 'LOUIS STYLES'

The wealthy class now began to enjoy the fortunes amassed by their merchant predecessors. Many turned to banking and finance and conducted their business from the comfort of opulent homes. Traders no longer stored goods in the attic but in warehouses elsewhere.

The preoccupation with all things French provided fertile ground for Huguenot refugees, such as Daniel Marot (1661–1752) and his assistants Jean and Anthony Coulon, who introduced French interior design with matching exteriors. Interiors were bathed in light thanks to stuccoed ceilings and tall sash windows (a French innovation), and everything from staircases to furniture was designed in harmony. Elegant bell gables, although first introduced around 1660, became commonplace at this time. Many architects did away with gables altogether in favour of richly decorated horizontal cornices.

The Louis XIV style, with its dignified symmetry and façades decorated with statuary and leaves, dominated until about 1750. It overlapped slightly with the Louis XV style (beginning around 1740), which brought asymmetrical rococo shapes resembling rocks and waves. Pilasters and pillars made a comeback around 1770 with Louis XVI designs.

WHAT TO SEE

At the late-Louis-style Felix Meritis Building (p86), note the enormous Corinthian half-columns designed by Jacob Otten Husly (1738–97).

The Maagdenhuis (Map pp292–3) on the Spui, designed by city architect Abraham van der Hart (1747–1820), is a much more sober interpretation of the new classicism. This classicist building was built in 1787 as a Catholic orphanage for girls and is now the administrative seat of the University of Amsterdam. Historical note: in 1969 it was occupied by students, a watershed in the development of students' rights in the country. Police cordoned off the building but the occupiers held out for five days, with supplies ferried across a bridge that supportive workers built over the alley.

19TH-CENTURY NEOSTYLES

Architecture stagnated in the first half of the 19th century as Amsterdam's economy struggled after the Napoleonic era. Safe neoclassicism held sway until the 1860s, when architects here and elsewhere in Europe began to rediscover other styles of the past.

The latter half of the century was dominated by neo-Gothic, harkening back to the grand Gothic cathedrals in which no design element was superfluous, and neo-Renaissance, which brought De Keyser's Dutch-Renaissance architecture back into the limelight. It was around this time that Catholics regained their freedom of worship in open churches, and neo-Gothic suited the boom in Catholic church building just fine; residential architects focused on neo-Renaissance.

One of the leading architects of this period was Pierre Cuypers (1827–1921), who built several neo-Gothic churches but often merged the two styles, as did CH Peters, while AC Bleijs created both monumental and smaller commercial buildings.

Around the turn of the century, Art Nouveau became popular across Europe, incorporating steel and glass with curvilinear designs resembling plants. In Amsterdam, Art Nouveau showed up mainly in shop fronts but little else; if you're looking for Art Nouveau, head to Den Haag (p233).

WHAT TO SEE

Pierre Cuypers designed two of the buildings any visitor to Amsterdam is likely to encounter: **Centraal Station** (see boxed text, p64) and the **Rijksmuseum** (p96). Here you can easily see the interplay of Gothic forms with Dutch-Renaissance brickwork. Another fine example of this mixture is CH Peters' general post office, now **Magna Plaza** (p69). Alfred Tepe's **Krijtberg** (p93) is more clearly Gothic (note the use of brick).

You can also view the ebullient neo-Renaissance façade of the **former milk factory** (Map pp292–3; Prinsengracht 739-741), built in 1876 to a design by Eduard Cuypers (Pierre's nephew). Until then, milk was brought into town from the surrounding countryside in wooden barrels and sold on the streets from open buckets.

Bleijs was the architect of the high profile **St Nicolaaskerk** (p65), while his intimate **PC Hooft Store** (1881; Map pp292–3; Keizersgracht 508), at the corner of Leidsestraat, is entirely different. This Dutch-Renaissance throwback with a Germanic tower was built for a cigar manufacturer and called the PC Hooft Store to commemorate the 300th birthday of the poet, playwright, historian and national icon, Pieter Cornelisz Hooft. The playful façade reliefs depict the various stages of tobacco preparation. Perhaps fittingly, it now houses a 'smart drug' shop.

Isaac Gosschalk used a similar approach in his 1879 design for the buildings at **Reguliersgracht 57-59**. The design is reminiscent of the city's medieval wooden houses, which makes sense since it was for a carpentry firm. Canal-boat operators fantasise that a midwife lived in the corner house at **No 92**, decorated with a statuette of a stork.

AL van Gendt's **Concertgebouw** (p95) is obviously neoclassical, but its interplay of red brick and white sandstone is Dutch Renaissance.

Van Gendt also designed the shopping arcade at Radhuisstraat towards Keizersgracht, for an insurance company, with sculptures of vicious animals to stress the dangers of life without insurance. Smoke bombs greeted Princess Beatrix's wedding coach as it passed this arcade in 1966.

Art Deco can be seen in a number of structures, most notably the **Greenpeace Building** (Map pp286–7; Keizersgracht 174-176). This tall building was built in 1905 for a life insurance company – the façade's huge tile tableau shows a guardian angel who seems to be peddling an insurance policy. Greenpeace no longer has its world headquarters here, but locals still know the building by that name. Other Art Nouveau structures are the **Amsterdam American Hotel** (p221), which occupies a prime location on the Leidseplein, and the riotous **Tuschinskitheater** (p178).

Art-Deco Greenpeace Building

BERLAGE & THE AMSTERDAM SCHOOL

The neo-styles and their reliance on the past were criticised by Hendrik Petrus Berlage (1856–1934), the father of modern Dutch architecture. Instead of expensive construction and excessive decoration, he favoured simplicity and rational use of materials.

Berlage's residential architecture approached a block of buildings as a whole, not as a collection of individual houses. In this he influenced the young architects of what became known as the Amsterdam School. Leading exponents of this style were Michel de Klerk (1884–1923), Piet Kramer (1881–1961) and Johan van der Mey (1878–1949).

Many architects of this school worked for the city council and designed the buildings of the ambitious 'Plan South', a large-scale expansion project mapped out by Berlage, with quality housing, wide boulevards and cosy squares. Humble brick housing blocks became sculpture, with curved corners, oddly placed windows and ornamental rocket-shaped towers. It was a period of frantic residential building activity beyond the Canal Belt. Close cooperation between housing corporations, city planners and council architects made the Amsterdam School more than just an architectural movement: it was a complete philosophy of city planning.

The Amsterdam School also coincided with the city's hosting of the Olympic Games in 1928, giving the architecture a worldwide platform.

WHAT TO SEE

Beurs van Berlage (p64) displayed Berlage's ideals to the full. Try to attend a concert or exhibit there or at least visit the café.

Johan van der Mey's remarkable Scheepvaarthuis (Shipping House, 1916; Map pp290–1; cnr Binnenkant & Prins Hendrikkade) was the first building in the Amsterdam School style and is still one of its finest examples. It uses the street layout to resemble a ship's bow, and note the many façade sculptures. It is now home to the GVB, the municipal transport company.

De Klerk's Het Schip (p81) in the Haarlem Quarter and Kramer's Cooperatiehof (Map p297) in the Pijp neighbourhood, have been described as fairytale fortresses rendered in a Dutch version of Art Deco. De Klerk also designed the idiosyncratic housing estates at Henriëtte Ronnerplein and Thérèse Schwartzeplein, near the Cooperatiehof. The eccentric details of these structures are worth noting: vertically laid bricks, letterboxes as works of art, asymmetric windows, oddly shaped doorways, funny chimneys, creative solutions for corners. While there, look up: sometimes the most interesting details are above the ground floor.

However, this 'form over function' ethic meant that their designs were not always fantastic to live in. Kitchens were tiny because residents were supposed to eat in a proper dining room; windows were set high because residents weren't supposed to look out but read a book.

FUNCTIONALISM

While Amsterdam School–type buildings were being erected, a new generation of architects began to rebel against the school's impractical, expensive structures. Influenced by the Bauhaus, Frank Lloyd Wright and Le Corbusier, they formed 'de 8' in 1927.

Architects such as Ben Merkelbach and Gerrit Rietveld believed that form should follow function and advocated steel, glass and concrete. Buildings should be spacious and practical structures with plenty of sunlight, not masses of art made in brick to glorify architects. The Committee of Aesthetics Control didn't agree and kept the functionalists out of the Canal Belt.

Functionalism finally came to the fore after WWII, with new suburbs west and south of the city. An acute housing shortage meant that these suburbs were built on a larger scale than originally planned, yet they still weren't sufficient. By the time the Bijlmermeer housing estates were built southeast of the centre in the 1960s and 1970s, there was resistance to such large-scale building.

In the inner city the emphasis shifted towards urban renewal, particularly in areas that had to be rebuilt after the construction of the metro line. Architects of this time include Aldo van Eyck and his student Theo Bosch, though their work remains controversial; critics call it 'parasite architecture' because it looks so out of place against 17th- and 18th-century surroundings.

WHAT TO SEE

Early ostracism or not, Rietveld left Amsterdam some high-profile works. Most prominently, he designed the **Van Gogh Museum** (p97), where the minimalist, open space allows the artist's works to shine. He also managed to penetrate the Canal Belt with some smaller projects. You can enjoy coffee inside his work at **M Café** (p143) atop Metz Department Store, and also **Café Walem** (p142).

Van Eyck's designs included the **Moederhuis** (Map pp290-1; Plantage Middenlaan 33); Bosch's included the **Pentagon Housing Estate** (1983; Map pp286-7; cnr St Antoniesbreestraat & Zwanenburgwal) a community housing project with a very contemporary glass wall that doubles as a waterfall (when the water's on).

THE PRESENT

Suburbs have been built on a more human scale since the 1970s, with low- and medium-rise apartments integrated with shops, schools and offices. Some of the old warehouse spaces were redone and now make very attractive live-and-work spaces.

The most significant developments, however, are taking place in the Eastern Docklands district. The Docklands were islands built into the IJ, with exotic names like Java and Borneo for the places they traded with – you'll find similar naming on warehouse buildings throughout town. The Docklands sat abandoned for decades in the 20th century until the city decided to add housing. An unsuccessful bid for the 1992 Olympics meant that Amsterdam had land on its hands. The hulking apartment complexes here don't feel like anything else you've seen in Amsterdam, but they certainly make a statement.

WHAT TO SEE

In the Eastern Islands, a must-see is the **Entrepotdok** (Map pp290-1; Entrepotdok 1), just across the bridge from the Plantage. This mid-80s redo of over 80 large 18th- and early-19th-century warehouses created mostly apartments, with studios and limited commercial space. Although the interior of the building was gutted to let in light for living space, the designers used existing façades and timber flooring.

Looking east from Centraal Station you can see the new **Muziekgebouw aan 't IJ** (p113).

Barcelonaplein, on KNSM Island, is a massive cylindrical edifice that is open on its south side, facing the city. It was designed by the Belgian architect Bruno Albert and features an iron 'fence' that completes a circular courtyard. On Sporenburg island, the 'Whale' (2000) is a mammoth, zinc-clad apartment building named for its sloping shape that's open at the top and bottom as if it's rearing its head and tail (you kind of have to imagine it).

A tall **pedestrian bridge** at the eastern end of Sporenburg links this peninsula to Borneo Eiland. It looks rather reptilian, but it is a work of art and walking across is quite an experience. It is rather high and exposed (vertigo sufferers take note) and will sway precariously if rocked. Plus, the steps are of unequal length and you can't see them properly on the way down. Great fun.

At the far end of Borneo, **Scheepstimmermanstraat** has homes where purchasers were allowed to build whatever they liked (within reason). This has resulted in some amazing solutions to problems such as car parking, maximising sun and ensuring an uninterrupted view of water and sky. It's a bizarre, wonderful patchwork, and if you're with a friend you will probably disagree over which houses you like.

The 1.5km Piet Heintunnel under the water between Sporenburg and Borneo (the longest tunnel in the country) links the Eastern Harbour District to **IJburg**, a huge new housing project under construction on a string of artificial islands. Two of these islands are linked by the stunning Enneus Heerma Brug, a futuristic steel construction designed by Nicholas Grimshaw & Partners. Locals call it the Dolly Parton Bridge, for reasons that should be apparent on sight.

History

History

THE RECENT PAST

The last few years have been ones of introspection for this outward-looking city. The widespread recession that began in 2001 suppressed real-estate prices, lowered tourism and made funding for the arts scarce. Whereas once the Dutch economy was the envy of Europe, the prospects for recovery – and the road to it – remain unclear. Emigration from the Netherlands reached a 50-year high of 49,000 people in 2004, mostly for economic and family reasons; increasing social tension was also cited.

Then, in late 2004, the film-maker Theo van Gogh was assassinated on an Amsterdam street, and the city's heart skipped a few beats. In this city famous for tolerance and acceptance of other cultures, what did it mean that a native Amsterdammer – of foreign descent though he may be – was behind this crime? Analysts say that related fears contributed to the 'no' vote by the Netherlands in the 2005 referendum on the European constitution.

New infrastructure and cultural centres are being built east of the city centre, and new office towers have arisen southeast, south and west of the city. A second metro (underground) line is under construction from Amsterdam North to the city's World Trade Centre. Even if many locals think it an eyesore and a waste of time and money, it also speaks of an optimism that may – again – come to the city's rescue.

TOP FIVE AMSTERDAM HISTORY BOOKS

- *Amsterdam: A Traveller's Literary Companion* Capital stories by top writers.
- *The Coffee Trader* by David Liss. Dark Amsterdam tale of a hill of beans.
- *The Diary of Anne Frank* Synonymous with wartime courage.
- *Tulip Fever* by Deborah Moggach. Historical novel of speculation in the time of Rembrandt.
- *Max Havelaar* by Multatuli. Narrow-mindedness of a colonial coffee merchant.

FROM THE BEGINNING

Most of the region that later became known as Holland (in the west of the present-day Netherlands) started out as a land of lakes, swamps and spongy peat at or below sea level; its contours shifted with fierce autumn storms and floods. This was certainly the case where the Amstel River emptied into the IJ (pronounced 'eye'), an arm of the shallow Zuiderzee or 'Southern Sea'. The oldest archaeological finds here – coins and a few artefacts – date from Roman times, when the IJ lay along the northern border of the Roman Empire; there is no evidence of settlement then.

Isolated farming communities gradually tamed the marshlands with ditches and dykes. Between 1150 and 1300 the south bank of the IJ was dyked from the Zuiderzee westwards to Haarlem, and dams were built across rivers with locks to let water out and boats in. Around 1200, a fishing community known as Aemstelredamme 'the dam built across the Amstel' sat at what is now the square known as the Dam. Under the count of Holland, local inhabitants created a network of work-and-maintenance groups and pooled their resources – a precursor to today's 'Polder Model' of public decision-making (p12).

On 27 October 1275 the count of Holland granted toll freedom to those who lived around the Amstel dam, freeing locals from paying tolls to sail through the locks and bridges of Holland. This event is reckoned as the official founding of Amsterdam.

TIMELINE	c 1150	1275
	Dams were built to retain the IJ between the Zuiderzee and Haarlem	The count of Holland grants freedom from tolls to residents along the Amstel; this is credited as the founding of the city

EARLY TRADE

Agriculture was difficult in this marshland, so fishing remained an important activity, but it was trade that provided the greatest growth. While other powerful Dutch cities concentrated on overland trade with Flanders and northern Italy, Amsterdam focused on maritime trade in the North and Baltic Seas, then dominated by the Hanseatic League (a group of powerful trading cities in present-day Germany, including Hamburg, Lübeck and Rostock).

Amsterdam's wharves churned out *cogs* – 100-tonne capacity merchant ships (five times the size of their predecessors) – revolutionising maritime trade and enabling the city to play a key role in the transit trade between Hanseatic cities and southern Europe.

Instead of joining the league, Amsterdam's *vrijbuiters* (booty-chasers) sailed straight to the Baltic, with cloth and salt to exchange for grain and timber. By the late 1400s, 60% of ships sailing to and from the Baltic Sea were from Holland, and the vast majority had Amsterdam as their base.

The original harbour in Damrak and Rokin had been extended into the IJ near what's now Centraal Station. Canals were cut to cater for merchant warehouses in the area of the present-day Medieval Centre. A fire in 1452 destroyed three-quarters of the city, including most of the wooden buildings, but it was soon rebuilt in brick.

In Amsterdam, skippers, sailors, merchants, artisans and opportunists from the Low Countries (roughly the present-day Netherlands, Belgium and Luxembourg) gained their livelihood through contact with the outside world. With no tradition of Church-sanctioned feudal relationships, no distinction between nobility and serfs, and little taxation, individualism and protocapitalism took hold.

Amsterdam also became a city of religious pilgrimage: in 1345 a dying man regurgitated the Host (communion wafer), which was thrown in the fire but did not burn. A miracle was proclaimed and soon the city boasted some 20 monasteries. In 1489 Holy Roman Emperor Maximilian recovered from an illness here and showed his gratitude by allowing the city to use the imperial crown on its documents, buildings and ships.

INDEPENDENT REPUBLIC

The Protestant Reformation was more than religious. It was a struggle for power between the 'new money', an emerging class of merchants and artisans, and the 'old money', the land-owning, aristocratic order sanctioned by the established Catholic Church.

The form of Protestantism that took hold in the Low Countries was the most radically moralistic stream of Calvinism. It stressed the might of God and treated humans as sinful creatures whose duty in life was sobriety and hard work. It scorned church hierarchy in favour of local communities led by lay elders.

Calvinism was integral to the struggle for independence from the fanatically Catholic King Philip II of Spain, who had acquired the Low Countries. In 1566, a coalition of Catholic and Calvinist nobles petitioned Philip not to introduce the Spanish Inquisition in the Low Countries, Philip refused; the resulting war of independence lasted more than 80 years.

Fanatical Calvinist brigands, wearing the disparaging nickname *geuzen* (beggars) as a badge of honour, roamed from city to city, murdering priests, nuns and Catholic sympathisers, and smashing 'papist idolatry' in the churches. Some took to the water and

COAT OF ARMS

Amsterdam's coat of arms consists of three St Andrew's crosses arranged vertically – a wonderfully simple design that is found on everything from VVV tourist brochures to the thousands of brown bollards or 'penises' (so-called *Amsterdammertjes*) that keep cars from veering off the streets or parking where they shouldn't. Its origins are unclear, though the St Andrew's Cross was a popular symbol in this part of the world before Amsterdam existed. It is also said that the three crosses represented protection from three persistent threats to the city: fire, flood and plague.

1345	1380
Miracle of Amsterdam proclaimed	Canals of the present-day Medieval Centre are dug; population 10,000

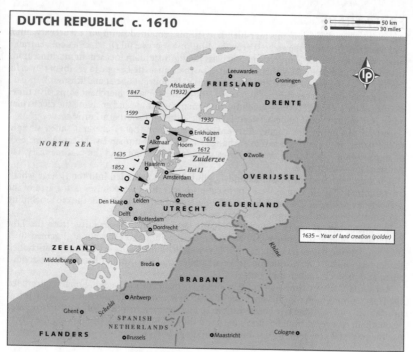

DUTCH REPUBLIC c. 1610

0 ——— 50 km
0 ——— 30 miles

Leeuwarden
Groningen
FRIESLAND
DRENTE
Afsluitdijk (1932)
1847
1599
1930
NORTH SEA
Enkhuizen
1631
Alkmaar Hoorn
1612
1635
Zwolle
Haarlem   Zuiderzee
1852
Het IJ
Amsterdam
OVERIJSSEL
H O L L A N D
Utrecht
Den Haag Leiden
GELDERLAND
Delft **UTRECHT**
Rotterdam
Dordrecht
1635 – Year of land creation (polder)
ZEELAND
Middelburg
Breda
Rhine
BRABANT
Antwerp
Ghent Scheldt
SPANISH
NETHERLANDS
FLANDERS Brussels Maastricht Cologne

harassed Spanish and other Catholic ships. Amsterdam was caught in the middle: its ruling merchants were pragmatic Catholics, but other merchants had adopted Calvinism along with most of the population, who resented heavy Spanish taxation. In 1578 the *geuzen* captured Amsterdam in a bloodless coup called the Alteration. In one of the most salient restrictions at home, Catholics were forced to worship in clandestine churches, a number of which still exist, including **Museum Amstelkring** (p67), **Begijnhof** (p72) and **De Rood Hoed** (p86).

With mighty Amsterdam now on their side, the seven northern provinces formed the Union of Utrecht and declared themselves to be an independent republic. The union was led by a *stadhouder* (chief magistrate), William the Silent of the House of Orange, who was the forefather of today's royal family (he was dubbed 'the Silent' because he wisely refused to enter into any religious debate). Their parliament, the Estates General, sat in Den Haag. The Seven United Provinces (the republic's official name) soon became known to the outside world as the Dutch Republic – or simply 'Holland' because of that province's dominance. Within Holland, Amsterdam towered over all the other cities put together.

GOLDEN AGE (1580–1700)

The city kept expanding. In the 1580s land was reclaimed from the IJ and Amstel to create the current Nieuwmarkt neighbourhood. Two decades later, work began on the Canal Belt that more than tripled the area of the city.

By 1600, Dutch ships dominated seaborne trade between England, France, Spain and the Baltic, and had a virtual monopoly on North Sea fishing and Arctic whaling. Jewish refugees taught Dutch mariners about trade routes, giving rise to the legendary United East India and West India Companies (see boxed text, opposite).

1566	1578
Nobles petition Spanish ruler not to introduce Spanish Inquisition; he refuses, touching off war of independence	Amsterdam captured by Calvinists; Dutch Republic declared a year later

Amsterdam's fortunes continued to rise when Antwerp, its major trading rival in the Low Countries, was retaken by the Spaniards. Half the population fled, and merchants, skippers and artisans flocked to Amsterdam with trade contacts and silk and printing industries – the world's first regular newspaper, full of trade news from around Europe, was printed in Amsterdam in 1618.

Amsterdam also welcomed persecuted Jews from Portugal and Spain, Germans provided a ready source of sailors and labourers, and a new wave of Jews came from Central and Eastern Europe, as did enterprising, persecuted Huguenots from France. Amsterdam had become a cosmopolitan city, where, in the absence of an overriding religion or dominant political entity, money reigned supreme.

By around 1620, Dutch traders were making an undeniable mark on the furthest reaches of the world. They rounded the tip of South America, naming it Cape Horn (after the city of Hoorn, north of Amsterdam). They expelled the Portuguese from the Moluccas (also known as the Spice Islands, in present-day Indonesia), and established outposts in the Pacific and Americas. By 1641 the Dutch had taken control of Formosa (Taiwan) and received sole trading rights to Japan. In 1652, Dutch sailors captured the Cape of Good Hope (South Africa); they booted the Portuguese out of Ceylon (Sri Lanka) soon after. They also explored the coastlines of New Zealand (named after the Dutch province of Zeeland) and New Holland (now Australia) but found nothing of value there.

Around 1650 the Dutch had more seagoing merchant vessels than England and France combined. Half of all ships sailing between Europe and Asia belonged to the Dutch; the exotic products traded eventually became commodities (coffee, tea, spices, tobacco, cotton,

THE FIRST MULTINATIONALS

It's hard to overstate the role played by the United East India Company (VOC; Vereenigde Oost-Indische Compagnie) and West India Company (WIC; West-Indische Compagnie) in Amsterdam's economic – and diplomatic – history.

More than just traders, these companies were authorised to negotiate with rulers overseas on behalf of the Dutch Republic, pursue trade opportunities as they saw fit, build forts and raise local militia. More than 1000 shareholders back home – merchants, artisans, clergy, shopkeepers, even servants – contributed capital, spreading risk and reaping rewards through generous dividends when risks paid off.

The VOC got its start in response to exclusion by the Portuguese from trade routes to the Orient. Some Amsterdam merchants sent a ship to break the Portuguese hold in 1595 and ships from other Dutch cities soon followed. The result: chaos. The counter-balance: 'Chambers' representing six Dutch cities came together to form the VOC, supervised by a group of 17 directors (the Heeren XVII, or '17 Gentlemen') on behalf of shareholders. Such was their importance that an Amsterdam canal was named after them, the Herengracht. The VOC was granted a Dutch government trading monopoly in 1602.

Batavia, now Jakarta, in Indonesia became the VOC's hub; a second hub opened on the island of Dejima, off Nagasaki, and became Japan's only gateway to European trade. Elaborate, often multilateral, trades involved Japan, Formosa (now Taiwan), China and Ceylon (now Sri Lanka), with goods including silks, spices, silver, gold, textiles, copper and, later, coffee and tea. Eventually, some 15 fleets of 65 ships plied the waters before the VOC was disbanded in 1795.

The WIC, meanwhile, consisted of five 'chambers' supervised by 19 directors (the Heeren XIX). Its ventures headed to the New World, establishing trade ports and colonies in New Netherland (now New York State and parts of neighbouring US states), the Netherlands Antilles, Suriname, Recife (Brazil) and Ghana. Piracy was another one of the aims of the WIC – the unlucky victims were largely Spanish ships. Its chief trade was in furs (from North America), sugar cane (from South America) and slaves (from Africa), a less than proud heritage.

In 1674, under pressure from British and Portuguese competition, the WIC folded officially but was reconstituted and continued to operate slave routes and colonies in the Antilles in Suriname until 1791, when it closed down for good. Its territories were placed under Dutch-government control.

Next time you think some of our modern-day multinationals are seeking world domination, remember in whose footsteps they're following.

1618	1688
World's first regular newspaper is printed in Amsterdam	William III of Orange marries Mary Stuart of England; England and the Netherlands join forces to defeat France

silk and porcelain). Dutch freight was unrivalled thanks to the availability of cheap Baltic hemp and timber, it being home to Europe's largest ship-building industry, and having abundant investment capital and low wages. Yet most wealth of Amsterdam proper was still generated by fishing and European trade.

In 1651, England passed the first of several Navigation Acts that posed a serious threat to Dutch trade, leading to several inconclusive naval wars; the Dutch lost New Amsterdam (New York City). Louis XIV of France took the opportunity to occupy much of the Low Countries two decades later.

The Dutch rallied behind their *stadhouder*, William III of Orange, who repelled the French with the help of Austria, Spain and Brandenburg (Prussia). A consummate politician, William then supported Protestant factions in England against their Catholic King James II. In 1688 William invaded England, where he and his wife, Mary Stuart (James II's Protestant daughter), were proclaimed king and queen.

WEALTHY DECLINE (1700–1814)

The Dutch Republic didn't have the military resources to continue fighting France and England head-on, but it had Amsterdam's money to buy them off and ensure freedom of the seas.

As more and more money went to this cause, Amsterdam went from being a place where everything (profitable) was possible, to a lethargic community where wealth creation was a matter of interest rates. Gone were the daring sea voyages, achievements in art, science and technology, the innovations of government and finance. Harbours such as London and Hamburg became powerful rivals.

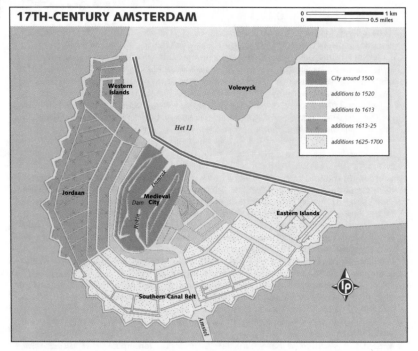

17TH-CENTURY AMSTERDAM

0 ——— 1 km
0 ——— 0.5 miles

City around 1500
additions to 1520
additions to 1613
additions 1613-25
additions 1625-1700

Western Islands
Volewyck
Het IJ
Jordaan
Damrak
Medieval City
Dam
Rokin
Eastern Islands
Southern Canal Belt
Amstel

1810	1813–14
The Netherlands is annexed into the French Empire	The French are overthrown and William I installed as king of the Netherlands

The decline in trade brought poverty, and exceptionally cold winters hampered transport and led to serious food shortages. The winters of 1740 and 1763 were so severe that some residents froze to death.

Amsterdam's support of the American War of Independence (1776) resulted in a British blockade of the Dutch coast followed by British conquests of Dutch trading posts around the world, eventually forcing the closure of the West India and East India Companies.

In 1794, the French revolutionary troops invaded the Low Countries, eventually installing a Batavian Republic and transforming the fragmented 'united provinces' into a centralised state with Amsterdam as its capital.

In 1806 this republic became a monarchy when Napoleon nominated his brother Louis Napoleon as king, and in 1808 the grand city hall on the Dam, symbol of the wealth and power of the merchant Republic, became his palace (now the Royal Palace, p70). Two years later Napoleon dismissed his brother and annexed the Netherlands into the French Empire.

Gothic Nieuwe Kerk (p69)

Britain responded by blockading the Continent and occupying the Dutch colonies. Amsterdam's trade and fishing industries came to a complete halt. Dutch society turned to agriculture and Amsterdam became a local market town.

After Napoleon's defeat in 1813, William VI of Orange was crowned as Dutch King William I in the **Nieuwe Kerk** (p69) in 1814. Louis Napoleon's palace became the new king's palace and has remained with the House of Orange ever since. The Britons returned the Dutch East Indies but kept the Cape of Good Hope and Ceylon. Amsterdam's seaborne economy recovered only slowly; domination of the seas had changed over to British hands.

NEW INFRASTRUCTURE (1814–1918)

Amsterdam in the first half of the 19th century was a lethargic place. Its harbour had been neglected, and the sand banks in the IJ, which were always an obstacle in the past, proved too great a barrier for modern ships. Rotterdam was set to become the country's premier port.

Things began to look up again as the country's first railway, between Amsterdam and Haarlem, opened in 1839. At this point, trade with the East Indies was the backbone of Amsterdam's economy, and a canal, eventually extended to the Rhine, allowed the city to benefit from the Industrial Revolution at home and in Germany.

The harbour was expanded to the east. The diamond industry boomed after the discovery of diamonds in South Africa. Amsterdam again attracted immigrants, and its population doubled in the second half of the 19th century. Speculators hastily erected new housing beyond the Canal Belt – dreary, shoddily built tenement blocks.

By 1887, restrictions imposed on Catholics in the Alteration were lifted, and Catholic churches were allowed to open again officially.

In 1889 the massive Centraal Station was built on a series of artificial islands in the IJ. Commentators saw this as the symbolic severing of Amsterdam's historical ties with the

1887	1940
Catholic churches allowed to reopen	Germany invades the Netherlands

sea. Towards the end of the 19th century some of the city's major waterways and smaller canals were filled in, both for hygienic reasons (such as several cholera epidemics) and to create roads.

The Netherlands remained neutral in WWI, but Amsterdam's trade with the East Indies suffered from naval blockades. There were riots over food shortages. An attempt to extend the socialist revolutions to the Netherlands was quickly put down by loyalist troops.

BOOM & DEPRESSION (1918–40)

After the war, Amsterdam remained the country's industrial centre. The Dutch Shipbuilding Company still operated the world's second-largest wharf and helped carry an extensive steel and diesel-motor industry. The harbour handled tropical produce that was processed locally (tobacco into cigars, cocoa into chocolate). Amsterdam is still the world's main distribution centre for cocoa.

The 1920s were boom years. In 1920 KLM (Koninklijke Luchtvaart Maatschappij; Royal Aviation Company) began the world's first regular air service, between Amsterdam and London, from an airstrip south of the city, and bought many of its planes from Anthony Fokker's aircraft factory north of the IJ. There were two huge breweries, a sizable clothing industry, and even a local car factory. The city hosted the Olympic Games in 1928.

By then the city had begun expanding north of the IJ, with housing projects for harbour workers and dockers in the new suburb of Amsterdam North. Then it expanded southwards, filling in the area between the Amstel and what was to become the Olympic Stadium.

The world Depression in the 1930s hit Amsterdam hard. Unemployment rose to 25%. Labour party members, who dominated the city council, resigned in protest at public-service salary cuts, and the conservative, spend-nothing national government of Hendrik Colijn (the Herbert Hoover of the Netherlands) had free reign.

Public-works projects did little to defuse the mounting tensions between socialists, communists and the small but vocal party of Dutch fascists. The city received some 25,000 Jewish refugees fleeing Germany; a shamefully large number were turned back at the border because of the Netherlands' neutrality policy.

WWII (1940–45)

The Netherlands tried to remain neutral in WWII, but Germany invaded in May 1940 and for the first time in almost 400 years Amsterdammers experienced war first-hand. Few wanted to believe that things would turn nasty (the Germans trumpeted that the Dutch were part of the 'Aryan brotherhood'). However, in February 1941 Amsterdam's working class protested restrictions placed on their Jewish compatriots in a general strike led by dockworkers. By then it was already too late. Only one in every 16 of Amsterdam's 90,000 Jews survived the war (one in seven in the Netherlands), the highest proportion of Jews murdered anywhere in Western Europe.

The resistance movement, set up by an unlikely alliance of Calvinists and Communists, only became large-scale when the increasingly desperate Germans began to round up able-bodied men to work in Germany.

During the 'Hunger Winter' of 1944 to 1945, the Allies had liberated the south of the country but were checked at Arnhem, and concentrated again on their push into Germany, thus managing to isolate the northwest and Amsterdam. Coal shipments ceased, many men aged between 17 and 50 had gone into hiding or to work in Germany, public utilities halted, and the Germans began to plunder anything that could assist their war effort. Although Amsterdam was spared the bombing and destruction that befell Rotterdam, thousands of lives were lost to severe cold and famine. Canadian troops finally liberated the city in May 1945, at the very end of the war in Europe.

1944–45	1975
Hunger Winter	The Netherlands decriminalises marijuana

POST-WAR GROWTH (1945–62)

The city's growth resumed after the war, with US aid through the Marshall Plan. Newly discovered fields of natural gas compensated for the loss of the East Indies, which became independent Indonesia after a four-year fight. The focus of the harbour moved westwards towards the widened North Sea Canal. The long-awaited Amsterdam-Rhine Canal opened in 1952.

Massive apartment blocks arose in areas annexed west of the city to meet the continued demand for housing, made more acute by the demographic shift away from extended families. The massive Bijlmermeer housing project (now called the Bijlmer) southeast of the city, begun in the mid-1960s and finished in the 1970s, was built in a similar vein.

In 1948 Queen Wilhelmina resigned in favour of her daughter Juliana.

CULTURAL REVOLUTION (1962–82)

Over the previous 80 years, Dutch society had become characterised by *verzuiling* (pillarisation), a social order in which each religion and political persuasion achieved the right to do its own thing, with its own institutions. Each persuasion represented a pillar that supported the status quo in a general 'agreement to disagree'. In the 1960s the old divisions were increasingly irrelevant, and the pillars came tumbling down.

Amsterdam became Europe's 'Magic Centre', an exciting place where anything was possible. The late 1960s saw an influx of hippies smoking dope on the Dam, unrolling sleeping bags in the Vondelpark and tripping in the nightlife hot spots. At the universities, students demanded a greater say and, in 1969, occupied the administrative centre of the University of Amsterdam. The women's movement began a campaign that fuelled the abortion debate throughout the 1970s.

In the early 1970s a fierce conflict developed between city planners and disaffected Amsterdammers over a proposed metro (underground railway) line through the Nieuwmarkt neighbourhood. Technology did not yet allow tunnelling through swampy ground and a

THE PROTESTING PROVOS

Mixing street theatre and serial anarchy, a movement called the Provos set the tone for Amsterdam in the days of the Magic Centre.

In 1962, window cleaner and self-professed sorcerer Robert Jasper Grootveld began to deface cigarette billboards with a huge letter 'K' (for *kanker*, cancer) to protest rampant, addictive commercialism. At get-togethers in his garage, he dressed as a medicine man, chanted antismoking mantras (under the influence of pot) and attracted other bizarre types: the poet Johnny van Doorn, also known as Johnny the Selfkicker, known for frenzied, stream-of-consciousness recitals; Bart Huges, who drilled a hole in his forehead (a 'third eye' to attain permanently expanded consciousness); and Rob Stolk, a working-class printer whose streetwise tactics helped the get-togethers become 'happenings'.

In summer 1965, happenings on the Spui attracted thousands, and were eventually disbanded by police using batons and issuing arbitrary arrests. Eyewitness accounts characterised it as police brutality against kids having fun, and soon the whole country was engaged in heated debate.

In 1965 to 1966, the Provos proposed a series of environmental 'White Plans', most famously a fleet of white bicycles to be provided free by the city. Provos were also behind the protests at the 1966 wedding of then-Princess Beatrix and the congenial German diplomat Claus von Amsberg, who had been a member of the Hitler Youth. Despite massive security, a live chicken was hurled at the royal coach, smoke bombs were ignited along the procession route, and bystanders chanted 'my bicycle back' – a reference to the many bikes commandeered by German soldiers. Naturally, it was all carried live on TV.

As much as anything, it was the Provos' own success that eventually did them in: society began to adopt their goals. Nowadays, even Queen Beatrix is passionately environmentalist.

1980	2003
Squatters disrupt celebrations for the coronation of Queen Beatrix	Her Royal Highness Catharina-Amalia Beatrix Carmen Victoria, second in line to the throne, is born

large portion of the derelict district had to be razed. The inhabitants became squatters and turned the area into a fortress. The district was eventually cleared with much violence on 'Blue Monday', 24 March 1975. Some 30 people, mostly policemen, were injured; surprisingly, no-one was killed. The episode became a watershed; subsequently the council set about renovating inner-city neighbourhoods for new housing. Nieuwmarkt was rebuilt with affordable council houses. The metro opened in 1980.

Still, families kept moving to the suburbs, the city became dominated by small households with modest means, and housing needs outstripped the council's ability to provide. A housing shortage fuelled speculation. Free-market rents – and purchase prices – shot out of reach of the average citizen. The waiting period for a council apartment was up to five years.

Many young people turned to squatting in buildings left empty by (assumed) speculators. Legislation made eviction difficult, giving rise to *knokploegen* (fighting groups) of track-suited heavies sent by owners to evict squatters by force. These new squatters, however, were prepared to defend themselves with barricades and a well-organised support network.

A few months after a particularly emphatic battle with authorities, squatters took to the streets on the occasion of the coronation of Queen Beatrix. In Amsterdam's largest-ever rioting, tear gas filled the air, and the term 'proletarian shopping' (ie looting) entered the national lexicon.

'Ordinary' Amsterdammers, initially sympathetic towards the housing shortage, became fed up with squatters jumping the queue and the violent riots. By the mid-1980s the movement had little or no outside support and was all but dead. Squatting still takes place now, but the rules are clear and the mood is far less confrontational.

NEW CONSENSUS (1982–2000)

Twenty years after the cultural revolution began, a new consensus, epitomised by the amiable mayor, Ed van Thijn, emphasised decentralised government. Neighbourhood councils were established with the goal of creating a more liveable city: integrating work, schools and shops within walking or cycling distance; decreased traffic; renovation rather than demolition; friendly neighbourhood police; a practical, nonmoralistic approach towards drugs; and legal recognition of homosexual couples. Social-housing construction peaked, with 40,000 affordable apartments easing the plight of 100,000 house hunters.

A combined city hall and opera house opened in 1986 on Waterlooplein, although opinions remain divided on its architectural success. Today it's known as the Stopera (p78) – a contraction of *stadhuis* (city hall) and opera, or of 'Stop the Opera', depending on your perspective.

By the early 1990s, families and small manufacturers, which dominated inner-city neighbourhoods in the early 1960s, had been replaced by professionals and a service industry of pubs, 'coffeeshops', restaurants and hotels. The ethnic make-up had changed too, with non-Dutch nationalities comprising over 45% of the population. The city's success in attracting large foreign businesses resulted in an influx of higher-income expatriates.

2004	2005
Activist film-maker Theo van Gogh is assassinated, touching off national worry and introspection	The Netherlands votes 'no' to the European constitution

Sights ■

Sights

Simply put, Amsterdam is one of Europe's most beautiful capitals. Add in some of the world's great cultural treasures, as well as sights that are quirky, gorgeous or just plain fun, and you've got a dream destination. And while other cities are grandiose and monumental, Amsterdam is intimate and accessible: you can walk across the city centre in about half an hour, and getting around on a bike is a snap.

One of the best ways to see this remarkable city is just to wander – the urge will be irresistible along some canals. That's how

Butterflies look back at you at Hortus Botanicus (p110)

we have found several of our favourite places. No doubt you will find some of your own favourites this way, and begin to understand what keeps drawing so many people back.

ITINERARIES

One Day

My goodness, but you're ambitious. Start (early, to beat the crowds) at the **Anne Frank Huis** (p85), followed by a trip across town to the **Van Gogh Museum** (p97) not long after it opens. **CoBrA Café** (p146) on Museumplein is a convenient lunch spot. From there you can browse **Nieuwe Spiegelstraat** and the department stores on **Kalverstraat** (p186) en route to the **Amsterdams Historisch Museum** (p71). After all this seriousness, you'll feel like a change of pace, and you can find it at the **Red Light District** (p66). Since you've only got one night in town, dine at Amsterdam's most renowned Dutch restaurant, **d'Vijff Vlieghen** (p132).

Three Days

Take in the one-day itinerary, but allow yourself time to pause and explore. For example: after the Anne Frank Huis, browse the shops of the **Negen Straatjes** (p84) and stay for lunch. Near the Van Gogh Museum, also take in the Dutch masters in the Philips Gallery of the **Rijksmuseum** (p96), catch a concert at the **Concertgebouw** (p176) or take the tour at **Coster Diamonds** (p200). Afterwards, stop for cake or quiche at **Taart van m'n Tante** (p150), then plunge into the diversity of the **Albert Cuypmarket** (p107). Stop for gelato at **Peppino's** (p150) or cheesecake at **Sarphaat** (p158), then take a well-earned rest. Dine at **Puyck** (p149) in De Pijp, but be sure to leave time for a night-time performance at the **Muziekgebouw aan 't IJ** (p113). You never know who will turn up for post-show drinks at the **Lloyd Hotel** (p228).

Leave a morning to stroll the **Begijnhof** (p72) – the nearly adjacent Amsterdams Historisch Museum makes a nice follow-up. To keep your mood mellow, see what's showing at the **Nieuwe Kerk** (p69) or feel like royalty at the **Hermitage Amsterdam** (p109) –

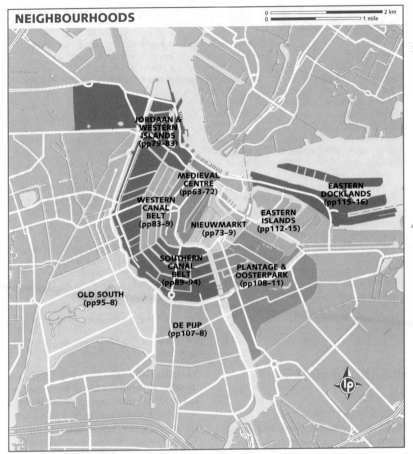

drink in that view of the Amstel. Dine at Art-Nouveau **Belhamel** (p140) or, if you're feeling rowdier, **de Blaffende Vis** (p137). Cap your stay with a Pils at the canalside brown **Café 't Smalle** (p157).

One Week

In addition to the above, don't miss Jewish Amsterdam: the **Joods Historisch Museum** (p75), a kosher lunch at **King Solomon** (p135) and a visit to the **Portuguese-Israelite Synagogue** (p77). At night, follow that ancient not-so-Jewish ritual of Chinese food, either on the Zeedijk (followed by karaoke at **Casablanca**, p174) or aboard the floating **Sea Palace restaurant** (p151).

Ride your bike to the IJ and a ferry to the **Eastern Docklands** (p46) to explore the intriguing new architecture. Stop at **Gare de l'Est** for dinner (p152) – it's different every night.

Take a day in the Plantage, visit the sobering memorial at the **Hollandsche Schouwburg** (p109) and feel uplifted at the **Verzetsmuseum** (p110); **Plancius** (p150) next door makes an excellent lunch stop or try the Orangery café at the **Hortus Botanicus** (p110). Then head north via the **Entrepotdok** (p112) to be entertained by retired engineers (really) at the technology museum **EnergeticA** (p113). Dine at historic **Koffiehuis van den Volksbond** (p151) or snappy **A Tavola** (p151).

Wrap up your stay with a visit to the seashore, the **Nederlands Scheepvaartmuseum** (p113) or, for a swan song, climb to the 11th floor of the Post Tower, above the Stedelijk Museum, for dinner at **11** (p151), whatever time it is, with city views that allow you to reminisce.

A MEDLEY OF MUSEUMS

Whether it's modern art or art about cats, stately homes or tropical cultures, stories of historical tragedy or miracles of modern technology, Amsterdam offers a range of museums for any taste (visit www.amsterdammuseums.nl).

Most of the leading museums in town display captions in English. If captions are in Dutch only, you can usually get an English-language brochure (often free) or borrow a binder explaining the exhibits. Many museums have pleasant cafés with gardens or courtyards – good places to relax or read up.

As to be expected, weekends tend to be the busiest times, along with Wednesday afternoons when many primary schools have the afternoon off and children are herded into museums. The most common museum closing day is Monday.

A handful of museums offer free entry, but most charge admission. Adult admissions run from about €2.50 to €10, which is pretty reasonable by the standards of world capitals; special exhibitions may cost extra. Discounts are available for those aged over 65 (though rarely) or under 18, for students and holders of other types of cards and passes (see p254).

If you plan to be in the Netherlands for a while, get the **Museumkaart** (Museum Card; ☎ 0900-404 09 10, per call €0.35; over/under 26yr €25/12.50 plus €4.95 fee for first-time registrants), which gives you free (mostly) or discounted (occasionally) admission to several hundred museums around the country for a year. It's valid for most museums in Amsterdam, although not the high-profile Anne Frank Huis or the Royal Palace. After five or six museums the card will have paid for itself. Inquire at participating museums.

If you are making just one quick trip to Amsterdam, you might consider the **I Amsterdam Card** (per 24/48/72hr €33/43/53). It includes many of the same museums as the Museumkaart (though, again, not the Anne Frank Huis or the Royal Palace), a free canal cruise, freebies and discounts at a number of shops and attractions and a transit pass good for anywhere the GVB goes. The pass can come in handy: although Amsterdam is not an enormous city, a half-hour walk between museums can certainly eat into your limited time. The I Amsterdam Card is available at tourist office (aka VVV) locations (p259).

The **Lovers Museum Boat** (p249; www.lovers.nl; adult/child €14.25/9.50) is also worth considering for the discounts offered with its day card.

ORGANISED TOURS

Bike Tours

MIKE'S BIKE TOURS

☎ 622 79 70; www.mikesbikeamsterdam.com; Kerkstraat 134; bike tour incl bike rental adult/ student/child 12yr & under/infant in bike seat €22/19/15/free, bike & boat tour €29/25/20/free; ☽ bike tour 12.30pm Mar–mid-May & Sep-Nov, 11am & 4pm mid-May–Aug; bike & boat tour noon Tue-Sun Jun-Aug

Readers have written to us in praise of Mike's fantastic four-hour tours, which take you both around the centre of town and into the countryside (where you can see windmills, cheese farms and so on). Guides are well known for their insider information about the city. It is likely you will find yourself at a pub when the tour is over. There's a new 'bike and boat' tour as well (about five hours), which includes drinks on board and a visit to the Vondel-park. Meeting place for the tours is the reflecting pool on Museumplein behind the Rijksmuseum.

YELLOW BIKE TOURS

☎ 620 69 40; www.yellowbike.nl; Nieuwezijds Kolk 29; city/countryside tour per person €18.50/25; ☽ city tour 9.30am & 1pm Sun-Fri, 9.30am & 2pm Sat, countryside tour 11am, all tours Apr-1 Nov

Yellow Bike was the original Amsterdam bike tour, so they've got it down pat. Choose from a three-hour city tour or a six-hour countryside tour through the waterland north of central Amsterdam. These tours are a little less youth-oriented than Mike's and are limited to 12 tour participants per guide. Tours depart from their office. Reservations recommended.

Boat Tours

The companies mentioned here offer a variety of boat tours (singular *rondvaart*, plural *rondvaarten*), from hour-long excursions on the inner canals (figure around €9 per person) to more expensive far-flung tours of architecture on the Eastern Docklands, jazz cruises, dinner cruises and candlelight cruises. Sure they're touristy, but on a clear night, they can be quite delightful. Details are constantly being revised, so check websites or phone for details. Some cruises are included in the I Amsterdam Card (p254).

CANAL BUS
☎ 623 98 86; www.canal.nl; Weteringschans 26; per adult/child 5-12yr €16/11
Offers a unique hop-on, hop-off canal boat service most of the big destinations. Routes vary depending on where you want to visit. At night, there is a 1½-hour jazz cruise (€43, runs 8pm and 10pm Saturdays from April to November). Sip wine, beer and soft drinks, enjoy light nibbles and watch the city lights go by.

HOLLAND INTERNATIONAL
☎ 622 77 88; www.hir.nl; Prins Hendrikkade 33A; 1hr cruise adult/child €8.50/5
Holland International's one-hour canal cruise (every 15 minutes 9am to 6pm and every 30 minutes 6pm to 10pm) attracts tourists like a visit to the Eiffel Tower does for Paris. They also have a roster of candlelight lunch and dinner cruises (adults €25 to €69, children €16 to €45).

REDERIJ LOVERS
☎ 530 10 90; www.lovers.nl; Prins Hendrikkade 25-27
Offers a number of night-time cruises, including the candlelight cruise (€24, runs 8.30pm nightly from spring to December, and most nights from January to spring), with wine and Dutch cheese.

WORTH NOTING
If you'd like to rent a bike and tour the city on your own, see bike rentals (p249) for information. Cycling tour info can be found on p123.

REEDERIJ NOORD-ZUID
☎ 679 13 70; www.canal-cruises.nl; Stadhouderskade 25; 75-min canal cruises adult/child 5-12yr/under 4yr €9/5.50/free; ☷ every 30min 10am-6pm Apr-Oct, every hr 10am-5pm Nov-Mar
Noord-Zuid's main tour clocks in at 75 minutes. Evening cruises (adult/child 5-12yr/under 4yr €13.50/9/free) are offered at least twice per night from April to October, and at 8pm only Thursday to Sunday throughout the rest of the year. Tour boats depart from the Noord-Zuid dock, just near the Rijksmuseum.

House Tours
URBAN HOME AND GARDEN TOURS
☎ 688 12 43; www.uhgt.nl; per person incl a drink €22.50; ☷ 10.15am Fri, 11.15am Sat, 12.15pm Sun Apr-Oct
These well-regarded tours look at Amsterdam dwellings from the perspective of home, garden, and even gable. Visits include 18th-century, 19th-century and contemporary homes. Tours take 2½ to three hours.

FOR CHILDREN
The **Vondelpark** (p97) is a natural with kids yet not too far for adults to travel. It's great for picnics, has a children's playground and ducks, and you can put the kids to work, making their own lunch at the park's **Kinderkookkafé** (p147). For something a bit more natural, the **Amsterdamse Bos** (p115) has a huge recreational area with an animal enclosure and a children's farm. Go on the right day, and you can take an historic tram from **Tram Museum Amsterdam** (p98) from near the Vondelpark to near the Bos, and what kid wouldn't love that?

If the weather doesn't cooperate, the **NEMO science and technology centre** (p114) is tailor made for kids; the **Tropenmuseum** (p111) has a separate children's section with activities focusing on exotic locations (although others tend to be in Dutch only); the **Joods Historisch Museum** (p75) also has a kids section, on Jewish life in Amsterdam; and the **Artis Zoo** (p108) has both indoor and outdoor pursuits. The **Nederlands Scheepvaartmuseum** (p113) has wonderful old ships, and a re-creation of a historic trading ship, usually staffed with costumed hosts. Artier museums may try your young'uns' patience, but the **Civic Guard Gallery** (p72) allows them to dip a toe in for free. If they like it, try giving them a little more – just like vegetables.

Speaking of dipping a toe in, kids may like the hi-tech **Mirandabad** (p184) public pool, or a unique ride aboard a canal bike (p181) or cruise (opposite). If you take the canal bike (p78), you won't be alone.

Kids of all ages love the madness of **Koninginnedag** (Queen's Day; p9) on 30 April. If your kids have talent (or even think they have), they can set up a little stage in the Vondelpark, and try to get people to pay them for it.

CANAL KNOWLEDGE

In Dutch, a canal is a *gracht*, pronounced 'khrakht', and Amsterdam has a lot of them. The best-known canals form the *Grachtengordel* (Canal Belt) around the city centre, and they are useful for naviagting you way around the city. The city area within the Canal Belt is referred to as Amsterdam Centrum. One of the charms of this part of town is that its history is evident simply from its geographical layout.

The extents of the medieval city came to be marked by the Kloveniersburgwal (a *burgwal* is a fortified embankment, though it sure looks like a canal to us, and the Kloveniers were a military group) and Geldersekade (*kade* means 'quay') on the Oude Zijde, and the Singel (moat) on the Nieuwe Zijde. During the late 15th century and early 16th century, this modest area received a city wall with fortified gates at strategic points. You can still see some of those gates today, though the walls have been largely torn down as the city grew and spilled over into the surrounding marshes.

This expansion continued through the 16th century until it was clear that modest measures, such as building islands east of the former city walls, would not be enough. In the 17th century an enormous urban construction project resulted in the semicircular Canal Belt, west and south of the Medieval Centre.

These canals came in two basic varieties: semicircular and radial. Semicircular canals form a ring around the centre, while radial canals radiate out from the middle, like spokes on a wheel. Starting from the centre of town, the major semicircular canals are the Singel, Herengracht, Keizersgracht and Prinsengracht. An easy mnemonic is that, apart from the singular Singel, these canals are in alphabetical order. Obvious though it may seem, it took us years to figure this out.

From west to east, the major radial canals are Brouwersgracht, Leidsegracht and Reguliersgracht, also in alphabetical order. East of the Reguliersgracht is another waterway that looks like a very broad canal; this is the river Amstel, and it ends in the IJ, the river that forms the northern border of the city centre.

The Canal Belt is enclosed by the Lijnbaansgracht and a zigzag-patterned canal originally called the Buitensingel (outer moat), now known as the Singelgracht.

An interesting quirk: many streets in modern Amsterdam also bear the name 'gracht'. That's because they were once canals as well, but they've since been filled in for reasons of sanitation or ease of transportation. Other streets have 'dwars' in their names, to indicate that they intersect (or intersected) with a canal, so Leidsedwarsstraat meets up with the Leidsegracht.

Here's a little quiz of canal fun facts for you to keep in mind as you read this chapter. We've given you clues in the form of page references where you'll find the answers:

1 – Canal best known for the floating flower market (p91)
2 – Collective Dutch name for the Canal Belt (p83)
3 – Dutch for 'canal' (above)
4 – Dutch for 'quay' (above)
5 – Dutch for 'fortified embankment' (above)
6 – Forms a zigzag around the city centre (above)
7 – Named for the Holy Roman Emperor Maximilian I (p84)
8 – Named for the 17 gentlemen of the Dutch East India Company (p51)
9 – Not a canal anymore, but a major thoroughfare through the Jordaan (p80)
10 – Site of canal parades during festivals such as Gay Pride and Queen's Day (p14)

A   Burgwal
B   Gracht
C   Grachtengordel
D   Herengracht
E   Kade
F   Keizersgracht
G   Prinsengracht
H   Rozengracht
I   Singel
J   Singelgracht

Answers: 1-I, 2-C, 3-B, 4-E, 5-A, 6-J, 7-F, 8-D, 9-H, 10-G

Other Tours

AMSTERDAM SEGWAY TOURS

☎ 06 4142 4344; www.glide.cc; per person €60;
🕙 10am & 8pm spring-Christmas
This relatively new outfit offers two daily
glide-by tours. The four-hour daytime tour
covers the major sights (museums, Jewish
quarter, Red Light District etc), while the
three-hour night tour clues you in on
lesser-known night spots in areas like De
Pijp. If you haven't been on a Segway
before, they'll train you. Capacity is up
to seven people, by reservation. Meet at
Nieuwmarkt by the Metro exit.

RED LIGHT DISTRICT TOUR

☎ 623 63 02; www.zoomamsterdam.com;
per person €15; 🕙 5pm
Zoom Amsterdam offers this 2½-hour tour
covering both the history and culture (if
you will) of the Red Light District. All questions answered. Meet at the café inside the
Schreierstoren (Prins Hendrikkade 94–95),
across from Centraal Station.

MEDIEVAL CENTRE

Eating p132; Shopping p187; Sleeping p215

This is where the city began, around a
dam built across the River Amstel at what
is now Dam Square ('Amstel' + 'Dam', or
'Aemstelredam' and later 'Amsterdam').
Two streets called Damrak and Rokin,
which run north and south from the Dam,
used to form the Amstel's final stretch. East
of the Damrak-Rokin axis is the 'Old Side' of
medieval Amsterdam, while the west bank is
the Nieuwe Zijde (New Side). In just one of
many oddities you'll discover in this quirky
city, the 'New Side' is actually older than the
'Old Side'; their names come from the parishes around the Oude Kerk (Old Church)
and the Nieuwe Kerk (New Church).

TRANSPORT

Tram lines 1, 2, 4, 5, 9, 13, 16, 17, 24 and 25 all terminate
at Centraal Station and run down either Damrak/Rokin
or Nieuwezijds Voorburgwal. Trams 1, 2 and 5 continue
down Nieuwezijds Voorburgwal to Spui Square and beyond. Trams 9 and 14 continue to Waterlooplein and
the Stopera. You can also catch the 'Opstapper' bus
between Centraal Station and Waterlooplein.

TOP FIVE MEDIEVAL CENTRE

- Take in the latest exhibit or concert at the **Oude
  Kerk** (p65), the city's oldest building, or the
  Nieuwe Kerk (p69), the coronation church of
  Dutch royalty.
- Feel positively regal inside the lavishly decorated
  salons of the **Royal Palace** (p70).
- Explore the edgy, the tawdry, the sexy and the
  silly in the **Red Light District** (p66).
- Spend a quiet interlude at the 14th-century
  Begijnhof (p72).
- Steep yourself in city history at the **Amsterdams
  Historisch Museum** (p71).

Exiting Centraal Station you're plunged
into the city pretty well immediately. Your
first obstacle: construction. Stationplein
(*plein* equates to 'square') is one of the
city's major construction hubs for the next
several years. Obstacle number 2: tram
tracks – please use caution, especially if
you're jet-lagged! To the right is a parking garage for 2500…bicycles, while across
the tram tracks is a small white building
housing branches of the tourist office (the
VVV), and the local transit bureau (the
GVB). Here you can collect information,
book hotels and purchase transit passes
and tickets. Tour boats dock on the channel before you reach the city (Canal Bus,
Holland International and Lovers among
them).

DAMRAK & OUDE ZIJDE

Although it's hard to imagine now, the
Damrak was the city's original harbour,
until it became unsuitable for large ships
that tied up to palisades along what is now
Centraal Station and unloaded onto light-
ers. Today's Damrak is an agonising stretch
of gaudy souvenir and sex shops, exchange
bureaus, cheap restaurants and claustrophobic, dumpy hotels. Its continuation,
Rokin, is much more agreeable.

East of the Damrak and Rokin is the Old
Side. It's a gorgeous and historic part of
town, yet it also contains one of Europe's
most notorious and visited locales, the Red
Light District. If you want to head directly
towards the red lights, you can skip ahead
to p66.

Warmoesstraat comprises one of the
original dykes along the Amstel – making

ALL ABOARD!

Although it may not be obvious, Centraal Station (1889) occupies an important place in architectural history. It's a Dutch-Renaissance edifice with Gothic additions, built to a design by Pierre Cuypers and AL van Gendt. Cuypers also designed the Rijksmuseum, and the structural similarity is instantly obvious; both buildings have a central section flanked by square towers with wings on either side. Van Gendt, meanwhile, was no slouch, having designed the Concertgebouw, said to have the best acoustics in Europe. Visitors familiar with Japan may also notice a resemblance to Tokyo station (1914) – that's how far this building's influence spread!

Most visitors arriving at Centraal Station exit the bustling front (south or city) side. If you think that's busy, exit to the rear (north or harbour side), and try to imagine the scene in the 17th and 18th centuries, when Amsterdam was the busiest harbour in the world.

it one of the oldest streets in town. It runs parallel to the Damrak behind the former warehouses that line the east bank of the river (the southern extension beyond the Dam is called Nes). The city's wealthiest merchants once lived here, and anyone else who could afford to.

Today it's a strip of restaurants, cheap hotels, coffeeshops, gay-oriented leather establishments and sex shops. Although that sounds rather tawdry, paradoxically the street also has a rather well-kept feeling to it. Condomerie Het Gulden Vlies (p187) and Geels & Co (p187) are two of the more interesting shops you'll find on the street.

ALLARD PIERSON MUSEUM

Map pp292-3

☎ 525 25 56; cf.uba.uva.nl/apm; Oude Turfmarkt 127; adult/child 4-16yr & senior/child under 4yr €5/2.50/free; ☷ 10am-5pm Tue-Fri, 1-5pm Sat & Sun
This museum, run by the University of Amsterdam, has one of the world's richest university-owned archaeological collections. You'll find an actual mummy, vases from ancient Greece and Mesopotamia, a very cool wagon from the royal tombs at Salamis (Cyprus) and galleries full of fascinating items from all over, providing real insight into daily life in ancient times. Each section is explained in a detailed overview via English signage, although most signage on the individual items is in Dutch only.

It may not in the same league as the country's largest collection of antiquities in Leiden, let alone the British Museum or the Louvre, but many visitors have found that the Allard Pierson Museum's scale and cosy intimacy make it far more accessible and comprehensible.

BEURS VAN BERLAGE Map pp286-7

☎ 530 41 41; Damrak 243
In the late 19th century the southern half of the Damrak was filled in for this new exchange (beurs) building, which was built in 1903 and is considered one of the most important landmarks of Dutch city architecture. It was named after the architect HP Berlage (p45), who was still designing it after work began. The large central hall, with its steel and glass roof, was the commodities exchange where coffee, tobacco, sugar, wine and colonial merchandise were traded. Traders eventually deserted the building in favour of the neoclassical Effectenbeurs (Stock Exchange), built in 1913 on the east side of Beursplein by Centraal Station's Pierre Cuypers.

In the 1970s the foundations of Berlage's Bourse were sinking and the building was slated for demolition. Saved by popular outcry, it is now home to the Netherlands Philharmonic Orchestra and occasional museum exhibitions – past shows have included Picasso's paintings, Frank Lloyd Wright's designs and Karel Appel's works that are too large for regular museums. Such is the importance of this building that on '02-02-02' Crown Prince Willem-Alexander married the Argentine Máxima Zorreguïeta here in the regulation civil ceremony, before proceeding to the Nieuwe Kerk for the church wedding.

Although the functional lines and stark, square clock tower contrast with the more exuberant designs of the age, there are clever details inside and out, visible in the museum and concert hall interiors. Even if there are no exhibitions or shows, the Beurs' B van B Café (p162) is open daily, and has worthwhile architectural details of its own (including three 1903 murals by Jan Toorop, representing past, present and future).

OUDE KERK Map pp286-7

Old Church; ☎ 625 82 84; Oudekerksplein 23;
adult/concession €4.50/3.50; ⏲ 11am-5pm
Mon-Sat, 1-5pm Sun

A few paces east of Warmoesstraat, through
Enge Kerksteeg, this Gothic church was
built early in the 14th century in honour
of the city's patron saint, St Nicholas – the
'water saint', protector of sailors, merchants,
pawnbrokers and children. The location of
the city's oldest surviving building (1306) is
one of Europe's great moral contradictions:
it's in full view of the Red Light District, with
passers-by getting chatted up a stone's
throw from the church walls.

The original basilica was replaced in 1340
by an intricately vaulted triple-hall church of
massive proportions that was miraculously
undamaged by the great fire of 1452. The
church's tower, built in 1565, is arguably the
most beautiful in Amsterdam and is well
worth climbing for the view; special **tours**
(☎ 689 25 65; €40, up to 25 people) can be
booked for this. The 47-bell carillon, installed
by the carillon master François Hemony in
1658, is considered one of the finest in the
country. The bell in the top of the tower
dates from 1450 and is the city's oldest.

Also note the stunning Müller organ
(1724), the gilded oak vaults (with remains
of paintings above the southern aisle) and
the stained-glass windows (1555). Check
the lively 15th-century carvings on the
choir stalls – some of them are downright
rude. Many famous and not so famous
Amsterdammers lie buried here under worn
tombstones, including Rembrandt's first
wife, Saskia van Uylenburgh (died 1642).
A Dutch Reformed service is held at 11am
Sunday (doors close at 11am sharp).

Historical notes: the church was once
due for further extensions, but these plans
ground to a halt as funds were diverted to
the Nieuwe Kerk. A century later, Calvinist
iconoclasts smashed and looted many of
the Oude Kerk's priceless paintings, statues
and altars. The Calvinist authorities kicked
out the hawkers and vagabonds who had
made the church their home, and changed
the official name from St Nicolaaskerk to
Oude Kerk (as it was commonly known anyway). In the mid-17th century the Nieuwe
Kerk took over as the city's main church.

ST NICOLAASKERK Map pp286-7

☎ 624 87 49; Prins Hendrikkade 73; admission free;
⏲ 11am-4pm Tue-Sat, noon-3pm Mon, worship
services 10.30am & 1pm Sun, 12.30pm Mon-Sat

Looking from Centraal station, across Prins
Hendrikkade (the large street across the
harbour) and to your left, you can't miss the
cupola and towers of this neo-Renaissance
edifice, the city's main Catholic church.
Designed by AC Bleijs and built in 1887, its
impressive interior (wooden vaulting with
square pillars of black marble) contains
paintings of the Stations of the Cross, and a
high altar with a representation of the crown
of Holy Roman Emperor Maximilian I. The
painter Jan Dunselman spent some 40 years
on the paintings. As St Nicholas is the patron
saint of seafarers, this was an important
symbol for the city. This church was the first
Catholic church to be built in the city after
restrictions were lifted on Catholic worship.

SEXMUSEUM AMSTERDAM Map pp286-7

Venustempel; ☎ 622 83 76; Damrak 18; admission
€2.50, age 16yr & over only; ⏲ 10am-11.30pm

Even if it seems rather tame amid the sex
shops right down the street, the Sexmuseum
gets loads of visitors, and if you're in the
right mood it's good for a giggle. Among its
many treasures are replicas of pornographic
Pompeian plates, erotic 14th-century Vien-
nese bronzes, some of the world's earliest
nude photographs, a music box that plays
'Edelweiss' and purports to show a couple
in flagrante delicto, and an eerie mannequin
of Marilyn Monroe re-enacting the sidewalk-
grate scene from *The Seven Year Itch.* The
route takes you through a 'bondage room'
('You could be shocked', warns a sign at its
entrance), a recreation of a bordello, and
mannequins with body hair à la Austin
Powers. Welcome to Amsterdam!

Gothic Oude Kerk

RED LIGHT DISTRICT

This (in)famous area with its houses of ill repute and countless distilleries has been sending sailors broke since the 14th century. The distilleries have gone, but prostitutes now display themselves in windows under red neon lights, touts at sex theatres lure passers-by with come-ons, and sex-shop displays leave nothing to the imagination.

All that aside, it is actually a very pretty part of town – well worth a stroll for the architecture – and the atmosphere is rather laid-back and far less threatening than in red-light districts elsewhere. Crowds of sightseers both foreign and local mingle with pimps, drunks, weirdos, drug dealers and Salvation Army soldiers. Police patrolling on foot chat with prostitutes. Female sightseers are not assumed to be soliciting and tend to be left alone as long as they exercise big-city street sense.

Colloquially the district is known as the *wallen* or *walletjes* for the canals that run down the middle. For a scenic view, face north on the bridge across Oudezijds Voorburgwal linking Lange Niezel and Korte Niezel. The formal border of the Red Light District is Warmoesstraat in the west, Zeedijk/Nieuwmarkt/Kloveniersburgwal in the east and Damstraat/Oude Doelenstraat/Oude Hoogstraat in the south. The best places for strolling window brothels are along Oudezijds Achterburgwal and in the alleys around the Oude Kerk, particularly to the south. Don't take photos of prostitutes or loiterers, or enter into conversation with a drug dealer.

CASA ROSSO Map pp286-7

☎ 627 89 54; Oudezijds Achterburgwal 106-108; admission with/without drinks €45/30; ☺ 7pm-2am

You're going to pass this place with its pink elephant logo, and you're going to wonder what's inside, so we're going to tell you. Briefly: live sex on stage, or, as we once heard a Casa Rosso barker put it, 'Quality sleaze and filth!'

Acts can be male, female, both or lesbian (although not gay…sorry boys!). Performers demonstrate everything from positions of the *kama sutra* to pole dances, incredible

THE RED LIGHT DISTRICT FAQS

- Year prostitution was legalised in the Netherlands: 1810
- Year brothels were legalised: 2000
- Percentage of Dutch public that claims to have 'no problems whatsoever with prostitution': 78%
- Percentage of working prostitutes born in the Netherlands: 5%
- Estimated percentage of prostitutes working illegally in the Netherlands: less than 5%
- Number of windows: approximately 380
- Number of prostitutes working each day in the windows: 1000 to 1200, comprising day, evening and night shifts
- Average rental cost per window (paid by prostitute): €40 to €100 per day, depending on location
- Typical base cost for either 'oral favours' or a 'quickie' in the Red Light District: €30
- Typical base cost for both: €50
- Typical duration of encounter with prostitute: 15 minutes
- Percentage of business from British clients: about 40%
- Most likely time to see prostitutes with Dutch patrons: Monday morning (when many businesses and most shops are closed)
- Do prostitutes pay taxes? Yes
- Are condoms required by law? No, but it's virtually impossible to find a prostitute who'll work without one
- Is there a union? Yes
- Are medical checkups required? No
- Is pimping legal? No
- Is trafficking in prostitutes legal? No
- Penalty for either of the above: maximum six years
- Are accommodations made if a patron can't perform? No
- What happens if a patron gets violent? Prostitutes' quarters are equipped with a button that, when pressed, activates a light outside. The offender had better hope that the police get there before the Hell's Angels do.
- Why red light? Because it's flattering. Especially when used in combination with black light, it makes teeth sparkle. Even as early as the 1300s, women carrying red lanterns met sailors near the port. Try it for yourself sometime.

tricks involving candles, and moves we commonly associate with competitive figure skating. Other acts are comedic, some maybe intentionally so. You may even catch a good old-fashioned striptease.

Apart from the content of the shows, Casa Rosso could pass for a theatre anywhere, with comfortable cinema-style seating, balcony and bar ('with drinks' price includes up to four drinks). Audience members are strictly prohibited from touching the performers.

EROTIC MUSEUM Map pp286-7

☎ 624 73 03; Oudezijds Achterburgwal 54; admission €5; ☻ 11am-1am Sun-Thu, 11am-2am Fri & Sat

Ho hum. Your usual assortment of bondage exhibits, erotic photos and cartoons. Although this museum has the advantage of location, it's less entertaining, not as well laid out, more expensive and a little seedy when compared with the Sexmuseum Amsterdam (p65) on the Damrak.

HASH & MARIJUANA MUSEUM

Map pp286-7

☎ 623 59 61; Oudezijds Achterburgwal 148; admission €5.70; ☻ 11am-11pm

Did you know that the first recorded use of marijuana was in 3727 BC in China? That's just one of the things we learned at this simply designed but informative museum. Exhibits cover pot botany, pipes of the world, the relationship between cannabis and religion, and the history of Amsterdam coffeeshops. Queen Victoria is said to have used marijuana for menstrual cramps, and hemp was used to cover wagons in the American Old West.

Dope-smoking is allowed inside, and if you're of a mind to you can watch (and watch and watch…) as the plants grow in a greenhouse in the back. The museum also sells seeds, books and hemp products.

MUSEUM AMSTELKRING Map pp286-7

☎ 624 66 04; Oudezijds Voorburgwal 40; adult/student/child 5-18yr €7/5/1; ☻ 10am-5pm Mon-Sat, 1-5pm Sun, extended hr during special exhibits

How odd is it to find one of Amsterdam's holiest (and most interesting) museums in the middle of the Red Light District?

The highlight here is Ons' Lieve Heer op Solder (Our Dear Lord in the Attic), one of several 'clandestine' Catholic churches. After the Calvinist coup in 1578, Catholic Church property was confiscated and Catholics were permitted to worship only in privately owned real estate, so long as it wasn't recognisable as a church and the entrance was hidden. The wealthy hosier Jan Hartman had this house built in 1663, complete with a small church in the attic dedicated to St Nicholas. It remained in use until 1887, when the large St Nicolaaskerk (p65) opened its doors on nearby Prins Hendrikkade, diagonally opposite Centraal Station.

In 1888 it became a museum and today houses the city's richest collection of Catholic art, with dozens of liturgical objects, many gilded in silver and gleaming brightly. As you navigate the museum's several floors via tiled staircases, you'll pass the original 'cupboard' bed in the chaplain's room (probably originally used by a servant), the Dutch Classical sael (reception hall; note the matching rectangular patterns on the floor, walls and ceiling) and items pertaining to the Miracle of Amsterdam (see boxed text, p71).

When you finally reach the church in the attic, the effect is quite unexpected. Although small, the church is very grand, with marble columns, an elaborate altar, choir, upstairs gallery and even an organ. It is the only clandestine church preserved as it was originally used, and it is still in use for special ceremonies (weddings, organ concerts and other services).

PROSTITUTION INFORMATION
CENTRE Map pp286-7

☎ 420 73 28; www.pic-amsterdam.com;
Enge Kerksteeg 3; ☺ noon-7pm Tue-Sat or by
appointment

For a donation of your choosing you can view a re-creation of a prostitute's working quarters, view historical photos of the Red Light District and browse some enlightening reading material. Established by a former prostitute and staffed by sex workers, the centre caters for study groups from around the world (including several police academies) and organises evening walks. It offers private tours by a former sex-worker (€12.50 per person, reservation-only), specialising in the life of a sex-worker. It also sells pamphlets on prostitution in the Netherlands and a nifty little map of the Red Light District, as well as a limited selection of Red Light District–themed souvenirs (private-label mirrors, photo frames etc) in its shop, the Wallenwinkel.

DAM SQUARE & NIEUWE ZIJDE

Beyond the Dam, Damrak becomes Rokin (a corruption of *rak-in*, literally, 'inner reach'), most of which was filled in during the 19th century. It is considerably more upmarket than Damrak, with office buildings (the modern Options Exchange at No 61), prestigious shops (the wood-panelled tobacconist Hajenius at No 92) and art dealers.

To the West of the Damrak-Rokin axis is the 'New Side' of the medieval city. It was actually settled slightly earlier than the Oude Zijde – the names date from the construction of the Nieuwe Kerk and division of the city into two parishes. The Rokin terminates at the attractive tower, the Munttoren.

The very first houses in Amsterdam probably stood on a dyke north of the Dam, no more than 25m wide, on what's now the street called Nieuwendijk. It used to link up with the road to Haarlem, and its shops and other businesses became adept at fleecing travellers on their way to Amsterdam's market on the Dam. Today this pedestrianised shopping street is still a down-and-dirty mix of souvenir shops,

'coffeeshops' and cheap hostels, but explore some of the narrow streets leading to the west are picturesquely medieval.

If you'd like to pass through a mini Red Light District without making an ordeal of it, take a quick walk down Oude Nieuwstraat.

South of the Dam is Kalverstraat. The name (Calves Street) presumably refers to the cattle that were led to market on the Dam. There is a good number of large department stores on the street (and pickpockets – please take care!). Crowds can be thick on weekends.

Along the Singel is the **Torensluis**, one of the widest bridges in the city. The view northwards is camera material. The 'toren' refers to a tower that once stood here and formed part of the city's fortifications; later the bridge was later built around it. After the tower was demolished in 1829, a 42m-wide esplanade remained; these days cafés line the bridge.

The **statue** seen on the bridge represents Multatuli, the pen name of the brilliant 19th-century author Eduard Douwes Dekker (see Multatuli Museum, p87).

THE DAM Map pp286-7

The Damrak ends in the Dam where the original dam was built across the Amstel. Once the central market square where everything happened, it used to be much smaller than it is today, reaching its current size only after buildings on all sides were gradually demolished. On busy days, and especially when it's warm, the square swarms with visitors – and pigeons!

The original dam was at the eastern end of the current square, with a sluice alongside so ships could pass through. From 1611 they had to lower their masts to pass under the stock exchange, which had been built over the sluice, until it was filled in for good in 1672.

These days there's some pretty high-priced real estate here, starting with the **Royal Palace** (p70). Clockwise, some of the significant buildings around the square are the **Nieuwe Kerk** (opposite), the department store **de Bijenkorf** (p188), the **NH Grand Hotel Krasnapolsky** (p216) and **Madame Tussaud's Amsterdam** (Map pp286–7; ☎ 523 06 23; www .madametussauds.nl; adult/senior/child €23/20/17.50; ☺ 10am-6.30pm, check for extended hours)

The phallic obelisk on the east side of the square is the **Nationaal Monument,** which was built in 1956 in memory of the people who died during WWII. Its many statues symbolise war (the four male figures), peace (woman with child) and resistance (men with dogs); the 12 urns at the rear contain earth from the 11 provinces and the Dutch East Indies. The war dead are still honoured here every year on 4 May.

By the early 1990s the monument had become seriously weakened by rain and frost, and was in danger of falling apart, but it was eventually restored (by a German firm – the irony!). The monument stands near the site of the old stock exchange (demolished in 1838).

MAGNA PLAZA Map pp286-7
☎ 626 91 99; Nieuwezijds Voorburgwal 182; 🕑 11am-7pm Mon, 10am-7pm Tue, Wed, Fri & Sat, 10am-9pm Thu, noon-7pm Sun

Back towards the Dam, facing the Royal Palace, this hulk, with its imposing orange-and-white façade, was the former General Post Office. It was built in 1895–99 by the government architect CH Peters, a pupil of Pierre Cuypers. It used to be one of the most impressive post offices in Europe, but has since been converted into a luxurious shopping centre dominated by clothing boutiques. Pop inside to admire the impressive hall – with three storeys of colonnades and an airy, skylit atrium – and look at some of the interesting shops.

Adjacent Nieuwezijds Voorburgwal was once the country's 'Fleet Street' where many newspapers had their head offices (they're now out in the suburbs).

NEWS PHOTO Map pp286-7
☎ 330 84 00; www.newsphoto.nl; Prins Hendrikkade 33; admission €5; 🕑 10am-6pm

Across from Centraal Station, this museum opened in mid-2005, and already it's one of our favourites. It displays enormous blowups (up to 60m long) of the photos that accompany headlines, by photographers from around the world. In fact the museum operates like something of a newsroom itself. Themed exhibitions (terrorism, the Tour de France etc) change every few weeks, but as news is made the curators use giant printers to print out the latest, and – *presto* – it's up on the conveniently magnetic walls.

News Photo has a gift shop, but it almost doesn't need one. If you like a photo you see in the main gallery, you can buy it right off the wall (€100 per sq metre while the exhibition is running, half-price thereafter). They can always print more.

NIEUWE KERK Map pp286-7
New Church; ☎ 638 69 09; the Dam; adult/child 6-15yr/under 6yr €5/4/free; 🕑 10am-6pm Fri-Wed, 10am-10pm Thu

Just north of the Royal Palace, this late-Gothic basilica is the coronation church of Dutch royalty, and reckons its origins back to the 14th century, making it the second-oldest church in the city. It is only 'new' in relation to the Oude Kerk (Old Church; p65) – the two competed to be the grandest church in the city. The Nieuwe Kerk was gutted by fire several times, and a planned, exceptionally high tower was never completed because funds were diverted to the city hall (now the Royal Palace) next door.

Of interest are the magnificently carved oak chancel, the bronze choir screen, the massive gilded organ (1645, designed by Jacob van Campen) and stained-glass windows. The church's oldest stained-glass

Magna Plaza (built 1895–99), a deluxe shopping centre

windows (1650) are directly opposite the entrance, depicting Count William IV presenting the coat of arms to the city founder. The upper portion of the window, with spectators and doves, was not added until 1977. The stained-glass work over the main entrance was created to commemorate the coronation of Queen Wilhelmina, who ascended the throne in 1898 at age 18.

The church also contains the mausoleum of the city's greatest naval hero, Admiral Michiel de Ruijter, who died fighting the French at Messina in 1676. Several other prominent Amsterdammers are buried here as well, including poets Joost van den Vondel and Pieter Cornelisz Hooft.

The building is used for exhibitions and organ concerts, but no longer as a church. Opening hours and admission fees may vary (eg during special exhibitions), so ring to check.

RONDE LUTHERSE KERK Map pp286-7
Round Lutheran Church; ☎ 623 15 72; cnr Singel 11; admission free; ⏲ 9am-1pm Mon-Fri & Sun
This domed church was built in 1668–71 to replace the old Lutheran church on the Spui. It is the only round Protestant church in the country, and is pure 17th-century baroque, though the white interior is suitably sober. The church was rebuilt after a disastrous fire in 1822, but falling attendances forced its closure in 1936 (ironically

---

THE WINNER BY A NARROW MARGIN

Canal-boat commentators like to point out the narrowest house in Amsterdam, explaining that property was taxed on frontage – the narrower the house the lower the tax, regardless of height. But each guide seems to have a different 'narrowest' house. So which is it?

The house at Oude Hoogstraat 22, east of the Dam, is 2.02m wide and 6m deep. Occupying a mere 12 sq metres, it could well be the least space-consuming self-contained house in Europe. The house at Singel 7 appears narrower still, just a door and a slim 1st-floor window, but canal-boat commentators fail to point out that it's actually the rear entrance of a house of normal proportions. On the other side of Singel, at No 144 is a house that measures only 1.8m across the front, though it widens to 5m at the rear.

So what do *you* think?

---

the old church on the Spui is still in use by Lutherans). It now serves as a conference centre for the nearby Renaissance Hotel.

Next door along the east side of Singel, where the former city wall used to run, the house at No 7 appears to be no wider than its door – except that this is actually the rear entrance of a house of normal proportions.

ROYAL PALACE Map pp286-7
Koninklijk Paleis; ☎ 620 40 60; www.koninklijk huis.nl; the Dam; adult/child 6-16yr & senior/child under 6yr €4.50/3.60/free, adult ticket with audio tour €6.50
The Dam's most imposing building, the palace began life as the grand *stadhuis* (city hall) of republican Amsterdam – in use since 1655, completed 1665. It replaced the old city hall on the same spot, which had burned down. The stunning interior is much more lavish than the stark exterior suggests and is well worth visiting.

The architect, Jacob van Campen, spared no costs for this display of Amsterdam's wealth that rivalled the grandest European buildings of the day. It was described at the time as the eighth wonder of the world, inspired by the Roman Forum (as the numerous columns of marble attest). The great hall (*burgerzaal* – citizens' hall) occupies the heart of the building and was designed to be freely accessible to any citizen. Van Campen envisioned this room as a schematic of the world, with Amsterdam as its centre – look carefully and you'll see motifs representing the four elements: birds (air), fish (water), fruit (earth) and fire (er, fire). On the far wall, a clock is constantly set to 11 o'clock, indicating that justice is possible even at the last hour. This room is still used for large royal functions.

Also worth noting are the balcony room, from where important announcements were made, and the council chamber with its elaborate paintings and murals depicting themes of giving advice, including owls and a painting of Moses by Jacob de Wit.

A century and a half after it was built, the building became the palace of King Louis, Napoleon Bonaparte's brother, who contributed one of the world's richest collections of Empire furniture but demolished the historic Weigh House in front of the building demolished because it spoiled his view. The building then passed to the members of the House of Orange, who stayed here occasionally. In 1935 the national government bought and restored it for state functions. Officially Queen Beatrix lives here and pays a symbolic rent, though she really lives in Den Haag.

Note that the Royal Palace does not accept the I Amsterdam Card or Museumkaart. The Palace is closed until 2008; ring or check the website for updates.

AROUND THE SPUI

Until 1882, the elongated Spui Square (referred to simply as the Spui, rhymes with 'how') used to be water. In the 14th century it marked the southern end of the city. The name means 'sluice' (or rather, the area inside a sluice) and it connected the Amstel with the watercourse running along Nieuwezijds Voorburgwal, the western side of the city, and later with the Singel.

The heart of the square is its western part where Nieuwezijds Voorburgwal meets Spuistraat. The statuette in the middle, called the Lieverdje (Little Darling), is an endearing rendition of an Amsterdam street-brat. It was donated by a cigarette company and became the focus for Provo 'happenings' in the mid-1960s (see boxed text, p55).

The Spui is now a meeting point for the city's intellectuals, who congregate in the pubs at the western end of the square – such as the old-style Luxembourg (p158), Hoppe (p156) and Dante (p158) – and in the surrounding bookshops, including the landmark Athenaeum bookshop and newsagency.

The Spui hosts weekly markets (see boxed text, p190).

Heiligeweg (the Holy Way) was travelled by Catholics on their annual procession to the chapel of the Miracle of Amsterdam. The route used to extend all the way from the village of Sloten, southwest of the city, along what is now the Overtoom (once a canal for towboats carrying produce) and through the current Leidsestraat, but only this final section has retained the original name. A procession still takes place every year on the Sunday closest to 15 March and attracts Catholics from Holland and abroad.

MIRACLES COME IN MANY FORMS

The Miracle of Amsterdam has a rather unappetising start.

In 1345 the final sacrament was administered to a dying man, but he was unable to keep the Host (communion wafer) down and – there's no way to put this delicately – vomited it up. Here's the miracle part: when the vomit was thrown on the fire, the Host would not burn. Shortly thereafter, a chapel (demolished 1908) was built on the site across Kalverstraat from what's now the museum and it soon became a pilgrimage area; the final approach is along the street now known as Heiligeweg. A commemorative column still remains in the pavement at Wijde Kapelsteeg.

In the Amsterdams Historisch Museum is a wooden chest reported to have once contained the Host. In 1578, when Catholic property was parcelled out, the chest ended up in an orphanage, and several children are said to have been cured of illnesses by sitting on it.

AMSTERDAMS HISTORISCH MUSEUM Map pp286-7

Amsterdam Historical Museum; ☎ 523 18 22; www.ahm.nl; Kalverstraat 92; adult/child 6-18yr/ under 6yr €6/3/free; ☺ 10am-5pm Mon-Fri, 11am-5pm Sat & Sun

Housed in the former civic orphanage (that existed here till 1960), this museum is quite extensive and pleasant. Begin with the large-screen TV depicting an aerial view of the evolution of the city from tiny settlement on the mouth of the Amstel, as it was filled in to create the metropolis we now know and love. Excavations, even in the city centre, have yielded several well-preserved artefacts: pottery, woollen cloth etc. Exhibited here are models of old homes, religious objects from churches and synagogues (including some relating to the Miracle of Amsterdam; see boxed text, above), silver, porcelain, exhibits on the trade guilds and a detailed history of Dutch trading. Exhibits on the 20th century include the spread of bicycle use, WWII (naturally), a re-creation of the original Café Het Mandje (a touchstone in the gay rights movement), well-meaning civic projects like the white cars and white bikes, and an examination of the city's drug policies.

Even if you give the museum a miss, it's worth walking into the courtyard (note the cupboards in which the orphans stored their possessions) or at least getting a taste of the amazing display of paintings in the Civic Guard Gallery (right).

BEGIJNHOF Map pp286-7

☎ 622 19 18; www.begijnhofamsterdam.nl; admission free; ☺ 8am-5pm

Hidden behind the intersection of the Spui and the Nieuwezijds Voorburgwal, this enclosed former convent dates from the early 14th century. It's a surreal oasis of peace, with tiny houses and postage stamp–sized gardens grouped around a well-kept courtyard. Inside these confines, you'd scarcely believe that the hustle and bustle of the city are mere steps away. Amsterdam has many such enclosed *hofjes* (literally, 'little courtyards'; see boxed text, p81) or almshouses (old people's homes run by charities), but this is the only one where the public is still welcome. How lucky we are for it.

The Beguines were a Catholic order of unmarried or widowed women from wealthy families, who cared for the elderly and lived a religious life without taking monastic vows; the last true Beguines died in the 1970s. They owned their houses, so these could not be confiscated after the Calvinist coup.

Contained within the *hof* is the Begijnhof Kapel (Begijnhof Chapel; ☎ 622 19 18; Begijnhof 30; admission free; ☺ Dutch-language Eucharist service 9am & 5pm Mon-Fri, 9am Sat, 10am Sun, French-language service 11.15am). After the loss of their Gothic church, the Beguines were forced to worship in this 'clandestine' church opposite. Go through the dog-leg entrance, and inside this lovely chapel you'll find marble columns, wooden pews, and paintings and stained-glass windows commemorating the Miracle of Amsterdam.

The other church in the Begijnhof is known as the Engelse Kerk (English Church; ☎ 624 96 65; Begijnhof 48; admission free; ☺ Presbyterian service in English 10.30am Sun), at the southern end of the Begijnhof courtyard. This Gothic church was built around 1392 and was used by the Beguines until it was taken away from them by the Calvinists. It was eventually rented out to the local community of English and Scottish Presbyterian refugees – the Pilgrim Fathers worshipped here – and still serves as the city's Presbyterian church. Some of the pulpit panels were designed by a young Piet Mondriaan.

Also note the house at No 34; it dates from around 1425, making it the oldest preserved wooden house in the country. There's a collection of biblical wall tablets on the blind wall to the left.

CIVIC GUARD GALLERY Map pp286-7

☎ 523 18 22; Kalverstraat 92; admission free; ☺ 10am-5pm Mon-Fri, 11am-5pm Sat & Sun

The enormous tableaux here represent a subgenre of Dutch painting: group portraits of medieval guards. The different divisions – *voetboog* (large crossbow), *kloveniers* (hackbut) etc – protected the city and played a large part in deposing the Spanish government; after the Peace of Munster in 1648, they took on more of a social function. This collection, together with the Rijksmuseum's (which includes the most famous of these paintings, Rembrandt's *Nightwatch*), is the world's largest, and given the repairs due to the Rijksmuseum over the next few years, the Civic Guard Gallery should be the best place in town to view a large number at once. English signage is excellent.

Technically, every man had to serve in these guard units, although not all were able because guardsmen had to pay for uniforms and weapons. Participation in the portraits, however, was voluntary, as each member paid his own way. The size of the paintings was determined by the size of the wall space in the guardhouses where the paintings were to be hung.

The gallery used to be a ditch separating the boys' and girls' sections of a previous orphanage. It ends by one entrance to the Begijnhof.

UNIVERSITY LIBRARY Map pp292-3

☎ 525 23 01; Singel 421-425; ☺ 8.30am-midnight Mon-Fri, 9.30am-5pm Sat, 11am-5pm Sun

Today's library is a concrete hulk, not nearly the beautiful building you'd expect from such an historic site. However, there's a small gallery that may be worth visiting depending on what's showing.

In any case, the history of the site is fascinating. Citizens' militias used to meet here: the 'hand-bow' (*handboog*) militia in No 421 and the 'foot-bow' (*voetboog*) militia in No 425, which also served as headquarters for the West India Company. Now you know where the names of the nearby streets Handboogstraat and Voetboogstraat come from. Their firing ranges at the rear reached to Kalverstraat.

NIEUWMARKT

Eating p135; Shopping p191; Sleeping p218

In the 17th century, ships used to sail from the IJ down Geldersekade to Nieuwmarkt (New Market) to take on board new anchors or load and unload produce. Today this square, east of the Red Light District, is a cheerful place ringed with cafés, shops and restaurants. It is also the centre of the city's New Year celebrations.

Many people can remember when this district wasn't so cheery. In the 1970s Nieuwmarkt's reputation bottomed out when it became the centre of Amsterdam's heroin trade. Drug dealers and international mobsters controlled the streets, to the point where a poster signed by the mayor recommended that people visit the miniature model at Madurodam (see boxed text, p235) if they wanted to see this historic part of town. The turning point was the murder of a policeman by a drug addict; the ensuing police campaign in the mid-1980s restored legitimate business and much of the old merriment. Although you might still encounter junkies (particularly along Geldersekade to the north of the square), they're far fewer and further between.

North of Nieuwmarkt Square is the Zeedijk, the original sea dyke that curved from the mouth of the Amstel to Nieuwmarkt Square and continued from there along what are now St Antoniesbreestraat, Jodenbreestraat and Muiderstraat.

The Zeedijk has a long (and ongoing) history as a street of wine, women and song, and was the first port of call for sailors after their long voyages. In the 1950s wine and song predominated and many of the world's great jazz musicians played in pubs such as the Casablanca (p174).

The house at Zeedijk 1 dates from the mid-1500s and is one of two timber-fronted houses still left in the city; the other, older one is in the Begijnhof (opposite). On the other side of the street stands the legendary Café Het Mandje, a touchstone in the gay-rights movement, and an early hangout among Dutch gays and lesbians. It closed in 1983, but if you want to see what it looked like inside, there's a replica at the Amsterdams Historisch Museum (p71).

The Zeedijk is also the main focal point for Amsterdam's 10,000-strong Chinese community, although a New Chinatown east of Centraal Station is on the books for completion by the end of the decade – the plan is for a combination of residences and entertainment facilities.

Incidentally, although Nieuwmarkt is very much an open space – arguably the grandest in town after the Dam – nobody adds the word *plein* (square) to the name. It's a little confusing because the whole neighbourhood to the east and southeast is also known as Nieuwmarkt.

The Nieuwmarkt neighbourhood, centred on Waterlooplein, is closely associated with Rembrandt, and until WWII it was the centre of Amsterdam's thriving Jewish community. Jews here enjoyed more freedom than elsewhere in Europe and made the city a centre for diamonds, tobacco, printing and clothing. They also gave Amsterdam an exceptional variety of lively markets, of which the current markets (p190) are mere wistful reminders. It is here that you'll find several important sites of Jewish interest (synagogues, current and former, the Jewish Historical Museum) and a controversial construction (the Stopera – city hall/opera house complex – and housing along busy St Antoniesbreestraat).

The busy roundabout east of the Mozes en Aäronkerk is Mr Visserplein. LE Visser was a Jewish president of the Supreme Court ('Mr' stands for *meester,* which means 'master', the Dutch lawyer's title) who was dismissed by the Nazis. He refused to wear the Star of David and berated the Jewish Council for helping the occupiers carry out their anti-Jewish policies. He died before the Germans could wreak revenge on him.

Nearby, south of the Portuguese synagogue, is the triangular Jonas Daniël (JD) Meijerplein, named after the country's first Jewish lawyer (actual name Joune Rintel), who did much to ensure the full emancipation of the Jews in the Napoleonic period.

TRANSPORT

Trams 9 and 14 head to the Nieuwmarkt neighbourhood; alight near Waterlooplein. For Nieuwmarkt Square, metro station Nieuwmarkt is just on the eastern edge. The metro also stops at Waterlooplein.

From Centraal Station you can also take the 'Opstapper' bus to Waterlooplein.

Sights

NIEUWMARKT

TOP FIVE NIEUWMARKT

- Celebrate local hero Rembrandt at **Museum Het Rembrandthuis** (p76).
- Follow the heartening success and the haunting downfall of Amsterdam's Jewish community at the **Joods Historisch Museum** (opposite).
- Give the kids a break at **TunFun** (p78).
- Stop for a coffee or a *biertje* in the cheery surrounds of Nieuwmarkt Square or at **Café de Sluyswacht** (p156) by the Oude Schans.
- The next wave? **Guan Yin Shrine** (right).

On the square, Mari Andriessen's **Dockworker statue** (1952; Map pp290–1) commemorates the general strike that began among dockworkers on 25 February 1941 to protest the treatment of Jews. The first deportation round-up had occurred here a few days earlier. The anniversary of the strike is still an occasion for wreath-laying but has become a low-key affair with the demise of the Communist Party.

The area southeast of here, the 'new' canals (Nieuwe Herengracht, Nieuwe Keizersgracht and Nieuwe Prinsengracht), intersected by the Weesperstraat traffic artery, was where the canal-belt project petered out around 1700. The canals on this far side of the Amstel were less in demand among the city's wealthy residents, and went to charities or were settled by well-off Jews from the Jewish quarter.

Waterlooplein, which is at the end of St Antoniesbreestraat and bordered by Jodenbreestraat and the Amstel, was once known as Vlooienburg and the heart of the Jewish quarter. Originally Waterlooplein was the site of the major Jewish flea market, where anything was available. There's still a **flea market** (9am-5pm Mon-Fri, 8.30am-5.30pm Sat) here, selling a wide range of goods. It's popular, not only tourists. Prices are a bit higher than at other markets, but it's worth a wander. Beware of pickpockets.

GASSAN DIAMONDS Map pp290–1
622 53 33; www.gassandiamonds.com; Nieuwe Uilenburgerstraat 173-175; admission free; 9am-5pm

A short walk from Waterlooplein, this vast diamond workshop offers regular, interestingly technical demonstrations of carving the hardest material known to humankind. You'll also get a quick primer in how to assess diamonds for quality, and of course there are opportunities to buy. There are several diamond outlets around town, but we think the tour here is the best and most comprehensive.

While you are there, you may notice that the factory sits on an island. This is Uilenburg, one of the rectangular islands reclaimed in the 1580s with the sudden influx of Sephardic Jews from Spain and Portugal. Shipyards that operated here soon moved out to the new area, Eastern Islands, making way for another wave of Jewish refugees, this time Ashkenazim. Another historical note: Gassan in the 1880s was the first diamond factory to use steam power.

GUAN YIN SHRINE Map pp286-7
Fo Guang Shan He Hua Temple; 420 23 57; www.ibps.nl; Zeedijk 106-118; admission free; noon-5pm Tue-Sat,10am-5pm Sun

Near the Nieuwmarkt end of the Zeedijk is Europe's first Chinese Imperial-style Buddhist temple, completed in 2000. It is dedicated to Guan Yin (aka Kannon), the Bodhisattva (Buddhist prophet) alternately depicted in male and female forms and sometimes known as the goddess of mercy. Guan Yin is commonly shown with many arms, to solve the many problems of supplicants, and this version is no exception. Images on the statue include a prayer bell, a lotus flower and a wheel (to symbolise the spread of Buddhist teaching), plus Guan Yin's own long ears to facilitate the hearing of prayer.

The building itself is unique in the city. The main gate is called the 'mountain gate', referring to the traditional mountain setting of Buddhist monasteries; not too many mountains in Amsterdam. It occupies several lots, and the sections on either end seem to echo the neighbouring row houses. The section in the middle is set back from the street and was designed along principles of feng shui.

Traditional Chinese-style recitations of the sutras (sayings of the Buddha) are held every Sunday at 10.30am and are open to the public. Meditations take place 10.30am to noon on the third Sunday of every month, except in the case of special events (check website).

HOLLAND EXPERIENCE Map pp286-7

☎ 422 22 33; www.hollandexperience.nl; Waterlooplein 17; adult/child 4-16yr & senior/child under 3yr €8.50/7.25/free, adult combination ticket with Rembrandthuis €13; ⓨ 10am-6pm (last show 5.30pm)

Oh dear. Next to the Rembrandthuis, this multimedia hype-fest tries to cram all of this little land's big attractions into an over-priced mish-mash of sights and sounds. The audience dons 3-D glasses and sits on a rotating platform that lurches along with a plotless half-hour film from tulips to windmills to threatened dykes. There's no narration or explanation, but a theme from *Swan Lake* gets played ad nauseam and an old-style car (a motif we don't understand) is your spirit guide through the journey. In one instance, a fish wags its tongue at the audience. In another, an on-screen dyke crumbles, room temperature plummets, and a Sony-augmented thunderstorm rages. As film-making it leaves a lot to be desired (hint: roll camera from *inside* the roller coaster, not *next* to it!), but we will say this: the six-year-olds in the audience howled with laughter over the sight gags (although even they fell silent after a while).

Our advice: get high first.

JOODS HISTORISCH MUSEUM

Map pp290-1

Jewish Historical Museum; ☎ 626 99 45; www .jhm.nl; JD Meijerplein 2-4; adult/senior or student/child 13-17yr/child 6-12yr €6.50/4/3/2; ⓨ 11am-5pm, closed Yom Kippur

This interesting and impressive museum (1987) is a beautifully restored complex of four Ashkenazic synagogues linked by glass-covered walkways. These are the Grote Sjoel (Great Synagogue, 1671), the first public synagogue in Western Europe; the Obbene Sjoel (Upstairs Synagogue, 1686); the Dritt Sjoel (Third Synagogue, 1700 with a 19th-century façade); and the Neie Sjoel (New Synagogue, 1752), the largest in the complex, but still dwarfed by the Portuguese Synagogue across the square.

Exhibits start with the pillars of Jewish identity and gradually give way to an engaging portrait of Jewish life in the city, through profiles of some important Jewish figures and displays of religious and secular articles. A more interactive kids' section is called 'Where Mokum is Home', and there's

Joods Historisch Museum

an excellent English-language audio tour (no extra charge).

The museum also contains a kosher-style coffeeshop.

MOZES EN AÄRONKERK Map pp290-1

☎ 624 75 97; www.mozeshuis.nl; Waterlooplein 205

This neoclassical Catholic church, built in 1841 on the northeastern corner of Water-looplein, shows that this wasn't exclusively a Jewish area. Despite its impressive organ, it is no longer used as a church, but rather for social, cultural and educational organisations, which often hold exhibitions (check listings for the latest) – otherwise the church is generally closed to the public

It replaced the 'clandestine' Catholic church that occupied two houses named Mozes and Aäron in what is now the rear of the church along Jodenbreestraat (note the wall tablet of Moses above the street corner).

One of the buildings demolished to make way for the new church was home to the Jewish philosopher Baruch de Spinoza (1632–77), who was born in Amsterdam but spent much of his life making lenses in Den Haag after rabbis proclaimed him a heretic. He is best known for his work *Ethics,* which proposes that the concept of God pos-sesses an infinite number of attributes.

JEWISH AMSTERDAM

It's hard to overstate the role that Jews played in the evolution of civic and commercial life of Amsterdam.

Although some histories trace the presence of Jews in Holland back to Roman times, their first documented Jewish presence goes back to the 12th century. Their numbers remained small through medieval times, but expulsion from Spain and Portugal in the 1580s brought a flood of Sephardic (Jews of Spanish, Middle-Eastern or North African heritage) refugees.

As in much of Europe, Jews in Amsterdam were barred from many professions. Monopolistic guilds kept most trades firmly closed. But some of the Sephardim were diamond-cutters, for which there was no guild. Other Sephardic Jews introduced printing and tobacco processing, or worked in similarly unrestricted trades such as retail on the streets, finance, medicine and the garment industry. The majority, however, eked out a meagre living as labourers and small-time traders on the margins of society, and lived in houses they could afford in the Nieuwmarkt area, which developed into the Jewish quarter.

Yet Amsterdam's Jews enjoyed freedoms unheard of elsewhere in Europe. They were not confined to a ghetto and, with some restrictions, could buy property. Although the Protestant establishment sought to impose restrictions, civic authorities were reluctant to restrict such productive members of society.

The 17th century saw another influx of Jewish refugees, this time Ashkenazim (Jews from Europe outside of Iberia) fleeing pogroms in Central and Eastern Europe. Amsterdam became the largest Jewish centre in Europe, some 10,000 strong by Napoleonic times.

The guilds and all remaining restrictions on Jews were abolished during the French occupation, and Amsterdam's Jewish community thrived in the 19th century.

All that came to an end, however, with WWII. The Nazis brought about the nearly complete annihilation of Amsterdam's Jewish community. Before the war, about 140,000 Jews lived in the Netherlands. Of these, about 90,000 lived in Amsterdam, comprising 13% of the city's population. Only about 5500 of these Amsterdam Jews survived the war, barely one in 16.

Today there are some 43,000 Jews in the Netherlands; of those around 20,000 live in Amsterdam. Among Dutch Jews, about 85% self-identify as Jewish, although only about 25% are members of synagogues while some 57% are non-practising. The rate of intermarriage among Dutch Jews is about 75%. New Jewish arrivals these days tend to be from Israel and, to a lesser extent, from Russia.

Ironically, Amsterdam's legendary tolerance may also portend difficulty ahead for its Jewish community. Recent decades have seen the arrival of Muslims from the Middle East and North Africa, and while there has not been the same level of friction here as elsewhere in Europe, there's anecdotal evidence of tension.

One lasting legacy of Jewish presence: Amsterdam slang incorporates many terms of Hebrew or Yiddish origin, such as the alternative name for Amsterdam, Mokum (from *makom aleph*, the best city of all); the cheery goodbye, *de mazzel* (good luck); *gabber* (friend, 'mate') from the Yiddish *chaver*, companion; and the put-down *kapsones maken* (to make unnecessary fuss; from *kapshones*, self-importance).

MUSEUM HET REMBRANDTHUIS

Map pp286-7

☎ 520 04 00; www.rembrandthuis.nl; Jodenbreestraat 4-6; adult/student/child 6-15yr/under 6yr €7.50/6/1.50/free, adult combination ticket with Holland Experience €13; ☽ 10am-5pm Mon-Sat, 11-5pm Sun

Rembrandt van Rijn lived and worked in this beautifully restored house dating from 1606. He bought the house in 1639 for a fortune thanks to his wealthy wife, Saskia van Uylenburgh, but chronic debt got the better of him and he had to bail out and move to the Jordaan in 1658. The years spent in this house were the high point of his career, when he was regarded as a star and ran the largest painting studio in Holland, before he ruined it all by making enemies and squandering his earnings.

Although it can be crowded, the museum is worth visiting for the almost complete collection of Rembrandt's etchings (250 of the 280 he is known to have made), although they are not all on display at once. Expect to see between 20 and 100 etchings on display at any one time, depending on the exhibit. Demonstrations of etching techniques take place several times daily.

Shows change a few times per year, often incorporating works by Rembrandt's peers, or contemporary paintings that somehow comment on Rembrandt's own pieces. The collection also includes several drawings and paintings by his pupils and his teacher, Pieter Lastman, and an etching by Albrecht Dürer.

The house itself has been completely restored. Thanks to the list of Rembrandt's possessions drawn up by the debt collector, as well as several drawings and paintings by the master himself, the interior now looks as it did when he lived there. The collection of objects alone is impressive: seashells, weaponry, musical instruments, a Roman bust and military helmets from as far away as Japan. No wonder he went bankrupt!

Recommended duration of a visit is 45 minutes to one hour.

PINTOHUIS (OPENBARE BIBLIOTHEEK) Map pp286-7

☎ 624 31 84; www.oba.nl; St Antoniesbreestraat 69; admission free; ☒ 2-8pm Mon & Wed, 2-5pm Fri, 11am-4pm Sat

The street that runs from Nieuwmarkt Square towards Waterlooplein is St Antoniesbreestraat, once a busy street that lost its old buildings during the construction of the metro line – the new houses incorporate rubber blocks in the foundations to absorb vibrations caused by the metro. One of the old buildings still standing is the Pintohuis, which used to belong to a wealthy Sephardic Jew, Isaac de Pinto, who had it remodelled with Italianate pilasters in the 1680s. In the 1970s a planned freeway to Centraal Station would have required the demolition of this building, but controversy stopped the freeway. It's now a library (bibliotheek) – pop inside to admire the beautiful ceilings.

PORTUGUESE-ISRAELITE SYNAGOGUE Map pp290-1

☎ 624 53 51; www.esnoga.com; Mr Visserplein 3; adult/child 10-15yr €6.50/5; ☒ 10am-4pm Sun-Fri Apr-Oct, 10am-4pm Sun-Thu, 10am-3pm Fri Sep-Mar

This edifice, built between 1671 and 1675 by the Sephardic community, was the largest synagogue in Europe at the time and is still impressive. The architect, Elias Bouman, was inspired by the Temple of Solomon, but the building's classical lines are typical of Amsterdam. It was restored after the war and is in use today. Check the website for the schedule of services.

The soaring interior features massive pillars that stand in contrast to some two dozen brass candelabra suspended from the ceiling (lit for night-time services). You can catch a short video presentation on some of the synagogue's implements and festivals. Inside you will find some short explanations of the various symbols.

The large library belonging to the Ets Haim seminary, on the synagogue grounds, is one of the oldest and most important Jewish libraries in Europe and contains many priceless works.

SCHREIERSTOREN Map pp286-7
Prins Hendrikkade 94-95

At the mouth of the Geldersekade, the canal east of the Zeedijk, is this small brick tower dating from around 1480 that used to form part of the city fortifications. It's the oldest such tower still standing. Its name comes from an old Dutch word for 'sharp', a reference to this sharp corner that jutted out into the IJ. Tourist literature prefers to call it the 'wailing tower' (from schreien, to weep or wail) and claims that sailors' wives stood here and cried their lungs out when ships set off for distant lands, which makes a far more interesting story. The women even have a plaque dedicated to them.

Nowadays you can enter the tower and take a break at the attractive café (☎ 428 82 91) inside.

FROM OLD AMSTERDAM TO NIEUW AMSTERDAM

Among the wall plaques on the Schreierstoren, one explains that the English captain Henry Hudson set sail from here in 1609 in his ship the Halve Maen (Half Moon). The United East India Company had enlisted him to find a northern passage to the East Indies, but instead he ended up exploring the North American river that now bears his name. On the return voyage his ship was seized in England and he was ordered never again to sail for a foreign nation.

His reports, however, made it back to base, and the Dutch soon established a fort on an island called Manhattan that developed into a settlement called Nieuw Amsterdam; in 1626 an agent of the recently established Dutch West India Company purchased the island from Native Americans for 60 guilders (often cited as the equivalent of US$24!). In 1664 the West India Company's local governor, the imperious, fanatically Calvinist Pieter Stuyvesant, surrendered the town to the British, who promptly renamed it New York. Stuyvesant retired to the Lower Manhattan market garden called Bouwerij, now known as the Bowery.

Fun fact: Manhattan's Wall Street, one of the centres of world finance, was originally the site of a fortified wall erected by the Dutch to keep out the British.

STOPERA Map pp292-3

☎ 551 81 17; Waterlooplein 22

This hulking complex occupies (in both senses) the space between Waterlooplein and the Amstel. Built in 1986, the 'St' part of its name stands for *stadhuis* (city hall) while the 'opera' part is obvious. Facing the Amstel is the **Muziektheater** (☎ 625 54 55; www.hetmuziektheater.nl; Amstel 3; ♥ advance tickets 10am-6pm Mon-Sat, 11.30am-6pm Sun; tickets also available at AUB Ticketshop, tourist information offices and online), while the city hall is closer to Waterlooplein.

The building, by the Austrian architect Wilhelm Holzbauer and his Dutch colleague Cees Dam, was the winner of a competition. However, opinions are not altogether positive – one critic said that the building had 'all the charm of an Ikea chair', and others sniff at the theatre's acoustics and rehearsal spaces. Our view: yea on the music theatre, nay on city hall.

Music and dance performances also take place in the theatre; there are usually free lunch-time concerts on Tuesdays. In any case, have a look at the little display in the arcade between city hall and the theatre about NAP, the country's water levels (see boxed text, below).

TAKING A NAP

It is widely known that Amsterdam (and indeed more than half the Netherlands) lies a couple of metres below sea level, but when's the last time you heard anyone ask which sea level? In fact, sea level varies around the globe and even around the Netherlands. The average level of the former Zuiderzee, in the lee of Holland, was slightly lower than that of the North Sea along Holland's exposed west coast.

A display in the arcade of the Stopera shows the ins and outs of Normaal Amsterdams Peil (NAP; Normal Amsterdam Level), established in the 17th century as the average high-water mark of the Zuiderzee. This still forms the zero reference for elevation anywhere in the country and is also used in Germany and several other European countries.

Water in the canals is kept at 40cm below NAP and many parts of the city lie lower still. Water columns represent different sea levels, as well as the highest level of disastrous floods in 1953 (4.55m above NAP). Information sheets explain the details.

TUNFUN Map pp290-1

☎ 689 43 00; www.tunfun.nl; Mr Visserplein 7; adult & child under 1yr/child 1-12yr free/€7.50; ♥ 10am-6pm (last entry 5pm)

Very odd, very cool and very Amsterdam, TunFun is an indoor playground in a former traffic underpass that was an unused eyesore for over a decade. Adriaan Van Hoogstraten and another local dad, Edward van der Marel, teamed up to enter the city's competition for the future of the tunnel, and their proposal beat 14 others. It took a year and lots of elbow grease, but TunFun opened in 2003, unmistakably child-oriented yet still urban. The owners even brought in artists to decorate the tunnel with new, kid-friendly graffiti. These days kids can build, climb, roll, draw, jump on trampolines and play on a soccer pitch. There's even a children's disco (this *is* Amsterdam). The café serves healthy-ish snacks and *poffertjes* (little pancakes). Note that kids can visit TunFun only if accompanied by an adult. It gets rather busy when the weather's bad.

WAAG Map pp286-7

☎ 422 77 72; Nieuwmarkt 4; admission free; ♥ 10am-1am

The Waag (Weigh House) dates from 1488, when it was known as St Anthoniespoort (St Anthony's Gate) and formed part of the city fortifications. A century later the city had expanded further east and the gate lost its original function. A section of Kloveniersburgwal was filled in to create the St Anthoniesmarkt (now the Nieuwmarkt). The central courtyard of the gate was covered and it became the city weigh house – the one on the Dam had become too small.

Several guilds occupied the upper floor, including the surgeons' guild, which commissioned Rembrandt to paint *The Anatomy Lesson of Dr Tulp* (displayed in the Mauritshuis in Den Haag) and added the octagonal central tower in 1691 to house its new Anatomical Theatre. The masons' guild was based in the tower facing the Zeedijk – note the superfine brickwork.

Public executions took place at the Waag from the early 19th century, after Louis Napoleon decreed that his palace on the Dam was no longer a suitable spot for such gory displays. In later years it served other purposes – fire station, vault for the city archives, home to the Amsterdams Historisch Museum and the Joods Historisch Museum.

The Stopera (p78), city hall and music theatre, on the Amstel

During WWII, Jews from the nearby Nieuwmarkt neighbourhood were assembled in front of the Waag for deportation.

Today it houses a bar-restaurant that is illuminated by huge candle-wheels for grand medieval effect.

ZUIDERKERK Map pp286-7

☎ 552 79 87; Zuiderkerkhof 72; admission free;
🕙 9am-4pm Mon-Fri, noon-4pm Sat

Off St Antoniesbreestraat, near the Pintohuis, a passageway through the modern Pentagon housing estate leads to the Zuiderkerk, the 'Southern Church' built by Hendrick de Keyser (p41) in 1603–11. His tower, 1m off plumb, dates from 1614. This was the first custom-built Protestant church in Amsterdam – still Catholic design but no choir – and served as a blueprint for the Westerkerk (p89). The final church service was held here in 1929 and at the end of WWII it served as a morgue.

The Zuiderkerk now houses the city government office, the Municipal Centre for Physical Planning and Public Housing and occasional, changing exhibits of art or displays on urban planning and the nature of the city. If you're hoping to be dazzled by the 17th-century church interior, dial back your anticipation: it's been pretty much modernised and hollowed out. However, you may be able to tour the tower for a great view over the city. Scheduled visits are usually held between June and September, but inquire ahead of time to avoid disappointment, as the tower was closed for maintenance as we went to press.

If you like what you see here, De Keyser also designed the tower on the nearby landmark **Montelbaanstoren** (p40).

JORDAAN & WESTERN ISLANDS

Eating p136; Shopping p192; Sleeping p218

The Jordaan neighbourhood was planned and built as a working-class district during the canal-belt project in the early 17th century. Here the canal-diggers, carpenters, bridge-builders, and stonemasons settled with their families. Here, too, came the tanneries, breweries, sugar refineries, smithies, cooperages and some other smelly or noisy industries banned from the upmarket Canal Belt, along with the residences of the artisans and labourers who worked in them.

The name Jordaan wasn't used until a century later, and its origin is unclear. The most popular theory is that it's a corruption of the French *jardin* (garden). After all, many Huguenots settled here in what used

TRANSPORT

Tram lines 13, 14 and 17 travel along Raadhuisstraat/Rozengracht and trams 3 and 10 travel down Marnixstraat, just to the west of the Jordaan.

Bus route 21 travels along Raadhuisstraat/Rozengracht; routes 18, 22 and 46 travel down Nieuwe Westerdokstraat, just north of Haarlemmerstraat, through the Haarlem Quarter.

to be the market gardens beyond the city walls, and many streets carry names of trees and flowers. Other historians contend that the name had biblical connotations and was a reference to the Jordan River.

For centuries, the Jordaan remained a working-class area and the authorities saw it as the unruly district of the city. It was the first precinct where tarred roads replaced brick paving because the latter could be turned into barricades and police-smashing projectiles during riots. Early in the 20th century, one in seven Amsterdammers lived in the Jordaan, with 1000 people packed to the hectare in squalid conditions.

In the late 19th and early 20th centuries, many of the Jordaan's ditches and narrow canals were filled in, mainly for reasons of sanitation. Their names still remain, however: Palmgracht, Lindengracht, Rozengracht (now a major thoroughfare) and Elandsgracht. Bloemgracht was the most upmarket of the canals (the 'Herengracht of the Jordaan') and, for that reason, was never filled in: many wealthy artisans built smaller versions of patrician canal houses.

In the 1960s and '70s many Jordaanese moved to the outlying 'garden suburbs'. Their places were taken by students, artists and tertiary-sector professionals who began to transform the Jordaan into a trendy area. The area south of Rozengracht has a heritage of workshops and artists' studios; a quick visit will turn up lots of galleries even today.

Popular ideas of the Jordaan linger: the 'heart and soul' of the 'real' Amsterdam epitomised in schmaltzy oompah ballads, where life happens on the streets or in corner pubs; where houses are tiny but tidy, with lace curtains and flowers in window boxes, behind which Auntie Cori eyes the street and her front door with the help of a *spionnetje* (little spy mirror) attached to the window-sill; and where living, working, shopping, schooling and entertainment are integrated in the one neighbourhood.

Such popular conceptions still hold true, as you will discover when you wander and soak up the atmosphere. Take your time and don't worry if you get lost (which you will); there are plenty of inviting pubs and restaurants, offbeat shops and weird little art galleries to grab your attention.

Haarlemmerstraat and Haarlemmerdijk end in **Haarlemmerpoort** (Haarlem Gate; Map pp282–3) on Haarlemmerplein, where travellers heading into town had to leave their horses and carts. The current structure dates from 1840 and was built as a tax office and a gateway for King William II to pass through on his coronation. It's since been converted to housing. It replaced the most monumental of all the city gates, built by Hendrick de Keyser in 1615 but demolished some 200 years later.

In the 17th century a canal was dug from here to Haarlem to transport passengers on horse-drawn barges. In the 19th century the railways took over, but the original canal-side road, Haarlemmerweg, is still a major road (which, for obvious reasons, no longer passes through the gate itself).

Halfway along Haarlemmerstraat you'll find Herenmarkt, which leads to the Brouwersgracht at the head of the Herengracht. This was planned as a market, but it never took off. Now it's a quiet oasis and a prestigious address. The building at the north end of the square used to be a meat hall before it became the **Westindisch Huis** (Map pp286–7), head office of the West India Company, from 1623 to 1654. In 1628 Admiral Piet Heyn captured the Spanish silver fleet off Cuba, and the booty was stored here in the cellars. Every Dutch person knows the nursery rhyme celebrating Heyn's small name and big deeds, sung by soccer supporters at international matches as a warning not to underestimate this small country.

Walk through the east entrance into the courtyard with its statue of Pieter Stuyvesant, the unpopular governor of Nieuw Netherlands in the 17th century. Today the building houses the **John Adams Institute**, a Dutch-US friendship society.

To the north, the Western Islands (West-elijke Eilanden) were built into the IJ in the first half of the 17th century. The main thoroughfare, Haarlemmerstraat, and its extension Haarlemmerdijk (collectively the 'Haarlemer Quarter') were part of the original sea dyke and the road to Haarlem. Warehouses sprang up as well; many have been converted to romantic housing. With train lines and expressways, this district has reverted to its more intimate character, and recent years have seen it boom as a centre for the same sorts of quirky shops, pubs and restaurants that characterise the Jordaan.

Beyond the Haarlemmer Quarter is Amsterdam's newest park and cultural area, the former gasworks of the Westergasfabriek.

HET SCHIP HOUSING ESTATE

Map pp282-3

☎ 418 28 85; www.hetschip.nl; Spaarndammerplantsoen 140; adult/senior/student €5/2.75/2; ⏱ 1-5pm Thu-Sun

Several minutes' walk northwest of the Haarlemmer Quarter (cross under the railway tracks), this housing estate (1920) is one of the signature buildings of the Amsterdam School of architecture (p45). What makes it unique is the high level of preservation and the fact that it welcomes visitors.

This triangular block, loosely resembling a ship, was designed by Michel de Klerk for a housing corporation of railway employees. The pointed tower at the short side of the block has no purpose whatsoever, apart from aesthetically linking the two wings of the complex – and serving as a major symbol of this architectural movement. There are several other Amsterdam School–designed housing blocks in this area.

The museum has just expanded to show workers' apartments, one as it would have been in the workers' days, complete with period furniture. Also, you can go inside the tower – there's little light but it's very interesting.

The former post office at the 'bow' of the 'ship' still has the original interior, all meticulously designed by De Klerk. It is now home to the Documentation Centre for Social Housing, with a permanent exhibition of Amsterdam School architecture called Poste Restante. It's not a conventional museum, however. The displays mostly take the form of videos at small stands; you listen via headphones (or read subtitles) to learn about living conditions for the average worker at the turn of the 20th century (squalid doesn't begin to describe it!), and how the Dutch government became responsible for ensuring basic housing standards. Among the other topics covered are Berlage's grand plan for southern Amsterdam, the relationship of the Amsterdam School to socialism, and how the city was laid out via the polder-and-ditch system. Architecture fans could spend an hour or more here.

Architectural details: the yellow *telefooncel*, in the section behind the former postal wickets, is where workers would dial the telephone numbers for customers; the *sprekcel* with its ingenious double doors is where the customer would sit and speak once the call was connected. Note the geometrical

HOFJES

A distinctive historical legacy of the Jordaan is its high concentration of *hofjes*, almshouses consisting of a courtyard surrounded by houses built by wealthy benefactors to house elderly people and widows – a noble act in the days before social security. Some *hofjes* are real gems, with beautifully restored houses and lovingly maintained gardens. Most entrances are unobtrusive and hidden behind doors. Unfortunately, *hofjes* became such popular tourist attractions that residents complained and they were closed to the public (the one exception being the Begijnhof, p72).

However, if you should find any of the following open, try to have a peek. The oldest *hofje* is the **Lindenhofje** (Lindengracht 94-112), dating from 1614; the **Suyckerhofje** (Lindengracht 149-163) is a charming *hofje* founded in 1670. **Karthuizerhofje** (Karthuizersstraat 89-171) is a *hofje* for widows, dating from 1650 and on the site of a former Carthusian monastery.

Claes Claeszhofje (Eerste Egelantiersdwarsstraat 3), also known as Anslo's Hofje, has three courtyards dating from around 1630. **St Andrieshofje** (Egelantiersgracht 107-141), the second-oldest surviving *hofje*, was finished in 1617, and founded by the cattle farmer Jeff Gerritzoon. **Venetiae** (Elandsstraat 106-136) was founded in the mid-1600s by a trader with Venice, and features a very pretty garden.

And if you're really motivated, Haarlem (p232) has a number of open *hofjes*.

designs of the leadlight windows and cast-iron counters, and the weird shapes of the tiled walls.

Outside on the pavement is a small collection of typical Amsterdam School street fixtures (letterbox, fire alarm etc). On the other side of the post office entrance, be sure to walk into the attractive courtyard through the arch. The fairy-tale garden house with its sculpted roof was intended as a meeting room.

HOUSEBOAT MUSEUM Map p285

☎ 427 07 50; www.houseboatmuseum.nl; Prinsengracht; adult/child under 152cm €3/2.25; ⏰ 11am-5pm Tue-Sun Mar-Oct, 11am-5pm Fri-Sun Nov-Feb, closed most of Jan

Along the canal from Elandsgracht, at Johnny Jordaanplein (named for a popular singer of local ballads), this museum offers a good sense of life on the water. The sailing barge (23m long by 4m wide) was built in 1914, and even if nobody lives here any more the museum's interior epitomises the Dutch term *gezelligheid* (see boxed text, p14). The collection itself is rather minimal, but you can view the iron hull up close, watch a slide show of pretty houseboats (and ugly houseboat disasters!), see sleeping, living, cooking and dining quarters with all mod cons, and try to imagine living here as the water gently rocks beneath. In case you were wondering, houseboat toilets, until this century, could drain directly into the canals, but they now must hook up to the city sewage system.

Look for the museum opposite No 296 Prinsengracht.

NOORDERKERK Map pp286-7

☎ 626 64 36; Noordermarkt 48; admission free; ⏰ 10.30am-3pm Mon, Wed & Thu, 11am-1pm Sat, 10am-noon & 7-8.30pm Sun

Near the northern end of the Prinsengracht, this imposing church was completed in 1623, to a design by Hendrick de Keyser (p41), as a Calvinist church for the 'common' people in the Jordaan (the upper classes attended his Westerkerk further south). It was built in the shape of a broad Greek cross (four arms of equal length) around a central pulpit, giving the entire congregation unimpeded access to the word of God in suitably sober surroundings. This design,

unusual at the time, would become common for Protestant churches throughout the country.

A sculpture near the entrance commemorates the bloody Jordaan riots of July 1934, when five people died protesting the government's austerity measures including a 12% reduction of the already pitiful unemployment benefits.

NOORDERMARKT Map pp286-7

Noorderstraat; ⏰ markets 8am-1pm Mon, 10am-3pm Sat

A market square since the early 1600s, the plaza in front of the Noorderkerk now hosts a lively flea market on Monday morning where you can find some wonderful bargains. Early on Saturday morning there's a bird market (caged birds, rabbits etc – a holdover from the former livestock market), followed till early/mid-afternoon by a *boerenmarkt* (farmer's market) with organic produce, herbs etc. There's a nice selection of cafés surrounding the square, including **Winkel** (p139) on the southwest corner, home of some of the city's best apple pie.

Hunt for a bargain at Noordermarkt

PIANOLA MUSEUM Map p285

☎ 627 96 24; www.pianola.nl; Westerstraat 106;
adult/student & senior/child under 12yr €5/4/3;
🕐 2-5pm Sun

Although its opening hours are limited, this
is a special place, crammed with pianolas
(only about a dozen of the 50 in the collection are on display at any one time), some
15,000 music rolls and even a player pipe
organ. You can hear concerts of player
pianos from the early 1900s, from Mozart to
Fats Waller and rare classical or jazz tunes
composed especially for the instrument. The
curator gives demonstrations with great zest.

STEDELIJK MUSEUM BUREAU
AMSTERDAM Map p285

☎ 422 04 71; www.smba.nl; Rozenstraat 59;
admission free; 🕐 11am-5pm Tue-Sun

Don't blink or you might walk right past this
unobtrusive outpost, a 'project space' of the
leading Stedelijk Museum; it's in a one-time
clothing workshop on a very quiet block.
Exhibits here – from painting and sculpture
to new media and installation pieces – mix
contemporary artists who have some connection to the city with some 'international
context'. In our experience, it's always
interesting and daring. Shows change about
every couple of weeks; ring to make sure it's
not closed while changing exhibitions.

WESTERGASFABRIEK Map pp282-3

☎ 586 07 10; www.westergasfabriek.nl;
Haarlemmerweg 8-10

Along busy Haarlemmerweg, this late-19th-
century Dutch Renaissance complex (14
hectares) was the city gasworks until it was
all but abandoned in the 1960s, its soil contaminated. That's all changed, thankfully, and
the *fabriek* is re-emerging from its cocoon
as a new cultural and recreational park. The
contaminated soil has been replaced with
lawns and a long pool suitable for wading
(bring the kids), sports facilities (including
korfball, p20) and even child care. As you
move west away from town, the aesthetic of
the parkland goes from urban plan to reedy
wilderness, with marshes and shallow water-
falls. It's surrounded by the long and varied
Westerpark; bike on in and stay a while.

Inside the main buildings, designed by
Isaac Gosschalk, are a mix of cinemas, cafés,
restaurants, nightspots and creative office
spaces. Watch for the Westergasterras (p168),
a new, slick, postindustrial party venue.

WESTERN CANAL BELT

Eating p139; Shopping p195; Sleeping p218

The canals bordered by the Brouwersgracht
and Leidsegracht (to the north and south
respectively), the Singel to the east and the
Prinsengracht to the west are among the
most desirable areas of town, for residents
and visitors alike. They are, quite simply
gorgeous, filled with stately homes, refined
museums and businesses, relaxing cafés and
some of the city's finest speciality shops in
the Negen Straatjes, near the southern end
of the western canals. You can eat and shop
to your heart's content.

This elegant area has its origins in the
end of the 16th century, when the city
burst out of its medieval walls with Jewish refugees from Portugal and Spain, and
Protestant refugees from Antwerp. In the
1580s new land was reclaimed from the
IJ and Amstel for the east side of town.
Here on the west side, meanwhile, in 1613
the authorities embarked on an ambitious
expansion project to more than triple the
city's area with canals on the western and
southern sides of the city. The plan was
drawn up by the city carpenter, Hendrick
Jacobsz Staets, comprising semicircular
and radial canals with bridges and connecting roads. Collectively, these new canals
have come to be called the Grachtengordel
(Canal Belt).

The plan called for the whole city to be
enclosed by a new outer moat, the zigzag
Buitensingel, now known as the Singel-
gracht. The moat's outer quays became
the current Nassaukade, named for the
Dutch royal House of Orange-Nassau, the
Stadhouderskade (for the magistrates) and
Mauritskade (named for Maurits of Nassau,
who played a pivotal role in liberating the
Netherlands from Spanish rule).

Work began at the Brouwersgracht and
headed south. Parcels of land were sold
along the way to finance the project, buildings arose gradually, and the Western Canal
Belt was completed by 1625.

TRANSPORT

The Western Canal Belt is steps away from the Nieuwe
Zijde of the Medieval Centre. Tram lines 13, 14 and
17 and bus route 21 all travel along Raadhuisstraat/
Rozengracht.

The western canals segregated the society into haves and have-nots. Until then, merchants lived more or less in their warehouses, mingling with their labourers and suppliers in the thick of the city's activities. Now the wealthiest among them escaped the sweat and the stench by building residential mansions along the delectable Herengracht (named after the Heeren XVII – 17 Gentlemen – of the United East India Company; see boxed text, p51). The Keizersgracht (Emperor's Canal), named in honour of Holy Roman Emperor Maximilian I, was similarly upmarket. Businesses that could be annoying or offensive were banned, and bridges were fixed to exclude large vessels – though this didn't prevent barges from unloading and loading goods at warehouses along these high-end canals.

The Prinsengracht – named for William the Silent, Prince of Orange and forefather of the royal family – was designed as a 'cheaper' canal with smaller residences, warehouses and workshops. It also acted as a barrier against the downmarket Jordaan neighbourhood that lay beyond. Today the Prinsengracht remains the liveliest of the canals. Instead of stately offices and banks, there are shops and cafés where you can sit outside in summer. The houses remain small and narrow, apartments are relatively affordable by canal standards, and houseboats line the quays. This is an area where anyone can feel comfortable.

At the northern end of the Canal Belt, Brouwersgracht (the Brewers' Canal) was

TOP FIVE WESTERN CANAL BELT

- Be moved by the story of the **Anne Frank Huis** (opposite) – get there early or late to avoid the crowds.
- Even nonshoppers may be charmed by the diverse offerings in the boutiques of the **Negen Straatjes** (below).
- Step 1: find yourself a seat at one of the many **brown cafés** (p157) lining the Prinsengracht. Step 2: relax.
- If the play's your thing, don't miss the excellent, handsome Theatermuseum at the **Theater Instituut Nederland** (p88).
- Go on, legs of steel: climb the tower of the **Westerkerk** (p89) for a gorgeous view.

named after the breweries that used to operate here. It's one of the most picturesque canals in town and a great place for a stroll, although it wasn't always so: throughout most of its history it was an industrial canal full of warehouses, workshops and factories banned from the residential Canal Belt. Businesses here included some of the smelliest: breweries, distilleries, tanneries, potash works, and whale-oil and sugar refineries, as well as more fragrant warehouses for spices, coffee and grain. The buildings were solidly constructed and many were converted to apartments in the 1970s and '80s. Note the almost uninterrupted row of former warehouses from No 172 to No 212. Houseboats add to the lazy, residential character.

Negen Straatjes (Nine Alleys; Map p84) sits like a tic-tac-toe board near the southern reaches of the Western Canal Belt, and is an area bounded by Reestraat, Hartenstraat and Gasthuismolensteeg to the north, Prinsengracht to the west, Singel to the east and Runstraat, Huidenstraat and Wijde Heisteeg to the south. The *straatjes* (little streets) are full of quirky little shops dealing in antiques, fashions, housewares and one-offs including everything from toothbrushes to antique eyeglass frames. It's all peppered with pubs, cafés and informal dining. Among our favourite shops are: Boekie Woekie (deals in books created by artists; p196), Laura Dols (vintage clothing; p196), Mendo (advertising agency with its own art gallery; p197) and De Kaaskamer (cheese; p196). For cafés, try Hein (p141), De Doffer (p157) or the lovely chocolate and cake shop, Pompadour (p163).

Negen Straatjes (Nine Alleys)

Map of Negen Straatjes showing canals Prinsengracht, Keizersgracht, Herengracht and Singel, with streets Reestr, Hartenstr, Gasthuismolenst, Berenstr, Wolvenstr, Oude Spiegelstr, Runstr, Huidenstr, Wijde Heist. Landmarks: Netherlands Media Art Institute, Felix Meritis Building. Scale 0–200 m.

AMSTERDAM TULIP MUSEUM Map p285

☎ 421 00 95; www.amsterdamtulipmuseum.com; Prinsengracht 112; adult/child €2/free; ☺ 10am-6pm Tue-Sat

It's amazing that Amsterdam never had a museum about its most famous flower until 2005. Sponsored by a bulb-growing company, this one is small and rather clinical as it traces the steps of this prince of petals from its beginnings in Turkey, Tulipmania (see boxed text, p92), bulbs as food in the war years, and present-day scientific methods of growing and harvesting. A highlight for us was the sampling of tulip paintings by 17th-century painter Judith Leijster, a student of Frans Hals (p28). The gift shop is one-stop shopping for all your tulip-themed souvenirs.

ANNE FRANK HUIS Map p285

☎ 556 71 05; www.annefrank.org; Prinsengracht 276; adult/child/under 10yr €7.50/3.50/free; ☺ 9am-9pm Apr-Aug, 9am-7pm Sep-Mar, closed Yom Kippur

It is one of Amsterdam's most compelling stories, indeed one of the most compelling of the 20th century: a young Jewish girl forced into hiding with her family and their friends to escape deportation by the Nazis (see boxed text, below). The house they used as a hideaway should be a highlight of any visit to Amsterdam; indeed, it gets over 900,000 visitors a year – go early or late in the day to avoid the crowds. The house itself is now contained within a modern, square shell.

It took the German army just five days to occupy all of the Netherlands, along with Belgium and much of France. Anne's famous diary describes how restrictions were gradually imposed on Dutch Jews: from being forbidden to ride streetcars to being forced to turn in their bicycles and not being allowed to visit Christian friends. These, of course, were only some of the mildest examples.

The focus of the museum is the *achterhuis* (rear house), also known as the **secret annexe**. It was this dark and airless space, where the Franks and others observed complete silence during the daytimes, outgrew their clothes, pasted photos of Hollywood stars on the walls and read Dickens, before being mysteriously betrayed and sent to their deaths.

It is the personalisation of the story that makes it so chilling. If you're like us, by the time you get to the diary itself, sitting alone in its case, you may well have a lump in your throat.

Sights

WESTERN CANAL BELT

ANNE FRANK

Anne Frank's father, Otto Frank, was a manufacturer of pectin (a gelling agent used in jam) who had the foresight to emigrate with his family from Frankfurt to Amsterdam in 1933. In December 1940 he bought what is now known as the Anne Frank Huis on the Prinsengracht and moved his business here from the Singel. By then the German occupiers had already tightened the noose around the city's Jewish inhabitants, and even though he signed the business over to his non-Jewish partner, Otto was forced to go into hiding in July 1942 with his family – his wife and daughters Anne (aged 13) and Margot (16).

They moved into the specially prepared rear of the building, along with another couple, the Van Daans, and their son Peter, and were joined later by a Mr van Dussel. The entrance hid behind a revolving bookcase, and the windows of the annexe were blacked out to prevent suspicion among people who might see it from surrounding houses (blackouts were common practice to disorient Allied bombers at night).

Here they survived until they were betrayed to the Gestapo in August 1944. The Franks were among the last Jews to be deported and Anne died in the Bergen-Belsen concentration camp in March 1945, only weeks before it was liberated. Otto was the only member of the family to survive, and after the war he published Anne's diary which was found among the litter in the annexe (the furniture had been carted away by the Nazis). Addressed to the fictitious Kitty, the diary – written in Dutch – traces the young teenager's development through puberty and persecution, and displays all the signs of a gifted writer in the making.

In 1957 the then-owner donated the house to the Anne Frank Foundation, which turned it into a museum on the persecution of Jews in WWII and the dangers of present-day racism and anti-Semitism.

The diary, meanwhile, has taken on a life of its own. It's been translated into some 60 languages and was made into a stage play performed in 34 countries, a 1959 Hollywood movie and a 2001 British movie. The diary has been reissued in recent years, complete with passages deleted by Otto about Anne's awakening sexuality and relationship problems with her mother, all of which only rounds out her character and reminds us that she was, among other things, an ordinary girl, unable to swim against the tide of extraordinary times.

Note that the Anne Frank Huis does not accept the Amsterdam Pass or the Museumkaart, and queues can be quite long at peak times. However, if you plan to visit late in the day (5pm to 8.30pm April to August, 4pm to 6.30pm September to March) you can purchase advance tickets (same price as regular tickets) at VVV offices in the city and airport, or the AUB Ticketshop on Leidseplein. There's a separate entrance for advance ticket holders, meaning that you don't have to queue up. Advance tickets are valid any day. Also note: there's no cloakroom, and no large rucksacks are permitted.

BIJBELS MUSEUM Map pp292-3

Bible Museum; ☎ 624 24 36; www.bijbelsmuseum .nl; Herengracht 366-368; adult/child 13-17yr/under 12yr €6/3/free; ⏰ 10am-5pm Mon-Sat, 1-5pm Sun

This very worthy museum originated as the life's work of Leendert Schouten (1828–1905), a minister of the Dutch Reformed Church who built a scale model of the Jewish Tabernacle described in Exodus, now on the museum's 3rd floor. So elaborate was the model that it is said to have attracted thousands of visitors even before it was completed in 1851. Schouten also collected Egyptian antiquities and Jewish ceremonial objects to illustrate the Israelites' 400 years in Egypt. An exhibit on the museum's 2nd floor examines the Temple Mount/Haram al-Sharif in Jerusalem from Christian, Jewish and Muslim perspectives. A collection of Dutch bibles includes the Delft Bible printed in 1477.

On the ground floor, you can sniff scents mentioned in the bible and stroll a garden of biblical trees. There are also beautiful 18th-century ceiling paintings by Jacob de Wit in a gallery of 17th-century paintings of biblical scenes.

The museum is housed in a landmark quartet of sandstone neck–gabled houses known as the Cromhouthuizen, designed in 1662 for wealthy merchant Jacob Cromhout by architect Philips Vingboons (p42).

DE ROOD HOED Map pp286-7

☎ 623 56 06; www.roodhoed.nl; Keizersgracht 102; admission free; ⏰ 8.30am-5.30pm except during special events

Since 1990 the Rood Hoed has been a cultural centre in these three early-17th-century canal houses. Its line-up includes lectures by world-renowned authors (eg Jonathan Safran Foer) and debates on the topics of the day, sometimes in English. It's worth a visit, even when nothing's on, to view the three-storey main auditorium, which was once the largest clandestine church in the Netherlands. The organ dates from about 1719. 'De Rood Hoed' means 'the red hat', named for the hat shop once housed in one of the houses – see if you can spot the tile on the façade that pays homage to this origin.

FELIX MERITIS BUILDING Map p285

☎ 623 13 11; www.felix.meritis.nl; Keizersgracht 324; ⏰ box office 9am-7pm

This centre for the performing arts was built in 1787 by Jacob Otten Husly for an organisation called Felix Meritis (Latin for 'Happy through Merit'), a society of wealthy residents who promoted the ideals of the Enlightenment through the study of science, arts and commerce. It became the city's main cultural centre in the 19th century. The colonnaded façade served as a model for that of the Concertgebouw, and its oval concert hall (where Brahms, Grieg and Saint Saëns performed) was copied as the Concertgebouw's Kleine Zaal (Small Hall) for chamber music.

The building later passed to a printing company and was gutted by fire in 1932. After WWII it became the headquarters of the Dutch Communist Party (and the offices of the party newspaper), and from 1968 to 1989 the Shaffy Theatre Company staged its avant-garde productions here. Nowdays the reconstituted Felix Meritis Foundation promotes European performing arts and literature; there are often musical performances, and on a sunny morning the café's huge windows make for a comfy warm seat.

HOMOMONUMENT Map p285

1987; cnr Keizersgracht & Radhuisstraat

Behind the Westerkerk is this cluster of three 10m x 10m x 10m triangles, embedded in the ground and straddling the narrow street. Made from pink granite (the pink triangle being the design of the patch the Nazis forced gay men to wear), these simple but evocative triangles were designed by Dutch artist Karin Daan to convey past persecution of gays and lesbians while projecting hope for the future.

One of the triangles (the water triangle) actually steps down into the Keizersgracht.

The Felix Meritis Building (opposite), a centre for performing arts on Keizersgracht

It is said to represent a jetty from which gays were sent to the concentration camps, while other interpretations say that stepping up from the canalside creates a rising symbol of hope. Another triangle (the text triangle) lies flat on the ground, while the podium triangle rises 60cm from the surface. If you walk by the monument without looking for it, you might not know, that it's there – an interesting metaphor for homosexuality.

Engraved in the text triangle is a quote from the gay Dutch poet Jacob Israel de Haan (1881–1924), 'Naar vriendschap zulk een mateloos verlangen' ('Such an endless longing for friendship').

Just south of the Homomonument is the **Pink Point** (noon-6pm Mar-Aug, limited hr rest of year). Part information point, part souvenir shop, it's a good place to pick up gay- and lesbian-themed publications, news about parties, events and social groups, as well as health info. It's volunteer-staffed, and all profits go to the care of the Homomonument (p86) and occasionally to other causes (and parties!).

HUIS MARSEILLE Map pp292-3
☎ 531 89 89; www.huismarseille.nl; Keizersgracht 401; adult/student/child under 17yr €5/3/free; 11am-6pm Tue-Sun
This well-curated photography museum stages large-scale, changing exhibitions, drawing from its own collection as well as from travelling shows. Themes might include portraiture, nature or regional photography, spread out over several floors and a 'summer house' behind the main house.

Huis Marseille is also noteworthy for its building. The name refers to its original owner, a French merchant in 1665, and the original structure (front house, courtyard and rear house) has remained largely intact since then. It was renovated in the late 1990s for use as a photography museum, but it retains some antique touches like the 18th-century fountain in the library, and a painting of Apollo, Minerva and the muses in the garden room.

Those with a serious interest in photography should also check out **FOAM** (p92) and **News Photo** (p69), or the **Nederlands Fotomuseum** in Rotterdam (p239).

MULTATULI MUSEUM Map pp286-7
☎ 638 19 38; www.multatuli-museum.nl; Korsjespoortsteeg 20; admission free; 10am-5pm Tue, noon-5pm Sat & Sun (closed Sat Jul & Aug)
Eduard Douwes Dekker (1820–87), better known by the pen name Multatuli (Latin for 'I have suffered greatly'), was a novel-ist best known for the novel *Max Havelaar* (1860), a seminal book for cultural anthro-pologists, about relations between white- and brown-skinned people. This small but thorough museum chronicles his life and works, and shows furniture and arte-facts from his life, particularly those from Indonesia.

Some visitors may find the book and the author's biography more interesting than the museum. As a youth, Dekker studied theology with the intention of becoming a Protestant vicar, but his father took him to Batavia (now Jakarta), where Eduard eventually worked in the colonial administration. This opportunity to observe the world of trade and colonisation left him profoundly disillusioned over relations between the colonial rulers and the local people, and even within local society in Indonesia. Dekker returned to Europe at age 37, and three years later published *Max Havelaar* under the name Multatuli. The book made him something of a social conscience for the Netherlands.

The book was novel in that Multatuli broke convention and told the story from several perspectives. DH Lawrence, no less, complained that the structure of the book was a mess.

The museum is located on a small street between the Herengracht and the Singel, south of the Brouwersgracht.

NETHERLANDS MEDIA ART INSTITUTE Map p285

☎ 623 71 01; www.montevideo.nl; Keizersgracht 264; adult/student €2.50/1.50; ⏰ gallery 1-6pm Tue-Sat & 1st Sun of month

From the hilarious to the ridiculous to the deep and the experimental, there's always something different in the gallery's changing exhibits. Don't expect to see works by the hit-makers or TV directors of tomorrow, though. The institute is specifically about video as art; there's an artist-in-residence program if you get inspired. The collection numbers some 1500 works, assembled since the institute was established in 1978. The mediatheek (admission free; ⏰ 1-5pm Mon-Fri) works like a library, complete with librarians to advise you.

POEZENBOOT Map pp286-7

Cat Boat; ☎ 625 87 94; admission free (but donations encouraged); ⏰ 1-3pm

This boat on the Singel is a must for cat-lovers…and hell for mouse-lovers. It was founded in 1966 by an eccentric woman who became legendary for looking after several hundred stray cats at a time. The boat has since been taken over by a foundation and holds a mere few dozen

kitties in proper pens, ready to be spayed, neutered, implanted with an identifying computer chip (as per Dutch law) and, hopefully, adopted out. In the meantime, the cats seem endearingly content with life as the boat rocks back and forth on the water and visitors come to stroke them. You'll find it just across from Singel 40.

THEATER INSTITUUT NEDERLAND

Map pp286-7

White House; ☎ 551 33 00; www.tin.nl; Herengracht 168; adult/senior, student or child €4.50/2.25; ⏰ 11am-5pm Mon-Fri, 1-5pm Sat & Sun

Theatre buffs will want to spend a good hour here at the Theatre Museum. Exhibits cover the history of Dutch theatre via dioramas (including the first theatre built in Amsterdam, in 1638); displays of costumes from lush to stark; heady sepia-toned early photographs of 19th-century actors; and video clips of famous modern-day productions. It's also a unique opportunity to learn about one of the most interesting legacies of the Dutch theatre: the *rederijkamers* (chambers of rhetoric), medieval literary societies that staged large-scale productions throughout the Netherlands and Flanders. Most signage is in English.

Major exhibits change annually, covering such topics as Rembrandt, 1000 years of Dutch theatre, and Dutch theatre during WWII.

Even if you're not really interested in theatre, the museum is worth visiting for the stunning interior, which was completely restyled in the 1730s with intricate plasterwork and extensive wall and ceiling paintings by Jacob de Wit and Isaac de Moucheron. A magnificent spiral staircase was added then too. In summer, the lovely garden out the back is the perfect spot to reflect on life. The façade dates back to 1620 (modified 1638) to a design by Philips Vingboons.

The museum spills over into the Bartolotti House (Herengracht 170-172), which has one of the most stunning facades in the city – a red-brick, Dutch-Renaissance job that follows the bend of the canal. It was built in 1615 by Hendrick de Keyser and his son Pieter, by order of the wealthy brewer Willem van den Heuvel, who later assumed the name of his Bolognese father-in-law so he could inherit his bank and develop it into a trading empire. The house was later split down the middle and both residences were inhabited by prominent Amsterdam families.

WESTERKERK Map p285

☎ 624 77 66; Westermarkt; church admission free, tower €5 by tour only; ⏰ church 11am-3pm Mon-Sat Apr-Sep, tower 10am-5pm Mon-Sat Apr-Sep, church services 10.30am Sun Apr-Sep

The church is the main gathering place for Amsterdam's Dutch Reformed community. It was built as a showcase Protestant church for the rich to a 1620 design by Hendrick de Keyser, who copied his design of the Zuiderkerk but increased the scale. De Keyser died in 1621 and the church was completed by Jacob van Campen in 1630. The square tower dates from 1638 – De Keyser would surely have made it hexagonal or octagonal. The nave, 29m wide and 28m high, is the largest in the Netherlands and is covered by a wooden barrel vault (the marshy ground precluded the use of heavy stone).

The huge main **organ** dates from 1686, with panels decorated with biblical scenes and instruments by Gerard de Lairesse. The secondary organ is used for Bach cantatas. Rembrandt, who died bankrupt at nearby Rozengracht, was buried in the church on 8 October 1669 but no-one knows exactly where – possibly near his son Titus' grave.

Another highlight of the church is its **belltower**, the highest church tower in the city (85m). It's topped by the imperial crown that Habsburg emperor Maximilian I bestowed to the city's coat of arms in 1489. A tourist logo of Amsterdam, the tower affords a tremendous view over the city, including the differing layouts of the Canal Belt and the streets in the Jordaan. The climb during the 60-minute tour is steep (186 steps) and claustrophobic (What do you want? You're in a bell tower!), but there are periodic landings where you can rest while the guide describes the bells and other workings of the massive carillon. Of the 50 bells, the largest is some 7500kg. You can also see the chamber where the night watchmen slept between keeping a lookout for fires.

Carillon recitals take place on Tuesdays between noon and 1pm; best listening is from the nearby Bloemgracht. The bells also chime mechanically every 15 minutes.

SOUTHERN CANAL BELT

Eating p142; Shopping p198; Sleeping p220

If the Western Canal Belt is upscale and refined, the Southern Canal Belt is more diverse and populist, though no less stately. The Southern Canal Belt spans the area from the radial Leidsegracht in the west to the Amstel in the east, anchored by two key nightlife districts: Leidseplein and Rembrandtplein. In between are the elegant antique and art shops of the Spiegel Quarter, the city's gay nightlife centre around Reguliersdwarsstraat, and the Golden Bend (see boxed text, p93), a stretch along the Herengracht that makes some Western Canal Belt houses look like servants' quarters.

The canal project, which began with the Western Canal Belt, stopped at the Leidsegracht in 1625 because of lack of funds, but it was picked up again at a later date. Even then, work on the southern section progressed much more slowly; it took 12 years to construct the western canals, but to extend the Canal Belt all the way to the Amstel took another 40. The Canal Belt was to have continued across the Amstel to the eastern IJ, but the only one ever completed was the (Nieuwe) Herengracht.

Heading east toward the Amstel, you'll see to your right the Amstelsluizen (sluices), built in 1674, that allowed the canals to be flushed with fresh water from the Amstel rather than salt water from the IJ, which made the city far more livable. They were still operated by hand until recently.

A very short walk west (and south) of the Amstel, Rembrandtplein is another hub of café culture and nightlife of any stripe. Originally called Reguliersplein and then Botermarkt (butter market), it now features a statue of the painter, gazing pensively towards the Jewish quarter where he lived until circumstances forced him to the Jordaan.

You won't have any trouble finding a café or restaurant on Rembrandtplein or

TRANSPORT

Tram lines 1, 2 and 5 travel on Leidsestraat; lines 16, 24 and 25 travel along Vijzelgracht; and line 4 along Utrechtsetraat. Lines 6, 7 and 10 skirt the southern edge of this Canal Belt, along Sarphatistraat and Weteringschans.

on neighbouring Thorbeckeplein (off Rembrandtplein's southwest corner). Many are large and spill onto the sidewalks, but our favourite is the more intimate Café Schiller (p161), an Art Deco marvel that's popular with the pre-theatre crowd. Heeren van Aemstel (p175) is a fun place to kick back a beer or to catch a performance. Gay visitors will want to head north on Halvemaansteeg and to the Amstel for a cluster of bars and cafés, or a block west across Vijzelstraat to the always busy Reguliersdwarsstraat; the friendly lesbian café Vivelavie (p173) is just east of Rembrandtplein.

The street running west from Rembrandtplein is Reguliersbreestraat. Before the construction of the Canal Belt, the nuns of the Regulier (Regular) order had a monastery outside the city walls roughly where Utrechtsestraat now crosses Keizersgracht, which explains the frequent use of the name in this area. Reguliersbreestraat is pretty busy, but about a third of the way along on the left you can see the Tuschinskitheater (p178), opened in 1921 and still the most glorious cinema in the country. The building's blend of Art Deco and Amsterdam School architecture, with its recently refurbished interior decorations, is a visual feast. Inquire about tours.

Off the southeast corner of Rembrandtplein is Utrechtsestraat, the city's best row of restaurants.

Southwest of Rembrandtplein, Thorbeckeplein is named after Jan Rudolf Thorbecke, the Liberal politician who created the Dutch parliamentary system in 1848. His statue faces outwards from the square, although he might have enjoyed its leafy car-free atmosphere. There are a number of cafés and clubs on both sides of the square, and the art market (10.30am-6pm Sun Mar-Oct) offers mostly modern pictorial work. Note that Thorbeckeplein used to be water – part of Reguliersgracht.

Opposite Thorbeckeplein on Herengracht is the beautiful Reguliersgracht, the 'canal of the seven bridges', cut in 1664. You can just about count them all when you stand on the Herengracht bridge. Canal tour boats halt here for photos because it's easier to count them from below, especially at night when the bridges are lit up and their graceful curves are reflected in the water.

Luckily, this lovely canal was spared from being filled at the turn of the 20th century to accommodate a tram line. Sights include

the house at No 34 with its massive eagle gable commemorating the original owner, Arent van den Bergh (arend is one of the Dutch words for eagle) and its unusual twin entrance against the side walls with V-shaped stairway for the upstairs and downstairs dwellings. Grab the camera for the superb scene back towards Herengracht from the east–west bridge at Keizersgracht and the lean of the two houses on the corner (not to mention the 15 bridges visible from here).

Magere Brug (Skinny Bridge) is the most photographed drawbridge in Amsterdam city. It links Kerkstraat across the Amstel to Nieuwe Kerkstraat and dates from the 1670s. This one-time pedestrian bridge was rebuilt and widened several times and torn down in 1929 to make way for a modern bridge, only to be rebuilt again in timber. It's still operated by hand and makes a very pretty sight during the day as well as at night when it's lit up. Stand in the middle and feel it seesaw under the passing traffic.

As the location of a never-completed church, Amstelveld has been kept free of buildings, and today it remains open and pleasant. A Monday market has been operating here since 1876 (before that it was on Rembrandtplein). This lively 'free market' had vendors from out of town peddling a wide range of goods (it still operates in the summer months, focusing on plants and flowers). A small statue by the Amstelkerk commemorates Professor Kokadorus, aka Meijer Linnewiel (1867–1934), the most colourful market vendor Amsterdam has known. People would buy anything from spoons to suspenders ('to hang up your mother-in-law') just to watch his performances interlaced with satirical comments about politics. The annihilation of the Jewish community in WWII put an end to the city's rich tradition of creative vending (though if you understand Dutch you can still pick up some great lines in the markets of the Jordaan).

These days the Monday market is mostly a garden market (8.30am-2pm Mar-Dec) with cheap flowers and potted plants, and an antiques and collectibles market (9am-6pm) has started on the last Friday of the month in warmer months. In summer the Amstelveld is a pleasant space where children play soccer, dogs run around, and patrons laze in the sun at Janvier restaurant (p142) against the south side of the Amstelkerk.

Leidseplein has always been busy as one of the liveliest squares in the city and the undisputed centre of nightlife. In the 17th century it was the gateway to Leiden and other points southwest, and travellers had to leave their carts and horses here when heading into town.

There's something here for every taste: the sidewalk cafés at the northern end of the square are perfect for watching interesting street artists and eccentric passers-by. There are countless pubs and clubs in the area that stay open till daylight, and a smorgasbord of restaurants in the surrounding streets. Cinemas and other entertainment venues radiate out from its centre, and Kerkstraat, a few streets away, has a cluster of gay friendly establishments.

Steps from Leidseplein, Max Euweplein is the austere building along the western side that used to be a prison. Now it houses a Hard Rock Café, the Comedy Café (p179) and an Irish pub. This is also where you'll find the Holland Casino (see boxed text, p165), built in the shape of a roulette table.

Even if you have neither the inclination nor the money to buy art, luxury antiques or collectables, it is well worth taking a look at Nieuwe Spiegelstraat (which begins at the Herengracht) and its pretty extension the Spiegelgracht (which ends across from the Rijksmuseum). Many of the shops and galleries here in the Spiegel Quarter feel like museums in their own right.

AMSTELKERK Map pp292-3
☎ 520 00 70; Amstelveld 10; admission free; ⏰ 9am-5pm
Near the intersection of Prinsengracht and Reguliersgracht is the Amstelveld, a large open square, with this church near its northwestern corner.

TOP FIVE SOUTHERN CANAL BELT

- Get an aerial view from the café of **Metz Department Store** (p93).
- See a stately home up close at **Museum van Loon** (p94).
- Join the throngs of visitors in the circus-like, busy Leidseplein or chill out at the comfy, quiet Amstelveld.
- See cutting-edge photography at **FOAM** (p92).
- Cap your day with a beer or dinner at **Café Schiller** (p161) on Rembrandtplein.

The unique, pinewood Amstelkerk was erected in 1668 as a *noodkerk* (makeshift church) under the direction of the city architect, Daniël Stalpaert. The idea was that the congregation would have somewhere to meet while a permanent church arose next to it. City planners had envisaged four new Protestant churches in the Southern Canal Belt, but the only one actually built was the Oosterkerk. It wasn't until the 1840s that plans for the stone church on the Amstelveld were abandoned, and the Amstelkerk's square interior was updated with neo-Gothic alterations, including a pipe organ.

The Amstelkerk fell into disrepair after the 20th century, and it even looked as if it would have to be demolished, until it was purchased by the Stadsherstel, a local city restoration group. Reopened in 1990, the building now houses Stadsherstel's offices – glassed-in spaces that complement the Gothic arches surprisingly well – and is a popular venue for concerts, weddings and the like.

BLOEMENMARKT Map pp292-3
Flower Market; Singel; ⏰ 9am-5pm, closed Sun in winter
The side of the Singel opposite the Munttoren (p42) is occupied by Amsterdam's most famous floating attraction, one of several flower markets since the 17th century. The market here dates from the 1860s and specialises in flowers, bulbs, pots, vases, some plants and lots of souvenirs. It's a very pretty sight and the place is packed with tourists and pickpockets. Prices are steep by Amsterdam standards but the quality is good. Just make sure that your home country allows you to import bulbs (bulbs destined for the USA are marked with a special label).

DE APPEL Map pp292-3
☎ 625 56 51; www.deappel.nl; Nieuwe Spiegelstraat 10; admission €4; ⏰ 11am-6pm Tue-Sun during exhibitions
Despite its location in the antiques district of the Spiegel Quarter, this contemporary arts foundation is anything but antique. Rather, it's a large art and media space with ever-changing exhibits of contemporary works: installation pieces, painting, sculpture, multimedia etc. Themes vary, but the aim is always to find something not otherwise readily available to the Dutch public. Phone or check the website to find out what's on.

TULIPMANIA

When it comes to investment frenzy, the Dutch tulip craze of 1636–37 ranks alongside the South Sea Bubble of 1720, the Great Crash of 1929, Enron, and the Netherlands' home-grown Ahold scandal.

Tulips originated as wildflowers in Central Asia and were first cultivated by the Turks, who filled their courts with these beautiful spring blossoms ('tulip' derives from the Turkish word for turban). In the mid-1500s the Habsburg ambassador to Istanbul brought some bulbs back to Vienna where the imperial botanist, Carolus Clusius, learned how to propagate them. In 1590 Clusius became director of the Hortus Botanicus in Leiden – Europe's oldest botanical garden – and had great success growing and cross-breeding tulips in Holland's cool, damp climate and fertile delta soil.

The more exotic specimens of tulip featured frilly petals and 'flamed' streaks of colour, which attracted the attention of wealthy merchants, who put them in their living rooms and hallways to impress visitors. Trickle-down wealth and savings stoked the taste for exotica in general, and tulip growers arose to service the demand.

Ironically, the frilly petals and colour streaks were symptoms of a virus – healthy tulips at the time were solid, smooth and monotone; the virus itself wasn't discovered until the 20th century. In the 17th century, Holland's most beautiful tulips were heavily cross-bred, making them even more susceptible to the virus and difficult to cultivate, and their blossoms unpredictable.

A speculative frenzy ensued, and people paid top florin for the finest bulbs, many of which changed hands time and again before they sprouted. Vast profits were made and speculators fell over themselves to outbid each other. Bidding often took place in taverns and was fuelled by alcohol, no doubt adding to the enthusiasm.

At the height of the Tulipmania in November 1636, a single bulb of the legendary *Semper augustus* variety fetched the equivalent of 10 years' wages for the average worker; a couple of *Viceroy* bulbs cost the equivalent of an Amsterdam canal house. One unfortunate foreign sailor made himself rather unpopular with his employer by slicing up what he thought was an onion as a garnish for his herring. An English amateur botanist, intrigued by an unknown bulb lying in his host's conservatory, proceeded to bisect it, and was put in jail until he could raise an astronomical 4000 guilders.

Of course, this bonanza couldn't last, and when several bulb traders in Haarlem failed to fetch their expected prices in February 1637, the bottom fell out of the market. Within weeks many of the country's wealthiest merchants went bankrupt and many more people of humbler origins lost everything. Speculators who were stuck with unsold bulbs, or with bulbs that had been reserved but not yet paid for (the concept of options was invented during the Tulipmania), appealed for government action but the authorities refused to become involved in what they considered to be gambling. Thus the speculation ended.

However, love of the unusual tulip endured, and cooler-headed growers perfected their craft. To this day, the Dutch continue to be the world leaders in tulip cultivation and supply most of the bulbs planted in Europe and North America. They also excel in other bulbs such as daffodils, hyacinths and crocuses.

So what happened to the flamed, frilly tulips of the past? They're still produced but have gone out of fashion, and are now known as Rembrandt tulips because of their depiction in so many 17th-century paintings.

DE DUIF Map pp292-3

The Dove; ☎ 520 00 70; Prinsengracht 756; ⏰ services 10am Sun

In 1796, shortly after the French-installed government proclaimed freedom of religion, De Duif was the first Catholic church to be built with a public entrance for over two centuries. Across the Prinsengracht from the Amstelkerk and the Amstelveld, it was re-built to its current design in the mid-1800s. These days it's undergoing another extensive renovation. Clay friezes of the Stations of the Cross decorate the right-hand wall. The pulpit carvings are of St Willebrordus of Utrecht, and the organ is a sight in its own right, reaching clear to the vaulted ceiling.

These days De Duif is no longer Catholic but Ecumenical, and also a venue for concerts, opera and private events.

FOAM (FOTOGRAFIE MUSEUM AMSTERDAM) Map pp292-3

☎ 551 65 00; www.foam.nl; Keizersgracht 609; adult/student & senior/child under 12yr €6/5/free; ⏰ 10am-5pm Sat-Wed, 10am-9pm Thu & Fri

Simple and functional but roomy galleries, some with skylights or grand windows for natural light, are the design created for this impressive museum for all genres of photography. Two storeys of exhibition space create a great setting for admiring the changing exhibits from photographers of world renown, including Sir Cecil Beaton, Annie Leibovitz and Henri Cartier-Bresson just to name a few. In case you become enthused after your visit, it also publishes the FOAM magazine.

GEELVINCK HINLOPEN HUIS
Map pp292-3
☎ 639 07 47; www.geelvinckhinlopenhuis.nl;
Herengracht 518; adult/student/child under 6yr
€4/3/free; ⏰ 11am-5pm Sun
Beyond Vijzelstraat, east of the mayor's residence at No 502, is this 17th-century house with stylish rooms, a formal garden and art in the carriage house. Though not quite as impressive as Museum Van Loon or Museum Willet-Holthuysen, it's more serene, and worth a look, especially if you can organise a private tour for your group on a weekday. Note: the entrance to the museum is around the back at Keizersgracht 633.

KATTENKABINET Map pp292-3
Cats' Cabinet; ☎ 626 53 78; Herengracht 497;
adult/child 4-16yr/under 3yr €5/2.50/free;
⏰ 11am-5pm Tue-Sun
One Golden Bend house that's open to the public is this museum, devoted to the feline presence in art. It was founded by a wealthy financier in memory of his red tomcat, John Pierpont Morgan III. The collection includes cats in art largely from Dutch and French artists (Theopile-Alexandre Steinlen, 1859–1923, figures prominently) as well as a small Rembrandt (a Madonna and Child with cat and snake) and Picasso's *Le Chat*. There's also a nice selection of 19th-century magazine covers and circus posters. The museum's worth visiting for the interior and views of the garden.

A note for the allergic: some real cats also live here.

KRIJTBERG Map pp292-3
☎ 623 19 23; Singel 446; ⏰ mass 12.30pm &
5.45pm Mon-Fri, 5.15pm Sat, 9am, 11am, 12.30pm
& 5.15pm Sun
On the southwestern side of Singel are the soaring turrets of this neo-Gothic church. Officially known as the St Franciscus Xaveriuskerk, it was completed in 1883 to a design by Alfred Tepe, replacing a clandestine Jesuit chapel on the same site; these days it's still a Jesuit church. The lavish paintings and statuary, recently restored to their full glory, make this one of the most beautiful churches in the city.

Krijtberg's name means 'chalk mountain', referring to one of the houses that once stood here, which belonged to a chalk merchant.

MAX EUWE CENTRUM Map pp292-3
☎ 625 70 17; www.maxeuwe.nl; Max Euweplein
30A-1; admission free; ⏰ 10.30am-4pm Tue-Fri &
1st Sat of month, limited hr Jul & Aug
Max Euwe (1901–81) was the Netherlands' only world chess champion, in the 1930s, and here you'll find a permanent exhibition devoted to the history of chess. You can play against live or digital opponents. An oversized chess board on the pavement of the square is often busy with players and onlookers.

METZ DEPARTMENT STORE
Map pp292-3
Cnr Keizersgracht & Leidsestraat
This building opened in 1891 to house the New York Life Insurance Company (hence the exterior and interior eagles), but soon passed to Metz, a purveyor of luxury furnishings, which still owns it today. The functionalist designer and architect Gerrit Rietveld added the gallery on the top floor where you can have lunch or (literally) high tea.

BENDING THE GOLDEN RULES

Amsterdam has always had a shortage of suitable land for building. When the authorities embarked on their expensive canal-belt project, they drew up detailed regulations to ensure that this scarce commodity would return maximum revenue.

On the outer bank of Herengracht, plots were limited to a width of 30ft and a depth of 190ft (these were pre-metric days). There were no limits on heights of buildings at the front of each plot, but the rear side could not be built higher than 10ft to ensure the unprecedented luxury of large gardens (even today, the gardens behind many Herengracht houses are magnificent). Buyers also had to pay for the brick quayside in front of their plots. Subdivisions were prohibited in order to keep these properties desirable and to maintain their value.

So much for the theory. In practice, the very wealthiest Amsterdammers got dispensation, as can be seen in the immense palaces along the 'Golden Bend' of Herengracht, between Leidsestraat and Vijzelstraat. Elsewhere, regulations were interpreted creatively – for instance, by buying two adjacent plots and building one house with two fronts; or conversely by building one house with two entrances, subdividing into upstairs and downstairs areas and selling the two separately.

MUSEUM VAN LOON Map pp292-3

☎ 624 52 55; www.museumvanloon.nl; Keizersgracht 672; adult/child 6-18yr/under 6yr €5/4/free; ⏰ 11am-5pm daily Jul & Aug, 11am-5pm Fri-Mon Sep-Jun
Our favourite house museum in town, this house was built in 1672 for a wealthy arms dealer. Portraitist Ferdinand Bol, a student of Rembrandt, rented the place for a while. In the late 1800s it was acquired by the Van Loons, one of the most prominent patrician families (thanks to the herring trade and the United East India Company of which the original Mr van Loon was a founder). Here they lived in a style befitting their status, and now the museum is a family trust.

Inside houses some important paintings, including the *Wedding Portrait* by Jan Miense Molenaer (1637; note the fine details, the cast of dozens and the fallen chair symbolising a brother who'd passed away before the event) and a collection of some 150 portraits of the Van Loon family. But the main point of the museum is to show it as a house. Quiet and unbusy, you can appreciate the fine architectural details and imagine canalside life when money was no object.

Historical note: in the 19th century, the Van Loon's an official representative of Queen Wilhelmina. The present Mrs van Loon is an assistant to Queen Beatrix.

MUSEUM WILLET-HOLTHUYSEN

Map pp292-3
☎ 523 18 22; www.willetholthuysen.nl; Herengracht 605; adult/child 6-18yr/under 6yr €4/2/free; ⏰ 10am-5pm Mon-Fri, 11am-5pm Sat & Sun
This impressive house museum, part of the Amsterdams Historisch Museum, dates from

1685 and is named after the widow who bequeathed the property to the city in the late 19th century. The sumptuous interior has been remodelled over the years, including extensive renovations several years ago. Some furnishings and artefacts come from other bequests, which accounts for the mix of 18th- and 19th-century styles.

Highlights include paintings by Jacob de Wit, the *place de milieu* (centrepiece) that was part of the family's 275-piece set of Meissen table service, and the intimate French-style garden with sundial – you can also peek at the garden through the iron fence at the Amstelstraat end. The top-floor galleries hold special exhibitions. Be sure to pick up the notebook of explanations at the front desk; it's got lots of details that make the house come alive (such as how meat was roasted and how windows were cleaned).

STADSSCHOUWBURG Map pp292-3

City Theatre; ☎ 624 23 11; Leidseplein 26; ⏰ advance ticket sales 10am-6pm Mon-Sat
This theatre, with its balcony arcade, dates from 1894. People criticised the building – as they criticised every city theatre before or since – and the funds for the exterior decorations never materialised. The architect, Jan Springer, couldn't handle this and retired.

The theatre is used for large-scale plays, operettas and festivals such as Julidans (p10). South across Marnixstraat, the Amsterdam American Hotel is an Art Nouveau landmark from 1902, foreshadowing the Amsterdam School's use of brick. You might grab a coffee in its stylish Café Americain.

Neo-Renaissance façade of Stadsschouwburg

OLD SOUTH (OUD ZUID)

Eating p146; Shopping p201; Sleeping p224

Simply put, this wedge-shaped district is one of Amsterdam's most genteel. It is roughly bordered by Stadhouderskade to the north, the Vondelpark to the west and Hobbemakade to the east. It's also variously known by its landmarks: some call it the 'Museum Quarter' (for the Rijks, Stedelijk and Van Gogh), the 'Concertgebouw area' or the 'Vondelpark area'. All are worthy emblems.

The origin of this gentility goes back to real estate. By the 1860s, the Canal Belt was no longer sufficiant for the population needs of this city, rapidly expanding with the industrial revolution.

If the Canal Belt was the essence of urban planning, this round of expansion was a pure expression of market capitalism. Cheap tenement housing was built across Hobbemakade in the neighbourhood that came to be known as De Pijp, but wealthy investors wanted an upmarket neighbourhood for themselves and saw to it that tenement blocks and businesses were prohibited on this side. Instead, they thought it a suitable spot for a grand national museum (the Rijksmuseum) and an equally grand new concert hall (the Concertgebouw).

In the centre of it all is the Museumplein, a large, grassy park that occupies the space between the Rijksmuseum, Van Gogh and Stedelijk Museums and Concertgebouw. Around it are a wealth of shopping and dining possibilities and some lovely places to stay. The district is also peppered with some stunning examples of Amsterdam School architecture. Museumplein had an auspicious beginning, hosting the World Exhibition in 1883, and it remains a venue for outdoor concerts and special events. At other times, it's a relaxing place to hang out, play hacky-sack, skateboard (ramp provided), throw a Frisbee or enjoy a picnic. See if you can spot the tic-tac-toe board that plays musical notes when you step on the different squares.

Many of the streets around the Museumplein are named for emblematic Dutch artists, musicians and writers.

For years the blocks of Pieter Cornelisz (PC) Hooftstraat between Stadhouderskade and the Vondelpark have been the shopping street for the cream of society and the nouveau riche. You'll find some of the world's leading brands here, both in shops of their own name and in others, as well as a few surprisingly friendly cafés for a break. Heading left (westward) on the PC Hooftstraat will deposit you in the lovely Vondelpark.

Hooft (1581–1647), by the way, was the son of a mayor of Amsterdam who grew up to become a historian, author and founder of a literary society that included Joost van den Vondel of Vondelpark fame. We wonder what Hooft would have made of the association of his name with such blatant commercialism.

CONCERTGEBOUW Map p296

☎ 671 83 45; www.concertgebouw.nl; Concertgebouwplein 2-6; ticket prices vary; ⏰ box office 10am-7pm

The literal name 'Concert Building' scarcely does justice to this world-class hall at the southwestern end of Museumplein. The Concertgebouw attracts some 833,000 visitors a year to 800 shows, making it the busiest concert hall in the world.

The Concertgebouw was completed in 1888 to a neo-Renaissance design by AL van Gendt. In spite of his limited musical knowledge, he managed to give the two-tiered Grote Zaal (Main Hall) near-perfect acoustics that are the envy of auditorium designers worldwide. Add in baroque trim, panels inscribed with names of classical composers, a massive pipe organ and a grand staircase via which conductors and soloists descend to the stage, and you've got a venue where the best performers consider it an honour to appear.

TRANSPORT

Tram lines 1, 2, 3, 5, 6, 7, 10, 12, 16 and 24 all head to this area. For the Vondelpark, use trams 1, 2, 3, 6 or 12.

Sights

OLD SOUTH (OUD ZUID)

AMSTERDAM'S POPULATION IN THE 19TH CENTURY

- 1830 – 200,000
- 1860 – 245,000
- 1880 – 320,000
- 1900 – over 500,000

Under the 50-year guidance of composer and conductor Willem Mengelberg (1871–1951), the Concertgebouw Orchestra (with the epithet 'Royal' since 1988) developed into one of the world's finest orchestras. The current conductor is Mariss Jansons.

In the 1980s the Concertgebouw threatened to collapse because its 2000 wooden piles were rotting. Thanks to new technology, the piles made way for a concrete foundation, and the building was thoroughly restored to mark its 100th anniversary. The architect Pi de Bruin added a glass foyer along the southern side that most people hate, though everyone agrees it's effective.

In 2004 the Grote Zaal was given a further renovation (including comfier seats) and now has a capacity of 1900. Recitals take place in the 19m x 15m, 450-seat Kleine Zaal (Recital Hall), a replica of the hall in the **Felix Meritis Building** (p86), and the 150-seat Koor Zaal (Choir Hall) is an intimate setting for jazz and other concerts.

RIJKSMUSEUM Map pp292-3
☎ 674 70 00; www.rijksmuseum.nl; Stadhouderskade 42; adult/child under 18yr €9/free; ⏲ 10am-5pm

The Rijksmuseum (National Museum) is the premier art museum of the Netherlands, and no self-respecting visitor to Amsterdam can afford to miss it. In normal times, 1.2 million visitors flock here each year.

However, these are not normal times. Much of the museum was due to be closed until 2009 at the time of research, though there is an excellent collection of the museum's masterpieces exhibited in a wing to the side (see boxed text, opposite). Since the exact works on display are subject to change, the information we are presenting here is mostly historical and architectural background.

The Rijksmuseum was conceived as a repository for several national collections, including the royal art collection that was first housed in the palace on the Dam. The collection includes some 5000 paintings, the most important of which are by Dutch and Flemish masters from the 15th to 19th centuries, with emphasis on the 17th-century Golden Age. Pride of place is taken by Rembrandt's *Nightwatch* (1650), showing the militia led by Frans Banning Cocq, a future mayor of the city – the painting only acquired its name in later years because it had become dark with grime (it's nice and clean now). Other 17th-century Dutch masters on this floor include Jan Vermeer *(The Kitchen Maid,* also known as *The Milkmaid,* and *Woman in Blue Reading a Letter),* Frans Hals *(The Merry Drinker)* and Jan Steen *(The Merry Family).*

The museum's other collections are Sculpture and Applied Art (delftware, dolls' houses, porcelain, furniture), Dutch History (though the Amsterdams Historisch Museum and Nederlands Scheepvaartmuseum do this better) and Asiatic Art (including the famous 12th-century *Dancing Shiva*). The museum's print collection includes some 800,000 prints and drawings.

Architecturally, the Rijksmuseum forms the gateway to the Museum Quarter, with a pedestrian and bicycle underpass connecting the city centre with Museumplein. It was completed in 1885 to a design by Pierre Cuypers, who also designed Centraal Station four years later. Both buildings are a mixture of neo-Gothic and Dutch Renaissance. The neo-Gothic elements (towers, stained-glass windows) elicited much criticism from Protestants including the king, who dubbed the building 'the archbishop's palace' (Cuypers was Catholic, and proudly so in his approach to architecture).

The **garden** at the back of the museum has flowerbeds, fountains and an eclectic collection of statues, pillars and fragments of demolished buildings and monuments from all over the country.

STEDELIJK MUSEUM BUILDING
Map pp292-3
Paulus Potterstraat 13

This is the permanent home of the National Museum of Modern Art, one of the world's great collections. However, at the time of writing it was scheduled to be closed for renovation and expansion until 2008, and until then its modernist statements appear on the 2nd and 3rd floors of a former post-office high-rise on Oosterdok Island, just east of Centraal Station. For the full details see p114.

The Stedelijk's permanent building was built in 1895 to a neo-Renaissance design by AM Weissman.

A BLESSING IN DISGUISE?

Art lovers may be disappointed at first that large parts of two of Amsterdam's most prized museums will be out of site, if not out of sight, for much of this decade. But take heart; management is looking after you, and actually rather well.

The **Rijksmuseum** is closed for a massive sweeping renovation until 2009, but a changing selection of the top 200 masterpieces is on display, and quite attractively, in the museum's **Philips Wing** (Map pp292–3; ☎ 674 70 00; www.rijksmuseum.nl; Jan Luijkenstraat 1; adult/child under 18yr €9/free; 9am-6pm daily) overlooking Museumplein. These include Rembrandt's *Nightwatch*, several Vermeers and a selection of delftware. There will also be travelling exhibits from the Rijksmuseum around the Netherlands (including at Schiphol airport) and in other countries. Check the website for further details, or if you want to make sure a specific piece will be on display, you can phone or email info@rijksmuseum.nl.

The nearby building of the **Stedelijk Museum** on Paulus Potterstraat will be shut until 2008 for renovations, and the Stedelijk has moved operations entirely to a high-rise (p114) once occupied by the post office, near the IJ and east of Centraal Station. We actually think the space has a great post-industrial vibe that complements the museum's contemporary core exhibitions, but don't tell them or they might not move back. Plus, the building's other floors allow visitors to catch other currents in design, and restaurant 11 (p151) on the top floor is worth a trip on its own.

VAN GOGH MUSEUM Map pp292-3

☎ 570 52 00; www.vangoghmuseum.nl; Paulus Potterstraat 7; adult/child/under 12yr €10/2.50/free, audio or palmtop tour €4; 10am-6pm Sat-Thu, 10am-10pm Fri

Next to the Stedelijk Museum building is the Van Gogh Museum, another of Amsterdam's must-sees. Opened in 1973 to house the collection of Vincent's younger brother Theo, it consists of about 200 paintings and 500 drawings by Vincent and his friends and contemporaries, such as Gauguin, Monet, Toulouse-Lautrec and Bernard.

Vincent van Gogh was born in 1853 and had a short but very productive life. Through his paintings, the museum chronicles his life's journey from Holland (where his work was characterised by a dark colour palette) to Paris (where, under the influence of the Impressionists, he discovered colour) to Arles (where it is said his career reached its peak).

Astoundingly, Vincent was self-taught and, even more astoundingly, his painting career lasted less than 10 years, from 1881 to 1890. It was in 1890 when, in a fatal depression, he shot himself (he had already cut off his ear after an argument with Gauguin). He survived for two more days before succumbing.

Famous works on display include *The Potato Eaters* (1885), a prime example of his sombre Dutch period, and *The Yellow House in Arles* (1888), *The Bedroom* (1888) and several self-portraits, sunflowers and other blossoms that show his vivid use of colour in the intense Mediterranean light. One of

his last paintings, *Wheatfield with Crows* (1890), is an ominous work foreshadowing his suicide.

The permanent collection also includes many of the artist's personal effects. He received a milk jug from Theo and used it in several of his works. There are also knots of wool which he used to study contrasts in colours.

Vincent's paintings are on the 1st floor; several other floors display his drawings and Japanese prints, and works by his friends, contemporaries and others he influenced, some of which are shown in rotation. The library (☎ 570 59 06; Museumplein 4; 10am-12.30pm & 1.30-5pm Mon-Fri) has a wealth of reference material for serious study.

The museum queues can be long. One way to (potentially) get around this is to visit on a Friday night, when the museum hosts special cultural events. These can be anything from lectures to chamber concerts, to dance to performance art, and are occasionally less crowded than daytimes.

The museum's main building was designed by the seminal Dutch architect Gerrit Rietveld. Behind it, stretching out on to Museumplein, is a separate exhibition wing (1999) designed by Kishio Kurokawa commonly referred to as 'the Mussel'.

VONDELPARK

This pleasant, English-style park with ponds, lawns, thickets and winding footpaths is about 1.5km long and 300m wide. Laid out on marshland beyond the Canal Belt in the 1860s and '70s as a park for the bourgeoisie (when the existing city park, the Plantage, became residential), it was soon surrounded by upmarket housing. It's named after poet and playwright Joost van den Vondel (1587–1679), the Shakespeare of the Netherlands.

During the late 1960s and early 1970s the authorities turned the park into an open-air dormitory to alleviate the lack of accommodation for hordes of hippies who descended on Amsterdam. The sleeping bags have long since gone and it's now illegal to sleep in the park, but there's still some evidence of Italian, French and Eastern European tourists stuck in the '70s.

The park is now used by one and all – joggers, in-line skaters, children chasing ducks or flying kites, couples in love, families with prams, teenagers playing soccer, even acrobats practising or performing – and can be crowded on weekends but never annoyingly so. There always seem to be people performing in the park, and on a summer day it may seem that everyone is sunbathing. Also check out the open-air theatre.

DE VONDELTUIN Map pp282-3

☎ 664 50 91; www.vondeltuin.nl; Vondelpark 7; skate rental 1/2/3+ hr adult €5/10/15, child €4/8/12; Mar-Oct

Near the Amstelveenseweg entrance at the southwestern end of the park, this stand rents in-line skates and gloves and has a café.

ELECTRISCHE MUSEUMTRAMLIJN AMSTERDAM Map pp282-3

Tram Museum Amsterdam; ☎ 673 75 38; www.museumtram.nl; Amstelveenseweg 264; return ticket adult/senior & child €3.50/1.80; 11am-5pm Sun mid-Apr–Oct, 1pm & 3pm Wed Jul & Aug

Beyond the southwestern extremities of the park, just north of the Olympic Stadium, is the former Haarlemmermeer Station, which houses the tram museum. Historic trams

sourced from all over Europe run between here and Amstelveen – a great outing for kids and adults. A return trip takes about 1¼ hours (contact the museum for a schedule) and skirts the large Amsterdamse Bos recreational area.

FILMMUSEUM Map pp282-3

☎ 589 14 00; www.filmmuseum.nl; Vondelpark 3

Close to Constantijn Huygensstraat is the former Vondelpark Pavilion (1881), now home to the Filmmuseum. Not a museum with displays and such, it has a large collection of memorabilia and a priceless archive of films that are screened in two theatres, often with live music and other accompaniments. One theatre contains the Art Deco interior of Cinema Parisien, an early Amsterdam cinema. Note that, at time of writing, some screenings were held at the Filmmuseum Cinerama (aka Calypso; p178) near Leidseplein; this was on an experimental basis but may be made permanent. Check website or local listings for details.

The museum's grand Café Vertigo, with its theatrical balcony and expansive ground-level terrace, is a popular meeting place and an ideal spot to spend a couple of hours watching the goings-on in the park; on summer evenings there are films on the outdoor terrace.

Adjoining the museum is an impressive information centre (☎ 589 14 35; Vondelstraat 69-71; admission free; 1-5pm Mon-Fri) with loads of books and videotapes that can be viewed in booths.

HOLLANDSE MANEGE Map pp282-3

☎ 618 09 42; Vondelstraat 140; vary

Just outside the park, west of the Filmmuseum, is the neoclassical Hollandse Manege, an indoor riding school inspired by the famous Spanish Riding School in Vienna. Designed by AL van Gendt and built in 1882, the building was fully restored in the 1980s, and it's worth walking through the passage to the door at the rear and up the stairs to the café. You can sip a cheap beer or coffee while enjoying the beautiful interior and watching the instructor put the horses through their paces. Opening times can vary – ring to avoid disappointment.

Nearby is the Vondelkerk (1880), built to a design by Pierre Cuypers, which now accommodates offices.

(Continued on page 107)

1 *A canalside café on Prinsengracht*
2 *The Other Side (p173), a coffee-shop on Reguliersdwarsstraat* 3 *The most common form of transport*
4 *Queen's Day celebrations (p9) on Thorbeckeplein*

1 *Traditional Amsterdam gabled buildings (boxed text, p4)*
2 *Stained-glass window at Nieuwe Kerk (p69), Medieval Centre*
3 *Centraal Station, Medieval Centre* 4 *Inside Het Schip Housing Estate (p81), Western Islands, signature building of the Amsterdam School of Architecture*

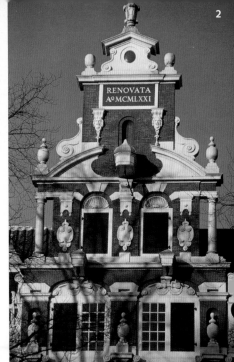

1 *Dutch modern architecture (p46) can be found in the Eastern Islands and the Western Islands* 2 *Bartolotti House (p88), Western Canal Belt* 3 *Gothic Oude Kerk (p65), Medieval Centre* 4 *Hotel de L'Europe (p215), Medieval Centre*

1 *Guan Yin Shrine (p74), Nieuw-markt* 2 *Royal Palace clock tower (p70), Medieval Centre* 3 *Anne Frank Huis (p85), Western Canal Belt* 4 *Westerkerk (p89), Western Canal Belt*

1 *Joods Historisch (Jewish Historical) Museum (p75), Nieuwmarkt* **2** *Museum Het Rembrandthuis (p76), Nieuwmarkt* **3** *The Dam and the Royal Palace (p70), Medieval Centre* **4** *Museum Van Loon (p94), Southern Canal Belt*

1 Night-time Amsterdam
2 Canal-tour boat 3 Visitors admire
architecture through the ages
4 Canals: an integral part of the
city (boxed text, p62)

1 *Wallen, Amsterdam's Red Light District (p66)* **2** *Thematic postcards in the Red Light District (p66)* **3** *Shopping in Nieuwmarkt (p73)* **4** *Coffeeshops (p165) come alive at night*

1 *Museumplein (p95), Old South*
2 *Artis Zoo (p108), Plantage*
3 *Vondelpark (p97), Old South*
4 *Statue of Rembrandt in Rembrandtplein (p89), Southern Canal Belt*

(Continued from page 98)

DE PIJP

Eating p147; Shopping p202; Sleeping p226

In the past as now, De Pijp has often been called the 'Quartier Latin' of Amsterdam thanks to its lively mix of people – labourers, intellectuals, recent immigrants, prostitutes (in a rather downmarket red-light district along Ruysdaelkade opposite Hobbemakade), and now gays, lesbians and an ever-increasing number of higher-income professionals.

Enclosed by the Amstel in the east, Stadhouderskade in the north, Hobbemakade in the west and the Amstelkanaal in the south, this district is a large island connected to the rest of the city by 16 bridges. The district's name, 'the Pipe' (originally the 'YY neighbourhood'), presumably reflects its straight, narrow streets that are said to resemble the stems of old clay pipes, but nobody really knows. There are a surprising number of attractions for an area that began as the city's first 19th-century slum.

Its early shoddy tenement blocks, some of which collapsed even as they were being built in the 1860s, provided cheap housing not just for newly arrived workers drawn by the city's industrial revolution, but also for students, artists, writers and other poverty-stricken individuals. In the 1960s and '70s, many of the working-class inhabitants left for greener pastures and the government began refurbishing the tenement blocks for immigrants from Morocco, Turkey, Suriname and the Netherlands Antilles. Now these immigrants are also moving out and the Pijp is attracting a wealthier breed of locals who are doing up apartments and lending the neighbourhood a more gentrified air.

South of Albert Cuypstraat is Sarphatipark, an English-style park named after the energetic 19th-century Jewish doctor and chemist Samuel Sarphati (1813–66). His diverse projects (a waste-disposal service, a slaughterhouse, a factory for cheap bread, trades and business schools, the Amstel

Albert Cuypmarkt can sell you anything

Sights

DE PIJP

Hotel and a mortgage bank) exasperated the dour city council, though many of these ventures survive to this day. The park contains a central fountain, nice lawns for having a picnick or sprawling, and enough trees for privacy or shade.

The street running along the south side of the park is Ceintuurbaan, a traffic artery that is of little interest to the casual observer except for the **Kabouterhuis** (Gnome House; Map pp282–3; Ceintuurbaan 251-255) near the Amstel. Its whimsical woodwork façade incorporates a couple of gnomes playing ball, a reference to the surname of the original owner, Van Ballegooijen (literally, 'of ball-throwing').

ALBERT CUYPMARKT Map p297

Albert Cuypstraat; ☺ 9am-5pm Mon-Sat

This is Amsterdam's largest and busiest market, which celebrated its 100th anniversary in 2005. The emphasis is on food of every description and nationality, but clothes and other general goods are on sale too, often cheaper than anywhere else. If you want to experience the 'real' Amsterdam at its multicultural best, this market is not to be missed. As always at busy markets, beware of pickpockets.

The surrounding streets hide cosy neighbourhood cafés, small (and usually very cheap) restaurants that offer a wide range of cuisines (check to the west of the market on Albert Cuypstraat), and an increasing number of stylish shops and bars (especially on Eerste van der Helststraat).

TRANSPORT

Tram lines 3, 6, 7, 10, 12, 16, 24 and 25 all head to this area. Trams 16 and 24 will take you right through the centre, on Ferdinand Bolstraat and Albert Cuypstraat.

GEMEENTEARCHIEF Map pp282-3

Municipal Archives; ☎ 572 02 02; Amsteldijk 67; admission free

In the former town hall of Nieuwe Amstel, a town annexed by Amsterdam during the late-19th-century expansion, are the Amsterdam city archives. Anyone interested in their family history or the history of the city can peruse the archives free of charge, and occasionally there some are very interesting exhibitions. There's a large library with books about Amsterdam in different languages on everything from housing to legal briefs and sports clubs.

Note that Gemeentearchief is moving to the former ABN-AMRO Bank building on Vijzelstraat. Ring for the latest or surf to www.gemeentearchief.amsterdam.nl (Dutch only).

HEINEKEN EXPERIENCE Map pp292-3

☎ 523 96 66; www.heinekenexperience.com; Stadhouderskade 78; admission €10 (under 18yr only with adult supervision); ☺ 10am-6pm Tue-Sun

On the site of a one-time (though not the original) Heineken brewery, you can take a self-guided tour through many forms of brew-worship. You'll learn the history of the Heineken family, find out how the typeface on the logo evolved, and follow the brewing process from water to malting to the addition of hops etc, all the way through to bottling. Along the way, you get to watch Heineken commercials from around the world, watch a multimedia video of the life of a Heineken bottle and drive a virtual Heineken horse.

Feel a little Heineken-overwhelmed? You can quell it at 'tasting' sessions included in the tour, at which three glasses per person may be consumed (note: smoking is not permitted). Homer Simpson would feel right at home. Allow 75 minutes for your visit.

If you're coming in summer or winter, expect lots of company on your tour.

The actual brewery closed in 1988 due to inner-city congestion, and since then the building has been used only for tours and administration; the company's directorate is in the low-key premises across the canal. Heineken beer is now brewed at a larger plant in 's-Hertogenbosch (Den Bosch), in the south of the country, that opened in 1950, and also at the largest brewery in Europe at Zoeterwoude near Leiden (opened in 1975).

THE WORLD'S ULTIMATE PICKUP LINE

Apart from his duties as international beer magnate, Freddy Heineken (1924–2002) had a reputation as a ladies' man. As the story goes, an attractive young lady approached the bar and uttered the familiar phrase: 'I'd like a Heineken, please.' Freddy (stationed nearby) replied: 'I'm right here.'

PLANTAGE & OOSTERPARK

Eating p150; Sleeping p227

Immediately east of the Nieuwmarkt neighbourhood is the stately district known as the Plantage.

The 19th-century discovery of diamonds in South Africa led to a revival of Amsterdam's diamond industry and the Jewish elite began to move into the Plantage (Plantation), where they built imposing town villas.

Until then the Plantage was a district of parks and gardens. In the 18th century, wealthy residents rented parcels of land here to use as gardens, and the area developed into a weekend getaway with teahouses, variety theatres and other establishments where the upper class relaxed in green surroundings.

PLANTAGE

ARTIS ZOO Map pp290-1

☎ 523 34 00; www.artis.nl; Plantage Kerklaan 38-40; adult/senior/child 3-9yr/under 3yr €16/15/12.50/free; ☺ 9am-5pm, to 6pm in summer

The zoo was founded by an association called Natura Artis Magistra (Latin for 'Nature is the Master of Art') back in 1838, which makes it the oldest zoo on the European continent, and the city's oldest park. Famous biologists studied and worked here among the rich collection of animals and plants. Even if some of the cramped enclosures hardly seem to have progressed since the 19th century, the zoo's layout – with ponds, statues and winding pathways through lush surroundings (remnants of some of the former Plantage gardens) – is very pleasant. Concerts and art exhibitions are also held here, in line with the original aim of the association: to link nature and art.

You'll find the usual assortment of apes, gazelles (unlike the city's Gazelle brand bikes, these have legs, not wheels), giraffes and elephants, tropical and polar birds, and an insectarium with creatures icky and alluring (if bugs creep you out, stick to the butterfly house). Another highlight is the **aquarium**, the oldest in the country (1882, renovated 1997), with some 2000 fish and imposing classical architecture. The zoo's exhibits include an Amazonian flooded forest, a tropical coral reef and an Amsterdam canal. There's a **planetarium** (Dutch commentary with a summary in English), and **zoological and geological museums**. The entrance fee includes all of these venues.

Although the zoo covers a vast swath of the Plantage, the only entrance to it is on Plantage Kerklaan, diagonally across from the Verzetsmuseum.

HERMITAGE AMSTERDAM Map pp290-1
☎ 530 87 51; Nieuwe Herengracht 14; www.hermitage.nl; adult/child under 16yr €6/free, combination ticket with Hortus Botanicus €9; ☉ 10am-5pm
Just as the Rijksmuseum and Stedelijk Museums were going under the knife, as it were, Russia came to the rescue with a new branch of the State Hermitage Museum of St Petersburg. It's not as random as you might think – the Hermitage had been holding special exhibits in the Nieuwe Kerk for many years already, and the building, a former almshouse for the aged called the Amstelhof, seemed like the perfect new venue.

Currently, the Hermitage Amsterdam occupies a small section (about 500sq metres) in the Neerlandia building. Long-term plans are for the museum to take over more of the Amstelhof, with over 4000 sq metres of exhibition space.

Exhibits change approximately twice per year, and they tend to be as stately and well-curated as you'd expect.

The Amstelhof (Amstel 51) is noteworthy in its own right. Its very construction as an almshouse in 1683 illustrates how the canal-belt project ran out of steam by the time it reached the Amstel. The wealthy had already bought their plots and built their mansions, and the Dutch Republic went into consolidation mode against the British and French, which meant there was little new wealth being created. Much of the land this side of the Amstel was given over to charities or turned into recreational space.

Over various renovations, the Amstelhof provided some advances in sanitation and humane care for the poor. In the 18th century, the building took the revolutionary step of housing its female wards in rooms of four, rather than massive dorms (men still lived in one, though, referred to as 'the pit'). Little remains of the old interiors, but the exterior is still handsome.

A combination admission ticket (€9, €12 if you purchased both separately) is available for the Hermitage and the Hortus Botanicus, about five minutes' walk away.

HOLLANDSCHE SCHOUWBURG
Map pp290-1
Dutch Theatre; ☎ 626 99 45; www.hollandscheschouwburg.nl; Plantage Middenlaan 24; admission free; ☉ 11am-4pm, closed Yom Kippur
It's ironic that a place of such joy became a place of such tragedy. Originally the house of the director of Artis Zoo, this building became the Artis Schouwburg (Artis Theatre) in 1892 and was soon one of the centres of Dutch theatrical life. In WWII, however, the Germans turned it into a theatre by and for Jews, and from 1942 they made it a detention centre for Jews awaiting deportation. Some 60,000 to 80,000 Jews passed through here on their way to Westerbork transit camp in the east of the country, and from there to the death camps.

After the war, people felt it unseemly to reopen the site as a theatre, and in 1961 it was demolished except for the façade and the area immediately behind it. Today there's a hollow shell of a lobby and, where the auditorium once provided laughter, a 10m-high memorial pylon dominates a courtyard; the effect is wrenching in its simplicity. Along the wall to the left of the lobby, glass panels are engraved with the names of all the Jewish families deported from the Netherlands. You may see stones at the foot of the panels, following the Jewish custom of placing a stone at a grave site. On the floor in front of the wall, an

Sights

PLANTAGE & OOSTERPARK

TRANSPORT
Tram lines 6, 9 and 14 travel though the Plantage; lines 3, 7 and 10 service Oosterpark. Metro station Weesperplein is on the western edge of Oosterpark, with Wibautstraat further to the south.

inscription in Dutch and Hebrew translates as: 'Watch me like you watch the iris of your eye, and hide me under your wings from the evil people lurking around me.'

Upstairs is a small exhibit hall with photos and artefacts of Jewish life before and during the war (signage here in Dutch only). The Hollandsche Schouwburg is part of the Joods Historisch Museum (p75).

HORTUS BOTANICUS Map pp290-1

☎ 625 90 21; www.hortus-botanicus.nl; Plantage Middenlaan 2A; adult/child €6/3, combination ticket with Hermitage Amsterdam €9; ☽ 9am-5pm Mon-Fri, 10am-5pm Sat & Sun, till 9pm daily Jul & Aug, till 4pm daily Dec & Jan

This botanical garden was established in 1638 as a medicinal herb garden for the city's doctors. After moving to this south-west corner of the Plantage in 1682, it became a repository for tropical seeds and plants (ornamental or otherwise) brought to Amsterdam by the ships of the West and East India Companies. Commercially exploitable plants such as those producing coffee, pineapple, cinnamon and palm oil were distributed from here throughout the world. The herb garden itself, the Hortus Medicus, won world renown for its research into cures for tropical diseases.

The garden is a must-see for anyone with an interest in botany, and even tree-haters may find something that fascinates: the 4000+ species are spread among a wonderful mixture of colonial and modern structures, including the restored, octagon-shaped seed house and a hyper-modern, three-climate glasshouse (1993) with sub-tropical, tropical (see if your glasses don't fog) and desert plants; catwalks in the greenhouses allow you to see the plants from below and up close. Inside the monu-mental palm house is a 300-year-old cycad, claimed to be the world's oldest potted plant (it bloomed in 1999, a rare event). The butterfly house is a hit with kids and stoned adults, and the Hortus Medicus still attracts students from around the globe.

All that said, it's not really a place for pleasant relaxation and communing with nature. You won't find expansive lawns, and don't even think of bringing a Frisbee. For that, go to the Vondelpark (p97) or the Westergasfabriek (p83). Closer by, the smaller Wertheimpark is across the street from the Hortus.

Guided tours (additional €1) are held at 2pm Sunday year round and also at 7.30pm Sunday in July and August.

The Hortus' café, the Orangery, recently reopened after refurbishment and is de-servedly popular, especially for its terrace. Jazz and world music evenings take place here on Friday evenings in July and August. Note that normal Hortus admission fees apply even to those only visiting the café.

A combination admission ticket (€9, €12 if you purchased both separately) is available for the Hortus and the Hermitage Amsterdam, about five minutes' walk away.

NATIONAAL VAKBONDSMUSEUM
Map pp290-1

National Trade Union Museum; ☎ 624 11 66; Henri Polaklaan 9; adult/concession or union member €2.50/1.25; ☽ 11am-5pm Tue-Fri, 1-5pm Sun, closed public holidays

The architect HP Berlage considered this building his most successful work, and it's easy to see why. Built in 1900 as the headquarters of the General Netherlands Diamond Workers' Union (ANDB), it soon became known as the 'Burcht van Berlage', Berlage's Fortress – a play on Beurs van Berlage, the bourse along Damrak (p64). It is a wonder from the diamond-shaped pin-nacle to the magnificent hall with its brick arches, the murals, ceramics and leadlight windows by famous artists of the day. The soaring, atrium-style staircase is graced with a three-storey tall chandelier – an Art-Deco marvel added in 1921 at the phenomenal cost (for the time) of 30,000 guilders (today 30,000 guilders would be roughly €15,000).

All that will probably be enough for most visitors. If you have a more abiding interest in labour issues and can read Dutch, the displays will be an extra bonus.

VERZETSMUSEUM Map pp290-1

Resistance Museum; ☎ 620 25 35; www.verzets museum.org; Plantage Kerklaan 61; adult/child 7-15yr/under 7yr €5/2.75/free; ☽ 10am-5pm Tue-Fri, noon-5pm Sat-Mon

It took less than one week in May 1940 for the Netherlands to be overrun by the German army, and from that moment the Dutch faced a choice: join or resist?

The choice was on all fronts: political, judicial, medical, scholarly, economic.

Germany tried to cosy up to the Dutch at first (declaring them part of the 'Germanic brotherhood'). Soon though, came the restrictions: changing the names of streets named for Jews, requiring doctors to join the Nazi Medical Chamber, banning of political movements, confiscation of 80% of radios and, naturally, unspeakable deportations and murders – all of which fomented mass resistance, even if much of it was below the surface.

This museum gives an excellent insight into the difficulties faced by those who fought the occupation from within – as well as the minority who chose to go along with the Nazis. Labels in Dutch and English help with the exhibits, many of them interactive, that explain such issues as active and passive resistance, how the illegal press operated, how 300,000 people were kept in hiding and how such activities were funded (a less glamorous but vital detail). The museum shows in no uncertain terms how much courage it takes to actively resist an adversary so ruthless that you can't trust neighbours, friends or even family. Just as importantly, it gives pause to think how each of us would handle such a situation.

OOSTERPARK

This southeastern district, named after the lush English-style park at its centre, was built in the 1880s. At the time, the city's diamond workers suddenly found they had money to spare, thanks to the discovery of diamonds in South Africa. About a third of Jewish families worked in the diamond industry, and many of these could finally afford to leave the Jewish quarter for this new district beyond the Plantage (the delectable parklands where only the wealthiest could afford to live). Signs of the lower-middle-class heritage have long since disappeared and now it's similar to the other 19th-century slums that arose around the Canal Belt. Much of the real estate in this area is owned by the University of Amsterdam.

TROPENMUSEUM Map pp290-1
☎ 568 82 15; www.kit.nl; Linnaeusstraat 2; adult/senior or student/child 6-17yr/under 6yr €7.50/5/3.75/free; ☻ 10am-5pm
This impressive complex was completed in 1926 to house the Royal Institute of the Tropics, still one of the leading research in-

stitutes for tropical hygiene and agriculture. Part of the building became a museum for the institute's collection of colonial artefacts, but this was overhauled in the 1970s to create the culturally aware and imaginatively presented displays you see today.

A huge central hall with galleries over three floors offers reconstructions of daily life in several tropical countries (eg African market, Mexican-style cantina, musical instruments you can hear via recordings). Separate exhibitions focus on theatre, religion, crafts, world trade, textiles and ecology, and there are special exhibitions throughout the year. Other exhibitions focus on regions (eg Latin America, Southeast Asia, Suriname). For Dutch-speaking children, the children's section, TM Junior, has special guided exhibits (ring for details and prices). There's also an extensive **library** (☎ 568 82 54; ☻ 10am-4.45pm Tue-Fri, noon-4.45pm Sun).

There's a shop selling books and gifts and unique CDs, and the pleasant Soeterijn Café and the **Ekeko Restaurant** (☎ 568 86 44) serve cuisine and snacks that relate to current exhibits and performances (despite its name, Ekeko is actually the less formal of the two).

The **Tropeninstituut Theater** (☎ 568 82 15; ☻ box office noon-4pm Mon-Sat) has a separate entrance and screens films as well as hosting music, dance, plays and other performances by visiting artists.

Among its other charms, the museum is a good place to spend a lazy Monday when most of the other museums around town are closed.

Gongs on display at the Tropenmuseum

EASTERN ISLANDS

Eating p151; Shopping p202; Sleeping p228

East of Centraal Station and north of the Medieval Centre, Nieuwmarkt and Plantage areas, the islands of Kattenburg, Wittenburg and Oostenburg were constructed in the 1650s to handle the rapidly expanding seaborne trade.

The United East India Company (VOC) set themselves up on the eastern island of **Oostenburg**, where it established warehouses, rope yards, workshops and docks for the maintenance of its fleet. Private shipyards and dockworkers' homes dominated the central island of Wittenburg – city architect Daniël Stalpaert's Oosterkerk (1671) on Wittenburgergracht was the last, and the least monumental, of the four 'compass churches' (the others were the Noorderkerk, Westerkerk and Zuiderkerk). Admiralty offices and buildings arose on the western island of Kattenburg, and warships were fitted out in the adjoining naval dockyards that are still in use today.

When the Plantage was constructed in the 1680s, the original sea dyke was moved north to what are now the Hoogte Kadijk and Laagte Kadijk (the high and low sections of the quay dyke). The stretch of water between the Plantage and this new sea dyke is the **Entrepotdok**, established in the 1820s as a storage zone for goods in transit. The 500m-long row of warehouses, once the largest storage depot in Europe, has been converted into desirable apartments and studios. They've won numerous awards for the preservation of their exteriors, while the interiors have been opened up significantly from the former cramped spaces. To see one from the inside, stop by for lunch or dinner at the dramatically remodelled café-restaurant **Kromhout** (p163).

Although this area may not have the intimacy or the unity of other areas of town, there's a lot to recommend it. We've also included information about other nearby islands in this section.

TRANSPORT

The Stedelijk Museum and NEMO are several minutes' walk from Centraal Station, or you can take the new tram lines 16 and 26. Bus lines 22, 32, 39, 43 and 59 spread throughout the Eastern Islands.

TOP FIVE EASTERN ISLANDS

- **Stedelijk Museum** (p114) Temporary home at Oosterdokseiland.
- **NEMO** (p114) Futuristic building, containing a science museum, that seems to float on its own in the harbour.
- **Nederlands Scheepvaartmuseum** (opposite) Maritime museum.
- **Entrepotdok** (left) Dramatically renovated former warehouses.
- **EnergeticA** (opposite) Relatively new super-cool museum of technology.

ARCAM Map pp290-1

Stichting Architectuur Centrum Amsterdam;
☎ 620 48 78; www.arcam.nl; Prins Hendrikkade 600; admission free; ⏲ 1-5pm Tue-Sat

Architecture buffs make a bee-line. The Amsterdam Architecture Foundation's wonderful office building and gallery (2003, by René van Zuuk) is a one-stop shop for all your architectural needs. Exhibits vary, but you are sure to find books, guide maps, suggestions for tours on foot, by bike and by public transport, and reference materials on just about anything built in town from early history to the very latest housing development.

Among the best titles are *25 Buildings You Should Have Seen* and *Eastern Docklands Map*. Check the website for the latest.

BIERBROUWERIJ 'T IJ Map pp290-1

☎ 622 83 25; Funenkade 7; admission free;
⏲ 3-7.45pm Wed-Sun

In 1985 the former public baths alongside the windmill were converted into this small brewery, producing six regular and several seasonal beers. Some are quite strong (up to 9% alcohol by volume), and all can be tasted in the comfortably grungy interior or on the terrace at the foot of the windmill. Apart from **De Bekeerde Suster** (p161), off Nieuwmarkt, it's the only brewery in town, and certainly the coolest.

The windmill itself dates from the 17th century and was used to mill grain. It's the sole survivor of five windmills that once stood in this part of the city. Originally located southwest of here, it was moved to its present location in 1814 when some barracks were built nearby, blocking the wind flow.

ENERGETICA Map pp290-1

☎ 422 12 27; Hoogte Kadijk 400; adult/child under 12yr €3/free; 🕙 10am-4pm Mon-Fri

If it has pistons, gears, wires, cables, tubes or shafts; if it clinks, clanks, buzzes, pops or clunks, you'll find it here. EnergeticA may be the quirkiest museum in Amsterdam, and it's also one of our favourites. It looks like a power station from the outside (which it was), volunteer guides act like retired engineers (which many are; average age, 70), and they'll enthusiastically escort you through centuries of technological history, demonstrating how things work as they go (some of them speak English extremely well).

Galleries are named for pioneering scientists (Marconi, Minckelers), and some of the ancient equipment in them – from steamship engines to antique toasters, early washing machines, electric lights and TVs – may remind you of science-fiction movies. The early refrigerators are, pardon the expression, very cool.

The highlight, though, is the soaring main hall, several storeys in what was the first power plant for the city's trams. It is filled with large-scale technological marvels from the past, including gas streetlamps, antique lifts (elevators) from Vienna and Paris, and high-voltage generators that send lightning between enormous v-shaped prongs. Chances are, you never imagined it could be this much fun to ride an escalator.

Note that each child under 12 years old needs to be accompanied by an adult (one adult supervising a group of kids is not going to do it!).

MUZIEKGEBOUW AAN 'T IJ Map pp282-3

tickets ☎ 788 20 00, office ☎ 788 20 10; www.muziekgebouw.nl; Piet Heinkade 1; bldg admission free, performance prices vary; ticket office 🕙 noon-7pm Mon-Sat

Amsterdam's newest landmark (opened spring 2005), the 'Music Building on the IJ' was some 20 years in the making. Designed by the Danish firm 3xNielsen, it is home to the long-standing music venues the IJsbreker (which changed its name to the new building) and the jazz house Bimhuis (p175), which retains its name and separate identity.

Even if you don't catch a show here, the Star Ferry café (🕙 10am-1am daily, until 2am Fri & Sat) is a great stop for snacks and views. A room for kids, featuring The Musical Tart (computerised musical installation art), should be open by the time you read this.

NEDERLANDS SCHEEPVAARTMUSEUM Map pp290-1

Netherlands Shipping Museum; ☎ 523 22 22; www.scheepvaartmuseum.nl; Kattenburgerplein 1; adult/senior/child 6-17yr/under 6yr/family €9/7/4.50/free/22.50; 🕙 10am-5pm mid-Jun–mid-Sep, 10am-5pm Tue-Sun Sep-May

The republic's naval arsenal was housed in this imposing building completed in 1656 to a design by Daniël Stalpaert. The admiralty vacated the building in 1973, and since 1981 it has housed this museum, with one of the most extensive collections of maritime memorabilia in the world.

The museum covers the history of Dutch seafaring from the ancient past to the present. Early shipping routes, maritime trade, naval combat, fishing and whaling are all explained in interesting displays, paintings and some 500 models of boats and ships. Lovers of charts, maps and navigational material will not want to miss it. There are also films throughout the day.

Moored alongside the museum is a full-scale replica of the United East India Company's 700-tonne *Amsterdam,* one of the largest ships of the fleet. It set sail on its maiden voyage in the winter of 1748–49 with 336 people on board, but got stuck off the English coast near Hastings; there it became a famous shipwreck that has become the subject of much research in recent years. Actors in 18th-century costume re-create shipboard life, and you can stroll through the cabins and cargo holds – the Great Cabin is beautifully set for an elegant dinner. Although it would have taken about six months to build the original *Amsterdam,* this one took six *years* (completed 1991).

Not to be missed is the Royal Barge, on display in its own gallery. This French-style craft (17m long by 2.6m wide, 6 tonnes, built 1818) is decorated from stem to stern in gold filigree, and on the bow there's an elaborate gold figure of Neptune driving a team of half-horse–half-fish beings. The barge the oldest existing vessel in the Royal Netherlands Navy.

NEMO Map pp290-1

☎ 0900-919 10 00, per min €0.35; www.e-nemo.nl; Oosterdok 2; adult/student/child under 4yr €11/6.50/free; ☉ 10am-5pm Tue-Sun, plus Mon Jul & Aug

Perched atop the entrance to the IJ-Tunnel (hold that thought) is the wedge-shaped museum of science and technology, the largest in the Netherlands. It's really meant for kids, but grown-ups will probably enjoy it too. There are loads of interactive exhibits, drawing with a laser, 'anti-gravity' trick mirrors and a 'lab' where you can answer questions like 'How black is black?' and 'How do you make cheese?' Signage is in English and Dutch.

Italian architect Renzo Piano (a Pritzker Prize winner whose works also include the Centre Pompidou in Paris, Kansai Airport near Osaka and Potsdamer Platz in Berlin) conceived of this design as the inverse of the tunnel below it. Less-kind critics had taken to calling this ship-shaped building the *Titanic,* for its colossal cost, but by all accounts it's doing very well, thank you.

In summer, the terraced rooftop plaza hosts **Nemo Beach** (admission €2.50, free with NEMO admission; ☉ vary). The 'beach' itself is actually a rather elaborate sandbox occupying just a small section of the roof, but further up DJs spin, and there's a bar, a convivial atmosphere and nice views. It can get very busy.

STEDELIJK MUSEUM Map pp290-1

☎ 573 29 11; www.stedelijk.nl; 2nd & 3rd floors, Post CS Bldg, Oosterdokskade 5; adult/child 7-16yr & senior/under 7yr €9/5/free; ☉ 10am-6pm

The Stedelijk focuses on modern art – paintings, sculptures, installations, videos, photography etc – from 1850 to the present. It's one of the world's leading museums of modern art, with an eclectic collection amassed by its postwar curator, Willem Sandberg. The permanent home of this important museum is under construction until 2008 (see boxed text, p97), so the exhibitions have been moved to this unlikely space in a former post-office tower during that time. To our surprise, we quite like it.

Check to see what's on while you are in town, but the permanent collection includes all the famous names: Monet, Van Gogh, Cézanne, Matisse, Picasso, Kirchner, Chagall. There are other modern 'classics', and some less famous but no less alluring, including a unique collection of some 50 works by the Russian artist Malevich. There are abstract works by Mondrian, Van Doesburg and Kandinsky, and a large, post-WWII selection of creations by Appel, De Kooning, Newman, Ryman, Judd, Warhol, Dibbets, Baselitz, Dubuffet, Lichtenstein, Polke and Klee, and furniture by Rietveld.

NEMO, a modern science museum

Sculptures include works by Rodin, Renoir, Moore, Laurens and Visser. More recent acquisitions include works by Damien Hirst and Julian Schnabel.

While you're here, take time to browse some of the upper floors, where design houses have their showrooms, as well as the café-restaurant 11 (p151). We'll let you guess which floor it's on.

WERFMUSEUM 'T KROMHOUT
Map pp290-1

☎ 627 67 77; www.machinekamer.nl; Hoogte Kadijk 147; adult/child €4.75/2.75; ⏲ 10am-3pm Tue
On the outer side of the dyke is an 18th-century wharf that still repairs boats in its western hall. The eastern hall is a museum devoted to shipbuilding and even more to the indestructible marine engines that were designed and built here. Anyone with an interest in marine engineering will love the place; others will probably want to move on. Signage is almost entirely in Dutch only.

EASTERN DOCKLANDS
Eating p152; Shopping p202; Sleeping p228
North and east of the Eastern Islands, this one-time shipyard and warehouse district sat derelict for decades, despite some excellent warehouse-style buildings. Recently, though, it's been the focus of a huge amount of attention from architects and architecture critics for the elaborate updates and extremely adventurous new construction. If you're looking for one place to see the cutting edge of Dutch – and indeed European – architecture, this is the place to come. When complete, there will be more than 8000 dwellings and 17,000 inhabitants.

Although there are no sights (museums, cultural points etc) in the Eastern Docklands, this new construction is well worth a look. See the Architecture chapter (p46) for details and the Walking & Cycling Tours chapter (p123) for a bicycle route through the islands.

TRANSPORT
Take the new tram lines 16 and 26 or the ferry from behind Centraal Station to the end of Java Eiland (€1).

OUTER DISTRICTS

Most of the rest of Amsterdam is taken up by suburbs planned in the 1930s as part of a general extension plan. The areas west of town (among them Bos en Lommer, Slotermeer, Osdorp and Slotervaart) came to be known as *tuinsteden* (garden cities) – with carefully planned traffic systems, lakes, sporting fields, greenery and abundant natural light. All of which goes to say that there's not a lot there to draw visitors.

Bijlmer, to the southeast, was designed to hold lots of people in a very small space, and it is largely occupied by immigrants, and now some second-generation residents, from the Netherlands Antilles and Suriname.

While still not much of a draw for visitors, Bijlmer does have a couple of high-profile entertainment venues. Most notable is the **Amsterdam ArenA** (p184), the large-scale venue where Amsterdam's Ajax football (soccer) club plays. It is also a concert venue, and visitors can take tours. Nearby are two more performance spaces, the **Heineken Music Hall** (p174) and **Pepsi Stage** (p174), both opened in this millennium. If they come up with the Milk Bowl, you'll see it here first.

The suburb of Amstelveen south of Amsterdam has a long history. During the 12th century it was a moor drained by the Amstel (*veen* means 'peat'). Local farmers built canals to drain the land for agriculture, thus turning the Amstel into a clearly defined river. As the soil along the Amstel compacted, the farming community moved farther west, which is why the west bank of the Amstel at this latitude is relatively uninhabited today. There's not a lot to draw you to Amstelveen, but a couple of attractions might be worth the trip.

AMSTERDAMSE BOS Map pp282-3
Amsterdam Woods; visitors centre ☎ 545 61 00; www.amsterdamsebos.nl; Bosbaanweg 5; admission free; ⏲ visitors centre 8.30am-5pm
This large recreational area was built as a work-creation project in the 1930s. Amsterdammers flock here on weekends, but it's so huge (940 hectares) that it never gets too crowded. Its only drawback is that it's close to Schiphol airport and a lot of low-flying aircraft.

There are lakes (notably the large Nieuwe Meer), wooded areas, meadows, an animal enclosure with bison, a goat farm, paths for walking, cycling and horse riding, a rowing course (the Bosbaan, with several water craft for hire), the open-air **Amsterdamse Bos Theatre** (p180) with plays in summer, a sports park, a pancake house, a **forestry museum** (☎ 676 21 52; admission free; ◷ 10am-5pm) with displays about the construction, flora and fauna of the area, and much more. To get here, take bus No 170, 171 or 172 from Centraal Station, or ride the historic tram from the Haarlemmermeer Station (p98). Bikes can be rented at the main entrance at Van Nijenrodeweg. By bike, the easiest way is to follow the Overtoom to the end, veer left onto Amstelveenseweg and stay on it past the Olympic Stadium and the Ring Rd, and you'll see it shortly on your right.

COBRA MUSEUM
☎ 547 50 50; www.cobra-museum.nl; Sandbergplein 1; adult/senior & student/child 6-16yr/under 6yr €7/4/2.50/free; ◷ 11am-5pm Tue-Sun

The CoBrA artistic movement was formed in the postwar years by a group of artists from Denmark, Belgium and the Netherlands – the name consists of the first letters of their capital cities. Members included Asger Jorn (Denmark), Corneille (Netherlands), Constant (Netherlands) and the great Karel Appel (Netherlands). The group lasted for just three years (1948–51),

so changing exhibits feature the work of artists from outside the movement as well as inside. Some critics hailed the CoBrA artists' work as bold, others thought it was derivative. Expect to see bold colours and busy designs, but the art is less of a unified whole than a philosophy, inspired by Marxism, of using materials at hand to create painting, sculpture, even poetry.

Especially now with the temporary relocation of the Stedelijk Museum, this contemporary, two-storey building is your best bet to see the work of this fascinating group, with paintings, ceramics, statuary, creative typography etc. It's really quite an impressive place, even if it doesn't have the history, cachet or location of its bigger siblings.

Take bus No 170 or 172 from Centraal Station or tram No 5 or 51 to the end of the line. From the tram line, walk through or around Vroom & Dreesman department store, through the Binnenhof and Rembrandt Hof shopping centres. Buses stop in front of the museum.

AMSTERDAM RAI
☎ 549 12 12; www.rai.nl; Europaplein 22
This exhibition and conference centre is the largest such complex in the country. It opened in the early 1960s and new halls are still being added. There's always some sort of exhibition or trade fair going on. Attendance varies with economic times, but it gets in the neighbourhood of two million visitors per year.

Walking & Cycling Tours

Walking & Cycling Tours

Amsterdam is a joy to discover on foot. Most of the sights are within easy walking distance in the compact city centre. You can get lost in Venice, but not as comprehensively as here.

Cycling is also an ideal way to get around town. You'll probably be able to make your own cycling tour just by going from sight to sight, but we've also given you a tour of the up-and-coming Eastern Docklands district. Biking is also a great way to see some very pretty countryside, often serene, unbelievably green, flat and a great escape if you need a break from the bustle of the city. Church steeples and the occasional windmill dot the horizon. Take a half- or full-day excursion, and you'll begin to understand how Dutch artists were inspired to paint such dramatic skies.

WALKING TOURS

In addition to the following, check at the Amsterdam tourist information offices for other suggested walking tours. Many come with excellent guidebooks. In the following walks, browsing time at the sights has not been factored in to the time allowed.

THE VEDDY CIVILISED WESTERN CANALS

Far from its farmland beginnings, today the **Dam 1** (p68) is dominated by the **Royal Palace 2** (p70), worth a visit for its grand interior and art collection. To the right, the impressive **Nieuwe Kerk 3** (p69) often stages excellent exhibitions, while **Madame Tussauds Scenerama 4** (good for kids) is to the left.

Head west, and across Nieuwezijds Voorburgwal you'll see the massive shopping complex **Magna Plaza 5** (p69) – check out its atrium lobby and, if you like, dozens of shops. Continue west and then head north towards the **Torensluis 6** (p68), the bridge over our first canal, the Singel. If you're craving coffee and apple pie, **Villa Zeezicht 7** (p134) has some of the best in town. The bridge features a **statue 8** of the Dutch literary giant Multatuli; there's a **museum 9** (p87) dedicated to him a few blocks north.

The Singel soon intersects with the pretty **Brouwersgracht 10**. Cross over Brouwersgracht and walk west to the head of the Herengracht, one of our favourite views in town, with boats passing in three directions. To the north, behind you, is Herenmarkt, with the 17th-century **Westindisch Huis 11** (p80). From here you can connect with our walking tour of the Wild Wild West (p122).

Nationaal Monument (1956; p69) on Dam Square

Continue west back along the Brouwersgracht, then turn south onto the western side of the Prinsengracht to the imposing **Noorderkerk 12** (p82): on the right day, you can visit a busy **market 13** (boxed text, p190). Dogleg left into Keizersgracht, with the curious **House with the Heads 14**. At peaceful Leliegracht, by the **Greenpeace Building 15** (p44), return to Prinsengracht to pass the **Anne Frank Huis 16** (p85) and the soaring tower of the **Westerkerk 17** (p89). Behind it is Karin Dann's quietly moving **Homomonument 18** (p86) and to its north the house where **René Descartes 19** stayed during his sojourn in Amsterdam. Further south on Prinsengracht is **Van Puffelen 20** (p158), an atmospheric brown café.

Back on Keizersgracht, you can't miss the quirky **Felix Meritis building 21** (p86), a one-time enlightenment society turned alternative theatre. Cross the canals again and head east to the **Bijbels Museum 22** (p86), with its impressive models of biblical sites, en route to the **Spui 23** (p71) for a coffee, beer or weekend book and art markets. The **Begijnhof 24** (p72) is just off the square. The **Amsterdams Historisch Museum 25** (p71) is just up the alley, along with the group portraits that fill its **Civic Guard Gallery** (p72). The busy shopping street **Kalverstraat 26** leads you back to the Dam.

WALK FACTS

Start/End The Dam
Distance 3.9km
Time One hour and 15 minutes

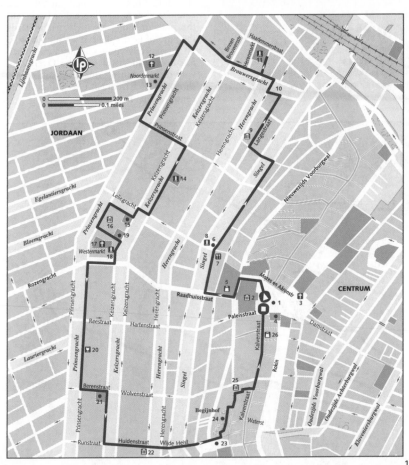

ARTS & FLOWERS WALK

Although the **Rijksmuseum 1** (p96) will be closed for construction until late this decade, its grand exterior makes a great starting point. Walk through the beautiful brick underpass to Museumplein, a monumental grassy expanse for lolling, strolling and open-air concerts. To your right, on the corner of Hobbemastraat, is **Coster Diamonds 2** (boxed text, p200), where you can take a free tour – diamonds are a kind of art, aren't they? Or you may prefer to continue along Paulus Potterstraat to the **Van Gogh Museum 3** (p97), with its modern, mussel-like annexe. The main building of the **Stedelijk Museum 4** (p96) is next door, though it's also closed for renovation. Across Paulus Potterstraat is the **Conservatorium 5** (p177), while the neoclassical **Concertgebouw 6** (p95) is diagonally across Van Baerlestraat – check schedules for free concerts at either venue. Otherwise pick up a picnic at the big **Albert Heijn supermarket 7** on Museumplein.

Weave northwest through a quiet residential quarter (shoppers may enjoy taking a detour to **Pieter Cornelisz Hoofstraat 8**, Amsterdam's answer to Rodeo Drive) towards the sprawling **Vondelpark 9**; highlights of the park include the **rose garden 10** and the **open-air theatre 11** (p180). Refreshment options abound: have a break and enjoy coffee and cake in **'t Blauwe Theehuis 12** (Round Blue Teahouse; p146) or the parkside **Vertigo 13** (p162) at the **Filmmuseum 14** (p98). Step out of the park to admire the **Vondelkerk 15**, a pretty 19th-century church that has been turned into an office complex, before heading either back into the park or along Vondelstraat towards the buzz of Leidseplein. It's a simple walk, or alternatively you could head one block north of Vondelstraat to the Overtoom, with its many furnishings and collectibles shops, to catch tram No 1 back towards the central Canal Belt.

WALK FACTS

Start Rijksmuseum
End Leidseplein
Distance 4km
Time Four hours

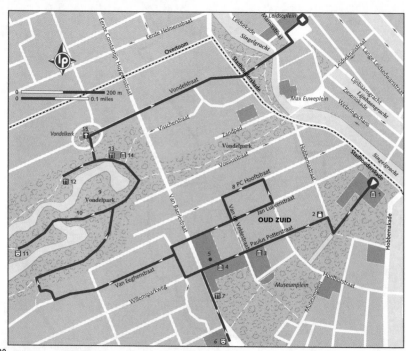

RED LIGHT RAMBLE

Begin at the **Nationaal Monument 1** (p69) and head north along the Damrak past the elegant **Beurs Van Berlage 2** (p64), designed by HP Berlage, founder of the Amsterdam School of architecture. Heading southeast along Oude Brugsteeg, you'll hit **Warmoesstraat 3**, where you can sample the city's wild side. If this is too much for you, turn back now! The venerable **Oude Kerk 4** (p65) is your gateway to the Red Light District proper. At the corner on Oudezijds Voorburgwal is the **Prostitution Information Centre 5** (p68), where you can pick up maps to your desires or see what a sex-worker's quarters look like from the inside (without paying for the sex worker, but please do leave a donation for the centre). North from here is the **Museum Amstelkring 6** (p67), with its clandestine Catholic church on the top floor. A jump over to the Oudezijds Achterburgwal and then south takes you past the low-key **Erotic Museum 7** (p67), the famous **Casa Rosso 8** (p66) erotic theatre, and the **Hash and Marijuana Museum 9** (p67).

Back up near the Erotic Museum, cross the canal and head east toward the **Guan Yin Shrine 10** (p74), and a good place to break for Chinese lunch or dinner along the Zeedijk

Walking & Cycling Tours   RED LIGHT RAMBLE

WALK FACTS

Start/End The Dam
Distance 4.5km
Time Three hours

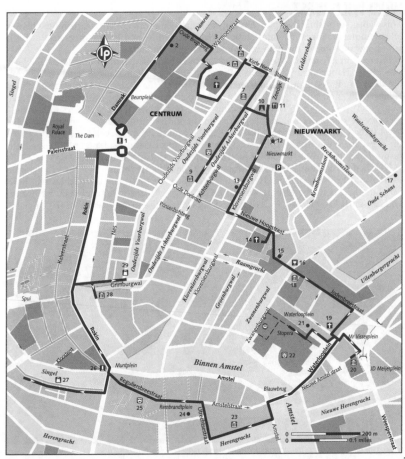

at **Nam Kee 11** (p135) or one of its compatriots. In Nieuwmarkt Square you'll find the historic and multitowered **Waag 12** (Weigh House; p78). Heading south from Nieuwmarkt, along Kloveniersburgwal, note the impossibly narrow **Kleine Trippenhuis 13**. Nieuwe Hoogstraat leads you to the elegant **Zuiderkerk 14** (p79), with the 17th-century **Pintohuis 15** (now a library; p77) nearly opposite.

Across the Oude Schans, **De Sluyswacht 16** (p156) makes an ideal beer break, with a classic view of the canal and the **Montelbaanstoren 17** (p40). The **Museum Het Rembrandthuis 18** (p76) is across the street. A sweep down Jodenbreestraat takes you past the **Mozes en Aäronkerk 19** (p75); 100m southeast is the **Joods (Jewish) Historisch Museum 20** (p75). The **Waterlooplein market 21** (p190) faces the **Stopera 22** (p78), which doubles as both opera house and city hall; check out the market before crossing the bridge Blauwbrug.

Stop at the charming **Museum Willet-Holthuysen 23** (p94) on the Herengracht. Turn right onto Utrechtsestraat toward **Rembrandtplein 24** (plenty of cafés here). Head northwest along Reguliersbreestraat, past the Art Nouveau **Tuschinskitheater 25** (p178) and the **Munttoren 26** (p42). The **Bloemenmarkt 27** (floating flower market; p91) is just the other side of the Singel, or head back toward the city centre on the wide street, the Rokin, to the right. Cross the Amstel to the **Allard Pierson Museum 28** (p64) and its antiquities, inspect the **jewellery shops 29** (p187) of Grimburgwal, then return to the Dam via Rokin.

WILD WILD WEST

This walk is surprisingly simple – basically a straight shot through the Haarlemmer Quarter (Haarlemmerstraat and its continuations Haarlemmerdijk and Haarlemmerweg) – but it will show you some of the newest, up-and-coming destinations in town.

From Centraal Station, head across Stationsplein and open harbour and across the busy street Prins Hendrikkade. Stop at **News Photo 1** (p69) to see photography literally taken from the day's headlines. Exit and head left (west), around the corner of Martelaarsgracht to Nieuwendijk, and turn right. Once you cross the Singel you'll be on Haarlemmerstraat. You won't need any help from us finding interesting sights, shops and cafés to browse – there are new ones opening all the time. Some of our favourites are the former head of the West India Company, **Westindisch Huis 2** (p80), the gourmet shop **Meeuwig & Zn 3** (p195) across the street, the grunge-plush coffeeshop **Barney's 4** (p166), **Unlimited Delicious 5** (p195) for adventurous bonbons and **5th Place Shirts & Juices 6**, as eclectic as its name implies.

Haarlemmerdijk ends at the **Haarlemmerpoort 7** (an old guardhouse that's been converted to housing) before becoming Haarlemmerweg. Stay on the right side of the street here. To your right is the handsome **Westerpark 8**. It's a great place to take a break, but wait if you can until you get to the city's newest showplace, the **Westergasfabriek 9** (p83), opened

Soak up the sunshine at one of the many outdoor cafés in Rembrandtplein, Southern Canal Belt

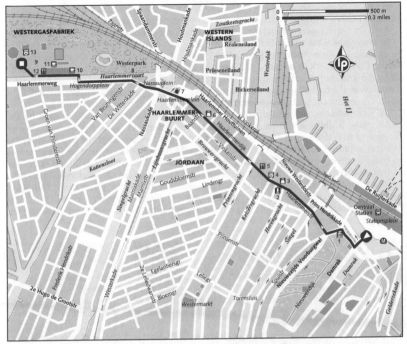

2005. If it looks like an old gasworks, that's because it was, but inside this complex you'll find cafés like **De Bakkerswinkel 10** and **Espressofabriek 11**, a lovely open meadow with a long pool to dangle your feet in, the café-restaurant **Pacific Parc 12** (p138), a court for korfball and the nightspot **Westergasterras 13** (p168).

You can walk back if you like (connect with our walking tour, the **Veddy Civilised Western Canals** (p118) at Westindisch Huis), otherwise you can catch bus No 46 along Haarlemmerweg back to Centraal Station.

CYCLING TOURS

ARCHITECTURE OF THE EASTERN DOCKLANDS

This tour endeavours to give you all of Amsterdam's most interesting contemporary architecture in one fell swoop. As many of these are private housing you won't be able to enter them, but they're still worthwhile for their exteriors.

From Centraal Station (main entrance), bear left past the bus stops to Oosterdokskade, where you'll see the Post CS building, the temporary home of the **Stedelijk Museum 1** (p114). Cross the narrow bridge (you may have to dismount here) to **Nemo 2** (p114), the science centre built on the entrance to the IJ-Tunnel.

Keeping Nemo on your left, head south toward Prins Hendrikkade, turn left and soon you'll come to **Arcam 3** (p112), the architecture resource centre and exhibition space where you can pick up detailed information on pretty much any building in town, particularly contemporary ones. From Arcam, bear left toward Kattenburgerstraat, where you'll pass the **Scheepvaartmuseum 4** (p113), maritime museum (not contemporary but very worthwhile).

Turn left when you reach Piet Heinkade, and the large building before you reach the water is the **Muziekgebouw aan 't IJ 5** (p113), well worth a visit or a beer overlooking the IJ at the Star Ferry Café. Continue back (east) along Piet Heinkade, and bear left onto Oostelijks Handelskade. The landmark **Lloyd Hotel 6** (p228) will be on your right; take a moment to explore the lobby bar and shop. Continue east to the intersection of C van Eesterenlaan and turn right. Turn left at the basketball court on Borneolaan (you're now on Borneo Island) and right again at the first corner (Blauwpijpstraat) which runs into Borneokade. Turn left.

As you pedal, across the shipping channel you'll see former warehouses used by the cocoa trade, while closer in are large yachts and commercial vessels. But once you round the end of the island onto Stokerkade, you'll get a good view across the former shipping channel to **Scheepstimmermanstraat 7**, a fascinating collection of houses where owners were free to build to their designs, making it the most colourful and diverse group of houses in this district. You can cross the little footbridge in the middle of the channel to see the homes from the front (although they're more interesting from the water side). You won't be able to ride your bike across the **red footbridge 8** – you'll barely be able to walk it – but it certainly demands a look-see. Take a left on Stuurmankade and head west. Take the flat bridge at Kwartermeesterstraat.

FIETS, DON'T FAIL ME NOW!

In Dutch, a bicycle is called a *rijwiel*, or to its friends, a *fiets*. Cyclists are called *fietsers*, a term we adore.

Cycling is our favourite way to explore the city. Although the distances in town are not extreme, saving 20 minutes between venues can buy you time to take in a few more sights each day. Plus, you'll feel like a native: sling your shopping bag from the Albert Heijn over the handlebars, hold on to the grip with one hand and your sandwich or mobile phone with the other, and you'll fit right in.

Don't bother bringing your bike from home. Your 21-speed racer with handbrakes and toe clips will get you attention, all right: (1) for its dashing looks and (2) for the pity you'll receive when it's stolen. Amsterdam's bike of choice seems to be the Gazelle, a gearless, Dutch-made dearie with pedal brakes and – most importantly – a bell. The more trashed the better. And what is this thing you call a 'helmet'? There are plenty of rental shops to set you up (p249); some lodgings also rent bikes.

It all sounds like fun, and indeed it can be, but there are some important rules of the road. So, if we may beg a few moments of your kind attention…

- There are 400km of bike paths in Amsterdam. Use them. You can identify them by signage and they are a different colour (reddish) from the road or the footpaths. Bike paths have their own dedicated traffic signals. Use those too.
- Watch for cars. Cyclists have the right of way, except when vehicles are entering from the right. However, that doesn't mean motorists are as careful as they should be.
- Watch for pedestrians too. Tourists (the poor things) tend to wander in and out of bike paths with no idea of the danger they're putting themselves in.
- The international 'no' sign with a picture of a bike on it (or a blue sign with pedestrians) means you need to walk your bike. If it reads *'fietsers afstappen'* (cyclists dismount), they're putting it in no uncertain terms. If there's a 'no-entry' sign and below it a sign with a picture of a bike and the word *'uitgezonderd'* (except), you may ride through. These are usually streets that are one way for cars. Construction sites are almost always no-biking zones.
- When approaching tram tracks, be careful. If your wheels get caught, you'll probably fall and it will hurt! Position your wheels as perpendicular to the tracks as possible.
- By law, after dusk you need to use the lights on your bike (front and rear) and have reflectors on both wheels. If your bike does not have lights, you need to use clip-on lights, both front and rear.
- It's polite to give a quick ring of your bell as a warning. If someone's about to hit you, a good sharp yell is highly effective.
- Chain your bike securely. Most bikes come with two locks, one for the front wheel (attach it to the frame) and the other for the back. One lock should also attach to something stationary.
- You'll see plenty of locals disobeying these rules, but that does not make it smart. Theoretically you could jump off a bridge and survive that too.
- Finally, weather: wind and rain are all too familiar features in Holland. A lightweight nylon jacket and cycling trousers or shorts will provide protection, but be sure to use a variety that 'breathes'. On other than warm days, a woollen cap or balaclava is a good idea to keep your ears from freezing.

The bridge deposits you by the 1999 **Whale 9** apartment building, the landmark of Sporenburg Island. Its sloping roof and base make it seem even more imposing than its dozen storeys would suggest, but also somehow more open and airy. Taking a short ride to the left, followed by a right turn, puts you on the Verbindingsdam to KNSM Island, named for the Royal Netherlands Shipping Company.

Once over the bridge, follow the bike path to the right and Levantkade. The heavy black buildings on the left are the stark **Piraeus 10** housing complex by Hans Kollhoff and Christian Rapp. Head around the inlet at Levantplein, and you'll see Bruno Albert's **Barcelonaplein 11** with its wrought-iron 'gate' spanning the entire height of the façade. Continue on Levantkade to the end and the 1996 **Venetië 12** housing complex.

From Venetië, head west along KNSM-Laan. The apartment buildings on the right are named for Greek philosophers, giving a whole new meaning to 'neoclassical'. The driveways of these buildings can take you through to the IJ, though the surface is not as smooth and you may prefer to stay on KNSM-Laan. Either route will take you to **Azartplein 13**, from where you can catch the bike path through the residential neighbourhood, parallel to Sumatrakade – take care at intersections, as cars may be crossing. The bike path provides your best views yet of what it feels like to live in these communities, with kids playing and locals localising.

The path ends near the **Jan Schaeferbrug 14**, the bridge named for an activist city councillor who famously said 'You can't live in claptrap', which about summarises this whole experience. You can take the bridge back toward Piet Heinkade (turn right and it eventually drops you at Centraal Station), or, for more fun and better views, you can dogleg to the right and take the journey back by **ferry 15** (€1, two or three times per hour); the pier is just across from Sumatrakade 1389.

CYCLE FACTS

Start/End Centraal Station
Distance 12km
Time Two hours

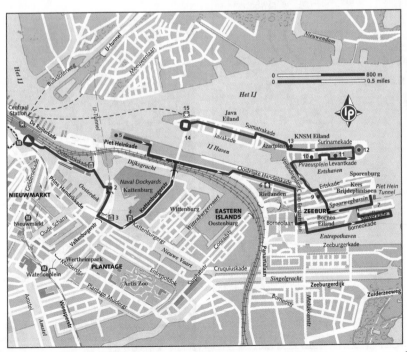

VILLAGES OF THE AMSTEL

This attractive, convenient route begins in the southern suburb of Amstelveen and takes in the Amstel River and some unexpectedly bucolic surrounds.

Leave from the **Amstelpark 1**, a pretty municipal park, about 300m south of the A10 motorway. Cycling isn't allowed in the park, which has a rose garden, an open-air theatre, cafés and other facilities.

A couple of kilometres south, along the quiet east bank of the Amstel, is **Ouderkerk aan de Amstel 2**, a pretty, affluent village (actually a few centuries older than Amsterdam) with plenty of riverside cafés and handsome houses.

At Ouderkerk, cross the bridge over the Bullewijk River and turn left (east) opposite the ancient Jewish cemetery, following the right bank of the Bullewijk. You pass under the A9 motorway, and 1km further on, at a spot with a pleasant restaurant, the Waver River comes in from the right (south) – follow that. You'll have great views of **De Ronde Hoep 3**, a wild, sparsely populated peat area drained by settlers about 1000 years ago. It attracts many birds, impervious to Amsterdam's skyscrapers looming in the distance. The Waver narrows and becomes the Oude Waver, and when you come to the two hand-operated bridges, you'll clearly see that the land is below sea level.

At the southwesternmost part of the route lies a squat riverside **bunker 4**, one of 38 defensive forts built around Amsterdam

CYCLE FACTS

Start/End Amstelpark
Distance 30km
Time Three to four hours

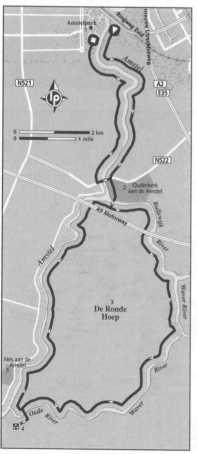

Boats on the Amstel River

at the turn of the 20th century (and outmoded by the 1920s). Here you rejoin the Amstel and turn right (north), following the eastern bank back toward Amstelveen. Just north of here, the village of **Nes aan de Amstel 5**, across the river, has some delightful wooden, café-filled terraces – admire them from a distance, as there's no bridge close by.

Crossing north under the A9, the final leg of the journey provides a view of the western edges of Amsterdam-Zuidoost. You could continue past Ouderkerk and return the way you came, along the east bank of the Amstel, but an interesting diversion takes you across the bridge at Ouderkerk to the west bank and around the fringes of the green Amstelland area, with oodles of all-too-cute garden allotments. The Amstelpark lies just to the north.

A DAM GOOD BIKE RIDE

This trip through the eastern half of the Waterland region, north of Amsterdam, is culture-shock material: 20 minutes from the centre of Amsterdam, but back a couple of centuries, with isolated farming communities and flocks of birds amid ditches, dykes and lakes.

Take the free Buiksloterweg ferry from behind Centraal Station across the IJ, then continue 1km along the west bank of the Noordhollands Kanaal. Do a loop onto and over the second bridge, continue along the east bank for a few hundred metres and turn right, under the freeway and along Nieuwendammerdijk past the Vliegenbos camping ground. At the end of Nieuwen-dammerdijk, do a dog-leg and continue along Schellingwouderdijk. Follow this under the two major road bridges, when it becomes Durgerdammerdijk, and you're on your way.

CYCLE FACTS

Start/End Centraal Station
Distance 37km (55km including Marken and Volendam)
Time Four to five hours (seven to ten hours including Marken and Volendam)

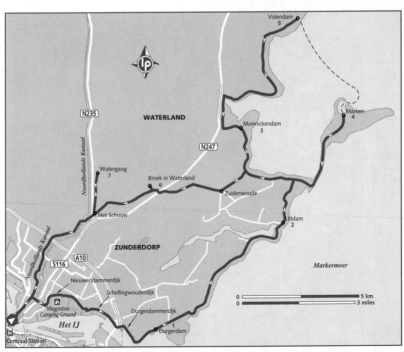

The pretty town of **Durgerdam 1**, spread along the dyke, looks out across the water to IJburg, a major land-reclamation project that will be home to 45,000 people in a few years' time. Further north, the dyke road passes several lakes and former sea inlets – low-lying, drained peat lands that were flooded during storms and now form important bird-breeding areas. Colonies include plovers, godwits, bitterns, goldeneyes, snipes, herons and spoonbills. Climb the dyke at one of the viewing points for uninterrupted views to both sides.

The road – now called Uitdammerdijk – passes the town of **Uitdam 2**, after which you turn left (west) towards **Monnickendam 3**, with its many old fishing homes and 15th-century church. Alternatively, you could turn right and proceed along the causeway to the former island of **Marken 4**, a one-time fishing community in an impressive setting, with houses on piles. After visiting Marken, you could take the summer ferry (one way adult/child €4/3, 30 minutes, ☯ 11.30am to 6pm, every 30 to 45 minutes April to mid-November) to **Volendam 5**. This picturesque former fishing port has reinvented itself as a tourist town – there are fewer tourists in the pretty streets behind the harbour. From Volendam, backtrack along the sea dyke to Monnickendam, or return over the causeway from Marken and rejoin the tour towards Monnickendam.

After visiting Monnickendam, return the way you came, but about 1.5km south of Monnickendam, turn right (southwest) towards Zuiderwoude. From there, continue to **Broek in Waterland 6**, a pretty town with old, wooden houses. Then cycle along the south bank of the Broekervaart canal towards Het Schouw on the Noordhollands Kanaal. Bird-watchers may want to head up the east bank towards **Watergang 7** and its bird-breeding areas. Otherwise, cross the Noordhollands Kanaal (the bridge is slightly to the north) and follow the west bank back down to Amsterdam Noord; it's straight cycling all the way to the ferry to Centraal Station.

Eating

Eating

Even if Amsterdam is not the food mecca that other European capitals are, there's a great diversity of choice. Italian, French, Indonesian, Thai and Chinese are commonplace, and sushi, Indian and Turkish are gaining in popularity. Plus there are some cuisines you may never have heard of (eg Surinamese) that may pleasantly surprise you. And don't neglect traditional Dutch cooking: while it may not be high cuisine, here you have the unique opportunity to try it.

One of the best things about dining in Amsterdam is the design of its restaurants. From the sumptuous interiors of the city's supper clubs, to places that wear their history like a fine suit, or just convivial canalside seating, you can feast your eyes as well as your stomach.

It's quite common for fine-dining restaurants to change menus seasonally, if not daily. Where we have listed individual dishes, they're either something that is always on the menu or a reference to give you an idea of the creativity of the cuisine. Most restaurants have a few vegetarian choices.

For a look at different cuisines available in Amsterdam, see p16.

Opening Hours

Dinner, the main meal of the day, is usually served between 6pm and 10pm, although some restaurants may serve an hour or so earlier or later. Most places that refer to themselves as restaurants (as opposed to cafés) open only for dinner, and popular places fill up by 7pm. Alternatively you could try arriving late: films and concerts usually start between 8.30pm and 9.30pm, and tables may become available then for a 'second sitting'.

Many kitchens close by 10pm (though the bars and dining rooms may stay open longer); vegetarian restaurants tend to close even earlier. Late at night, a smattering of restaurants are still open around Leidseplein, and falafel or pizza joints city-wide.

For lunch, your best bets are cafés (see the Entertainment chapter). They're everywhere, and meals tend to be reliable, though not life-changing – soups, sandwiches, salads etc. Many open as early as 10am, and the standard time for serving lunch is 11am to 2.30pm; cafés have the added bonus of staying open late (though usually not their kitchens) and being great places to hang out. Many places listed as serving lunch may also stay open until late afternoon.

Breakfast before 10am can be problematic. Unless your hotel serves breakfast, you may need to wait until the cafés open, or find a bakery.

Many restaurants are open daily; otherwise the most popular closing days are Sunday and Monday. During the busiest tourist months of July and (especially) August, some restaurants go on holiday or operate at reduced hours, so phone ahead to avoid disappointment.

How Much?

Amsterdam used to be known as one of Western Europe's least-expensive capitals. It remains reasonable by comparison to some other places (hello, London and Paris), but prices have gone up significantly – particularly, locals complain, since the introduction of the euro.

TOP FIVE EAT STREETS

- **Utrechtsestraat** (p142) Hands down our favourite dining street.
- **Negen Straatjes** (p139) A great place to browse for clothing or lunch, home wares or dinner.
- **Haarlemmerstraat** (p136) This newly trendy strip on the way out of town has some cool new spots and is within striking distance of some not-so-new spots.
- **Leidseplein and surrounds** (p142) Included for quantity if not necessarily quality. There's absolutely everything here, prices are reasonable, and it's minutes' walk from entertainment.
- **Albert Cuypstraat** (p146) West of the famous market you'll find an unparalleled assortment of exotic choices including Cambodian, Kurdish and Surinamese.

Lunch prices range from €2.50 for a simple cheese sandwich to €10 for a more elaborate salad; most sandwiches are under €5. Main courses at moderate restaurants run between €8 and €18 (lunch or dinner). To keep costs down, look for restaurants serving a *dagschotel* (dish of the day). For the heartier appetite, many restaurants offer the *dagmenu*, a set menu of three or more courses for around €9 to €15 for lunch and from about €20 for dinner. Except at top-end restaurants, it's rare to see a main course above €27.50 (usually something like lobster) or a four-course menu above €50. Main-course servings are usually generous.

We find breakfast overpriced: at a café, you can expect to pay upwards of €5 for coffee, something baked and maybe some orange juice. If your hotel doesn't serve breakfast, buy something the night before (see Self-Catering), or for an occasion you can splurge at a fabulous hotel buffet. At bakeries, muffins and croissants start from about €0.80. Takeaway shops and stands have specialities (sandwiches, fish etc) from around €1.75.

A beer will generally set you back around €2; nonalcoholic drinks are slightly less. House wines by the glass are generally €3 to €5, although the sky's the limit on full bottles – bottles that cost €4.50 in the shops can sell for up to €20 in a café or restaurant.

Many restaurants do *not* accept credit cards; check in advance.

Booking Tables

Virtually everyone speaks English very well, and except at the busiest upper-crust restaurants, booking a table is rarely a problem. Apart from Fridays and Saturdays, a simple phone call a day or two before your arrival should do the trick. Seating at most cafés is first-come-first-served.

Tipping

If you're from a 'service-with-a-smile' kind of society, service in Amsterdam may strike you as inattentive, impersonal, off-putting and just plain slow.

Our advice: (1) don't take it personally – it's not directed at you; and (2) turn it to your advantage. If it's taking forever for your main course to arrive, savour the delicate bouquet of your beer. If you and your friends have to wait an eternity for the bill, just be *gezellig* – you're enjoying each other's company, so what's the problem?

Service is included in the bill, but unless your server does something truly rude, inept or egregious, a modest tip is in order. A good guideline is to round up to the next number, around 5%; 10% is considered very generous. In practical terms, if your bill comes to €9.50, you can leave €10; if it's €14.75, round up to €15.50. Tax is always figured into the bill before it's presented to you.

If you're paying by credit card or need change, state the amount you want to pay, including tip, as you hand your payment to your server (this will usually elicit a proper 'thank you'!). Credit-card users: note that servers generally appreciate being tipped in cash – in some restaurants they do not receive tips until after the credit-card payment has cleared.

TOP FIVE TAKEAWAYS

Some of these even have seating areas:

- **Pasta di Mamma** (p143) Country Italian for a getaway in the Vondelpark.
- **Small World Catering** (p139) Tiny though well-regarded catering shop in the Haarlemmer Quarter.
- **Turkiye** (p149) Turkish takeaway in De Pijp.
- **Uliveto** (p145) Eat in, take away or take a class.
- **Waroeng Asje** (p147) Comfy Indonesian in the Old West.

Self-Catering

Amsterdam is blessed with a number of excellent takeaway shops (*traiteurs*; literally, 'caterers'). The current trend is mostly Mediterranean, but you will also find Middle Eastern and Indonesian. Department stores like De Bijenkorf (p188) and Vroom & Dreesman (p191) have worthwhile cafeterias. The chains Volendamer Vishandel (fish, sandwiches, snacks and more) and Bakkerij Bart (bakers) can be found in large shopping complexes such as Marie Heinekenplein in De Pijp and Brazilië in the Eastern Docklands. AH To Go has branches in heavy-traffic areas.

Among supermarkets, Albert Heijn is the most prominent (look for the white logo that looks something like a bow, on a blue background), although a tad expensive. Less-expensive supermarkets include Dirk van den Broek (on Marie Heinekenplein), Edah and Aldi. In the Eastern Docklands you'll find the C1000 Supermarket. Farmers markets are held throughout town (p190).

The chain Gall & Gall sells alcohol; you can usually find it adjacent to Albert Heijn supermarkets. Check out speciality shops Arnold Cornelis (p193) and Hart's Wijnhandel (p199) for fine wines, and De Bierkoning (p188) for an amazing selection of beers.

TOP FIVE RESTAURANT VIEWS

- **De Belhamel** (p140) In summer, try for an outdoor table overlooking the canal: you'll have the beautiful Browersgracht alongside you and the handsome Herengracht at your feet.
- **11** (p151) Panoramic views from the city's only skyscraper, also the temporary location of the Stedelijk.
- **La Rive** (p142) As if two Michelin stars weren't enough, this restaurant at the Intercontinental Hotel sits right on the Amstel for riverfront views.
- **M Café** (p143) Drink in the views from the top floor of the Metz & Co department store on the Keizersgracht.
- **Sea Palace** (p151) This floating Chinese restaurant is pleasing on the eye, and pleasing on the IJ.

MEDIEVAL CENTRE

The city centre offers everything from supremely elegant Dutch cuisine to the hippest restaurants and DJ clubs. Some of the highest-end places are where you'd least expect them, such as the Red Light District.

D'Vijff Vlieghen restaurant on Spuistraat

BLAUW AAN DE WAL

Map pp286-7   International

☎ 330 22 57; Oudezijds Achterburgwal 99; mains €24-27, 3-course menu €40; ☾ dinner Mon-Sat

Oasis, rose among thorns, minor miracle: a long, often graffiti-covered hallway in the middle of the Red Light District leads you to a place of unexpected refinement. Originally a 17th-century herb warehouse, the whitewashed, exposed brick, multilevel space still features old steel weights and measures, plus friendly, knowledgeable service and contemporary French- and Italian-inspired cooking. In summer, grab a table in the romantic garden.

D'VIJFF VLIEGHEN

Map pp286-7   Contemporary Dutch

☎ 530 40 60; www.thefiveflies.com; Spuistraat 294-302; mains €20-28, set menus from €39; ☾ dinner

So what if every tourist and business visitor eats here? Sometimes the herd gets it right. The Five Flies is a classic, spread out over five 17th-century canal houses. Old-wood dining rooms teem with character, Delft tiles and works by Rembrandt and Breitner. Some chairs have brass plates commemorating celebrities who've sat in them, but you don't have to be famous to receive silver service and chichi contemporary Dutch food.

DE KEUKEN VAN 1870

Map pp286-7   Traditional Dutch

☎ 620 40 18; Spuistraat 4; mains €6.50-14, 3-course menu €7.50; 🕐 lunch & dinner Mon-Sat

Thanks to a recent redo, you'd never guess that this central and smart-looking place was once a restaurant for the poor. It still keeps up that heritage, though, with decent cooking (think *stamppot* or couscous) at exceedingly decent prices. If you know a better three-course meal in town for the price, tell us, though we doubt it's possible.

GETTO Map pp286-7   International

☎ 421 51 51; Warmoesstraat 51; mains €10.50-14.50; 🕐 dinner Tue-Sun

Getto's fab-trashy, disco-pad interior is a great place to chill while you indulge in a few cocktails, a burger or the cranberry crumble. There are cool tunes, a lounge room in the back, customers from twinks to leather boys, and some of Warmoesstraat's best people-watching.

GREEN PLANET Map pp286-7   Vegetarian

☎ 625 82 80; Spuistraat 122; mains €10-16.50, sandwiches & salads €6-10; 🕐 dinner Mon-Sat

This modern veggie eatery cares…about your health, biodegradable packaging, peace, love and decent food. Come for a soup, salad, antipasto or cake. Mains include goulash, dumplings and Indian masala.

HAESJE CLAES

Map pp286-7   Traditional Dutch

☎ 624 99 98; www.haesjeclaes.nl; Spuistraat 273-275; mains €13.30-20, set menus from €28.50; 🕐 lunch & dinner

Haesje Claes' warm surrounds, with lots of dark wooden panelling and antique knick-knacks, is just the place to sample comforting pea soup and endive *stamppot*. The fish starter has a great sampling of Dutch fishes. This restaurant gets lots of tourists, but with good reason.

KAM YIN Map pp286-7   Surinamese/Chinese

☎ 625 31 15; Warmoesstraat 6-8; mains €4-15 (most under €10); 🕐 lunch & dinner

There is zero atmosphere, and it may even be a bit dingy around the edges, but this bustling place is filled with ethnic Surinamese who know what's good: curries, plates of roast chicken, lamb or pork etc. Wash it down with Chinese tea or a can of coconut juice.

LUCIUS Map pp286-7   Seafood

☎ 624 18 31; Spuistraat 247; mains €17.50-28, set menus €35; 🕐 dinner

Simple, delicious and simply delicious, Lucius is known for fresh ingredients and for not mucking them up with lots of sauce and spice. The interior, all fish tanks and tiles, is workmanlike and professional, just like the service.

ORIENTAL CITY Map pp286-7   Chinese

☎ 626 83 52; Oudezijds Voorburgwal 177-179; mains €8.50-24, dim sum €2.50-4.50; 🕐 lunch & dinner

This huge Hong Kong–style restaurant with the requisite red lanterns is always lively. Join gaggles of local Chinese for daily dim sum (11.30am to 4.30pm; we like the meaty, flavoursome *cha sieuw bao* pork buns) and a 24-page menu (!) of classic Canto cuisine.

PANNENKOEKENHUIS UPSTAIRS

Map pp286-7   Contemporary Dutch

☎ 626 56 03; Grimburgwal 2; mains €4-10; 🕐 noon-5pm

Climb some of the steepest stairs in town to reach this small-as-a-stamp restaurant. The lure? Pancakes that are flavoursome, inexpensive (most under €7.50) and filling. We like the one with bacon, cheese and ginger. It's a one-man show, so service operates at its own pace.

TOP FIVE MEDIEVAL CENTRE DINING

- **Blauw aan de Wal** (opposite) Sophisticated French dining in a most unexpected place.
- **Lucius** (above) Fish and seafood prepared simply in an understated setting.
- **Supper Club** (p134) For when dinner has to be a scene.
- **d' Vijff Vlieghen** (opposite) Everyone visits this old line Dutch place, with good reason.
- **Vlaams Friteshuis** (p135) Because everyone should try Flemish-style fries once (or twice, or three times…).

SUITE Map pp286-7 International

☎ 344 64 06; www.suite.nu; Sint Nicolaasstraat 43; dishes €3-8, 6-course 'surprise' menu €32.50; ☾ dinner Tue-Sun, plus Mon Sep-May

The folks who brought you Supper Club have opened this more sedate 'rest-o-bar' in a rambling suite of rooms: think a salon with fish tank and cat, or the lounge room, a chill space with embroidered sofas, hassocks and still-lifes. Dishes are eclectic small plates, from rib eye in tomato sauce to Vietnamese spring rolls and watermelon soup.

SUPPER CLUB

Map pp286-7 Contemporary Dutch

☎ 638 05 13; www.supperclub.nl; Jonge Roelensteeg 21; 5-course menu €65; ☾ dinner

If you're looking for a scene, you've found one. Enter the theatrical, all-white room, snuggle up on enormous mattresses and snack on platters of victuals as DJs spin platters of house music, then head upstairs later to dance. Even if the food and service are so-so and the prices are expensive (mitigating factor: you don't need to pay club admission later), it's an experience that's hard to forget. The crew applies the same concept to a boat trip on the IJ with **Supper Club Cruise**, which leaves from dock 14 behind Centraal Station.

VILLA ZEEZICHT Map pp286-7 Café

☎ 626 74 33; Torensteeg 7; mains €3-21; ☾ breakfast, lunch & dinner

Although you *could* try sandwiches and pastas here, half the patrons seem to be eating the famous apple pie. For €4.40 you get a mountain of apples dusted in cinnamon, surrounded by warm pastry and fresh cream. In warm weather, they set up tables on the bridge over the Singel. Drawback: since everyone seems to know that the pie is famous, the staff sometimes act accordingly superior.

CHEAP EATS

DOLORES Map pp286-7 Organic

☎ 620 33 02; Nieuwezijds Voorburgwal; mains €2.50-8.70; ☾ lunch & afternoon

Biologische (organic) is the name of the game at this tiny shop, which resembles a kiddie train station in the traffic island. Try organic burgers, *tostis*, chicken and *frites*. Service has been known to take its time, but it is fun to watch the world go by at the picnic-table seating outdoors. It is on Nieuwezijds Voorburgwal, opposite No 289.

DUTCH FOUR Map pp286-7 Sandwich Shop

☎ 626 33 88; Zoutsteeg 6; sandwiches €2.30-4.30; ☾ breakfast & lunch

This three-table shop has a 20-year history, a kindly owner, immaculate fresh fish and a great, central location – a quiet refuge from the madness of Damrak.

KANTJIL TO GO Map pp292-3 Indonesian

☎ 620 09 94; www.kantjil.nl; Nieuwezijds Voorburgwal 342; combos €3.50-6.50; ☾ lunch & dinner

The large Kantjil en de Tijger restaurant (Spuistraat 291–293) has a spotty reputation for sit-down meals, but everyone seems to agree that its new takeaway shop is a good deal. Cobble your own combo from rice, noodle, meat and veggie options.

VAN DEN BERG'S BROODJESBAR

Map pp286-7 Sandwich Shop

☎ 622 83 56; Zoutsteeg 4; sandwiches €1.60-4.45; ☾ 9am-6pm Mon-Fri

Tiny, friendly, clean, family-run and utterly without pretension, you can linger over the newspaper and commune with local office people. Our favourite sandwich is the *gehakt*, thin slices of a giant meatball, served warm and eaten with killer-hot mustard.

SEE ALSO

- **Café Dante** (p158) Popular for its café scene and also for its art gallery.
- **Café De Jaren** (p158) Multi-level space with drop-dead views of the inner Amstel.
- **De Brakke Grond** (p161) Restaurant at the Flemish Cultural Centre.
- **De Schutter** (p156) Ever-popular student café. Cheap, cheap, cheap.
- **De Sluyswacht** (p156) Historic watch-house that looks like it's listing in the wind.
- **Luxembourg** (p158) One of the grandest grand cafés, facing the Spui.
- **Winter Garden** at Grand Hotel Krasnapolsky (p216) Have brunch in a national landmark.

VLAAMS FRITESHUIS

Map pp292-3   Takeaway

☎ 624 60 75; Voetboogstraat 33; small/large €1.50/1.90, sauces €0.40; ⏲ 11am-6pm Tue-Sat, noon-6pm Sun & Mon

At this hole-in-the-wall takeaway off the Spui, join queues of locals for Amsterdam's best-loved *frites* (french fries). The standard is smothered in mayonnaise, though you can ask for ketchup, peanut sauce or choose from a variety of spicy mayos including our favourite, with green peppercorns. It's been an institution since 1887.

NIEUWMARKT

Amsterdam's liveliest square (and one of its loveliest) and its surrounds brim with restaurants, of which we can only list a sample. Two highlights: the little Chinatown in and around Zeedijk, and the kosher restaurants around the old Jewish quarter.

CAFÉ BERN Map pp286-7   Swiss

☎ 622 00 34; Nieuwmarkt 9; mains €9-14; ⏲ dinner

Indulge in a fondue frenzy at this delightfully well-worn brown café. People have been flocking here for nearly 30 years for the gruyère fondue as well as the entrecôte. Note: it's generally closed for a large part of the summer, but do you really want fondue in hot weather anyway? Reservations advised.

HEMELSE MODDER

Map pp290-1   Contemporary Dutch

☎ 624 32 03; Oude Waal 9; mains €16, 3-/4-/5-course menus €26/29/32; ⏲ dinner

A little hard to locate, but worth it. Extraordinary care goes into dishes – you might find pot-au-feu with chicken or polenta soufflé – and you may even find a sprig of mint in your carafe of water. Desserts are wonderful, including the namesake *hemelse modder* (heavenly mud) chocolate mousse. The dining room is spare yet comfy, or snag a table out back on a warm night.

KING SOLOMON Map pp290-1   Kosher

☎ 625 58 60; Waterlooplein 239; mains €14-22; ⏲ lunch & dinner except Jewish Sabbath & holidays

Close your eyes and you could be in Tel Aviv, thanks to the Hebrew-speaking staff and patrons, informality, streetside seating and, of course, food. Try the veal schnitzel, as well as small plates including hummus, falafel and gefilte fish imported from the Holy Land. It's right near many sights of Jewish interest.

KRUA THAI Map pp292-3   Thai

☎ 622 95 33; Staalstraat 22; mains €6.75-25, set menus €19.50-23; ⏲ dinner Tue-Sun

Top-shelf soups, duck or shrimp curries, and noodle dishes are the order of the day at this sophisticated restaurant with bright art. Note: some locals refer to it by its old name, Tom Yam. A pre-theatre menu is available.

NAM KEE Map pp286-7   Chinese

☎ 624 34 70; www.namkee.net; Zeedijk 113-116; mains €6-16.50; ⏲ lunch & dinner

It won't win any design awards, but year in, year out, Nam Kee's the most popular Chinese spot in town. And why not: there's good roast anything, and service is snappy. A new, fancier location has opened at Geldersekade 117 (Map pp286–7).

NEW KING Map pp286-7   Chinese

☎ 625 21 80; www.newking.nl; Zeedijk 115; mains €4-16; ⏲ lunch & dinner

If you want Chinese on the Zeedijk but don't want to feel like you're slumming it, New King is about the fanciest on the block. The roast meats may have you asking 'how much is that duckie in the window?' (€24 with the full service of different courses.)

CHEAP EATS

STERK STAALTJE Map pp292-3   Takeaway

☎ 624 9065; Staalstraat 12; prices vary; ⏲ lunch

Squarely between the Amstel, the Red Light District and Nieuwmarkt is this handsome, *rustique* takeaway shop with lasagne, savoury pies, and lovely olives and cheeses. Lunch will set you back about €5.

VILLAGE BAGELS

Maps pp292-3   Sandwich Shop

☎ 427 22 13; Vijzelstraat 139; bagel sandwiches €2.95-5.10; ⏲ breakfast & lunch

The shop that brought bagel-chic to Amsterdam is still going strong. You may feel like a New Yorker as you dive into a bagel with salmon, chive cream cheese and capers, especially if you grab the newspaper, but you'll know you're in Amsterdam sitting on the canalside terrace at the Stromarkt branch (Map pp286–7; ☎ 528 91 52; Stromarkt 2).

JORDAAN & WESTERN ISLANDS

The restaurants of this western part of the city centre are typified by the conviviality that has long been a hallmark of the Jordaan, and Haarlemmerstraat and its surrounds have become cool virtually overnight. It will be tempting to lose your way in the narrow backstreets. Let it happen, and you may discover the next hot spot.

BALTHAZAR'S KEUKEN

Map p285   French-Mediterranean
☎ 420 21 14; Elandsgracht 108; 3-course set menu €25; ☿ dinner Wed-Fri

Consistently one of Amsterdam's top-rated restaurants. Don't expect a wide-ranging menu – the byword is basically 'whatever we have on hand', but whatever they have is reliably delicious. Plus, there's a modern-rustic look and attentive service. Reservations recommended.

BLENDER   French-Mediterranean

☎ 486 98 60; Van der Palmkade 16; mains €19.50-22; ☿ dinner daily, lunch Sat & Sun

Way out west, Blender's cheeky, curvy, 1970s airport-lounge interior (think lots of orange swivel chairs) is just the place to sip cocktails, sample inventive French-Med food and socialise as DJs spin deep house and soul. People love it and hate it for the same reason (self-conscious hipness), but there's no doubt it's a scene.

BORDEWIJK Map pp286-7   French

☎ 624 38 99; Noordermarkt 7; mains €24-29, set menus €37-52; ☿ dinner Tue-Sun

Other places may have grander reputations, but many locals consider Bordewijk the best in town. The interior is so minimal that there's little to do but appreciate the spectacular French/Italian cooking. The chefs are not afraid to take risks (we once saw lamb's testicles on the menu), but professional staff handle special needs (eg vegetarians) with ease and aplomb.

BURGER'S PATIO Map p285   International

☎ 623 68 54; Tweede Tuindwarsstraat 12; mains €12.50-18.50, 3-course menu €25; ☿ dinner

Despite its name, this is no hamburger joint. Rather, an air of easy-going cool permeates

the modern interior, and the namesake patio is a fun hideout. Meats are free-range, pastas are popular, and touches like crudités, aioli and tapenade make the prices seem more reasonable than they already are.

CAFÉ REIBACH Map pp286-7   Café

☎ 626 77 08; Brouwersgracht 139; mains €2.80-12.50; ☿ breakfast & lunch

This window-lined corner place in the Jordaan serves a magnificent, fresh-made breakfast (€12.50), laden with Dutch cheese, pâté, smoked salmon, eggs, coffee and fresh juice. It's also pleasant for afternoon cake and coffee (try the cheesecake or nut tart). We love the sassy service that describes itself as 'straight-friendly'.

CAFÉ-RESTAURANT AMSTERDAM

Map pp282-3   French International
☎ 682 26 66; Watertorenplein 6; mains €10-21; ☿ lunch & dinner

One of the city's hippest eateries is housed in a former water-processing plant. Expect classic French brasserie cooking (steak bearnaise, mussels, roasted garlic chicken). Note the 30m high wooden ceilings (with hanging metal hooks and chains) and the huge floodlights rescued from the former Ajax and Olympic stadiums.

CINEMA PARADISO Map p285   Italian

☎ 623 73 44; Westerstraat 184-186; mains €9-15; ☿ dinner Tue-Sun

Action! Cinema Paradiso opened in 2002 in a former movie theatre, and glitterati have been appearing in the dining room ever since. Direct yourself into a booth or table near the open kitchen, and enjoy pastas, pizzas, lots of antipasti and stargazing. Go for cocktails and drink in the atmosphere.

TOP FIVE JORDAAN & WESTERN ISLANDS DINING

- **Bordewijk** (left) A sure hand in the kitchen, and service that knows what it's doing.
- **Café Reibach** (above) A big brunch and big windows.
- **Duende** (opposite) For tapas and music.
- **Local** (p138) Convivial setting, food on skewers and cocktails for dessert.
- **Small World Catering** (p139) One of the city's best-loved takeaway shops.

Patrons enjoying breakfast, coffee and newspapers at Café Reibach (opposite)

DE BLAFFENDE VIS

Map p285   Contemporary Dutch

☎ 625 17 21; Westerstraat 118; mains under €8.50; ✆ breakfast, lunch & dinner

Meals at the rowdy, corner 'barking fish' are better than they need to be for the price (contemporary Dutch – steak, fish, chicken – changing daily). Students and 30-somethings happily bop and swish beer while listening to music with a beat.

DE VLIEGENDE SCHOTEL

Map p285   Vegetarian

☎ 625 20 41; Nieuwe Leliestraat 162-68; mains €8.50-13; ✆ dinner

Service can be spotty at 'the flying saucer', but if you're prepared to take your time in the summer camp–chic dining room, you'll enjoy some of the city's favourite veggie gratins, lasagnes and Indian-inflected meals. There's a decent wine list.

DIVAN Map p285   Turkish

☎ 626 82 39; Elandsgracht 14; mains €13-16.50; ✆ lunch Fri & Sat, dinner nightly

In a town where 'Turkish' usually means 'takeaway' (or 'pizza'), Divan offers a calming alternative. For €23.50 you get the *meze* combo starter of 10 assorted dips, skewers and salads, and we loved *ali nazik* (minced lamb with aubergines in yogurt garlic sauce), but it was the gracious, sweet service that will take us back. It's packaged in a brown café–style setting.

DUENDE Map pp286-7   Spanish

☎ 420 66 92; Lindengracht 62; tapas €3-9.50; ✆ dinner

Flamenco music (Saturday night), big shared tables and reasonably priced tapas guarantee Duende's popularity. It's great for a party with a big group of friends – or strangers. The front room is the more lively (and attractive) of the two. Note: you have to order at the bar, which, once you get past the hassle, gives you an excuse to mingle.

JAPANESE PANCAKE WORLD

Map p285   Japanese

☎ 320 44 47; www.japanesepancakeworld.com; Tweede Egelantiersdwarsstraat 24A; mains €8-19; ✆ noon-10pm

If the Dutch are famous for pancakes of meat, seafood and veggies, so are the Japanese. At the continent's only shop specialising in *okonomiyaki* (literally, 'cook as you like'), you'll get yours in a hot iron dish with your choice of fillings and topped with flakes of dried bonito. There's a J-pop backdrop and barely two dozen seats; the action's around the griddle.

JEAN JEAN Map p285 — French
☎ 627 71 53; Eerste Anjeliersdwarsstraat 14; mains €16-19, 4-course menu €32.50; ☾ dinner Tue-Sun
One of the hottest places in town, this cosy neighbourhood bistro offers honest and affordable Gallic comfort food: soups, meat and fish dishes etc. The setting is understated yet sophisticated, and service is professional.

LOCAL Map p285 — International
☎ 423 40 39; Westerstraat 136; mains €7-19.50; ☾ dinner
This eel's nest of contempo-cool, with long, tall tables stretching its entire length, ensures that you will never eat alone. Go with friends, and it's an instant party. In keeping with the 'long and thin' theme, main dishes are grilled on skewers: there's an international selection from yakitori to beef stroganoff, all served with potatoes, salad and appropriate sauces. For dessert: cocktails!

LOF Map pp286-7 — Fusion
☎ 620 29 97; Haarlemmerstraat 62; mains €20, 3-course menu €35; ☾ dinner Tue-Sun
Chef Sander Louwerens combines Southeast Asian and Mediterranean flavours in complex and complementary ways. This is evidenced in dishes such as pike served with fennel and miso sauce. Schoolhouse-surplus décor manages to feel cool. Staff are known for being attentive.

MOEDERS Map p285 — Traditional Dutch
☎ 626 79 57; Rozengracht 251; mains €13-17.50, 3-course menus €23-25; ☾ dinner
Mum's the word at 'mothers'. When this friendly place opened a few years ago, they asked customers to bring their own plates, flatware and photos of their own mums as donations, and the result is still a delightful hodgepodge. So is the food, including *stamppot*, seafood, Moroccan dishes, a vegetarian frittata and a *rijsttafel* of traditional Dutch dishes.

MOEDER'S POT EETHUISJE
Map pp286-7 — Traditional Dutch
☎ 623 76 43; Vinkenstraat 119; mains €3.60-11.35, 6-course set menus €12.50-15; ☾ dinner Mon-Sat
Moeder (mother) is probably in his 60s (yes, his…he's big and gruff and probably a sweetheart inside), and he's been serving up solid, inexpensive meals for decades. The tiny kitsch-laden shop serves home cookin': beefsteaks, schnitzels and chicken with potatoes and vegetables (some canned) like your own *moeder* always wanted you to eat. The set menus are a steal.

NOMADS Map p285 — Middle Eastern
☎ 344 64 01; Rozengracht 133; mezze plates €3-8.25, couscous €15-21.50, 3-course set menu €45; ☾ dinner Tue-Sun
It's the Supper Club concept on the road to Morocco. Wine, dine and recline on mattresses amid decadent decorations, and graze on platters of mod Middle Eastern snacks while being entertained by belly dancers and DJs. Fancy-trancey and superbly sexy.

NOODLE & GO Map pp286-7 — Takeaway
☎ 773 09 13; Brouwersgracht 125; dishes €4-6.50; ☾ lunch & dinner
Here's the formula: choose from noodles or fried rice, add meat (like chicken saté, coconut beef, spicy pork) and a vegetable, and you're on your way. It ain't gourmet, but it's quick and honest. There are a few seats, plus a TV or people-watching.

PACIFIC PARC Map pp282-3 — International
☎ 488 77 78; Polonceaukade 23; lunch dishes €2.90-9, dinner mains €12-15, 3-course menu €25; ☾ lunch & dinner
Among the many venues in the newly refurbished Westergasfabriek, Pacific Parc is the most established and, arguably, the most interesting. Lunch-time is typically sandwiches, pastas and salads, although dinner can get pretty adventurous with selections like ceviche and stuffed lamb shanks. Late at night expect to see DJs and guest performers.

RAKANG THAI Map p285 — Thai
☎ 627 50 12; Elandsgracht 29; mains €17.50-21, 4-course menus €27-32; ☾ dinner
Chairs wrapped in straitjackets, bright art on the walls, neckties in the tables (it makes sense when you see it), a *mai pen rai* (no problem) atmosphere and delicious cooking (go for the almost buttery *tom kha gai* soup or crunchy, spicy duck salad) keep it busy here night after night.

SEE ALSO

- **Arnold Cornelis** (p193) Bake shop and patisserie with savoury pastries and challenging chocolates.
- **De Reiger** (p157) Classic and civilised brown café, known for excellent food.

STOUT Map pp286-7   Fusion Café

☎ 616 36 64; Haarlemmerstraat 73; lunch mains €4.30-12.50, dinner mains €15-21; ☺ lunch & dinner
Slick, hip couples congregate at this airy, artful café to air-kiss, read design magazines, gossip and share imaginative fusion dishes (carrot and coriander soup with spicy tempeh, Thai chicken burger with kimchi) and fruit shakes. In warm weather, sit on an outdoor cushion and watch the world go by.

CHEAP EATS

BROODJE MOKUM Map p285   Sandwich Shop

☎ 623 19 66; Rozengracht 26; sandwiches from €2; ☺ breakfast & lunch Mon-Sat
With several tables and outdoor seating, it's larger than your average *broodjeswinkel* (sandwich shop) but has a great workaday feeling that may remind you of your favourite burger stand at home. Our strategy for ordering: point at what you want, and the staff will tell you how much it is.

SMALL WORLD CATERING

Map pp286-7   Takeaway
☎ 420 27 74; Binnen Oranjestraat 14; sandwiches €5.45-7.50, other mains €4-6; ☺ 10.30am-8pm Tue-Sat, noon-8pm Sun
This Australian-run company is known for quality. Small cases house gorgeous prepared vegetables and meat dishes, and you can get a variety of quiches and sandwiches including fresh tuna, tapenade and artichoke hearts.

WINKEL Map pp286-7   Café

☎ 623 02 23; Noordermarkt 43; mains €2.50-6; ☺ breakfast, lunch & dinner
This sprawling, indoor-outdoor space is great for people-watching, popular for coffees and small meals, and out-of-the-park for its tall, cakey apple pie (€2.50). On market days (Mondays and Saturdays) there's almost always a queue out the door.

WESTERN CANAL BELT

It may not have the ethnic dining diversity of other parts of town, but the Canal Belt makes up for it with some interesting and surprisingly fashionable options. Notably, the Negen Straatjes (Map p84) are filled with cafés and small restaurants to match their lovely boutiques.

BUFFET VAN ODETTE & YVETTE

Map pp286-7   Café
☎ 423 60 34; Herengracht 309; mains €3-12; ☺ 8.30am-5.30pm Mon-Fri, 10am-5.30pm Sat, noon-5.30pm Sun
Not a buffet but a sit-down café, Odette and Yvette show how good simple cooking can taste when you start with great ingredients and a dash of creativity. Soups, sandwiches, pastas and quiches are mostly organic, and you might find smart little extras like pine nuts in your quiche. Sit by the window for one of the city's prettiest canal views.

CASA PERÚ Map pp292-3   Peruvian

☎ 620 37 49; Leidsegracht 68; mains €12-20
When the weather's good, there's nothing quite like enjoying a *crema de ajo* (cream of garlic) soup or *lomo saltado* (beef with onion, tomato and French fries) while looking out over the Leidsegracht and the Prinsengracht. Indoors, it's busy and homely.

CHRISTOPHE Map pp286-7   French

☎ 625 08 07; www.christophe.nl; Leliegracht 46; mains €31-53, 4-course set menus €45-65; ☺ dinner Tue-Sat
Lobster dishes, duck-liver terrine and an unusual elegance keep Jean-Christophe Royer's Michelin-star restaurant busy every night.

TOP FIVE WESTERN CANAL BELT DINING

- **Buffet van Odette & Yvette** (above) Cosy corner café with smart takes on the classics.
- **De Belhamel** (p140) Especially on a summer night sitting canalside.
- **Christophe** (above) This Michelin-rated restaurant is a splurge and worth it.
- **'t Kuyltje** (p141) Negen Straatjes sandwich bar that'll take you back a generation.
- **Zuid Zeeland** (p141) Sophisticated and knowledgeable yet friendly.

Eating

WESTERN CANAL BELT

However, the excellent, caring service puts it over the top in our book, making this an extraordinary restaurant by world, and not just Amsterdam, standards.

CILUBANG Map pp292-3 — Indonesian

☎ 626 97 55; www.cilubang.com; Runstraat 10; mains €7.25-18, rijsttafel €21-37; ☯ dinner Tue-Sun

In the Negen Straatjes, cute, cosy and slightly romantic, celadon-hued Cilubang soothes the stomach and soul with *rijsttafel* and attentive, personal service. They've been at it for 2½ decades. The food is west Javanese style, and with any luck you'll hear gamelan music too.

DE BELHAMEL Map pp286-7 — French

☎ 622 10 95; Brouwersgracht 60; mains €18-21, set menu €31; ☯ dinner

In warm weather the canalside tables at the head of the Herengracht are an aphrodisiac, and the sumptuous Art Nouveau interior provides the perfect backdrop for excellent, French- and Italian-inspired dishes like silky roast beef.

DE BOLHOED Map pp286-7 — Vegetarian

☎ 626 18 03; Prinsengracht 60-62; lunch mains €3.50-11.50, dinner mains €9.50-14.50, 3-course menu €22; ☯ lunch & dinner

The 'Charlie Brown's pumpkin patch goes to India' interior is a nice setting to tuck into enormous, organic Mexican, Asian and Italian-inspired dishes; in warm weather, there's a verdant little canalside terrace. Leave room for the banana cream pie. Veggies swear by it – reserve.

Visit De Belhamel restaurant for dinner

DE STRUISVOGEL Map p285 — French

☎ 423 38 17; Keizersgracht 312; 3-course menu €19; ☯ dinner

This former kitchen to some large canal houses offers a great deal. It's in the basement (*struisvogel* means 'ostrich'), and yes they do serve the bird, along with a nightly rotating menu – generous portions of more conventional French-inspired choices. It gets crowded; book ahead.

DE 2 GRIEKEN Map pp286-7 — Greek

☎ 625 53 17; Prinsenstraat 20; mains €13-17; ☯ dinner

Craving stewed mountain goat or some juicy lamb chops? This relaxed, family-run bistro caters to your carnivorous desires with great grills and gets '*opa!*'s from locals. In nice weather, grab a seat on the flower-lined terrace out back. If you're a fan of Greek wines, this is the place to go.

DYLAN Map p285 — International

☎ 530 20 10; Dylan Hotel, Keizersgracht 384; mains €28-38; ☯ breakfast daily, lunch Mon-Fri, dinner Mon-Sat

Dylan Hotel's restaurant is swank central, baby, thanks to the dazzlingly elegant interior with well-spaced power tables, ultra-smooth service, cuisine that fuses French, Italian, Japanese and Thai, and an ever-present smattering of international celebs. Diners also get access to one of Amsterdam's most excellent lounge scenes. Reserve.

FOODISM Map pp286-7 — Café

☎ 427 51 03; www.foodism.nl; Oude Leliestraat 8; mains €2.75-10; ☯ lunch & dinner

A hip, colourful little joint run by a fun, relaxed crew. All-day breakfasts and sandwiches like chicken mango and salads make up the day menu; night-time sees patrons tucking into platefuls of pasta – try the 'Kung Funghi' (with three kinds of mushrooms, parsley, walnuts and cream).

GOODIES Map pp292-3 — Café

☎ 625 61 22; Huidenstraat 9; dishes €2.75-10; ☯ lunch & dinner

This once-country place in the Negen Straatjes with rustic picnic tables has gone glam with a slick makeover, a bar and even occasional DJ nights. Recently they've joined the tapas wave, but it's still popular for creative sandwiches like grilled chicken with salad and pine nuts.

GREKAS Map pp286-7   Greek
☎ 620 35 90; Singel 311; mains €8-10;
🕑 1.30-9.30pm Wed-Sun

What started as a catering shop has bloomed into one of the city's best-loved Greek restaurants. Low overheads (there's almost no seating) means low prices with high quality, generous portions of Greek home cooking: moussaka, roasted artichokes, chicken in lemon sauce… Salads and smaller dishes are available for €1.40 to €4.20 per 100g.

HEIN Map p285   Café
☎ 623 10 48; Berenstraat 20; mains €4-10;
🕑 breakfast & lunch

Hein simply loves to cook, and it shows in her simple, stylish, sky-lit café – you have to walk through the kitchen to reach the dining room. Media types, doing business over brunch, comment that she has a great touch with simple dishes: *croque monsieur* or *madame*, smoked salmon etc.

KOH-I-NOOR Map p285   Indian
☎ 623 31 33; Westermarkt 29; mains €10-18.50;
🕑 dinner

Long-standing Koh-I-Noor's interior is all cinnabars and blue-and-white tapestries, and the curries, tandoori and biryani dishes (especially the king-prawn biryani) are about as good as you get in town. Tables are rather close together, but hospitable staff help alleviate any pressure.

L'INDOCHINE Map pp292-3   Indonesian
☎ 627 57 55; Beulingstraat 9; mains €19.50-25, 4-course menus €35; 🕑 dinner Tue-Sun

A swanky, white-linen Thai-Vietnamese place, known for using only the finest ingredients. Dishes like *bo luc lac* (filet mignon with garlic) and *tom xao bo toi* (king prawns with garlic butter) are enough to get upscale diners into this restaurant, and the nice crockery and nicer service keep them coming back.

LUST Map pp292-3   Café
☎ 626 57 91; Runstraat 13; mains €2.75-8.50;
🕑 breakfast & lunch

Parquet floors and walls, super-mod ceiling lamps, and Brazilian dance beats animate this glam café. It's a fair bet you'll spot models nibbling focaccia sandwiches, *tostis* (grilled sandwiches), generous salads or the popular grilled chicken club with avocado.

SEE ALSO
- **Brix** (p165) Slick new bar with consistently interesting small plates.
- **Urban Picnic** (p197) Picnic shop that also sells smart takeaway food.

NIELSEN Map p285   Café
☎ 330 60 06; Berenstraat 19; dishes €3.60-10;
🕑 breakfast & lunch Tue-Sun

This sunny café, with its bright interior filled with fresh flowers, has a tasty set breakfast – eggs, toast, fruit, juice and coffee (€7.50). During lunch a large variety of salads and sandwiches are served: try the BLT or gigantic chicken club sandwich, and top it off with lemon cake.

PANCAKE BAKERY
Map pp286-7   Contemporary Dutch
☎ 625 13 33; Prinsengracht 191;
mains €4.95-11.50; 🕑 lunch & dinner

This basement restaurant in a restored warehouse features a dizzying 79 varieties of this Dutch speciality from sweet (chocolate) to savoury (the 'Egyptian', topped with lamb, sweet peppers, garlic sauce). There are also omelettes, soups, desserts and lots of tourists given its proximity to the Westerkerk and Anne Frank Huis, but plenty of locals too.

ZUID ZEELAND Map pp292-3   International
☎ 624 31 54; Herengracht 413; mains €23-26, 3-/4-/5-course menu €32/37/50; 🕑 lunch Mon-Fri, dinner nightly

Popular with artists, authors, Bohemians and the US Democratic Party, Zuid Zeeland is known for cuisine that whispers quality and its low-key celebrity clientele. The contemporary room is attractive but not imposing, much like the French-international cuisine. Finish with the port-infused Stilton.

CHEAP EATS
'T KUYLTJE Map pp286-7   Sandwich Shop
☎ 620 10 45; Gasthuismolensteeg 9; sandwiches €1.75-3.10; 🕑 breakfast & lunch

You've got to love the timeless antiseptic-atmospheric, tile-lined look of this little sandwich shop. We like the pastrami, but there are lots of ways to eat raw meat too. Plus, the menu tops out at around €3.

Eating   WESTERN CANAL BELT

SOUTHERN CANAL BELT

All roads in Amsterdam seem to lead to Leidseplein, but we don't really recommend eating there. While cheap and cheerful, establishments there tend to be not particularly distinctive. A short walk away, however, are some very attractive options.

Much the same could also be said for Rembrandtplein. Instead of eating there, walk a few steps to Utrechtsestraat, Amsterdam's finest restaurant row.

BOJO Map pp292-3 · Indonesian
☎ 622 74 34; Lange Leidsedwarsstraat 51; mains €7.25-11.50; ☽ lunch Sat & Sun, dinner daily (open until 2am)

After a night on the town, there's nothing like a little Indonesian. Bojo is a late-night institution. Clubbers come for sizzling satés, filling fried rice and steaming bowls of noodle soup. The quality may be uneven, but the food is certainly well priced.

CAFÉ MORLANG Map pp292-3 · Café
☎ 625 26 81; Keizersgracht 451; lunch mains €3.50-18, dinner mains €10-18; ☽ lunch & dinner

Grab a fashion magazine, order tomato soup or tarte tatin, or choose from a rotating menu with influences from Italy to Thailand. The canalside terrace is fab in warm weather; indoors enjoy the high ceilings and gigantic portraits of staff members painted on the back wall. Friday nights it's a low-key gay hangout, so low-key that you may not realise it.

CAFÉ WALEM Map pp292-3 · Café
☎ 625 35 44; Keizersgracht 449; lunch mains €4.50-9.50, dinner mains €9.50-17.50; ☽ breakfast, lunch & dinner

The industrial-mod building by Gerrit Rietveld, two terraces, friendly service and a changing menu keep this place busy. There's a popular carpaccio sandwich, mains including fish and duck, a neat line of soups and salads, and coffee from Illy.

GOLDEN TEMPLE Map pp292-3 · Vegetarian
☎ 626 85 60; Utrechtsestraat 126; mains €7-13.50; ☽ dinner

Golden Temple's quietly upscale setting means that you don't have to feel like you're back in school just because you're eating vegetarian food. Its international menu of Indian thali, Middle Eastern and Mexican platters is good and inexpensive. Leave room for the totally wicked banana-cream pie.

IGUAZU Map pp292-3 · Argentine/Brazilian
☎ 420 39 10; Prinsengracht 703; mains €13.50-35, most under €25; ☽ lunch & dinner

In a city where impersonal Argentine chains dominate, Iguazu offers quality and personal service. In addition to great Argentine steaks – from special butchers and served with powerful chimchurri sauce – you'll find Brazilian specialities like feijoada. Sip caipirinhas by the canal in nice weather.

JANVIER Map pp292-3 · International
☎ 626 11 99; Amstelveld 12; lunch mains €5.50-14, dinner mains €10.50-17; ☽ lunch & dinner

The gathering of fine, fashionable folks on the terrace might remind you more of Paris than Amsterdam. Janvier's speciality is tastings – ham, cheese, wine, beer – but the Caesar salad sets standards, and even humble croquettes are served handsomely. Watch for DJ events.

LA RIVE Map pp290-1 · French
☎ 622 60 60; Amstel Intercontinental Hotel, Professor Tulpplein 1; mains €38-58; ☽ breakfast daily, lunch Mon-Fri, dinner Mon-Sat

Two Michelin stars and a formal dining room with graciously spaced tables and views over the Amstel make La Rive the perfect venue for an out-to-impress lunch or dinner. The menu changes frequently, but standbys include turbot and truffle in potato pasta, or, as you'd expect, a starter of caviar.

TOP FIVE SOUTHERN CANAL BELT DINING

- **Iguazu** (above) Friendly, informal Argentine/Brazilian; steaks are a cut above.
- **La Rive** (above) It's hard to get more elegant than the Amstel Hotel's top-flight restaurant.
- **Segugio** (p144) Chic Italian with staying power.
- **Tempo Doeloe** (p144) Some of the city's best Indonesian, which is saying something.
- **Uliveto** (p145) Our favourite takeaway/eat-in shop in town.

M CAFÉ Map pp292-3   Café

☎ 520 78 48; Keizersgracht 455; mains €4-12;
🕒 10am-5pm

Drink in that amazing, panoramic view! The location, high above the Keizersgracht in the top-floor gallery of the ritzy Metz & Co department store, gives new meaning to 'high tea' (€12) although other dishes are nothing you can't find elsewhere (soup, salads or sandwiches).

PASTA DI MAMMA

Map pp292-3   Italian/Takeaway

☎ 664 83 14; PC Hooftstraat 52; sandwiches €3.10-5;
antipasti per 100g €2.75-4.80; 🕒 9am-7pm Mon-Sat,
noon-7pm Sun

Casual, friendly Pasta di Mamma is supremely located for picking up a picnic to take to the Vondelpark. You can choose from dozens of antipasti, gorgeous salads and more substantial plates. The countrified-cafeteria space is also pleasant for eating in.

PASTA E BASTA Map pp292-3   Italian

☎ 422 22 26; Nieuwe Spiegelstraat 8;
3-course menu €35; 🕒 dinner

There may be better Italian food in town, but Pasta e Basta is popular with large groups year in, year out thanks to its singing waitstaff, who perform opera, standards and more. Regulars swear by the antipasto buffet and grilled meats. Reserve well in advance.

PASTINI Map pp292-3   Italian

☎ 622 17 01; Leidsegracht 29; mains €10-19;
🕒 dinner

With a *gezellig*, rustic-renaissance interior and a can't-beat-it location facing two canals, Pastini wins praise for its looks, pastas and prices. Another speciality is the antipasto starter (€10.25 for five choices), but save room for dessert.

PATA NEGRA Map pp292-3   Spanish

☎ 422 62 50; Utrechtsestraat 142; tapas €3.50-16,
most under €9; 🕒 lunch & dinner

Tapas and only tapas. The alluringly tiled exterior is matched by a vibrant crowd inside, especially on weekends downing sangria by the jug and all those small plates (the garlic-fried shrimps and grilled sardines are standouts). Margaritas are made with freshly squeezed lime juice, as they should be. Arrive before 6.30pm or reserve.

Visit Pata Negra restaurant for tapas or a drink

PIET DE LEEUW Map pp292-3   Steakhouse

☎ 623 71 81; Noorderstraat 11; mains €11.50-18;
🕒 lunch Mon-Fri, dinner nightly

The building dates from 1900, it's been a steakhouse and hangout since the 1940s, and the dark and cosy atmosphere has barely changed since. If you don't get your own table, you may meet folks from all over (including, admittedly, tourists) at a common table, over well-priced steaks with toppings like onions, mushrooms or bacon, served with salad and piping-hot *frites*.

PYGMA-LION Map pp292-3   African

☎ 420 70 22; Nieuwe Spiegelstraat 5A;
mains €19.50-23; 🕒 dinner Tue-Sun

This modern South African bistro plates up animals you normally have to go to a zoo to see, like ostrich, springbok, zebra (the last might be in a quince-port sauce). Squeamish stomachs will still find more domesticated options: vegetarian dishes, 'tipsy' tart and blackcurrant scones.

RISTORANTE D'ANTICA

Map pp292-3   Italian

☎ 623 38 62; Reguliersdwarsstraat 80-82; mains
€12-42, course menus from €35; 🕒 dinner Tue-Sun

Although D'Antica's three dining rooms get their share of celebrities, you'd be hard pressed to find a more welcoming restaurant in town. There's a familiar selection of pastas and meats, but cognoscenti order spaghetti al parmigiano (not on the menu) assembled tableside – the entire room may pause to watch as waiters whirr steaming green pasta inside a huge wheel of cheese.

ROSE'S CANTINA Map pp292-3   Mexican
☎ 625 97 97; Reguliersdwarsstraat 38-40; dishes €4-17.50; ☻ dinner
Even if the Californians and Texans (not to mention Mexicans) among us wouldn't recognise the food as authentic, it's hard not to love the gorgeous garden courtyard and fiesta interior. Fajitas, quesadillas and enchiladas are super-sized, and margaritas taste good on any continent.

SATURNINO Map pp292-3   Italian
☎ 639 01 02; Reguliersdwarsstraat 5; mains €7.25-24; ☻ lunch & dinner
The menu at this Italian bistro is as long as the phone book in a village in Tuscany. Stunning gay couples pack the different levels of this Art Nouveau tiled-and-styled space for pizzas, pasta and playful flirting, or have a low-key lunch with your fashion-industry friends.

SEGUGIO Map pp292-3   Italian
☎ 330 15 03; Utrechtsestraat 96; pastas €15-17, mains €23-27; ☻ dinner Mon-Sat
This fashionably minimalist storefront with two levels of seating is the sort of place other chefs go for a good dinner. It's known for risotto and high-quality ingredients combined with a sure hand. Book ahead – it's almost always busy.

FEBO A-GO-GO
Our approach to the fast-food chain **Febo** (fay-bo) is pretty much the way Amsterdammers approach sex and drugs: you may well encounter it while you're in town, so you might as well educate yourself before you decide whether to partake.

Febo's grease-laden snacks are much-maligned but also secretly loved, not least because they're cheap (mostly between €1 and €2). Then there's the presentation: along one wall of these tiny shops, the delicacies practically wink at you from behind little glass doors like ugly kids on the make at a school dance: kroketten of veal or beef, the kipburger (made from chicken), the Feboburger (beef with grill sauce and lettuce) and a half-dozen others. Insert a coin or two into a slot, open the door, and pull out your snack.

It's down and dirty, all right, but as long as you keep your wits about you, there's nothing wrong with an occasional dalliance; plus, if you duck in and out quickly, who's gonna know?

SLUIZER Map pp292-3   International
☎ 622 63 76; Utrechtsestraat 43-45; mains €13.50-25, 3-course menu €19.50; ☻ dinner
This old-line institution – with its romantic, enclosed garden terrace – historically comprises two restaurants: a Parisian-style 'meat' restaurant (No 43) and a fish restaurant (No 45), though both menus are available in both restaurants. Spare ribs are the speciality of the former and bouillabaisse the speciality of the latter.

SZMULEWICZ Map pp292-3   International
☎ 620 28 22; Bakkersstraat 12; mains €10-17; ☻ dinner
Szmulewicz's décor is at once slick and breezy (trompe l'oeil marble walls, sculpted lighting), a diversity reflected in its menu of reliable, ever-changing international cooking: pastas, tapas, Greek dishes, beef fillets, and vegetarian specialities. In summer, buskers play outside on this quiet block off Rembrandtplein.

TAKE THAI Map pp292-3   Thai
☎ 622 05 77; Utrechtsestraat 87; mains €11.25-20, set menus €25-38; ☻ dinner
This modern, all-white restaurant plates up some of the best Thai food in the city. Choose from a variety of curries spiced according to your palate. The Penang beef curry is a winner, as is the fish fried in lemongrass and Thai basil.

TEMPO DOELOE Map pp292-3   Indonesian
☎ 625 67 18; Utrechtsestraat 75; mains €19.50-25, rijsttafel & set menus €27-49; ☻ dinner Mon-Sat
One of the best Indonesian restaurants in the city (it charges accordingly), Tempo Doeloe's setting and service are pleasant and decorous without being overdone. Dishes bring out subtle flavours amid the spice, and staff are happy to accommodate vegetarians. Plus, there's an extraordinary wine list. Downside: a bit supercilious – you have to ring a doorbell to enter.

THAI CORNER Map pp292-3   Thai
☎ 320 66 84; Kerkstraat 66; mains €9.50-19.50, set menus €23-28; ☻ dinner
Don't dismiss this cute little place: it does seriously authentic Thai. Locals and restaurant critics swoon over squid with garlic pepper and tofu with Thai basil, and stare agog at the over-the-top, carved wooden

Try Penang beef curry at Take Thai (opposite)

ramen, Japanese curries and fried noodles or rice. Some dishes have been prettied up for Western palates, but that doesn't stop them from being good.

ZUSHI Map pp292-3 — Japanese
☎ 330 68 82; Amstel 20; dishes €2.55-8.50;
☽ lunch & dinner
You're heading to the Stopera or returning from a bike ride and you need sushi, stat. This conveyor-belt sushi shop features post-industrial chic décor (stainless steel, brick and blondwood), club tunes, lightning service, and new grilled dishes. Add up the colours of your plates to figure out how much you owe.

CHEAP EATS
BROODJE VAN KOOTJE
Map pp292-3 — Sandwich Shop
☎ 623 20 36; Leidseplein 20; broodjes from €2;
☽ lunch & dinner
This is Amsterdam's longest-running sand-wich bar, although you'd never know it by its appearance (Micky D's has more charm). Still, it's open from lunch until late, the quality is solid, and you can't beat the central locations of Leidseplein and Spui (Map pp292–3; ☎ 623 74 51; Spui 28).

LOEKIE Map pp292-3 — Sandwich Shop
☎ 624 42 30; Prinsengracht 705; broodjes €2.25-5.50; ☽ lunch & dinner
Steps from Leidseplein, this butcher shop has over 150 types of meat, fish and cheese, which they'll gladly stuff into a *broodje* for you. Some are typically Dutch (*osseworst* – raw beef sausage), while others evoke Italy or Thailand.

bar at the back of the room. Other restaurants could afford to take lessons from the self-effacing service.

TUJUH MARET Map pp292-3 — Indonesian
☎ 427 98 65; Utrechtsestraat 73; mains €13.50-19.50, rijsttafel €19-24; ☽ lunch Mon-Sat, dinner nightly
Dare we say it? Tujuh Maret, next door to Tempo Doeloe, is just as good but attitude-free and cheaper. Grab a wicker chair and tuck into spicy Sulawesi-style dishes like dried, fried beef or chicken in red pepper sauce. *Rijsttafel* is laid out according to spice intensity, and *makanan kecil* is a mini-*rijsttafel* for €15.

ULIVETO Map pp292-3 — Takeaway
☎ 423 00 99; Weteringschans 118; dishes €4.50-10.50; ☽ 11am-8pm Mon-Fri, noon-6pm Sat
In a capacious, spare atmosphere of under-stated luxury, this shop is lined with huge crocks of olive oil and splendid displays of Italian specialities. If you prefer to dine in, try the long white marble table when cooking demonstrations or classes are not being held there.

WAGAMAMA Map pp292-3 — Japanese
☎ 528 77 78; Max Euweplein 10; mains €8-13;
☽ lunch & dinner
Long rows of rectangular tables, laid out cafeteria-style, are often filled with hipsters fortifying themselves for days on bikes or nights on the town. Staples include chicken

SEE ALSO
- **Amstel Haven** (p163) *Uitsmijters* – and sometimes dancing – on the Amstel.
- **Café Americain** (p159) Art Nouveau masterpiece in the Amsterdam American Hotel.
- **Café Het Molenpad** (p157) Gallery-café with Dutch-Med cuisine.
- **Café Schiller** (p161) Clubby Art Deco café on Rembrandtplein.
- **De Smoeshan** (p162) Intimate theatre café off Leidseplein.

Eating

SOUTHERN CANAL BELT

SEE ALSO

- **Deshima** (p198) Vegetarian shop, with a fine takeaway counter

MAOZ FALAFEL Map pp292-3   Israeli
☎ 420 74 35; Muntplein 1; sandwiches €2.80-4.30;
☺ lunch & dinner
Its flagship falafel sandwich is always crispy, hot and very authentic, with endless toppings from the self-service salad bar. There's a half-dozen branches around town, most open good and late.

VAN DOBBEN Map pp292-3   Sandwich Shop
☎ 624 42 00; Korte Reguliersdwarsstraat 5;
dishes €2-7.50; ☺ breakfast, lunch & dinner
This tiny stand has been kicking around ever since 1945, with Amsterdam's best *kroketten* (€2) – most other places seem to get theirs supplied from here. It's also much beloved for sandwiches, soups and omelettes. Its location just off Rembrandtplein makes it a compulsory stop on a pub crawl.

OLD SOUTH

As you'd expect in the part of town that hosts the Concertgebouw, major museums and the city's fanciest shopping, the Old South is home to some very chichi places. We've also listed the area off the Overtoom in this section – though technically it's in the Old West – as it's developing into a trove of interesting ethnic choices.

'T BLAUWE THEEHUIS Map pp282-3   Café
Round Blue Teahouse; ☎ 662 02 54; Vondelpark 5;
lunch €3.50-4, dinner mains €14.50-18.50;
☺ 9am-10pm
The functionalist teahouse from 1936 is a wonderful multilevel building that serves coffee, cake and alcohol; its terrace and balcony are great for a beer on a sunny day, even in winter when the heaters are on.

BARK Map p296   Seafood
☎ 675 02 10; Van Baerlestraat 120; mains
€14.50-22; ☺ lunch Mon-Fri, dinner nightly
Thanks to the location a quick hop from the Concertgebouw, this genteel, old-line place does a big pre- and post-performance business. For starters, choose from a long

shellfish menu or try the blinis of smoked oilfish. For mains, we like the grilled tuna steak with bacon and balsamic sauce. Some dishes can be a little salty, so let them know if you're sensitive.

COBRA CAFÉ-RESTAURANT
Map pp292-3   International
☎ 470 01 11; www.cobracafe.com/nl/ Hobbema-straat 18; mains €4.70-11.50; ☺ lunch & dinner
This arty glass cube of a restaurant, full of original works by Corneille and Appel, sure is touristy. But when you're all museumed out and need a salad, massive club sandwich or slice of 'Karel Appel taart', you'll hardly notice. The hi-tech toilets are almost worth the €0.50 admission.

HAP HMM Map pp292-3   Traditional Dutch
☎ 618 18 84; Eerste Helmersstraat 33;
mains €5.20-6.70; ☺ 4.30-8pm Mon-Fri
Elsewhere €6 might buy you a bowl of soup, but at this wood-panelled neighbourhood place €6 might buy an entire dinner: simple Dutch cooking (meat + veggies + potatoes), served on stainless steel dishes. Beer is cheap too.

LA FALOTE Map p296   Traditional Dutch
☎ 622 54 54; Roelof Hartstraat 26; mains €7.30-14;
☺ dinner Mon-Sat
Every resident of the Old South knows this place and its home-style Dutch cooking. Apart from the food, one of the best things on offer is Peter, the dashing, ever-smiling owner. If he brings out the accordion, you may not know what hit you.

LALIBELA Map pp282-3   Ethiopian
☎ 683 83 32; Eerste Helmersstraat 249;
mains €8-12.50; ☺ dinner
This shop front off the Overtoom was the Netherlands' first Ethiopian restaurant, and

TOP FIVE OLD SOUTH DINING

- **Bark** (left) Ocean catches in old-world surrounds.
- **CoBrA Cafe-Restaurant** (above) A winner for its setting, because sometimes you just want to relax overlooking the Museumplein.
- **Lalibela** (above) A mini-escape to Ethiopia.
- **Sama Sebo** (opposite) Tastes: Indonesian. Looks: brown café.
- **Mansion** (opposite) Pan-Asian cooking and a scene.

TOO TIRED TO COOK?

The **Kinderkookkafé** (Map pp282–3; ☎ 625 32 57; Vondelpark 6; ☿ ring for hours and reservations) lets the kids take over the kitchen, with careful supervision of course. Kids prepare meals from pancakes to pizzas to Moroccan, write up the menus, and even clean (well, just a little).

it's still our favourite in town. Aksumite-hide paintings with Christian motifs hang on the walls, drink Ethiopian beer from a half-gourd, and taste your stews, egg and vegetable dishes eaten with your hands using *endjera,* a spongy pancake, instead of utensils. Unique, trippy music rounds out the experience.

MANSION Map pp292-3   Asian/Fusion

☎ 616 66 64; Hobbemastraat 2; mains €12-21; ☿ dinner Tue-Sun

There's no sign out front, just black lac-quered doors. It's all about a little mystery and a whole lot of cool. Inside, the Mansion melds 21st-century opulence (gauzy purple curtains, chandeliers) with specialities like soft-shell crab with chilli-garlic marinade and lobster in XO sauce. Modelling agen-cies hold their parties here. Need we say more? Reservations required.

PALOMA BLANCA Map pp282-3   Moroccan

☎ 612 64 85; Jan Pieter Heijestraat 145; mains €12.50-18; ☿ dinner Tue-Sun

Yes, we know the name is Spanish, but the lanterns, dishware and mosaic-top tables at this undersung storefront could have come from the souk in Marrakech. Try the starter of olives and *brik* (spicy tuna spread), mains of couscous and *tajine* (Mo-roccan stew), or mixed grills like *merguez* (spicy sausage), lamb cutlets and chicken.

SABOR DE MARIA

Map p296   Mediterranean Tapas

☎ 662 62 76; Roelof Hartstraat 60; mains €9; ☿ lunch & dinner Mon-Sat

This catering shop sells tapas from €1.25 per 100g, such as meatballs, stuffed grape leaves and garlic chicken wings, and main dishes like rib eye with pepper sauce, vege-table lasagne and Spanish chicken. For us, though, the well-chosen salad bar (around

€3.50) is usually plenty. Take it away, or there are a few tables where you can eat.

SAMA SEBO Map pp292-3   Indonesian

☎ 662 81 46; www.samasebo.com; PC Hooftstraat 27; rijsttafel per person €27, lunch specials per person €14.50, individual dishes €1.25-6.30; ☿ lunch & dinner Mon-Sat

Sama Sebo looks more like a brown café than a trip to the South Seas, and that's OK. The *rijsttafel* is 17 dishes (four to seven at lunch-time), and you can get individual plates if that's too much. They've had the same formula since 1970, so who are we to question?

WAROENG ASJE

Map pp282-3   Javanese/Surinamese

☎ 616 65 89; Jan Pieter Heijestraat 180; mains €5-12, rijsttafel €28; ☿ lunch Mon-Fri, dinner nightly

This counter-service shop serves *rijsttafel,* but you can get some of the same food in human portions with the *nasi rames* special (€9) – a heaped plate of roasted meats, on skewers or in spicy stews, with stir-fried or pickled vegetables, and a deep-fried hard-boiled egg.

SEE ALSO

- **Hotel Okura** (p227) Two restaurants have Michelin stars here: Yamazato (Japanese) and Ciel Bleu (continental).
- **Café Vertigo** (p162) The Filmmuseum's café has an excellent patio for people- or park-watching.

DE PIJP

Anything can happen in De Pijp – funky, frilly, fashionable and fun. Albert Cuyp-straat, west of the Albert Cuypmarkt, is lined with unique ethnic spots.

ALBERT CUYP 67 Map p297   Surinamese

☎ 671 13 96; Albert Cuypstraat 67; mains €3.20-8.40; ☿ lunch & dinner

If you're looking for stylish surrounds, turn away now. If, however, you're after quality examples of Surinamese food, take a seat. A colossal portion of *roti kip* (chicken curry, flaky roti bread, potatoes, cabbage and egg) is a fine replenishment after a couple of hours at Albert Cuypmarkt.

Eating

DE PIJP

WORTH THE TRIP

- **Betty's** (Map pp282-3; ☎ 644 58 96; Rijnstraat 75; mains €18-20; ☻ lunch Wed-Fri, dinner Wed-Sun) Some consider it the top vegetarian restaurant in the country. The menu's small on any given day, but there's always something new. It's rounded out by tiny tables and a decent wine selection, and everyone says to save room for dessert.
- **Gary's Muffins** (☎ 412 30 25; Kinkerstraat 140; dishes €1.50-4.35; ☻ 8.30am-6pm Mon-Fri, 9am-6pm Sat, 10am-6pm Sun) This long-standing bakery serves fresh bagels, chocolate brownies from Gary's grandma's recipe, and sweet and savoury muffins for anyone craving a healthy(ish) mini-munch.
- **Sal Meijer** (Map p297; ☎ 673 13 13; Scheldestraat 45; dishes €2-4.75; ☻ 10am-7.30pm Sun-Thu, 10am-3pm Fri) This kosher delicatessen is a fixture of the local Jewish community. There's little to no atmosphere, but when you have a refrigerator case lined with pretty scoops of salmon, potato and egg salads, how can you complain? Order the heaping corned beef sandwich – get it warm, you'll thank us – and the kosher *kroketten* will give Mr van Dobben a run for his money if word leaks out. We love the kicky ginger cake for dessert.

BALTI HOUSE Map p297   Indian
☎ 470 89 17; Albert Cuypstraat 41; mains €10.50-18;
☻ dinner
One of the best-kept secrets in De Pijp is this exceedingly friendly, quick-serving, always-tasty spot. The butter chicken masala (€12.50) is consistently smooth and tender but the fiery tandooris and biryanis won't disappoint either. Start with a rich mango lassi and a chapatti *amuse-bouche* on the shady terrace.

BAZAR AMSTERDAM
Map p297   Middle Eastern/Fusion
☎ 675 05 44; www.bazaramsterdam.nl; Albert Cuypstraat 182; mains €8-14, 3-course menu €15;
☻ breakfast, lunch & dinner
Every so often, a new restaurant makes us say '*oh* yeah!' Beneath a golden angel in the middle of the Albert Cuypmarkt, this

one-time Dutch Reformed church has fab-u-lous tile murals and 10,001 Arabian lights to complement the cuisine: from Morocco through Turkey, Lebanon through Persia. Even the plates are gorgeous and exotic. Breakfast and lunch are served all day, or just come for a beer or coffee, baklava or apple pie.

CAFÉ DE PIJP Map p297   Café
☎ 618 16 69; Ferdinand Bolstraat 17-19; mains €13.50-15; ☻ lunch & dinner
De Pijp, the restaurant, is a fitting emblem of De Pijp, the neighbourhood: bright, young, cheerful, colourful, reasonably priced and good-looking both outside and in. You might see skinny young things digging into enormous plates of fish paella or tempura-style shrimp.

CAMBODJA CITY Map p297   Cambodian
☎ 671 49 30; Albert Cuypstraat 58-60; mains €3.50-13.50; set dinner for 2 from €24;
☻ dinner Tue-Sun
The owner's welcome is warm and friendly, and the flavours are from across Southeast Asia – *loempias* (spring rolls), Vietnamese noodle soups, Thai curries etc. Set menus also reflect the different traditions, and there are fab displays of takeaway foods in case you don't feel like eating in.

MAMOUCHE Map p297   Moroccan
☎ 673 63 61; Quellijnstraat 104; mains €14.50-22;
☻ dinner Tue-Sun
Mamouche gets serious acclaim for modern Moroccan amid minimalism. Exposed floor-ing, mottled walls and slat-beam ceilings

Sweet snacks and sweet staff at Gary's Muffins

complement the changing selection of couscous, lamb and fish dishes. Check out the brass fixtures in the loo – if you can find it. Reservations are a must.

MÁS TAPAS Map p297 — Spanish
☎ 664 00 66; Saenredamstraat 37; tapas per plate from €3; ✆ dinner

While 'tapas' has become Amsterdamese for anything served on a small plate, this cool, whitewashed room serves the real thing and is full of funsters having a garlicky good time. It wins raves from old and new customers alike.

NIEUW ALBINA Map p297 — Surinamese
☎ 379 02 23; Albert Cuypstraat 49; mains €4.50-11.50; ✆ lunch & dinner Wed-Mon

Nieuw Albina is more polished and more expensive than Albert Cuyp 67, but the flavours are just as bold. One of the cheapest dishes on the menu, *moksi meti* (roast mixed meats over rice), is also one of the best.

PUYCK Map p297 — International
☎ 676 76 77; Ceintuurbaan 147; set menus from €38.50; ✆ dinner Mon-Sat

This place near Sarphatipark offers neither games nor pretension, just imaginative, sophisticated cooking appropriate for a nice night out. Think baby lobster with lettuce, duck breast in Chinese five-spices, or a white wine–poached pear, all served with flair. If they have the Thai curry sorbet, consider yourself lucky.

TURKIYE Map p297 — Turkish
Ferdinand Bolstraat 48; mains €6.50-15.50; ✆ breakfast, lunch & dinner

English may not work at this simple shop, but it doesn't matter: the dishes inside the

glass case are plenty eloquent. Locals value Turkiye for its grilled mains and small plates like stuffed tomatoes and Turkish pizza (€1 to €3.50). Eat-in or takeaway.

ZAGROS Map p297 — Kurdish
☎ 670 04 61; Albert Cuypstraat 50; mains €10.50-15.50; ✆ dinner

Never tried Kurdish food? Neither had we, but we're glad we did. Just as Kurdistan straddles Greece and Persia, so does the cuisine, with grills and stews (mostly lamb and chicken), salads of cucumber, tomato or onion, and starters like hummus and *dumast* (thick, dry yoghurt).

ZEN Map p297 — Japanese
☎ 627 06 07; Frans Halsstraat 38; mains €6.80-17; ✆ lunch & dinner Tue-Sat

Let's be frank: many Japanese restaurants are lovely, elegant poseurs. Zen, however, offers cooking like *okāsan* (mum) used to make: *domburi* (bowls of rice with various ingredients on top), sushi and *tonkatsu* (deep-fried pork cutlet) are just the start. Décor: minimalist Dutch-meets-Japanese. It's also popular for takeaway.

CHEAP EATS
BAGELS & BEANS
Map pp292-3 — Sandwich Shop
☎ 330 55 08; Keizersgracht 504; bagels €2.50-5.50; ✆ breakfast & lunch Mon-Fri, lunch Sat & Sun

At the Ferdinand Bolstraat location (Map p297; ☎ 672 16 10, Ferdinand Bolstraat 70), join the crowds on the square near the Albert Cuypmarkt for bagels with all the usual toppings, plus some new-fangled ones (smoked chicken with avocado and pesto). In poor weather the interiors at both locations are light and airy. Top it all off with a slice of dense fig cake; it goes exceedingly well with coffee.

BAKKEN MET PASSIE Map p297 — Bakery
☎ 670 13 76; Albert Cuypstraat 51-53; ✆ 8am-6pm Tue-Sat

Say your sweetie hates ethnic food but you desperately want something exotic on the Albert Cuyp. This quietly fancy shop bakes the appropriate bribes like yummy Valrhona chocolate tart (€3.85 per slice) or lemon cake (€6.50 per small loaf).

TOP FIVE DE PIJP DINING

- **Bazar** (opposite) Modern Middle Eastern in a rockin' yet civilised setting.
- **Mamouche** (opposite) Super-popular neo-Moroccan in a very cool space.
- **Nieuw Albina** (above) If you've never tried Surinamese, you may be pleasantly surprised.
- **Puyck** (above) Understated, smart, adventurous.
- **Taarte van m'n Tante** (p150) Which are more kitsch? The tasty cakes or the pink décor?

DE SOEPWINKEL Map p297 — Soup

☎ 673 22 93; Eerste Sweelinckstraat 19F; soups €3.50-10; ☼ 11am-8pm Mon-Fri, 11am-6pm Sat
Slurping out loud is positively encouraged at this renowned shop. A welcome alternative to fast-food joints, this sleek, airy eatery does an ever-changing selection of seasonal soups, as well as home-made quiches, cakes and tarts.

GELATERIA ITALIANO PEPPINO

Map p297 — Sweets
☎ 676 49 10; Eerste Sweelinckstraat 16; gelati from €0.90; ☼ 11am-11pm
Ignore those packaged ice-cream cones at the Albert Cuypstraat Market and instead head around the corner for a cone of lemon, mango, Malaga wine or a dozen-plus other flavours. What the heck – take a gamble and let them scoop you some of whatever is currently spinning in the ice-cream maker.

TAART VAN M'N TANTE

Map pp292-3 — Sweets
☎ 776 46 00; Ferdinand Bolstraat 10; cakes per slice around €4; ☼ 10am-6pm
One of Amsterdam's best-loved cake shops operates from this über-kitsch parlour at the entrance to De Pijp: apple pies (Dutch, French or 'tipsy'), pecan pie, and tarts with ingredients like truffles and marzipan with strawberry liqueur. Savouries include the mozzarella-pesto quiche. Hot-pink walls accent cakes dressed like Barbie dolls – or are they Barbies dressed like cakes?

PLANTAGE & OOSTERPARK

The Plantage may be just steps from Nieuwmarkt, but what a difference those few steps make, taking you to an area that's quiet yet close to some important sights. Locations in Oosterpark are a little far out but worth the trip.

ABE VENETO Map pp290-1 — Italian

☎ 639 23 64; Plantage Kerklaan 2; mains €4.50-12.50; ☼ lunch & dinner
Sometimes you just want a corner place with decent food at honest prices. The pizza menu tops out at €9.50 and has

SEE ALSO

- **Café Koosje** (p158) Corner café at the crossroads of everything.
- **Orangery** at the Hortus Botanicus (p110) Lovely dishes in a lovely setting.
- **Soeterijn Café Restaurant** inside the Tropenmuseum (p111) Exotic meals, often themed to the museum's shows.

45 choices – the gorgonzola pizza puts this stinky cheese to excellent use. Other options include pastas, salads and meat dishes. In summer, a terrace is set up by the canal.

DE KAS Map pp282-3 — International

☎ 462 45 62; Kamerlingh Onneslaan 3, Frankendael Park; 5-course menu €42; ☼ lunch Mon-Fri, dinner Mon-Sat
Admired by gourmets city-wide, De Kas has an organic attitude to match its chic glass greenhouse setting – try to go during a thunderstorm! They grow most of their own herbs and produce right there (if it's not busy you might be offered a tour), and the result is incredibly pure flavours with innovative combinations. Romantic and toney.

LA SALA Map pp290-1 — Portuguese/Spanish

☎ 624 48 46; Plantage Kerklaan 41; mains €15-17, tapas €2.70-6.50; ☼ dinner Tue-Sun
Amid a city full of Spanish tapas bars, popular La Sala serves Portuguese dishes as well; *bacalhão* (salt cod) and *espetada de porco* (skewered pork) are favourites. Tapas are generous, varied and colourful. The simple, blue-tiled room is more functional than exotic, but there is busy sidewalk seating in warm weather.

PLANCIUS Map pp290-1 — International

☎ 330 94 69; Plantage Kerklaan 61A; mains €16-19; ☼ lunch & dinner
Next to the Resistance Museum and opposite the Artis Zoo, this dramatically stylish space (bright red bar at the back) is where TV execs head to cut deals over big serves of upmarket comfort food. Lunch is typically sandwiches, salads and pastas. The menu changes quarterly, and there are friendly, good-looking waiters.

TO DINE Map pp290-1
Fusion
☎ 850 24 00; Hotel Arena, 's Gravesandestraat 51; mains €11-21; ☽ lunch & dinner

The main restaurant of the hip Hotel Arena offers adventurous dishes (beef with shallot tarte tatin, mullet with violet artichoke and lobster foam) with influences from France, Spain, the Middle East and Japan. Dance those calories away at the hotel's ToNight club next door.

EASTERN ISLANDS

In this district, a lot of our favourite places are by (or in some cases, literally on) the water. Choose from the historic and homely to world-class slick.

A TAVOLA Map pp290-1
Italian
☎ 625 49 94; Kadijksplein 9; mains €11.50-20; ☽ dinner

Overlooked by most tourists, this authentic Italian restaurant, that's near the Shipping Museum, serves a small but well-chosen menu of meats and pastas that cry out for a selection from its excellent wine list. Even if the service can be a little iffy, the quality of the cooking is consistent and strong. Reservations are a must.

11 Map pp290-1
International
☎ 625 59 99; Oosterdokskade 3-5; lunch mains €4-8.50, 4-course menu €30; ☽ lunch & dinner

On the top floor of the former post office tower (temporary home of the Stedelijk Museum), you'll find one of the city's grandest spaces and the best views bar none. At lunch-time, tuck into sandwiches, pastas and focaccias (think eggplant, hummus and *arugula*), or try the changing four-course dinner menu. At night, 11 is variously a cultural centre with lectures on art and the like and a dance club with an emphasis on electronica.

FIFTEEN Map pp282-3
International
☎ 0900-343 83 36; www.fifteen.nl; Jollemanhof 9; mains €17.50-21, 4-course set menu with wine €42.50; ☽ dinner

'Naked chef' Jamie Oliver has brought to Amsterdam a concept he began in London: take 15 young people from underprivileged backgrounds and train them for a year in the restaurant biz. Results: noble intention, sometimes spotty execution. The setting,

Can you still float after eating dim sum at Sea Palace?

however, is beyond question: Fifteen faces the IJ, and the busy, open-kitchen space is city-cool, with graffiti walls and exposed wood beams.

KOFFIEHUIS VAN DEN VOLKSBOND
Map pp290-1
International
☎ 622 12 09; Kadijksplein 4; mains €11.50-15.50; ☽ dinner

This laid-back place began life as a charitable coffee house for dockers, and it still has a fashionably grungy vibe – wood floors, a giant red-rose mural and tall candles on the tables. The ever-changing menu is huge plates of comfort food with ingredients like mussels and *merguez,* or try the risotto. The Belgian chocolate terrine has fans all over town.

SEA PALACE Map pp290-1
Chinese
☎ 626 47 77; Oosterdokskade 8; mains €9.60-36, yum-cha courses €13.50-15; ☽ lunch & dinner

Funny thing about floating Chinese restaurants: they look like tourist traps and may well be, but from Hong Kong to Holland many are admired for good food. The Sea Palace's three floors are busy with Chinese and non, who come not just for great views of the city from across the IJ. Even if you order dim sum from a menu instead of a cart, the shrimp in the *ha kow* dumplings go pop in your mouth just the same.

> ## SEE ALSO
> - **Kromhout** (p163) Your chance to get inside one of those oh-so-cool Entrepotdok warehouses.

EASTERN DOCKLANDS

This is it: the end of the line, but many agree that the trek is worth it for the adventuresome and beautiful restaurants.

GARE DE L'EST Map pp282-3   International

☎ 463 06 20; Cruquiusweg 9; 4-course set menu €27; ⏰ dinner

Gare de l'Est has both the smallest menu in Amsterdam and also the largest. They say that because four chefs (from traditions including North African, Mediterranean and Asian) take turns nightly in the kitchen, and what their course menus lack in length they make up for in variety over the course of a year. Portuguese tiles and glowing Middle Eastern lamps adorn the interior, and courtyard seating exudes good vibes.

ODESSA Map pp290-1   International

☎ 419 30 10; Veemkade 259; lunch mains €2.75-8.50, dinner mains €16.50-22; ⏰ lunch & dinner

Odessa rocks. Literally. This groovy boat, with indoor and outdoor eating decks and a 1970s-themed 'plush-porno' décor, is just the sort of place where Hugh Hefner would hold a debauched pyjama party – as if to emphasise that fact, DJs take over late at night. The menu changes frequently, and although opinions on food and service run the gamut from 'love it' to 'hate it', there's no denying it's a scene.

SEE ALSO

- Lloyd Hotel (p228) Marvellous open space and a swinging bar in this historic hotel/cultural centre.
- KHL (p164) Try simple fare and, if you're lucky, catch a live band.

PANAMA Map pp290-1   International

☎ 311 86 89; Oostelijke Handelskade 4; mains €11-18; ⏰ lunch & dinner

The Eastern Harbour's first grown-up restaurant has an enormous, sleek dining room, Mondrian colour scheme and steel light fixtures, a good place to fortify yourself before hitting the nightclub on the same premises. Gucci-garbed couples splurge on oysters (in season) and a weekly changing menu of pastas and grills. Wash it down with the – wait for it – Panamartini (vodka, crema ciocolata, espresso).

VOORBIJ HET EINDE Map pp282-3   French

☎ 419 11 33; Sumatrakade 613; mains €24, set menus €33-66; ⏰ dinner Wed-Sat

It means 'beyond the end', and on your trek out here to Java Eiland you may begin to question your judgement. Don't. This place, with its super-mod architectural interior (frosted glass walls, lots of right angles), wins high praise for high French in high style – the menu changes every month or so.

Ententertainment

Entertainment

Call it Sin City. Call it quaint and classic. Call it the party capital of Europe. Call it smart. Call it libertine.

Whatever you call it, chances are Amsterdam has a way to fulfil your taste: from cosy cafés where you can chat all day to wild parties where you can dance all night, from the Concertgebouw to the Red Light District, from smacking a ball to smoking a bowl, from stadium concerts to ice-skating. Intimate jazz pubs, Afro-Latino-electro-boho-trendo, gay, straight or undecided – you name it and Amsterdam probably has it. No wonder people have so many names for this city.

That said, Amsterdam is far from out of control. Part of the reason the nightlife thrives goes back to the ethic of 'do what you want as long as nobody else is harmed'. That has begun to change a bit. Amsterdam is part of the Netherlands, and the Netherlands is part of Europe, from where there's pressure to clamp down, specifically on drugs. Whereas the authorities once had an attitude of *gedoogbeleid* (turning a blind eye) to illegal activities, now that eye is not quite so blind. To read more, see the Night Mayors boxed text, p168.

In reality though, most folk don't seem to notice much. Amsterdammers, it seems, always find ways to party on. To do just that, the busiest nightlife districts are in the Southern Canal Belt, concentrated around Rembrandtplein and Leidseplein (some large music clubs are near the latter), although the Jordaan can also be busy. Students will find plenty of company around the Spui, while Reguliersdwarsstraat is the centre of Amsterdam's gay scene. The variety of marijuana bars throughout the Centrum should be enough to keep anyone happy.

Lovers of the performing arts will find venues throughout town, including the Old South (the Concertgebouw), the Eastern Islands (the Muziekgebouw aan 't IJ) and Nieuwmarkt area (the Stopera).

DRINKING

Given Amsterdam's wild reputation, it may surprise the first-time visitor that, in the mainstream, Amsterdam is very much a café society.

When the Dutch say 'café', they mean a pub, and there are over 1000 of them in the city. More than just drinking houses, they're places to go and hang out for hours if you like. Amsterdam's cafés are stunning in their variety; some have regular customers or a certain type of clientele that's been coming there for years, if not generations.

Many cafés have outside seating on a *terras* (terrace), glorious in summer, and sometimes covered and heated in winter. These are great places to relax and watch people pass by, soak up the sun, read a paper or write postcards. Once you've ordered a drink you'll probably be left alone, but you might be expected to order the occasional top-up. If all tables are occupied, don't be shy about asking if a seat is taken and sharing a table.

Most of these cafés serve food as well. Less adventurous chefs get by on soups, sandwiches, salads, *tostis* (ingredients such as cheese and tomato or pesto grilled between two slices of bread) and the like. Cafés that take their food seriously call themselves *eetcafé*, and their food can be very good indeed.

TOP FIVE DRINKING

- Feel like you're part of history over a beer at **Hoppe** (p156).
- Taste Amsterdam's own at **Bierbrouwerij 't IJ** (p112).
- See what it's like to drink from Amsterdam's shortest pipes at **Pilsener Club** (p156).
- Get a brew with a view at **Café de Jaren** (p158).
- Contemplate the gorgeous canal outside **'t Smalle** (p157).

The price for a standard beer varies from around €1.25 in the outer suburbs to €2.50 in the popular Leidseplein and Rembrandtplein areas; a mixed drink (eg scotch and coke) will set you back €3 to €5. If you occupy a table or sit at the bar, it's common to put drinks on a tab and to pay when you leave.

Lager beer is the staple, served cool and topped by a two finger–thick head of froth – supposedly to trap the flavour. Requests of 'no head please' will be met with a steely response. *Een bier, een pils* or *een vaas* will get you a normal glass; *een kleintje pils* is a small glass and *een fluitje* is a small, thin, Cologne-style glass. Many places also serve half-litre mugs *(een grote pils)* to please tourists, but somehow draught lager doesn't taste the same in a mug and goes flat if you don't drink it quickly! Better to do as the locals do.

Popular brands include Heineken, Amstel, Grolsch, Oranjeboom, Dommelsch, Bavaria and the cheap Brouwersbier put out by the Albert Heijn supermarket chain. They contain about 5% alcohol by volume, so a few of those seemingly small glasses can pack quite a wallop. Tasty and stronger Belgian beers, such as Duvel and Westmalle Triple, are also very popular and reasonably priced. *Witbier* ('white beer', eg the Dutch Wieckse Witte, the Belgian Hoegaarden) is a somewhat murky, crisp, somewhat citrusy blonde beer that's drunk in summer with a slice of lemon. The dark, sweet *bokbier* is available in autumn. Don't be surprised if the beer sold in supermarkets is not much cheaper than beer in pubs.

Dutch gin *(genever,* pronounced 'ya-*nay*-ver') is made from juniper berries and is drunk chilled from a tiny glass filled to the brim. Most people prefer *jonge* (young) *genever,* which is smooth and relatively easy to drink; *oude* (old) *genever* has a strong juniper flavour and can be an acquired taste. A common combination, known as a *kopstoot* (head banger), is a glass of *genever* with a beer chaser – few people can handle more than two or three of those. Brandy is known as *vieux* or *brandewijn.* There are plenty of indigenous liqueurs, including *advocaat* (a kind of eggnog) and the herb-based *Beerenburg,* a Frisian schnapps.

Wines in all varieties are very popular. The average Amsterdam supermarket stocks wines from every corner of Europe (with excellent value from Spain and Bulgaria) and many countries further afield, such as Chile, South Africa and Australia. The most expensive bottle in a supermarket rarely costs more than €8 and will be quite drinkable.

The proper toast is *prost,* but the Italian *cin-cin* is also fine.

NO MORE MUD IN YOUR EYE

In Amsterdam, if you order a white beer, a soda water, or any cold drink served with a lemon slice, it will almost invariably be served with a plastic stick, like a swizzle stick on one end, with a plastic disc or clover with little spikes sticking out on the other.

The stick is called a *stamper* – sometimes they're referred to as *stampertjes* (little stampers). You use the spiked end to crush the lemon in the bottom of the glass. No more lemon juice in your partner's eye, and no wasted lemon juice either.

Entertainment

DRINKING

Lots of clubs have wall displays of their patrons, especially the regulars

BROWN CAFÉS

The most historic and famous type of café is the brown café (*bruin café*). The name comes from the interior, stained with smoke from centuries of use (recent aspirants simply slap on the brown paint). You may well find sand on the wooden floor or Persian rugs on the tables to soak up spilled beer, and some sell snacks or full meals. Most importantly: they provide an atmosphere conducive to deep, meaningful and often convivial conversation.

Medieval Centre

CAFÉ DE DOELEN Map pp292-3
☎ 624 90 23; Kloveniersburgwal 125
On a busy canalside crossroads between the Amstel and Red Light District, this café dates back to 1895 and looks it: carved wooden goat's head, stained leaded glass lamps, sand on the floor. Still, it's far from stuffy, there's a fun, youthful atmosphere here, and during fine weather the tables spill across the street for picture-perfect canal views.

DE SCHUTTER Map pp292-3
☎ 622 46 08; Voetboogstraat 13-15
This large student *eetcafé* has a brown-café look, a relaxed vibe and inexpensive, tasty *dagschotels* (dishes of the day). It's open for lunch and dinner, and is a good place to fortify yourself on the cheap before a night on the town.

DE ZWART Map pp292-3
☎ 624 65 11; Spuistraat 334
'Not everyone has knowledge of beer, but those who have it drink it here', is the translation of the slogan on a panel above this atmospheric bar with the original tile floor from 1921. Just across the alley from Hoppe, De Zwart gets a different (though amicable) crowd of left-wing journalists and writers, as well as local-government people.

HOPPE Map pp292-3
☎ 420 44 20; Spui 18-20
Go on. Do your bit to ensure Hoppe maintains one of the highest beer turnovers in the city. Since 1670, drinkers have been enticed behind that velvet curtain into the dark interior to down a few glasses – the entrance is to the right of the pub-with-terrace of the same name. In summer, Hoppe's crowd of boisterous business boys spills over onto the pavement of the Spui.

OPORTO Map pp286-7
☎ 638 07 02; Zoutsteeg 1
This tiny brown café is worth visiting just for the inlaid woodwork behind the bar (check out the Zodiac signs). Its wrought-iron-and-parchment lighting fixtures are said to have been the same for 60 years.

PILSENER CLUB Map pp286-7
☎ 623 17 77; Begijnensteeg 4
Also known as Engelse Reet (ask the bartender for a translation), this small, narrow and ramshackle place doesn't allow you to do anything but drink and talk, which is what a 'real' brown café is all about. It opened in 1893 and has hardly changed since. Beer comes straight from the kegs in the back via the 'shortest pipes in Amsterdam' (most places have vats in a cellar or side room with long hoses to the bar); connoisseurs say they can taste the difference.

Nieuwmarkt

DE SLUYSWACHT Map pp286-7
☎ 625 76 11; Jodenbreestraat 1
Listing like a ship in a high wind, this tiny black building was once a lock-keeper's house on the Oude Schans. Today, the canalside terrace is one of the nicest spots we know in town to relax and down a beer (Dommelsch is the house speciality) with gorgeous views of the **Montelbaanstoren** (p40).

LOKAAL 'T LOOSJE Map pp286-7
☎ 627 26 35; Nieuwmarkt 32-35
With its beautiful etched-glass windows and tile tableaux on the walls, this is one of the oldest and prettiest cafés in the Nieuwmarkt area. It attracts a vibrant mix of students, locals and tourists.

Jordaan

CAFÉ 'T MONUMENTJE Map p285
☎ 624 35 41; Westerstraat 120
Diagonally opposite Café Nol, this slightly scruffy café is always full of barflies, backgammon players and locals. It's a good spot for a beer and a snack after shopping at the Westermarkt.

CAFÉ 'T SMALLE Map p285
☎ 623 96 17; Egelantiersgracht 12
Take your boat and dock right on 't Smalle's pretty terrace – there's hardly a more convivial setting in the daytime or a more romantic one at night. It's equally charming inside – dating back to 1786 as a *genever* distillery and tasting house, and restored during the 1970s with antique porcelain beer pumps and leadlight windows.

CAFÉ NOL Map p285
☎ 624 53 80; Westerstraat 109
Hipsters may cringe, but Café Nol epitomises the old-style Jordaan café with a must-see, kitsch interior. It's the sort of place where the original Jordanese (ie before students, artists and professionals moved in) still sing oompah ballads with drunken abandon; nowadays, everyone from athletic types to drag queens might join in. Here comes the neighbourhood. Note: it doesn't open until 9pm.

DE REIGER Map p285
☎ 624 74 26; Nieuwe Leliestraat 34
Assiduously local but highly atmospheric, this café has a quiet front bar and a noisy, more spacious dining section at the back serving a short menu (eg steaks or duck with peppercorns).

DE TUIN Map p285
☎ 624 45 59; Tweede Tuindwarsstraat 13
Always a good place to start the evening – join the youngish clientele enjoying the wide selection of Belgian beers, good food and funky soul music.

Western Canal Belt

CAFÉ HET MOLENPAD Map pp292-3
☎ 625 96 80; Prinsengracht 653
This place attracts a nice mix of artists – some of whose work adorns the walls of this gallery-café – students and tourists. Lunch is the standard sandwich-and-salad affair, but dinner dishes are more interesting, with a mix of Dutch and Mediterranean flavours.

DE DOFFER Map pp292-3
☎ 622 66 86; Runstraat 12-14
Writers, students and artists congregate at this popular café (with adjoining bar) for affordable food and good conversation. The dining room, with its old Heineken posters, large wooden tables and, occasionally, fresh flowers, is particularly ambient at night.

DE PIEPER Map pp292-3
☎ 626 47 75; Prinsengracht 424
Considered by some customers to be the king of the brown cafés, De Pieper is small, unassuming and unmistakably old (1665). The interior features stained-glass windows, fresh sand on the floors, antique Delft beer mugs hanging from the bar and a working Belgian beer pump (1875). It's a friendly, sweet place for a late-night Wieckse Witte.

DE PRINS Map p285
☎ 624 93 82; Prinsengracht 124
Close to the **Anne Frank Huis** (p85), this pleasant and popular brown café prepares good lunch-time sandwiches, a terrific blue-cheese fondue at night, and international dishes like vegetarian wraps.

DE II PRINSEN Map pp286-7
☎ 624 97 22; Prinsenstraat 27
With its large windows, chandelier, mosaic floor and big terrace, this café looks suitably restrained. You may be surprised then by the pumping disco music inside; all those students munching on tasty sandwiches don't seem to mind.

DE TWEE ZWAANTJES Map p285
☎ 625 27 29; Prinsengracht 114; ⏰ ring for opening hr
The small, authentic 'Two Swans' is at its hilarious best on weekend nights, when you can join some 100 people belting out torch songs and pop standards. Hours are erratic, so ring ahead first.

HET PAPENEILAND Map pp286-7
☎ 624 19 89; Prinsengracht 2
You won't be the only tourist visiting this café, but that doesn't make it any less worthwhile. It's a 1642 gem with Delft-blue tiles and a central stove. The name, 'Papists' Island', goes back to the Reformation when there was a clandestine Catholic church across the canal, allegedly linked to the other side by a once-secret tunnel that is still visible from the top of the stairs.

VAN PUFFELEN Map p285

☎ 624 62 70; Prinsengracht 377

This large café-restaurant, popular among cashed-up professionals and intellectual types, has lots of nooks and crannies for nice, cosy drinks, and big, communal tables for sharing meals like antipasto and large salads.

Southern Canal Belt

EYLDERS Map pp292-3

☎ 624 27 04; Korte Leidsedwarsstraat 47

During WWII, Eylders was a meeting place for artists who refused to toe the cultural line imposed by the Nazis, and the spirit lingers on. It's still an artists' café with exhibits, and makes a quiet retreat from the Leidseplein.

OOSTERLING Map pp292-3

☎ 623 41 40; Utrechtsestraat 140

Opened in the 1700s as a tea and coffee outlet for the United East India Company, Oosterling is as authentic as it gets – run by the same family since 1877. These days it's packed with the after-work-drinks crowd from the bank across the square and is one of the very few cafés that has a bottle-shop (liquor-store) permit.

Old South

WILDSCHUT Map p296

☎ 676 82 20; Roelof Hartplein 1

A real gathering place for the Old South. When the weather's warm, pretty much everyone heads to the terrace, with views of the Amsterdam School buildings. And when the weather's not great, soak up the atmosphere in the Art Deco interior.

De Pijp

PILSVOGEL Map p297

☎ 664 64 83; Gerard Douplein 14

The kitchen dispenses small plates (€2.50 to €4.50) and *dagschotels* (€11.50) to a 20-something crowd, but that's really secondary when you're sitting on De Pijp's loveliest, busiest corner. Watch the world go by, or at least its ambassadors.

SARPHAAT Map p297

☎ 675 15 65; Ceintuurbaan 157

Grab an outdoor table by the Sarphatipark, tuck into a slice of Boston cheesecake and a coffee, and see if you don't feel like a local.

Plantage

CAFÉ KOOSJE Map pp290-1

☎ 320 08 17; Plantage Middenlaan 37

If the three catch-words for real estate are location, location and location, then Koosje's got a lock on the market, between the Artis Zoo (p108) and the Hollandsche Schouwburg (p109). There are lots of windows to watch the action outside, a great corner vibe, and small plates and sandwiches, most under €6.

GRAND CAFÉS

Grand cafés are spacious and have comfortable furniture. A good tradition in many grand cafés is the indoor reading table with the day's papers and news magazines, including one or two in English. Another difference: they all have food menus, some quite elaborate. Some are very grand indeed, and when they open at 10am they're perfect for a lazy brunch with relaxing chamber music tinkling away in the background.

Check out the CoBrA Café (p146) or Bazar Amsterdam (p148).

Medieval Centre

CAFÉ DANTE Map pp292-3

☎ 638 88 39; Spuistraat 320

This big, Art Deco–style space is peaceful during the day, but after 5pm weeknights it transforms into a lively bar full of stockbrokers and suits. Plus, you get your choice of outside views: the busy Spui out front or the lovely Singel in the back. Upstairs is the Herman Brood Galerie (p190).

CAFÉ DE JAREN Map pp292-3

☎ 625 57 71; Nieuwe Doelenstraat 20

Watch the Amstel flow by from the balcony and waterside terraces of this soaring, bright and *very* grand café, one of our favourites. Find a foreign publication at the great reading table and settle down for Sunday brunch (try the smoked-salmon rolls) or an afternoon snack like banana-cream pie.

LUXEMBOURG Map pp292-3

☎ 620 62 64; Spui 24

Join gaggles of glam locals and tourists at this permanently busy café. Grab a paper

Luxembourg (opposite), one of Amsterdam's grand cafés

(from the reading table or the Athenaeum newsagency across the square), procure a sunny seat on the terrace, order the 'Royale' snack platter (bread, cured meats, Dutch cheese and deep-fried croquettes) and watch the world go by. Inside are parquet floors, a marble bar and Art Deco stained-glass skylight.

Nieuwmarkt
CAFÉ-RESTAURANT DANTZIG
Map pp292-3

☎ 620 90 39; Zwanenburgwal 15

Located in the Stopera building, Dantzig doesn't have the history of some of the other cafés in town, but that doesn't make it any less appealing. The great Amstel-side terrace is always busy in summer, with excellent views over the water and lots of sunlight.

Western Islands
DULAC Map pp286-7

☎ 624 42 65; Haarlemmerstraat 118

This former bank building is outrageously decked-out in a kooky, but kind of spooky, mixture of styles (think Turkish, Art Nouveau and Amsterdam School, with a few Gothic accents). There are DJs Thursday through to Saturday nights, a pool table and an amiable mix of students, older folks and Americans.

Western Canal Belt
CAFÉ DE VERGULDE GAPER
Map pp286-7

☎ 624 89 75; Prinsenstraat 30

Decorated with old chemists' bottles and vintage posters, this former pharmacy (it translates as 'the golden mortar') has nice amiable staff and a terrace with copious afternoon sun. It gets busy late afternoons with 20- and 30-somethings, as well as media types meeting for after-work drinks and big plates of fried snacks or dinner salads.

Southern Canal Belt
CAFÉ AMERICAIN Map pp292-3

☎ 556 32 32; Amsterdam American Hotel, Leidsekade 97

This Art Deco monument, opened in 1902, was a grand café before the concept even existed, with huge stained-glass windows overlooking Leidseplein, a lovely, library-like reading table and a great terrace.

DE KROON Map pp292-3

☎ 625 20 11; Rembrandtplein 17-1

A popular venue for media events and movie-premiere parties, with high ceilings, velvet chairs, and the chance to wave at the Little People below on the Rembrandtplein. There is a lift to get up the two storeys, but climb the two flights instead and you'll be rewarded with an Art Deco tiled staircase.

IRISH & ENGLISH PUBS

You won't have any trouble finding an Irish or English pub. We've listed just a few of our favourites.

Medieval Centre

DURTY NELLY'S Map pp286-7
☎ 638 01 25; Warmoesstraat 117
Huge, dark and always busy, this Red Light District pub attracts foreign visitors from the cheap hotels in the area with fun, drinks, darts and pool. It serves a first-rate Irish breakfast and has Internet access too.

MOLLY MALONE'S Map pp286-7
☎ 624 11 50; Oudezijds Kolk 9
Regularly packed with Irish folk, this dark, woody pub holds spontaneous folk music sessions – bring your own guitar.

TARA Map pp286-7
☎ 427 46 57; Rokin 85-89
This expat meeting place combines Irish folksiness with Amsterdam chic. In its maze of rooms (the one-time home of German expressionist Max Beckmann) you'll find warm fireplaces, a cool bar, gorgeous wall carvings and seats salvaged from an old Irish church. Catch frequent musical happenings and sports on the telly. Meals include Irish stew, and beef and Guinness pie (mains €10.50 to €13.50).

Southern Canal Belt

In addition to the following, you'll also find Irish-style pubs around the Leidseplein (it teems with them) and Rembrandtplein.

MULLIGANS Map pp292-3
☎ 622 13 30; Amstel 100
This is probably the most 'authentic' pub, at least music-wise. There's a congenial atmosphere, Guinness on tap and live Irish music most nights from 9pm (no cover charge). Sunday *sesiàns* let you participate. BYOI (instrument) and T (talent).

TASTING HOUSES

There are also a few tasting houses (*proeflokalen*), generally small affairs where you can try dozens of *genevers* (Dutch gin) and liqueurs. Some are attached to distilleries (a

holdover from the 17th century when many small distilleries operated around town), while others are simply affiliated.

Medieval Centre

DE BLAUWE PARADE Map pp286-7
☎ 624 48 60; Nieuwezijds Voorburgwal 176-180
The building, now the Hotel Die Poort van Cleve, was the site of the original Heineken brewery, so it seems an appropriate place for tastings (of *genevers* though, not beers). While there, feast your eyes on the Delft-blue tile mural (1870s), a parade of children bearing gifts to an emperor.

DE DRIE FLESCHJES Map pp286-7
☎ 624 84 43; Gravenstraat 18
Behind the Nieuwe Kerk, the distiller Bootz's tasting room dates from 1650. It is dominated by 52 vats that are rented out to businesses that entertain clients here. It specialises in liqueurs (although you can also get *genevers*) – the macaroon liqueur is quite nice. Take a peek at the collection of *kalkoentjes*, small bottles with hand-painted portraits of former mayors.

PROEFLOKAAL WIJNAND FOCKINCK
Map pp286-7
☎ 639 26 95; Pijlsteeg 31; ⏰ 3-9pm
This small tasting house (dating from 1679) has scores of *genevers* and liqueurs – some quite expensive and potent. It's in an arcade behind Grand Hotel Krasnapolsky, and although there are no seats or stools, it is an intimate place to knock back a taste or two with a friend. We particularly enjoy the *boswandeling* ('walk in the woods'), a vivacious combination of young *genever*, herb bitters and orange liqueur – the effect is like cloves. Note: large groups are not welcome.

Western Canal Belt

DE ADMIRAAL Map pp286-7
☎ 625 43 34; Herengracht 319; ⏰ 5pm-midnight Mon-Sat
The grandest and largest of Amsterdam's tasting houses, De Admiraal is also a restaurant and party venue. Although some grumble that they pour only their own house brands (16 *genevers* and 60 liqueurs made by Van Wees, an Amsterdam distiller), it's hard to quibble over the lovely setting and pleasant staff.

BEER CAFÉS

Beer cafés specialise in the brew, with many seasonal and potent brands on tap and in the bottle.

Medieval Centre

IN DE WILDEMAN Map pp286-7
☎ 638 23 48; Kolksteeg 3

This former distillery tasting house has been transformed into an atmospheric yet quiet beer café with over 200 bottled beers, 18 varieties on tap and a smokefree area. Locals rave about the choice of Trappist ales, the huge selection from Belgium and the Netherlands, and the potent French 'Belzebuth' (13% alcohol!).

Nieuwmarkt

DE BEKEERDE SUSTER Map pp286-7
☎ 423 01 12; Kloveniersburgwal 6-8

It's got the brew tanks, it's got the beautiful hardwood interior, it's even got the history: a 16th-century brewery-cloister run by nuns. Stop in for a meal of pub grub, or make it a start of an evening on Nieuwmarkt Square.

Western Canal Belt

GOLLEM Map pp286-7
☎ 626 66 45; Raamsteeg 4

Gollem, the pioneer of Amsterdam's beer cafés, is a minuscule space covered all over in beer paraphernalia (old coasters, bottles and posters). The 200 beers on tap and in the bottle attract lots of drinkers.

'T ARENDSNEST Map pp286-7
☎ 421 20 57; Herengracht 90

This gorgeous, restyled brown café, with its glowing, copper *genever* boilers behind the bar, specialises in Dutch beer served by helpful staff. Be sure to try the herby, powerful Jopen Koyt, brewed from a 1407 recipe.

Eastern Islands

BROUWERIJ 'T IJ Map pp290-1
☎ 622 83 25; Funenkade 7; ☽ 3-8pm Wed-Sun

The tasting room of Amsterdam's leading microbrewery (p112) has a cosy, down-and-dirty beer-hall feel (walls lined with bottles from around the world and dried hops) and the house brew is on tap. In nice weather

you can enjoy your beer on the terrace at the foot of the windmill. Where better to sample a *zatte* (drunk) or a sweet, orange-coloured *struis* (ostrich)?

THEATRE CAFÉS

Theatre cafés are normally attached or adjacent to theatres, serving meals before and drinks after performances. Generally they're good places to catch performers after the show, though they'd be lovely spots even without that attraction.

Medieval Centre

DE BRAKKE GROND Map pp286-7
☎ 626 00 44; Nes 43

Part of the Flemish Cultural Centre, this café overlooking a quiet square does an honest trade in Flemish beer (try a magnum bottle from a Belgian abbey) and home-style food (think steak *au poivre* or salmon with Ardennes ham).

Western Canal Belt

FELIX MERITIS CAFÉ Map p285
☎ 626 23 21; Felix Meritis Bldg, Keizersgracht 324

Join performing artists from around Europe and the city's cultural cognoscenti imbibing in this high-ceilinged, quietly refined room (think theatrical lighting). Huge windows overlooking the canal make it a sunny place for breakfast (from 9am).

Southern Canal Belt

CAFÉ SCHILLER Map pp292-3
☎ 624 98 46; Rembrandtplein 26

Most cafés would pay a fortune to have Schiller's fabulous Deco interior, but this is original. Walls are lined with portraits of Dutch actors and cabaret artists from the 1920s and '30s. Bar stools and booths are often occupied by tippling journalists and artists, and folks tucking into pre- and post-theatre menus.

DE BALIE Map pp292-3
☎ 623 36 73; Kleine Gartmanplantsoen 10

In the Balie performance space, lovely Deco-meets-industrial design attracts a diverse crowd of artists, politicians, journalists, actors, film-makers and anyone else looking for a decent lunch.

DRINKING

DE SMOESHAAN Map pp292-3
☎ 625 03 68; Leidsekade 90
Theater Bellevue's café gets pretty lively, both before and after the shows, with theatre visitors and performers. During daytimes it's a nice place to relax by the Singelgracht. The pub food is better than it needs to be (try the *gehakt* at lunchtime) and there's a good full-on restaurant upstairs too (restaurant closed July to mid-August).

Old South
Worth visiting in this area are 't Blauwe Theehuis (p146) and Kriterion (p178).

CAFÉ VERTIGO Map pp282-3
☎ 612 30 21; Vondelpark 3
Bonus: this is both a theatre café (at the main hall of the Filmmuseum, p98) and, in nice weather, a great place to linger outdoors watching the cyclists and families go by in the Vondelpark. Try the *uitsmijter* Vertigo (egg sandwich with bacon, mushrooms, tomato and melted cheese for €7.50). Main dishes cost €14.50 to €27.

Eastern Islands

STAR FERRY Map pp282-3
☎ 788 20 90; Piet Heinkade 1
It's practically a commandment nowadays that any newly built performing space worth the name has to have a flash café, and the café at the new Muziekgebouw aan 't IJ is hard to beat for location and views. Several storeys of glass give you an IJ's-eye perspective.

OTHER CAFÉS
Medieval Centre

B VAN B CAFÉ Map pp286-7
☎ 638 39 14; Beursplein 1; ⏰ 9am-5pm Mon-Wed, 10am-6pm Thu-Sat, 11am-6pm Sun
The café in the Beurs van Berlage (p64), one of the city's most spectacular buildings, boasts original brick and tilework, and murals by Jan Toorop (1903) representing past, present and future. Food includes lasagne, croquettes, steaks and the usual assortment of sandwiches and salads. Unless the main building is reopened to the public (such as for a concert), this is your only sure way to get inside.

CAFÉ CUBA Map pp286-7
☎ 627 26 35; Nieuwmarkt 3
If a brown café was beamed to the tropical Atlantic, it would probably have Café Cuba's air of faded elegance. Slouch into a table with names etched into it, and quaff blender drinks like mai-tais, planter's punch and the legendary mojito. It may remind you of Hemingway or the Buena Vista Social Club, although we can't help wondering whether Café Cuba's attractive 20- and 30-something crowd has even heard of them.

CAFÉ-RESTAURANT KAPITEIN ZEPPO'S Map pp286-7
☎ 624 20 57; Gebed Zonder End 5
This site, off Grimburgwal, has assumed many guises over the centuries: a cloister during the 15th, a horse-carriage storehouse in the 17th and a cigar factory in the 19th. These days it's festive, attractive and almost romantic, with a beautiful garden and Belgian beers. There's live music Sunday from 4pm (cover groups and big bands).

WAAG CAFÉ Map pp286-7
☎ 422 77 72; Nieuwmarkt 4
This former 15th-century weigh house (and later, gallows! – see p78) is now an impressive café-restaurant combining old-world accents (massive, circular wrought-iron candelabras) with new-world drinks and food, though it's rather expensive. It serves pretty good sandwiches (try the Club) and salads too, and there's *so*-not-medieval wireless Internet access.

I GET AROUND...
We suppose it was only a matter of time before someone combined two legendary Amsterdam pastimes: cycling and beer. Het Fietscafé (Bike Café; ☎ 06 5386 4090; www.fietscafe.nl; per hr/day €75/275, plus delivery fee of Mon-Fri/Sat & Sun €190/238; 30/50L keg €50/75) is a pedal-powered party, shaped like an open-sided trolley car with a bar down the middle and barstools on either side. Here, though, the barstools sit atop pedals, which you and up to 16 of your mates can use to go anywhere cars can (except highways). Designate a bartender and a driver (who's not allowed to drink), pop your favourite CD in the player, and you're on your way.

Jordaan

CAFÉ THIJSSEN Map pp286-7

☎ 623 89 94; Brouwersgracht 107

The glowing umber, Art Deco inspired interior with stained-glass windows and big tables is a crowd-puller. It's busy on weekends with groups of neo-Jordanese yuppies meeting up for a late brunch and staying on until dinner.

Western Canal Belt

POMPADOUR Map pp292-3

☎ 623 95 54; Huidenstraat 12

Join society ladies sipping top-notch tea and nibbling away at home-made Belgian-style chocolates and pastries at this chichi little tearoom in the Negen Straatjes. If you just want the chocolates, they're €4.30 per 100g. Note: it's not open on Sundays, but a new branch is, at Kerkstraat 148 (pp292–3).

WERCK Map p285

☎ 627 40 79; Prinsengracht 277

Finally, a café that is worthy of the high-profile location between the Anne Frank Huis and Westerkerk. You can choose from an assortment of sandwiches and snacks (€3 to €8), steaks and more involved mains (€14 to €18.50; think chicken with smoked bacon or black tagliatelle with morel sauce), but the real reason to be here is to see and be seen on the crushed-white-stone terrace.

Southern Canal Belt

AMSTEL BAR & BRASSERIE Map pp290-1

☎ 622 60 60; Amstel Hotel, Professor Tulpplein 1

So you need to entertain a client. She's very high powered and you can't leave things to chance. The bar at the Amstel Intercontinental Hotel is dignified and appropriately clubby, and its river-view location is the power spot in town. We expect you'll get that contract you wanted and may even rub elbows with famous financiers for your next deal.

DE KOE Map pp292-3

☎ 625 44 82; Marnixstraat 381

'The Cow' is loved by a 25-plus crowd of locals for its gezellig atmosphere, fun pop quizzes, darts tournaments, good (cheap)

WORTH NOTING

Near Leidseplein, Marnixstraat has a clutch of funky and busy bars. Join the perpetually clamorous din of 20-something arts students, designers and stylish city workers drinking and dancing:

- **Lux** (Map pp292–3; ☎ 422 14 12; Marnix-straat 403)
- **Kamer 401** (Map pp292–3; ☎ 320 45 80; Marnixstraat 401)
- **Weber** (Map pp292–3; ☎ 627 05 74; Marnixstraat 397)

restaurant and free performances by local rock bands.

TWINS BACKSTAGE Map pp292-3

☎ 622 36 38; Utrechtsedwarsstraat 67

Actual twins Greg and Gary Christmas once had a song-and-dance act, and in the 1970s they opened this café as a sideline. Greg passed away several years ago, and Gary keeps things going with substantial help from the neighbours. Don't expect crisp service or top-notch food, but do expect encompassing kitsch, from mannequins in crocheted shawls to flower power decals. No matter your sexual orientation, you'll find a titillating photo on the washroom wall.

Plantage

AMSTEL HAVEN Map pp282-3

☎ 665 26 72; Mauritskade 1

Bike or boat up to where the Amstel meets the Singelgracht, snag a canalside table under an umbrella, and have yourself a swell view of the water and skyscrapers. Daytimes, munch on uitsmijters, sandwiches and mains, and on weekend nights, the dining room becomes a dance floor with DJs or live music.

Eastern Islands

KROMHOUT Map pp290-1

☎ 330 09 29; Entrepotdok 36

You've always wanted to see those lovely buildings of the Entrepotdok from the inside? Now you can, at this dark and cosy café-restaurant. Amid the brick and beams, enjoy a beer or coffee, and meals are better than they need to be (lunch around €7, three-course menus around €20).

Eastern Docklands

KHL Map pp282-3

☎ 779 15 75; Oostelijke Handelskade 44

Proof of how far this district has come, KHL is a one-time squatter café gone legit. Next to the Lloyd Hotel, it's a historic brick building with great tilework, and the garden is worth a glass or two. There's often music on weekends, everything from Latin to pop to Klezmer.

DESIGNER BARS

There are a number of 'loungey' designer bars. Some are ultramodern, some retro, others shabby-chic.

Medieval Centre

BAR BEP Map pp286-7

☎ 626 56 49; Nieuwezijds Voorburgwal 260

With its olive-green vinyl couches and ruby-red walls, Bep resembles a kitsch, 1950s Eastern European cabaret lounge. It gets groovy with film-makers, photographers and artists. The heat is off since its heyday, and we prefer it.

DIEP Map pp286-7

☎ 420 20 20; Nieuwezijds Voorburgwal 256

Located just next door to Bar Bep, Diep does first-rate quirky decorations. You might find chandeliers made of bubble wrap, a 6ft fibreglass hammerhead shark, illuminated electronic signs above the bar and a similarly creative crowd.

Nieuwmarkt

LIME Map pp286-7

☎ 639 30 20; Zeedijk 104

Small but perfectly formed Lime, with its ever-changing, kitsch-cool interior and upbeat grooves, is the perfect pre-club pit stop.

Jordaan

FINCH Map pp286-7

☎ 626 24 61; Noordermarkt 5

This funkalicious bar, with its retro décor (deliberately mismatched yet somehow harmonious) is just the spot to hang out and knock back a few beers after a visit to the market. It's known for an arty–designy clientele, and lipstick lesbians.

PROUST Map pp286-7

☎ 623 91 45; Noordermarkt 4

Next door to Finch, this bar is sleek and hip with mod colours, and the crowd changes as the hour does – families in the daytime, students (and older) at night. It's also known for its hot chocolate.

Western Canal Belt

DYLAN Map p285

☎ 530 20 10; Keizersgracht 384

Like the hotel surrounding it, the Dylan's lobby bar is super-posh – sleek black and white with Indonesian influences, and a great place to pose…if you can get in. Restaurant patrons get seating priority.

PLACES TO PLAY

You'll have ample opportunity for mind games at Amsterdam's bars and clubs, but for something more traditional, try one of the following. Some are pretty down-and-dirty. Hours vary, but these places generally open from early afternoon through the evening.

- **Snookerclub Final Touch** (Map pp292-3; ☎ 620 92 52; Prinsengracht 735) This two-storey spot with six snooker tables and five pool tables feels studenty but gets a mixed crowd. Other games include backgammon, darts and chess.
- **Schaakhuis Gambit** (Map p285; ☎ 622 18 01; Bloemgracht 20) Chess players won't want to miss Gambit's 10 intimate, well-worn tables. Daytimes the crowd skews older, while the sharks come out at night. Refreshments include coffee, beer and *tostis*.
- **Snookerclub De Keizers** (Map p285; ☎ 623 15 86; Keizersgracht 256) De Keizers five storeys feel like something out of *The Shining*, a once-grand 18th-century canal house whose huge rooms now contain just one or two tables each. You can get drinks and bar snacks, and it's always pretty quiet. It's bittersweet to see such faded glory; on the other hand, it's soooo cool that it exists.
- **Max Euweplein** (Map pp292-3) Enthusiastic chess players can play and schmooze around the oversized outdoor chessboard.

You might swear that all the beautiful people surrounding you stepped off the pages of the fashion magazines on the coffee tables.

BRIX Map pp286-7
☎ 639 03 51; Wolvenstraat 16
The mod lounge setting at this new spot makes it a great place to chill over a beer or enjoy small plates like herring and salmon carpaccio, and chicken lemongrass sticks with banana chutney. There's live jazz Sunday and Monday nights from about 9pm.

Southern Canal Belt

DE HUYSCHKAEMER Map pp292-3
☎ 627 05 75; Utrechtsestraat 137
A one-time restaurant, De Huyschkaemer has made the transition to a full-time designer bar, with a mixed crowd – gay and straight, expat and local, old and young. The setting is minimalist, with spare walls and booths.

SUZY WONG Map pp292-3
☎ 626 67 69; Korte Leidsedwarsstraat 45
This sure-to-impress bar bustles with Dutch trendies and actors. The look? Victorian drawing room on speed, with red velveteen wallpaper and a bamboo garden; a photo of Andy Warhol observes. A worthy place to fortify yourself before heading across to Jimmy Woo's (p169).

De Pijp

BAR ÇA Map p297
☎ 470 41 44; Marie Heinekenplein 30-31
Bursting on the scene in 2005 and probably the hottest café in town, this 'Barcelona in Amsterdam' themed club has brought real life to Marie Heinekenplein. Hang in the posh plush-red and darkwood interior, or spread out onto the terrace.

18 TWINTIG Map p297
☎ 470 06 51; Ferdinand Bolstraat 18-20
This bar facing Marie Heinekenplein is all pastels, mints and tiny Buddhas to make anyone look glam, not that the good-looking 20- and 30-somethings need enhancement. There's a contemporary, diverse food menu (mains €16.50 to €21.50).

GAMBLING
Rounding out the cavalcade of vices that make up Amsterdam, the **Holland Casino** (Map pp292-3; ☎ 521 11 11; www.hollandcasino.nl; Max Euweplein 62; ☽ 1.30pm-3am) is prominently located by the Singelgracht, an easy walk from the Leidseplein. More new Amsterdam than old, it's a splashy place with blackjack, touch-bet roulette, 700 slot machines and, our favourite game name, 'Caribbean stud poker'. According to the tourist bureau, the casino's one of the top attractions in town.

As with Amsterdam's other vices, an ethic of 'know before you go' prevails. A rack of booklets sits near the entrance in several languages explaining the rules of the games and various strategies for playing. Government-issued photo ID (displaying date of birth) is required for admission.

SMOKING

First things first: in Amsterdam-speak, a *coffeeshop* is a place that sells cannabis. A *koffiehuis* (say 'coffee house') is an espresso bar or sandwich shop. If you try to toke up at the latter, you'll receive something between a look of revulsion and a hostile expulsion. The Dutch are nice people; don't push it.

In the former, though, you are free to purchase and smoke away. Many coffeeshops also live up to their literal name and serve coffee (as well as beer, other drinks and snacks). There are also a few *hashcafés*.

You'll have no trouble finding a coffeeshop; there are some 200 of them. It's a safe bet that a place showing palm leaves and Rastafarian colours (red, gold and green) will have something to do with marijuana; others are barely distinguishable from cafés.

Ask at the bar for the list of goods on offer, usually packaged in small bags for €4 to €12 (the better the quality, the less the bag will contain). You can also buy ready-made joints in nifty, reusable packaging (a good idea because the stuff can be potent).

Most cannabis products used to be imported, but today the country has top-notch home produce, so-called *nederwiet* (nay-der-weet) developed by horticulturists and grown in greenhouses with up to five harvests a year. Even the police admit it's a superior product, especially the potent 'super skunk' with up to 13% of THC, the active substance (Nigerian grass has 5% and Colombian 7%). According to a government-sponsored poll of coffeeshop owners, *nederwiet* has captured over half the market, and hash is in decline even among tourists.

'Space' cakes and cookies are sold in a rather low-key fashion, mainly because tourists have problems with them. If you're unused to their effects, or the time they can take to kick in and run their course, you could be in for a rather involved experience. Ask the staff how much you should take and *heed their advice*, even if nothing happens after an hour. Some coffeeshops sell magic mushrooms – legal because they're an untreated, natural product – but if you're after serious mushies and other mind-altering products, see smart-drug shops listings in the Shopping chapter.

Price and quality are OK – you won't get ripped off in a coffeeshop. Most shops are open 10am to 1am Sunday to Thursday, and until 3am Friday and Saturday.

Note that many coffeeshops don't have phones, but we've noted some coffeeshop websites that our *friends* tell us are great to view while stoned.

Medieval Centre

ABRAXAS Map pp286-7

☎ 625 57 63; Jonge Roelensteeg 12

Hands down the most beautiful coffeeshop in town. Choose from southwest USA, Middle Eastern and other styles of décor spread over three floors. There are live DJs, extra-friendly staff and Internet usage with a drink purchase.

DAMPKRING Map pp292-3

☎ 638 07 05; Handboogstraat 29

You saw it in *Ocean's Twelve*, now see it up close. Consistently a winner of the Cannabis Cup, Dampkring is dark-ish, young-ish and decorated rather hobbit-ish. Its name means the ring of the Earth's atmosphere where smaller items combust.

DUTCH FLOWERS Map pp292-3

☎ 624 76 24; Singel 387

Were it not for this shop's main wares, you'd be hard pressed to distinguish it from a brown café, with the game on TV and a lovely view of the Singel. It all means that you needn't slum it with the college kids or feel as if you've gone to Jamaica or India in order to enjoy a toke.

EL GUAPO Map pp286-7

Nieuwe Nieuwstraat 32

Sorta Latin, sorta caveman, this shop is populated by friendly people and is known for some of the best hash in town. You can bring your own music and ask them to play it – just remember to get it back when you leave.

GREENHOUSE Map pp286-7

☎ 627 17 39; www.greenhouse.org; Oudezijds Voorburgwal 191

One of the most popular coffeeshops in town – smokers love the funky music, multicoloured mosaics, psychedelic stained-glass windows and the high-quality weed and hash. The alcohol licence doesn't hurt either.

HOMEGROWN FANTASY Map pp286-7

☎ 627 56 83; Nieuwezijds Voorburgwal 87A

Quality Dutch-grown product, pleasant staff, good tunes and famous space cakes make this popular with backpackers from nearby hostels. Patrons make use of the 3m-long glass bongs to smoke hydroponic weed.

Western Islands

BARNEY'S Map pp286-7

☎ 625 97 61; www.barneys.biz; Haarlemmerstraat 98 & 102

Ever-popular Barney's is more famous for its enormous all-day breakfasts (€5.70 to €10.50; the traditional Irish is the most popular) than its quality weed and hash. Go figure. Non-smokers can just go for the food at its new café down the block.

TO SPLIFF OR NOT TO SPLIFF? THAT WAS THE QUESTION

Well, not exactly, but we couldn't resist the title.

At the beginning of this century, the Dutch health ministry announced that smoking would be banned in bars, cafés and restaurants around the country – the disposition of coffeeshops was tabled for later. The volley that followed between the ministry and the hospitality industry was enough to make a tennis referee dizzy, and the imposition of the law was delayed from 2004 to 2005 to 2006. Nobody's sure it will ever take effect.

poetry slams, acoustic concerts, DJ nights and even horoscope readings.

Southern Canal Belt

BULLDOG Map pp292-3
☎ 625 62 78; www.bulldog.nl; Leidseplein 13-17
Amsterdam's most famous coffeeshop chain has evolved into its own empire, with multiple locations (some double as cafés), a hotel, bike rental, even its own brand of energy drink. This flagship location on the Leidseplein is in a former police station. How times have changed.

GLOBAL CHILLAGE Map pp292-3
☎ 777 97 77; Kerkstraat 51
This relaxed shop with friendly staff looks like a little forest with trippy murals and chilled-out music (African and jazzy beats), populated by happy smokers relaxing on comfortable couches.

Bulldog 'coffeeshop' is in a former police station

Western Canal Belt

GREY AREA Map pp286-7
☎ 420 43 01; www.greyarea.nl; Oude Leliestraat 2;
⏰ noon-8pm Tue-Sun
Owned by a couple of laid-back American guys, this tiny shop introduced the extra-sticky, flavoursome 'Double Bubble Gum' weed to the city's smokers. They also keep up the wonderful American tradition of coffee refills (it's organic). It keeps shorter hours than most coffeeshops.

LA TERTULIA Map p285
Prinsengracht 312; ⏰ 11am-7pm Tue-Sat
A backpackers' favourite, this mother-and-daughter–run coffeeshop has a greenhouse feel. You can either sit outside by the Van Gogh–inspired murals, play some board games, or take in those Jurassic-sized crystals by the counter.

SIBERIË Map pp286-7
☎ 623 59 09; www.siberie.nl; Brouwersgracht 11
It's a comfortable, living room–like setting and the owners are known for supplementing their wares with cultural events like

CLUBBING

Thursday and Saturday are the most popular club nights, and not much happens before midnight. Most of the venues listed here close at 4am on Thursday and Sunday and 5am on Friday and Saturday. If you're looking for recovery parties, keep an eye out for flyers at record shops, smart-drug and club-wear stores, or ask around the club. Record shops that specialise in club music (see boxed text, p197) are known for keeping a bead on the scene.

For a long time, dress at Amsterdam's clubs was decidedly informal, but that's beginning to change. If you end up at a club with a bouncer or hostess, you may well be given the once-over. At larger venues, don't

---

TOP FIVE CLUBS

- **To Night** (p169) A little out of the way, but worth it for the hip and diverse grooves.
- **Dansen bij Jansen** (p168) Students make a bee-line for this legendary club.
- **11** (p151) Smart programming and can't-be-beat views.
- **Jimmy Woo** (p169) A little bit classy, very new and, in a word, a scene.
- **Melkweg** (p170) 300,000 people a year can't be wrong.

be surprised if you have to pass through metal detectors, check your bags and even be frisked before entering.

Some clubs charge exorbitant admission (up to €20); others are free. If there's no entrance fee, it's good etiquette to slip the doorperson a couple of euros as you leave. Also, have a bit of change (€0.50) handy for when you visit the toilet or check a bag.

Individual club nights change periodically, so consult local listings or the venues' websites or ask around for the hot places.

Note also the mega-venues Melkweg and Paradiso (p170).

Medieval Centre

BITTERZOET Map pp286-7
☎ 521 30 01; www.bitterzoet.com; Spuistraat 2
Always full, always changing. This is the freshest, friendliest and best-regarded among the new venues – different nights might see pulse, roots, drum'n'bass, Latin, Afro-beat, Old School jazz or hip-hop groove.

DANSEN BIJ JANSEN Map pp292-3
☎ 620 17 79; www.dansenbijjansen.nl; Handboogstraat 11
For over a generation, this rambling space has been Amsterdam's most famous student

nightclub, and it still thumps nightly. The secret? Cheap drinks, a fun selection of classic disco and house, and a relaxed dress code. Valid student cards are required for entry.

MEANDER Map pp292-3
☎ 625 84 30; www.cafémeander.com; Voetboogstraat 5
In the student club district near the Spui, this venue (capacity up to 350) has a variety of bands, some popular house DJs and, if you're lucky, ridiculously cheap beer.

WINSTON INTERNATIONAL Map pp286-7
☎ 623 13 80; www.winston.nl; Hotel Winston, Warmoesstraat 127
Changing theme nights (think the 'sexy, trashy and sauve' Club Vegas on Sundays) and a fine line-up of local DJs make Winston a popular destination; very hip, very cool and very Amsterdam. It's part of our favourite artist-designed hotel in town.

Western Islands

WESTERGASTERRAS Map pp282-3
☎ 475 14 12; www.westergasterras.nl; Klönneplein 4
In the Westergasfabriek is this post-industrial cool new indoor-outdoor space, with Friday clubs like Tropical and various events the

NIGHT MAYORS BATTLE NIGHTMARES

Amsterdam has one famous *Nachtwacht* (Night Watch) already (courtesy of a certain Mr Rembrandt), but there's another, newer one you may not have heard of. In response to mounting concern over restrictions on the city's nightlife, in 2003 a local councilman organised elections for a board of *nachtburgemeesters* (night mayors).

Collectively called the Nachtwacht, this board of eight includes club hosts and promoters, a sociologist, a restaurant owner, a concert programmer and a DJ. Although they have no government mandate, they view their volunteer job as a matter of the survival of the city's nightlife. Explains *nachtburgemeester* (and club promoter) Maz Weston, Amsterdam's once-unique reputation as a place for outrageous clubs and parties 'has been taken over by the nightlife in cities such as Barcelona, Berlin, and of course Ibiza'.

Part of that may be simple evolution, but the conventional wisdom is that shifting political winds are forcing the change. Political pressure has brought an increase in police raids on clubs, which, Weston says, 'have certainly shaken Amsterdammers up; the discussion over the wrongs or rights of the action has involved everyone from the local greengrocer to the chief of police'.

Either despite the raids, or perhaps because of them, some of the raided clubs have seen an increase in business. 'For clubbers,' Weston says, 'the injustice…has created a *we're-in-this-together* attitude not seen since the beginning of the house scene in the '80s.'

Not that things are *all* bad here. It's still quite possible for club-goers to spend all night in a variety of DJ-cafés (and never pay a cent in entry fees!); the coffeeshop scene is still going strong; and in summer there are regular festivals along area beaches.

For an update of the activities of the *burgemeesters*, check out www.nachtwachtamsterdam.nl. The public is welcome to attend the monthly meetings of the Nachtwacht (Studio 80, Amstel 80 – see website for dates and times). They're followed by an 'open stage' for anyone who wants to present his or her special talent.

rest of the week. Tapas is served too. Go after dinner or a movie at the Westergasfabriek and make an evening of it.

Southern Canal Belt

ESCAPE Map pp292-3

☎ 622 11 11; www.escape.nl; Rembrandtplein 11
A fixture of Amsterdam nightlife since 1987, it's all lights and video screens. Now it's a venue for special parties: first Friday most months is Salvation, one of Amsterdam's leading gay dance clubs.

JIMMY WOO Map pp292-3

☎ 626 31 50; Korte Leidsedwarsstraat 18
If you're of the school that any nightclub worth the name needs a queue out the door, look no further. This fabulous spot holds up to 700 people. Fridays are eclectic, Saturdays a little more alternative, and the lighting and sound systems have to be experienced at least once.

ODEON Map pp292-3

☎ 521 85 55; www.odeonamsterdam.nl; Singel 460
My, my, my. This long-standing venue (the site dates back to the 1660s) was given a top-to-toe glam renovation in 2005. The bar looks out over the Singel, but you may not be able to take your eyes off the murals of models. In addition to club nights and concerts in the grand hall upstairs, you can enjoy the café and restaurant, open both day and night.

RAIN Map pp292-3

☎ 626 70 78; www.rain-amsterdam.com; Rembrandtplein 44
The city's newest club has rapidly become one of its busiest. Offerings can be eclectic, ranging from lounge to deep soul, funk and Latin house. If you need nourishment, there's an eclectic world menu in the restaurant.

SUGAR FACTORY Map pp292-3

☎ 626 50 06; www.sugarfactory.nl; Lijnbaansgracht 238
Cool spot, excellent location and a varied line-up are the hallmarks here. Most nights have both early programs (live music, cinema or spoken word) and late-night fun including DJs and dancing.

TOP FIVE ONE-STOP ENTERTAINMENT

A number of Amsterdam restaurants turn into clubs late at night. Prices run on the high side, but you can rationalise it, sort of, with the idea that it's money you would have spent on club admission fees anyway.

- **Nomads** (p138)
- **Odessa** (p152)
- **Supper Club** (p134)
- **Supper Club Cruise** (p134)
- **Mansion** (p147)

Oosterpark

TO NIGHT Map pp290-1

☎ 694 74 44; www.hotelarena.nl; Hotel Arena, 's-Gravesandestraat 51
In keeping with the hotel's theme, the club goes by the moniker To Night, and each night is different – everything from dance classics to salsa. It's worth a visit just for the magnificent interior; the chapel of this one-time orphanage has been given a solid redo. Even the loos are worth checking out.

Eastern Islands

11 Map pp290-1

☎ 625 59 99; www.ilove11.nl; Osterdokskade 3-5
11 could probably get by merely on its looks, or rather the looks you get from it. It's right by the IJ and at the top of the old post-office building that now houses the Stedelijk Museum, which means that it's the only venue in town with 360-degree city views. Inside, it's slick, urbane and quite a sight. Go for DJ nights and food that's better than you would have expected (p151).

Eastern Docklands

PANAMA Map pp290-1

☎ 311 86 86; www.panama.nl; Oostelijke Handelskade 4
A brilliant and luxe venue aimed at 25- to 35-year-olds, Panama has a salsa-tango dance salon, a restaurant (p152) and a glamorous nightclub that programs Latin, house, progressive, Ibiza vibes, Cuban big bands and much more.

MEGA VENUES

You never know what to expect at the following venues. One night might be an international pop star, then next might be dance or a classical concert, or even a club night. What's for sure is that every Amsterdammer knows them.

- **Amsterdam ArenA** (☎ 311 13 33; www.amsterdamarena.nl; Arena Blvd 1, Bijlmermeer) This ultimate stadium venue – home of the Ajax soccer club – seats 52,000 and produces shows that are big on lights, screens and production – crowd-pulling performers like the Rolling Stones, Eminem and 50 Cent feature. You might also catch an opera or a mega dance party.
- **Koninklijk Theater Carré** (Map pp290-1; ☎ 0900-252 52 55; www.theatercarre.nl; Amstel 115-125) The largest theatre in town puts on big-budget, international shows, cabaret, circuses and Broadway and West End musicals; most presentations are in Dutch, but others require no translation. Backstage tours are also available by **reservation** (☎ 524 94 52; adult/child €8/4; ☽ 11am Sat).
- **Melkweg** (Map pp292-30; ☎ 531 81 81; www.melkweg.nl; Lijnbaansgracht 234A) 'The Milky Way' has seemingly infinite goings-on, attracting over 300,000 people per year. There's live music almost every night (an eclectic international line-up of everything from Afro-Celtic to thrash), plus dance halls, cinema, lounges and art galleries.
- **Paradiso** (Map pp292-3; ☎ 626 45 21; www.paradiso.nl; Weteringschans 6) This large former church has been the city's premier rock venue since the 1960s. Big-name acts like Bright Eyes, Jurassic 5, Wilco and Lucinda have all appeared recently, and its regular dance evenings like Paradisco and Paradisoul are legendary.
- **Stadsschouwburg** (Map pp292-3; ☎ 624 23 11; www.stadsschouwburgamsterdam.nl; Leidseplein 26) The city's most beautiful theatre, built in 1894 and refurbished in the 1990s, features large-scale productions, operettas, dance, summer English-language productions and performances by the stolid Toneelgroep Amsterdam. Most major festivals also seem to have a presence here.

Other Districts

POWERZONE Map pp282-3

☎ 0900-7693796; www.thepowerzone.nl; Daniel Goedkoopstraat 1-3

This multilevel dance factory has a capacity of 3500, and sometimes it almost feels full. Different DJs mean that each space seems to have its own vibe. And, there's no tipping allowed. Take the metro to Spaklerweg.

VAKZUID Map pp282-3

☎ 570 84 00; www.vakzuid.nl; Olympic Stadium 35

A glamorous club-restaurant at the 1928 Olympic Stadium, Vakzuid has a large dance floor and loads of comfortable lounges to pose on. There's a lot of house, some '80s and disco thrown in for good measure.

GAY & LESBIAN

Amsterdam's gay scene is the biggest in Europe, with close to 100 gay and lesbian bars, cafés, clubs, shops and hotels. There are also queer club nights at larger venues, but they don't generally last more than a few years (at least not under the same name). For websites and publications specialising in the gay scene, see p254.

Medieval Centre

Gay clubs in the Medieval Centre tend to me more hard core than elsewhere. Kinky Amsterdam congregates on the Warmoesstraat, next to the Red Light District, at clubs catering to lovers of leather, rubber, piercings, slings, darkrooms and hard-core porn.

ARGOS Map pp286-7

☎ 622 65 95; www.argosbar.com; Warmoesstraat 95

Amsterdam's oldest leather bar still hosts leather boys of all ages in its famous darkrooms. The regular 'SOS' (Sex On Sunday) party is always wild (though safe) – dress code: nude or semi-nude.

COCKRING Map pp286-7

☎ 623 96 04; www.clubcockring.com; Warmoesstraat 96

This popular club has a disco downstairs playing techno and trance, while upstairs is a hot cruising area; leather boys are welcome, but so are others. Look for live strip shows and 'shoes only' nude parties.

CUCKOO'S NEST Map pp286-7

☎ 627 17 52; Nieuwezijds Kolk 6

A small, busy bar said to have the largest 'playroom' in Europe. You could spend a whole night exploring the labyrinth of cubicles and glory holes.

Melkweg (p170) – a cinema, gallery, multimedia centre, café and music venue

GETTO Map pp286-7

☎ 421 51 51; www.getto.nl; Warmoesstraat 51;
☾ Tue-Sun

This groovy, long alley of a restaurant and bar is much loved for its fun nightly entertainment (tarot readers, DJs, bingo competitions, cocktail happy hours), the Warmoesstraat's best people-watching from the streetside, and a loungey area in the back where you can chill quite nicely. It's patronised by a hip and up-for-it crowd, and a diverse cross-section of the gay community.

QUEEN'S HEAD Map pp286-7

☎ 420 24 75; www.queenshead.nl; Zeedijk 20

Beautifully decorated, canal-view, old-world-style café. It used to be run by the outrageous, legendary drag queen Dusty, but new owners have taken over and the place has toned down a bit. There are still drag shows on Tuesdays, but the crowd is more mixed: leather, drag, even straights are welcome.

WEB Map pp286-7

☎ 623 67 58; St Jacobsstraat 6

Cruisey, well-established leather and clone bar with darkrooms and 'bear nights'. No, the pit below the grate in the floor is not a real loo.

Jordaan

COC AMSTERDAM Map p285

☎ 623 40 79; www.cocamsterdam.nl; Rozenstraat 14

The Amsterdam branch of the national gay and lesbian organisation holds a variety of gay, lesbian and mixed club nights every weekend – great for people who want to emphasise the social atmosphere over the trappings of some other establishments. It also has loads of information on gay health, local support groups, special events and programs for men, women, under 26, over 30…check the website.

TOP FIVE GAY & LESBIAN

- Spend a night (or two or three) barhopping along the Reguliersdwarsstraat, including **April** (p172), **SoHo** (p173) and **ARC** (p173).
- Drink in a bit of lesbian history at friendly **Saarein** (p172).
- Belt out tunes with cute boys at **Montmartre** (p173).
- Explore the legendary darkrooms at **Argos** (opposite) or the **Cockring** (opposite).
- Join the congenial crowds at regular dance nights (and dozens of other events) at the lesbian and gay centre, **COC** (above).

IJ LOVE THE NIGHTLIFE

Can't afford Ibiza this year? Don't worry. For the warm, long and languid days of summer, Amsterdam's ever-inventive club promoters have come up with the next best thing: parties on Amsterdam's waterways.

The last few summers have seen a growing number of 'city beaches' along the IJ. They can be as simple as the glorified sandbox atop the Nemo science museum, to a full-on beach of trucked-in sand – check these listings before setting out because locations and offerings are subject to change.

One 'you've got to see it to believe it' beach party is **Blijburg** (☎ 416 03 30; www.blijburg.nl), in the fast-growing IJburg suburb east of the city centre. Parties here can be anything from jazz to hippie scene, India, trance and a singer-songwriter soirée. The new tram 26 takes you there from Centraal Station in 15 minutes. Other beaches include **Strand West** (Map pp282–3; www.strand-west.nl), off Sparndammerstraat (take tram 22 from Centraal Station) and **Amsterdam Plage** (Map pp282–3; ☎ 06 4601 6005; www.amsterdamplage.nl), a few hundred metres from Centraal Station – walk or take tram 3 to Zoutkeetsgracht. And the good folks at **Supper Club Cruise** (p134) also operate Oase, a cruise around the IJ – when the weather cooperates. **Ship of Fools** (www.azart.org; Azartplein 117) is part floating theatre troupe, part party boat based in the Eastern Docklands, it might turn up at any party near the beach. Look for your host, wearing pointy ears.

More voracious party animals will want to head to Bloemendaal Beach, about a half-hour trip west of town, on Sundays from June to October. Thousands of flamboyant clubbers crowd into, and spill out of, massive and quite sophisticated beach-tents, each with a different musical style: the imposing Bloomingdales; Republiek (www.republiek.tv) attracting hordes of house fans with brilliant local DJs; and Woodstock, keeping the party sticky and sexy with soulful house. From Centraal Station, take the train to Haarlem station and catch the bus to Bloemendaal aan Zee. It's near Zandvoort which has some 2km of beach pavilions of its own. Whatever you do, don't try to drive out there: traffic is almost certain to be a horror.

Also out of town: **Dance Valley Festival** (www.dancevalley.nl) runs for two days in August. Some 130 of the world's best DJs and bands perform in 15 tents and two outdoor stages to 80,000 enthusiastic dance-music lovers. It's spawned a lot of imitators, all quite popular.

DE TRUT Map pp282-3

☎ 612 35 24; Bilderdijkstraat 165E; ☯ 11pm Sun

Just west of the Jordaan, this Sunday-night club is a lesbian and gay institution held in the basement of a former squat. It means 'the tart' (and no, we don't mean pie), and comes with the appropriate party posture. Arrive well before its 11pm opening time and be prepared for the strict 'door police'; heteros are definitely not welcome.

SAAREIN Map p285

☎ 623 49 01; Elandsstraat 119

During the late-1970s Saarein was the focal point of the feminist movement, and it's still a premier meeting place for lesbians. The café itself dates from the early 1600s, and some vestiges remain. It offers a small menu with tapas, great soups and daily specials. Bar staff can give you tips on lesbian nightlife. Typical of this friendly place, gay men are welcome too.

Southern Canal Belt

Activity in the Southern Canal Belt centres on the Reguliersdwarsstraat, with some of Amsterdam's longest-running gay favourites. On warm weekend nights, 'de straat' can

seem like a giant block party, attracting beautiful boys who schmooze and cruise their way along the street. Crowds tend to vary with the time of happy hour – it shifts from bar to bar, and so will you in all likelihood.

APRIL Map pp292-3

☎ 625 95 72; Reguliersdwarsstraat 37

April is equally famous for its happy hour, a relaxed atmosphere (even when it's packed) and beautiful guys who cram into the space to flirt and drink. The revolving bar in the back can make for quite a giddy experience after too many cocktails.

AMSTEL TAVERNE Map pp292-3

☎ 623 42 54; Amstel 54

While many of Amsterdam's gay bars have could-be-anywhere décor (not that there's anything wrong with that), the Amstel Taverne feels only-in-Amsterdam. On cooler nights, a 40s-and-up crowd gathers in perhaps the brownest of the brown cafés in the area (Dutch master reproduction, Delft-blue tiles and mugs hanging over the bar). On warm nights, the entire bar might spill out onto the street and mix very amicably with passers-by.

ARC Map pp292-3
☎ 689 70 70; www.bararc.com;
Reguliersdwarsstraat 44

This classy, well-regarded restaurant/bar has a minimalist interior, making it a fitting backdrop for the beautiful, fashionable crowd (predominantly gay, though also lesbian and straight). Fancy flavoured martinis are the drink *du jour,* though bartenders are certainly also happy to pour you a beer. The kitchen serves up some adventurous fusion cuisine.

DE SPIJKER Map pp292-3
☎ 620 59 19; Kerkstraat 4A

Leather boys and clones feel right at home at this friendly bar. Entertainment is in the form of pool tables, hard-core videos (mixed in with, er, Daffy Duck) and a very busy darkroom; not far from Leidseplein, a visit here could be your warm-up before heading to Thermos Sauna down the street.

ENTRE NOUS Map pp292-3
☎ 623 17 00; Halvemaansteeg 14

If you need to recover after a visit to Montmartre, this bar across the street with red wallpaper is an understated, friendly choice.

EXIT Map pp292-3
☎ 625 87 88; Reguliersdwarsstraat 42

This multistorey nightclub plays underground house and has a selection of bars, dance floors and a busy darkroom. The occasional 'Drag Planet' night is a scream.

LELLEBEL Map pp292-3
☎ 427 51 39; www.lellebel.nl; Utrechtsestraat 4

For those who can never get enough drag, this tiny bar just off Rembrandtplein has shows – singing, comedy etc – Friday, Saturday and Sunday. It can get pretty bitchy, but always in the funniest possible way. Most shows are in Dutch, but drag is the international language, *n'est-ce pas?*

MONTMARTRE Map pp292-3
☎ 620 76 22; Halvemaansteeg 17

Year-in, year-out, Montmartre has been voted the most popular gay bar in the Netherlands and Belgium, and one visit on a busy weekend night will show why. Patrons sing along at the top of their voices to recordings of Dutch ballads and top-40 songs (think Abba, or the Dutch equiva-

lent of German *schlager,* with occasional numbers in English) and bop around to the extent possible – it can be packed! It's like a camp Eurovision song contest beneath outrageous ceiling decorations.

OTHER SIDE Map pp292-3
☎ 421 10 14; www.theotherside.nl; Reguliersdwarsstraat 6

This coffeeshop caters to the gay community with grass from Jamaica, Thailand and very strong Dutch super-skunk, and hash from central Asia, north Africa and more. Music: a mix of disco, funk and soul.

SAPPHO Map pp292-3
☎ 06 2868 4906; Vijzelstraat 103

A new, arty lesbian bar, it gets a mixed crowd most of the week but is women-only on Fridays. Look for events like poetry readings and art shows.

SOHO Map pp292-3
☎ 616 13 12; Reguliersdwarsstraat 36

Kitschly decorated – imagine an old-world English library on the *Titanic* – this huge, two-storey bar pumps with a young, friendly and ridiculously pretty clientele, drinking and flirting around the bar or on the upstairs Chesterfield sofas.

VIVELAVIE Map pp292-3
☎ 624 01 14; Amstelstraat 7

Just off Rembrandtplein, this lively place is probably Amsterdam's most popular lesbian café. It has flirty girls, good-natured staff, loud music and large windows. In summer the outdoor terrace buzzes.

Gay Saunas
THERMOS DAY SAUNA Map pp292-3
☎ 623 91 58; www.thermos.nl; Raamstraat 33; admission €18; ☽ noon-11pm Mon-Fri, noon-10pm Sat, 11am-10pm Sun

Thermos is a sprawling, popular place for sexual contacts, with porn movies, private

---

YIPPEE KI YI 0-73!

The hottest game in town is gay Super Bingo at **Taart van m'n Tante** (Map pp292-3; ☎ 776 46 00; Ferdinand Bolstraat 10; ☽ 8pm first Wed of month). Theme: all-American rodeo. No guns allowed.

(or not so private) darkrooms, roof deck, hair salon and restaurant.

THERMOS NIGHT SAUNA Map pp292-3
☎ 623 49 36; www.thermos.nl; Kerkstraat 58-60; admission €18; ☽ 11pm-8am Sun-Fri, 11pm-10am Sat

Thermos Day's night-owl brother is the place to let it all hang out after the clubs close. It's similar to the day sauna, except there's no restaurant, roof deck or hair salon. Thermos has been keeping it up (so to speak) for four decades yet still manages to keep it clean and current.

LIVE MUSIC

At many of the venues listed below, usually you can just turn up at the door and pay to get in. You might want to book ahead, however, for famous acts – see boxed text (below). For information on the development of the music scene in Amsterdam, see p31.

ROCK

In addition to the usual sources of live performance info, try music stores (p189) for rock performances.

> ### HOW TO FIND IT, HOW TO BOOK IT
>
> For current listings of performances, consult local publications such as the *Amsterdam Weekly* and *Day by Day* (both in English) or the Dutch-language *Uitgids*, *NL20*, *Zone 020* and the PS weekend supplement in *Het Parool* newspaper, or visit the website of the Amsterdams Uitburo, www.aub.nl. If a venue's website is in Dutch only, click on 'Programma' or 'Agenda' to see the calendar.
>
> To purchase tickets, contact the venues directly; box office hours are generally 10am to 6pm Monday to Saturday and an hour before the performance. In many cases you can purchase tickets (a surcharge may apply) via the **AUB Ticketshop** (Map pp292-3; ☎ 0900-01 91, per min €0.40; www.aub.nl; cnr Leidsestraat & Marnixstraat; ☽ 10am-7.30pm Mon-Sat, noon-7.30pm Sun). **Ticket Service** (☎ 0900-300 12 50, per min €0.45; www.ticketservice.nl) and **Top Ticketline** (☎ 0900-300 50 00; www.topticketline.nl) may also be able to help.
>
> Occasionally the AUB Ticketshop has last-minute tickets available for half price.

Southern Canal Belt
KORSAKOFF Map p285
☎ 625 78 54; www.korsakoffamsterdam.nl; Lijnbaansgracht 161

Going since the late '80s and still grungy after all these years, this hard-rock and alternative-music venue attracts a young clientele for lashings of punk, metal and goth. It opens late (10pm or 11pm nightly) and closes late too (3am or 4am).

Outer Districts
HEINEKEN MUSIC HALL
☎ 0900-687 42 42; www.heineken-music-hall.nl; Arena Blvd 590, Bijlmermeer

A steady stream of international acts (John Legend, Riverdance and Holland's own Golden Earring) perform at this mid-sized entertainment venue, praised for its high-quality acoustics and amazing lights.

PEPSI STAGE
☎ 0900-737 74 78; www.pepsistage.nl; Arena Blvd 584, Bijlmermeer

Near the Heineken Music Hall is another venue named for a beverage, a relatively intimate (up to 1600 people) hall with acts like Elvis Costello, Sarah McLachlan, Brian Wilson and the Gipsy Kings.

JAZZ, BLUES & LATIN

Jazz is popular in Amsterdam and there's a lot happening in cafés around town; blues thrives less. The world's largest jazz festival is the North Sea Jazz Festival in Den Haag in July (p10), and throughout that month many international greats take the opportunity to take to the stage in Amsterdam too. See also **KHL** (p164).

Medieval Centre
CASABLANCA Map pp286-7
☎ 625 56 85; www.casablanca-amsterdam.nl; Zeedijk 26

This jazz café has an illustrious history. Even if its glory days are over, they still book big bands four nights a week and other kinds of jazz the rest of the time. Wednesday to Saturday sees singing and dancing, including karaoke. It's sometimes referred to as Casablanca Muziek, to differentiate it from **Casablanca Variété** (p179).

COTTON CLUB Map pp286-7
☎ 626 61 92; Nieuwmarkt 5
Squish into this dark, bustling brown café every Saturday (5pm to 8pm) for live, vibrant jazz. There's salsa on Tuesdays.

MEANDER Map pp292-3
☎ 625 84 30; www.cafémeander.nl; Voetboogstraat 3
Catch live bands at this multilevel club often followed up by DJs spinning funk, garage, soul and jazzy beats for a studenty crowd.

Southern Canal Belt
BOURBON STREET JAZZ & BLUES CLUB Map pp292-3
☎ 623 34 40; www.bourbonstreet.nl; Leidsekruisstraat 6-8; ⏰ 10pm-4am Sun-Thu, 10pm-5am Fri & Sat
Catch blues, funk, soul, and rock'n'roll performances in this intimate venue filled with local and international performers (and visited over the years by the likes of Sting and the legendary, departed Dutch musician Herman Brood, p190). There are weekly jam sessions and unplugged nights too. Ages 23 and up.

BRASIL MUSIC BAR Map pp292-3
☎ 626 15 00; www.brasilmusicbar.com; Lange Leidsedwarsstraat 68-70
Get jiggy at this popular little club; there's live Brazilian and Caribbean music three nights a week, and R&B and Brazilian DJs at other times. The club, like the dancing, is hot and steamy.

DE HEEREN VAN AEMSTEL Map pp292-3
☎ 620 21 73; www.deheerenvanaemstel.nl; Thorbeckeplein 5
Office workers and students cram into this grand café–style club to enjoy the roster of live big bands and pop and rock cover bands most nights.

JAZZ CAFÉ ALTO Map pp292-3
☎ 626 32 49; www.jazz-café-alto.nl; Korte Leidsedwarsstraat 115; ⏰ 9pm-3am Sun-Thu, 9pm-4am Fri & Sat
A slightly older crowd of jazz lovers toe-taps to serious jazz and blues at this small brown café; try to catch tenor saxophonist Hans Dulfer and band. Look for the big sax on the façade.

MALOE MELO Map p285
☎ 420 45 92; www.maloemelo.com; Lijnbaansgracht 163
This small venue is home to the city's blues scene with local and international musicians playing everything from Cajun zydeco and swing to Texas blues and rockabilly.

Eastern Docklands
BIMHUIS Map pp282-3
☎ 788 21 50; www.bimhuis.nl; Piet Heinkade 3
The Bimhuis has been Amsterdam's main jazz venue for years, and stylish new digs and rock-star location in the Muziekgebouw aan 't IJ (p113) have suddenly given it an even higher profile than before. It attracts Dutch and international jazz greats and offers workshops. The intimate auditorium has huge windows giving a view over the city, and a spiffy bar.

WORLD MUSIC
Amsterdam is a major European centre for music from exotic parts of the world. In addition to the venues listed below, look into Melkweg (p170), Paradiso (p170) and Latin bars.

A trumpeter belts it out at Bimhuis

Medieval Centre

AKHNATON Map pp286-7
☎ 624 33 96; www.akhnaton.nl;
Nieuwezijds Kolk 25
A young, multicultural crowd jams this club
(going strong for 50-plus years!) to catch
live hip-hop, Latin and Afrocentric acts.

Old South

DE BADCUYP Map p297
☎ 675 96 69; www.badcuyp.nl; Eerste
Sweelinckstraat 10
A low-down and very cool venue off the
Albert Cuypmarkt, De Badcuyp has regular World Jam and Open Kuip (open mic)
nights, African dance cafés, musical offerings including South Indian, jazz and
Latin, and loads of special evenings and
workshops.

Oosterpark

TROPENINSTITUUT THEATER
Map pp290-1
☎ 568 85 00; www.kit.nl; Tropenmuseum,
Linnaeusstraat 2
Come here for sterling live music, mainly
South American, Indian and African, films
and performances like Japanese geisha.
Make a night of it too: the adjoining
restaurant serves food to match the per-
formances. It's one of the venues for the
Amsterdam Roots Festival.

CLASSICAL

In addition to regular performances, a
wonderful Amsterdam music tradition is
free lunch-time concerts throughout the
city. These generally run from 12.30pm to
1.30pm, although concerts are suspended
in June, July or August, when everyone goes
on holidays. The Muziektheater inside the
Stopera offers free concerts of 20th-century
music on Tuesdays in the Boekmanzaal;
on Wednesdays the Concertgebouw has a
series of chamber-music recitals and the
like in its recital hall, but you won't be the
only visitor taking advantage of these; and
on Fridays the Bethaniënklooster puts on
whatever takes their fancy, from medieval
to contemporary music.

See also **Koninklijk Theater Carré** and **Stadsschouwburg** (see boxed text, p170).

Medieval Centre

BETHANIËNKLOOSTER Map pp286-7
☎ 625 00 78; www.bethanienklooster.nl;
Barndesteeg 6B
A small former monastery near Nieuwmarkt
Square with a glorious ballroom, it's the
perfect place to take in some Stravinsky or
Indian sitar.

BEURS VAN BERLAGE Map pp286-7
☎ 627 04 66; www.beursvanberlage.nl;
Damrak 243
This former commodities exchange houses
two small concert halls with comfortable
seats and underwhelming acoustics. Resident companies, the Netherlands Chamber
Orchestra and the Netherlands Philharmonic,
play a varied menu of Mozart, Beethoven,
Bach, Mahler and Wagner. The building itself
is famous for its architecture (p64).

MUZIEKTHEATER Map pp292-3
☎ 625 54 55; www.hetmuziektheater.nl;
Waterlooplein 22
This swanky, large-scale theatre inside the
Stopera is the official residence of the Netherlands Opera, National Ballet and Netherlands
Ballet Orchestra. Renowned international
dance companies like Merce Cunningham
and Martha Graham perform here too.

Old South

CONCERTGEBOUW Map p296
☎ 671 83 45; www.concertgebouw.nl;
Concertgebouwplein 2-6
One of the world's great concert halls, the
Concertgebouw has near-perfect acoustics

HEAVENLY VENUES

A great way to get inside many of Amsterdam's
landmark churches is during performances. Offerings
cover everything from world music to avant-garde and
classical, and if you can catch an organ recital you're in
for a treat. Look for the following in local listings:
- **Amstelkerk** (p91)
- **De Duif** (p92)
- **Engelse Kerk** (p72)
- **Nieuwe Kerk** (p69)
- **Noorderkerk** (p82)
- **Oude Kerk** (p65)
- **Ronde Lutherse Kerk** (p70)

and is home to the Royal Concertgebouw Orchestra led by chief conductor Mariss Jansons.

Among the 650 or so performances here per year, the orchestra performs works by Ravel, Stravinsky and Shostakovich. Alternatively, you can catch visiting international soloists, visiting classical orchestras, jazz performers like Dianne Reeves and Sonny Rollins and world music including Portuguese fado and Indian sitar. Some concerts are held in the smaller recital hall or the intimate 'Koorzaal'.

You can purchase tickets any day on the telephone between 10am and 5pm, or at the box office till 7pm (after 7pm you can only get tickets for that evening's performance). The VVV and AUB Ticketshop (see boxed text, p174) also sell tickets. Visitors up to age 27 can purchase rush tickets (when available) beginning 30 minutes before the show. At just €7, they may be the best deal in town. Proof of age will be required.

There are free 'lunch concerts' in the Kleine Zaal at 12.30pm Wednesdays between September and June. Arrive early.

CONSERVATORIUM VAN AMSTERDAM Map pp292-3
☎ 527 75 50; www.cva.ahk.nl; Van Baerlestraat 27
Students at the Netherlands' largest conservatory of music offer recitals, which give them practical experience performing before audiences. Give them a try, and you may discover someone special.

Eastern Islands
MUZIEKGEBOUW AAN 'T IJ Map pp282-3
tickets ☎ 788 20 00, office ☎ 788 20 10; www.muziekgebouw.nl; Piet Heinkade 1; performance prices vary; ticket office ☺ noon-7pm Mon-Sat
Opened in spring 2005, Muziekgebouw is home to the long-standing music venues the IJsbreker (which changed its name to that of the new building) and the jazz house Bimhuis (p175). The outside may be curiously clad in glass, but the core attraction is the concert halls; the Muziekgebouw has 735 seats, simple maple-slat walls (backlit by LEDs for dramatic effect), a flexible stage layout and great acoustics. The Bimhuis' black, backstagey performance space (also part of this complex) is more intimate.

CINEMA
There is usually a good choice of films screening in Amsterdam, which includes plenty of 'art' movies for discriminating cinephiles. The 'film ladder' – the listing of what's on – is pinned up at cinemas and in many pubs, online at www.amsterdam.filmladder.nl (in Dutch) or in the newspaper on Thursday, when weekly programs change. *AL* means *alle leeftijden* (all ages) and 12 or 16 indicates the minimum age for admission.

Films are almost always screened in their original language with Dutch subtitles; the exceptions are children's matinees where the latest Disney creation may come with Dutch voices.

Ticket prices are generally between €4.50 and €8.75, depending on the theatre and time of the day of you want to go – prices tend to be lowest for the first weekday screenings at the mainstream Hollywood cinemas. See p36 for information on the Dutch film industry.

Big multiplexes include the Pathé cinemas (☎ 0900-14 58; per min €0.35) with branches in the city (Map pp292-3; Kleine Gartmanplantsoen 15-19) and De Munt (Map pp292-3; Vijzelstraat 15). The following cinemas are some of the more interesting venues.

Jordaan & Western Islands
HET KETELHUIS Map pp282-3
☎ 684 00 90; www.ketelhuis.nl; Westergasfabriek, Haarlemmerweg 8-10
In the old gas works, soaring ceilings, wooden floors, pegboard walls, comfy chairs and a post-industrial vibe provide a great platform for art-house films (especially Dutch ones). It has three screening rooms and a café.

MOVIES Map pp282-3
☎ 638 60 16; www.themovies.nl; Haarlemmerdijk 161
Interesting, arty films are shown alongside independent American and British movies and big studio releases at this beautiful Art Deco cinema. Treat yourself to dinner in the highly regarded restaurant (the three-course 'dinner and a movie' costs a reasonable €29) and – bam! – it's a great evening out.

Southern Canal Belt

CINECENTER Map pp292-3
☎ 623 66 15; Lijnbaansgracht 236
Euro and American art-house fare is the flavour of the day. The last Monday of the month is devoted to queer films (except in summer). The hip bar with white padded walls closes after the last screening begins.

DE UITKIJK Map pp292-3
☎ 623 74 60; www.uitkijk.nl; Prinsengracht 452
This cosy art-house stalwart is the city's oldest surviving cinema (1913). In an old canal house, it attracts film buffs who know their Fuller from their Fellini, as well as more contemporary fare.

FILMMUSEUM CINERAMA Map pp292-3
Calypso; ☎ 623 78 14; www.filmmuseum.nl; Marnixstraat 400
At the time of writing, the three halls of this cinema screened regular offerings of fare from the Filmmuseum. It's a great venue for this worthy endeavour, but nobody is sure whether it will last. We hope it does.

TUSCHINSKITHEATER Map pp292-3
☎ 623 15 10, 0900-14 58, per min €0.35; www.pathe.nl/tuschinski; Reguliersbreestraat 26-34
Extensively refurbished, Amsterdam's most famous cinema is a monument worth visiting for its sumptuous Art Deco/Amsterdam School interior alone. Expect to see mainstream blockbusters, or inquire about 90-minute tours (€7; 10am Sunday and Monday in July and August).

Old South

FILMMUSEUM Map pp282-3
☎ 589 14 00; www.filmmuseum.nl; Vondelpark 3
The esteemed Filmmuseum's program appeals to a broad audience. Its two small cinemas (60 and 80 seats) screen cult shlock-horror movies, cutting-edge foreign films (think Iran or Korea) and specials devoted to screen legends and genres such as Bollywood musicals.

De Pijp

RIALTO CINEMA Map p297
☎ 676 87 00; www.rialtofilm.nl; Ceintuurbaan 338
Great old cinema on the main drag near Sarphatipark, it concentrates on premieres and gets eclectic art-house fare from around the world.

Oosterpark

KRITERION Map pp290-1
☎ 623 17 08; www.kriterion.nl; Roeterstraat 170
Come to this UvA-student-run theatre-café for premieres, theme parties, cult movies, classics, kids' flicks and sneaks. It's in a former diamond factory – and a very cool Amsterdam School space – turned into a movie theatre after WWII to help resistance fighters earn an income. Drinks are cheap, and there's a limited food menu.

COMEDY
Southern Canal Belt

BOOM CHICAGO Map pp292-3
☎ 423 01 01; www.boomchicago.nl; Leidseplein Theater, Leidseplein 12
Amsterdam's – indeed the Continent's – premier theatre for English-language stand-up and improv comedy; the best way to see it is over dinner and a few drinks. Fortunately, the food is decent, as is the café, boomBar, with DJs spinning a few nights a week and a quiz night on Mondays. See boxed text, below.

WHEN IMPROV HITS AMSTERDAM, WHAT SOUND DOES IT MAKE?

With legendary improv-comedy venues like Second City, Chicago has long been a jumping-off point for some of the world's most famous comedians. But Chicago comedy in Amsterdam? In the early 1990s the idea was about as sexy as a cold croquette.

Yet three Americans had the vision to set up **Boom Chicago** (above), a comedy nightclub that has evolved into the best (English-language) improvisational and comedy club in the Netherlands. Shows are superfast, musical, political, very funny and, against all odds, really popular with locals as well as visitors. What's more, Boom has begun to join its hometown (and Los Angeles and New York) counterparts on the fast track to the likes of Mad TV, Saturday Night Live and even Broadway, and on to international stardom. See a show here and who knows? You may catch the next John Belushi, Mike Myers or Will Ferrell.

Boom Chicago (opposite), at the Leidseplein Theater, offers English-language improv and stand-up comedy

COMEDY CAFÉ AMSTERDAM
Map pp292-3

☎ 638 39 71; www.comedycafé.nl;
Max Euweplein 43-45

If Boom Chicago is improv, the Comedy Café books-in Dutch and international stand-up comics. Sundays are regularly reserved for English-speaking acts, although you might catch them other nights as well.

DE KLEINE KOMEDIE Map pp292-3
☎ 624 05 34; www.dekleinekomedie.nl;
Amstel 56-58

This internationally renowned theatre, founded in 1786, focuses on concerts, dance, comedy and cabaret, sometimes in English.

THEATRE, DANCE & SPOKEN WORD

There are about 50 theatres in Amsterdam – the ones listed here are merely a selection. Performances are mostly in Dutch, sometimes in English (especially in summer) and sometimes language doesn't matter. See also **Koninklijk Theater Carré** and **Stadsschouwburg** (boxed text, p170).

Medieval Centre
AMSTERDAMS MARIONETTEN THEATER Map pp290-1
☎ 620 80 27; www.marionet.demon.nl; Nieuwe Jonkerstraat 8; adult/child from €12/6;
☽ ring or check website for showtimes

In a former blacksmith's shop, this intimate theatre presents big culture for little people, with marionettes performing elaborate productions like *The Magic Flute*. Grown-ups will appreciate it too, especially the skill of the puppeteers. Lunch and dinner-time performances carry an extra fee. If you can't catch them here, the company also tours Europe.

DE BRAKKE GROND Map pp286-7
☎ 626 68 66; Flemish Cultural Centre, Nes 45

A fantastic array of music, experimental video, modern dance and exciting, young theatre is performed in Brakke Grond's striking 150-seat theatre.

CASABLANCA VARIÉTÉ Map pp286-7
☎ 625 56 85; www.casablanca-amsterdam.nl;
Zeedijk 24; dinner & show €29, show only €5

The other half of Casablanca contains the Netherlands' only theatre devoted to the art of circus performance – sleight of hand,

179

magic, variety shows and singers. The interior is kitsch redefined, but the theatre itself is quite small (meaning no large animal acts, darn it!).

COSMIC THEATER Map pp286-7
☎ 626 68 66; www.cosmictheater.nl; Nes 75-87
This theatre originated in Curaçao and has made it all the way to the big city, staging plays representing a variety of cultures. Emphasis is on Surinamese, African, Turkish and Moroccan. There's also a competition for young writers.

FRASCATI Map pp286-7
☎ 626 68 66; www.nestheaters.nl; Nes 63
This experimental theatre spotlights young Dutch directors, choreographers and producers. There are multicultural dance and music performances, as well as hip-hop, rap and breakdancing. In May it is host for the urban dance festival, which is definitely worth checking out if dance is your thing.

Western Canal Belt
DE BALIE Map pp292-3
☎ 553 51 51; Kleine Gartmanplantsoen 10
International productions spotlighting multicultural and political issues are the focus here. De Balie also holds short-film festivals and political debates and has new-media facilities and a stylish bar.

FELIX MERITIS Map p285
☎ 623 13 11; Keizersgracht 324
The city's former cultural centre now presents innovative, modern theatre, music and dance, with lots of cooperative productions between Eastern and Western European artists. It has also got very cool loos.

THEATER BELLEVUE Map pp292-3
☎ 530 53 01; www.theaterbellevue.nl; Leidsekade 90
Come here for experimental theatre, international cabaret and modern dance, mainly in Dutch. Its affiliate theatre **Nieuwe de la Mar** (Map pp292–3; ☎ 530 53 01; Marnixstraat 404) presents road shows (sometimes in English), international festivals and occasionally light kids' plays. The box office for both theatres is at Leidsekade 90.

LEND AN EAR
If you find yourself with some spare time on an early Friday night, the **Van Gogh Museum** (p97) has a new, weekly cultural series, running the gamut from classical music recitals to modern dance, lectures and singers. Some nights are happenings with up to 2000 spectators; others are quiet and civilised. Tear yourself away from the performance, and the absence of the daytime hordes means that you can devote to Van Gogh's masterworks the attention they deserve.

Old South
AMSTERDAMSE BOS THEATRE
Map pp282-3
☎ 643 32 86; www.bostheater.nl; Amsterdamse Bos
This large open-air amphitheatre in the park stages plays in Dutch (Shakespeare, Brecht, Chekhov) in summer. We love it when the actors pause as planes pass overhead.

OPENLUCHTTHEATER Map pp282-3
Vondelpark Open-Air Theatre; ☎ 673 14 99; www.openluchttheater.nl, Vondelpark
From June to August, the park hosts free concerts in its intimate theatre; it doesn't have the classical lines of other park buildings, but that won't matter when you watch the performances, from classical to hip-hop, world music, dance and children's performances. For the calendar, check local listings or click 'programma' on the website.

ACTIVITIES
OUTDOOR ACTIVITIES
Soccer, ice-skating, cycling, tennis, swimming and sailing are just a few activities that keep the locals fit – and of course jogging, which is popular in the Vondelpark and other parks. The Amsterdamse Bos has several walking and jogging trails for serious exercise. Bikes are available for rent in many corners of town.

The whole coast of Holland is one long beach, backed by extensive dunes that are ideal for walks. The closest seaside resort is Zandvoort, but quieter resorts can be found further north, such as Castricum north of IJmuiden, or Egmond and Bergen a bit further north near Alkmaar.

For information about sport and leisure activities and venues, visit the **City Hall Information Centre** (Map pp292–3; ☎ 624 11 11; Amstel 1) in the arcade between the Stopera and the city hall. Local community centres (in the phone book under Buurtcentrum) organise fitness courses.

Canal Bikes

Explore the city from a different perspective with a pedal around the canals. Don't worry, it isn't as much work as it sounds. As long as you don't mind getting a little bit wet, it is lots of fun.

CANAL BIKE

Per hr per person €8, more than 2 people per boat €7, plus €50 deposit; ☾ 10am-6pm Apr-Oct, later on warm nights in summer
Affiliated with **Canal Bus** (p61), Canal Bike allows you to explore the canals yourself at water level. Landing stages are by the Rijksmuseum, Leidseplein, Anne Frank Huis and the corner of Keizersgracht and Leidsestraat. The Rijksmuseum location (Map pp292–3) is open daily until 5.30pm all year, and there are limited hours at other locations.

Golf

Golf was long derided as something for the elite but has become increasingly popular in recent years, but don't go expecting a Scottish-style course. The Netherlands space crunch means that land is usually more profitably put to other uses. Look under *Golfbanen* in the pink pages of the phone book for several other options.

FRIDAY NIGHT SKATE

This weekly event (www.fridaynightskate.com) is a great way to see the city. You'll also get to meet new people: hundreds of in-line skaters (perhaps thousands in peak season) gather at 8pm near the Filmmuseum in the Vondelpark, for departure at 8.30pm. The route varies each week, but generally it's between 15km and 20km; expect the whole skate to finish by 10.30pm.

Skaters should be advanced, bring helmet and knee protection and be able to brake well. Even so, organisers caution, skating is at your own risk. The skate is cancelled if streets are wet, meaning that on average it actually takes place about twice a month.

BORCHLAND SPORTCENTRUM

☎ 563 33 33; www.borchland.nl; Borchlandweg 6-12; 9 holes from €10, from €15 after 4pm and on weekends; ☾ 8am-11pm Mon-Fri, 8am-9pm Sat & Sun
Borchland has a nine-hole all par-three course. Call for course hours or to set up a lesson. Take metro Strandvliet.

OPENBARE GOLFBAAN SLOTEN

Map pp282-3
☎ 614 24 02; Sloterweg 1045; 9 holes €13-18; ☾ 8.30am-dusk May-Aug, 8.30am-8pm Mon-Fri Sep-Apr
Located on the southwest side of town, this course also consists of nine holes. Take bus No 145.

Hockey

Dutch (field) hockey teams compete at world-championship level. In contrast to soccer, which is played mainly by boys in school yards, streets and parks, hockey is still a somewhat elitist sport played by either sex on expensive club fields. For this reason, visitors will have a hard time playing unless they can become affiliated with a team. The season is similar to that for soccer. For information and matches, contact **Hockey Club Hurley** (☎ 645 44 68; Amsterdamse Bos, Nieuwe Kalfjeslaan 21; ☾ 4pm-midnight Mon-Fri, 8.30am-6pm Sat, 8.30am-8pm Sun).

Ice-Skating

When the canals freeze over in winter (which doesn't happen enough) everyone goes for a skate. Lakes and waterways in the countryside fill up with colourfully clad skaters making trips tens of kilometres long. It's a wonderful experience, though painful on the ankles and butt if you're learning. Be aware that people do drown under ice every year. Stay away from the ice unless you see large groups of people, and be very careful at the edges and under bridges (such areas often don't freeze properly).

You can only rent skates at a skating rink. Buying a pair of simple hockey skates costs upwards of €50 at department stores and sports shops. Hockey skates are probably the best choice for learners: figure skates are difficult to master. Speed skates put a lot of strain on the ankles but are definitely the go if you want to make serious trips. Wood-framed skates that you tie under your shoes can be picked up cheaply at antique and bric-a-brac shops. Don't dismiss them: they're fast if they're sharpened, and make great souvenirs.

The **Ijscomplex Jaap Eden** (Map pp282–3; ☎ 694 96 52; Radioweg 64; adult/child under 15yr & senior €5.10/3.20; ❉ Oct–mid-Mar, ring for hours) in the eastern suburb of Watergraafsmeer has an indoor and outdoor rink. Get there on tram No 9 to Kruislaan/Middenweg.

In winter you can also skate on the pond on Museumplein.

Korfball

This sport (see also p20) elicits giggles from foreigners who don't understand how appealing the game can be. It's a cross between netball, volleyball and basketball, where mixed-sex teams toss a ball around and try to throw it into the opposing team's hoop, which is 3.5m off the ground; players can only mark opponents of the same sex. There's a lively local-club scene. For information, contact the **Amsterdam Sport Council** (☎ 552 24 90). They also provide information on other sports in town.

Sailing

The Dutch are avid sailors – windsurfing is a national sport, but so is yachting which is curbed only by its expense (the word 'yacht', after all, comes from the Dutch *jachtschip*, 'chase ship'). This includes modern open boats and yachts, but also the more traditional kind, which are revered here like nowhere else. On weekends a fleet of restored flat-bottomed boats, called the 'brown fleet' because of their reddish-brown sails, crisscross the IJsselmeer. Some are privately owned but many are rented, and sailing one is an unforgettable experience.

The cheapest options are *botters* (from about €350 per day), former fishing boats with sleeping space (usually for around eight people) below deck. Larger groups could rent a converted freight barge known as a *tjalk* (from about €575 per day), originally a Frisian design with jib and spritsail rig, though modern designs are made of steel and have diesel motors. Other vessels include anything from ancient pilot boats

to massive clippers. Inquire at VVV offices or boat docks for more information.

Costs are quite reasonable if you can muster a group of fellow enthusiasts. Some places only rent boats for day trips, but it's much more fun to go for the full weekend experience. The usual arrangement is that you arrive at the boat Friday at 8pm, sleep on board, sail out early the next morning, and visit several places around the IJsselmeer before returning on Sunday between 4pm and 6pm. Food is not included in the packages, nor is cancellation insurance (trips are cancelled if wind is stronger than 7 Beaufort), but you do get a skipper.

Tennis & Squash

More courts are listed under *Tennisbanen* and *Squashbanen* in the pink pages of the phone book.

BORCHLAND SPORTCENTRUM

☎ 563 33 33; Borchlandweg 6-12; per hr tennis 8am-4pm Mon-Fri €15.50, 4-10pm Mon-Fri, all day Sat & Sun €23, squash until 4pm Mon-Thu €8, after 4pm Mon-Thu €15, after 4pm Fri, all day Sat & Sun €10; ❉ 8am-11pm
A huge complex next to the Amsterdam ArenA in the Bijlmer, it has tennis, squash and badminton courts, bowling alleys, golf and other facilities including a restaurant. Take the metro Strandvliet.

SQUASH CITY Map pp286-7

☎ 626 78 83; www.squashcity.com; Ketelmaker-straat 6; day pass €7-14, month pass €32-75; ❉ 8.45am-midnight Mon, 7am-midnight Tue-Thu, 7am-11.30pm Fri, 8.45am-7.30pm Sat & Sun
Located across the railway line Haarlemmer-plein, at Bickerseiland, west of Centraal Station. Sauna is included with squash-court hire, as is use of a well-equipped fitness centre. Admission price depends on the services you want to use.

TENNISCENTRUM AMSTELPARK
Map pp282-3

☎ 301 07 00; www.amstelpark.nl; Koenenkade 8; court hire per hr summer €20, per hr winter outdoor/indoor €20/25
Amstelpark has 42 open and covered courts and runs the country's biggest tennis school. It's conveniently close to the World Trade Center and RAI exhibition buildings, and there are fitness facilities as well.

HEALTH & FITNESS

With the northern European climate, indoor fitness is quite popular in Amsterdam.

Gyms

In addition to the places listed below, several hotels also have fitness centres available for day use, including the Splash Fitnessclub at the **Renaissance Hotel** (Map pp292–3; ☎ 621 22 23; Kattengat 1), Amsterdam Fitness & Health Club at the NH Amsterdam Centre (p225) and the gym at the Hotel Okura (p227). Squash City also has full facilities.

BARRY'S HEALTH CENTRE Map pp292-3

☎ 626 10 36; www.barryshealthcentre.nl; Lijnbaansgracht 350; day/week pass €15/€28; ☼ 7am-11pm Mon-Fri, 8am-8pm Sat & Sun

Large, well-equipped facility to make you large and well equipped, recently renovated with a full complement of the latest machines and classes, plus sauna, steam, tanning beds and a 'cardio theatre'.

FITNESS FIRST Map pp286-7

☎ 530 03 40; www2.fitnessfirst.nl; Nieuwezijds Kolk 15; day pass €16, month pass from €29; ☼ 7am-11pm Mon-Fri, 9am-6pm Sat & Sun

A central location is not the only thing this modern gym has going for it. There's a full range of cardio and weightlifting equipment, group classes, sauna, steam and aroma rooms, sun beds, beauty treatments and free video loans for members.

GARDEN GYM Map pp290-1

☎ 626 87 72; www.thegarden.nl; Jodenbreestraat 158; day pass €9-12.50, month pass €40-61; ☼ 9am-11pm Mon, Wed & Fri, noon-11pm Tue, noon-10pm Thu, 9am-4pm Sat, 9am-5pm Sun

Recently rated Amsterdam's best gym for women, the Garden Gym offers aerobics and feel-good activities, including sauna, massage, physiotherapy and dietary advice. It was renovated in 2005.

Saunas & Baths

Saunas are mixed and there's no prudish swimsuit nonsense, though they may cater for people who have a problem with this – ask and see. Note that gay saunas have another purpose entirely.

HAMMAM Map pp282-3

☎ 681 48 18; www.hammamamsterdam.nl; Zaanstraat 88; adult/child 2-5yr/6-12yr €15/4/11; ☼ noon-10pm Tue-Fri, noon-8pm Sat & Sun, last entry 2½hr before closing

In the northwest beyond the Haarlemmerpoort, Hammam is an attractive Turkish-style place for women only, offering a range of spa treatments and vittles like baklava.

KOAN FLOAT Map pp286-7

☎ 555 00 33; www.koanfloat.nl; Herengracht 321; floating 45/60min €30/38; ☼ 9.30am-11pm

It's not a sauna, but come here for salt-water floatation tanks – have music piped in if you like – and massages. Management swears that 45 minutes of soaking is the equivalent of four hours' sleep, and great for jet lag. Massages are also available. Inquire about special deals.

SAUNA DECO Map pp286-7

☎ 623 82 15; www.saunadeco.nl; Herengracht 115; admission noon-3pm Mon-Fri €14, all other times €15; ☼ noon-11pm Mon-Sat, 1-6pm Sun

Sauna Deco is a respectable, elegant sauna with good facilities including a snack bar. The building itself is an early creation of the architect HP Berlage, and its Art Deco furnishings used to grace a Parisian department store. Massages and facials are also available. Inquire for rates. Credit cards and PIN cards are not accepted.

Swimming

Amsterdam has a number of indoor pools and summer outdoor pools, some of them historic and very cool. However, we strongly recommend that you phone before you set out. In recent years, some public pools have been shut down, and hours can vary from day to day or season to season. Few are open past 7pm.

Also, note that there are often restricted sessions – nude, Muslim, children, women, seniors, clubs, lap swimming etc.

BIJLMERSPORTCENTRUM Map pp282-3

☎ 697 25 01; Bijlmerpark 76, Bijlmer; adult/child €2.90/2.60; ☼ Tue, Thu, Sat & Sun, ring for times

Near metro Bijlmer station, this sport centre has indoor and outdoor pools with a mixture of lane swimming and family free swims.

DE MIRANDABAD Map pp282-3

☎ 536 44 44; De Mirandalaan 9; adult/concession €3.30/2.60; ⏰ ring for times

A tropical 'aquatic centre', complete with beach and wave machine, indoor and outdoor pools, tanning booths and waterslide, Mirandabad is south of the city centre. It also has squash courts.

FLEVOPARKBAD Map pp282-3

☎ 692 50 30; Insulindeweg 1002; adult/senior/child 3-15yr €2.50/1.90/2.40; ⏰ 10am-5.30pm May–early Sep (to 7pm in hot weather)

Located east of the city centre, there's only an outdoor pool here. Take tram 7 or 14 to the end.

FLORAPARKBAD Map pp282-3

☎ 632 90 30; Sneeuwbalweg 5, Amsterdam North; adult/child €3.50/3

Florapark has indoor and outdoor pools, a 65m slide (!), kids' play area and a good sunbathing section, sauna and lots of classes.

SLOTERPARKBAD Map pp282-3

☎ 506 35 06; Slotermeerlaan 2-4; adult or child €3.75, child under 2yr free; ⏰ Tue-Sun

Set in an attractive recreational area with a yacht harbour in the western suburbs, next to the terminus of tram No 14, this place has indoor and outdoor pools. In summer, on cold, rainy days the indoor pool opens. The outdoor pools can get overcrowded, but this bath is known for a less frequented nudist island, past the pools and across a causeway.

ZUIDERBAD Map pp292-3

☎ 678 13 90; Hobbemastraat 26; adult/child €3/2.70

This 1912 edifice behind the Rijksmuseum has been restored to its original glory. Now it's unique and full of character.

WATCHING SPORT
Football (Soccer)

Local club Ajax usually qualifies for the UEFA Champions League, Europe's top competition. Other Dutch leaders are PSV (the Philips Sport Association) from Eindhoven and Feyenoord from Rotterdam, and if any of these clubs play against one another, it's a big event. Dutch soccer is 'cool' and 'technical', characterised by keep-

Impressive Amsterdam ArenA

the-ball play and surgical strikes. Local hooligans are every bit as hot-headed as their British counterparts but you should be quite safe if you buy seat tickets (as opposed to standing-room tickets).

Amsterdam ArenA (☎ 311 13 33; www.amster damarena.nl; Arena Blvd 1, Bijlmermeer) is where Ajax plays. This massive, expensive, hi-tech complex with a retractable roof seats 52,000 spectators and has an Ajax museum with cups and other paraphernalia. Soccer games usually take place Saturday evening and Sunday afternoon during the playing season (early September to early June, with a winter break from just before Christmas to the end of January). Take the metro to Bijlmer or Strandvliet/ArenA station.

Readers have recommended the one-hour guided stadium tour (☎ 311 13 36; adult/child €10/8.50; ⏰ 11am-4.30pm daily Apr-Sep, noon-4pm Mon-Sat Oct-Mar, except on game days or major events). The tour includes a walk on the hallowed turf and entry to the museum.

Football (American)

American football started in Europe from nothing several years ago and has had a bit of trouble gaining traction as teams have shifted from city to city. As of this writing, there were six teams in the NFL (National Football League) Europe in the Netherlands and Germany including the Amsterdam Admirals. Players are predominately American, but there are a number of European and even Japanese players. Home games, complete with cheerleaders, take place at the Amsterdam ArenA. Unlike in the States, the European football season is in the spring.

Shopping

Shopping

During the 17th century, Amsterdam was the warehouse of the world, stuffed with riches from neighbours and far-off colonies. Even if the Dutch empire has since crumbled, its capital remains a shopper's paradise. In particular, Amsterdam's speciality shops and markets truly stand out. Sure, you may be able to find glowing Mexican shrines or banana-flavoured condoms back home, but Amsterdam has whole shops devoted to such items and, of course, dope, flower bulbs, clogs, wheels of cheese, and obscure types of *genever* (Dutch gin).

Fantastic bargains are rare, but it may be worth chasing pictorial or photographic art, music, clothing from Dutch designers, vintage clothes, diamonds and collectors' books (especially art, antiquarian and comic books). Look for the occasional sale at department stores and speciality shops. The Damrak and the area around Leidseplein teem with tourist shops, but for a souvenir of quality, try elsewhere for a Delft-blue tulip vase or bulbs to plant back home (customs legislation permitting).

Shopping Streets

The busiest shopping streets are the down- to mid-market Nieuwendijk and the more up-scale Kalverstraat and Leidsestraat, with department stores and clothing boutiques serving large crowds, especially on Saturday and Sunday. Well-heeled shoppers head for the expensive shops along PC Hooftstraat and the chic boutiques and cafés of the Negen Straatjes (Nine Alleys) in the Western Canal Belt, while antique and art buffs head for the Spiegel Quarter in the Southern Canal Belt. The Jordaan is also full of galleries and quirky shops.

Opening Hours

Generally, shops are open between 9am and 6pm Tuesday to Saturday, although Thursday is late-night shopping until 9pm. Monday and Sunday tend to have shorter hours, from noon till 6pm. Art galleries keep limited hours and are often only open afternoons from Wednesday to Sunday. Shops selling smart drugs tend to stay open into the evenings. Where hours vary significantly from these opening times, we've noted it in individual listings. Note, however, that many shops close on Sundays and operate on limited schedules during summer holidays.

Consumer Taxes

The Dutch abbreviation for value-added tax is BTW, and the rate is about 15.97% of the purchase price. However, if you are a non-citizen of the European Union, and you are buying expensive items that you will export from the European Union within three months, you may be entitled to a refund of the tax, minus a service fee.

The store must subscribe to the Global Refund system (look for the sticker in the window), your purchase there must total at least €137 in a single day, and you must request a Global Refund cheque at the time.

If you are departing the EU from Schiphol airport, present your goods along with your receipt, passport, air ticket and your Global Refund cheque at the Global Refund office in terminal 3. You can receive cash, a credit to your credit card or a bank cheque.

If you are departing the EU from another airport, inquire locally, but generally you must take your goods and documents to customs for authorisation.

MEDIEVAL CENTRE

The centre contains Amsterdam's greatest concentration of shops, from storeyed department stores to boudoir wear for you to create your own stories.

DAMRAK & OUDE ZIJDE

3-D HOLOGRAMMEN

Map pp286-7   Speciality Shop

☎ 624 72 25; www.3-dhologramman.com; Grimburgwal 2; ☽ noon-6pm Tue-Fri, noon-5.30pm Sat, 1-5.30pm Sun & Mon

This fascinating (and trippy) collection of holographic pictures, jewellery and stickers will delight even the most jaded peepers.

BEAUFORT Map pp286-7   Jewellery

☎ 625 91 31; Grimburgwal 11; ☽ Tue-Sat

Exquisite handcrafted contemporary jewellery is created on site; many of the pieces combine silver and gold. The necklaces and rings are particularly beautiful.

CLOTHING SIZES

Measurements approximate only, try before you buy

Women's Clothing

Aus/UK	8	10	12	14	16	18
Europe	36	38	40	42	44	46
Japan	5	7	9	11	13	15
USA	6	8	10	12	14	16

Women's Shoes

Aus/USA	5	6	7	8	9	10
Europe	35	36	37	38	39	40
France only	35	36	38	39	40	42
Japan	22	23	24	25	26	27
UK	3½	4½	5½	6½	7½	8½

Men's Clothing

Aus	92	96	100	104	108	112
Europe	46	48	50	52	54	56
Japan	S		M	M		L
UK/USA	35	36	37	38	39	40

Men's Shirts (Collar Sizes)

Aus/Japan	38	39	40	41	42	43
Europe	38	39	40	41	42	43
UK/USA	15	15½	16	16½	17	17½

Men's Shoes

Aus/UK	7	8	9	10	11	12
Europe	41	42	43	44½	46	47
Japan	26	27	27½	28	29	30
USA	7½	8½	9½	10½	11½	12½

BOOK EXCHANGE Map pp286-7   Books

☎ 626 62 66; Kloveniersburgwal 58

Near the University, this rabbit warren features four rooms of second-hand books, with temptingly priced occult, sci-fi and detective novels, many of them in English.

C&A Map pp286-7   Clothing

☎ 530 71 50; Beurspassage 2

There's little fancy about this Euro-chain (what's a designer brand?), but it's a fine choice if you need inexpensive knockabout clothes. Choose carefully, and you may even find some wares with style.

CONDOMERIE HET GULDEN VLIES

Map pp286-7   Speciality Shop

☎ 627 41 74; www.condomerie.nl; Warmoesstraat 141, ☽ closed Sun

Where the well-dressed Johnson shops. Perfectly positioned for the Red Light District, this boutique stocks hundreds of types of condoms, lubricants and saucy gifts. Some of the condoms are decorated like minitropical scenes, or may remind you of your favourite cartoon character.

GEELS & CO Map pp286-7   Food & Drink

☎ 624 06 83; Warmoesstraat 67; ☽ Mon-Sat

Operating from this glorious, aromatic store for over 140 years, the distinguished tea-and-coffee merchant also sells chocolate, teapots and coffee plungers. Be sure to visit the interesting little museum upstairs (museum hours: 2pm to 4.30pm, Tuesday and Saturday).

HANS APPENZELLER

Map pp286-7   Jewellery

☎ 626 82 18; Grimburgwal 1; ☽ Tue-Sat

Appenzeller is one of Amsterdam's leading designers in gold and stone, known for the simplicity and strength of his designs. If his sparse work is not to your taste, all along the same street is a row of jewellery shops of all kinds.

HIMALAYA Map pp286-7   Speciality shop

☎ 626 08 99; Warmoesstraat 56; ☽ Mon-Sat

What a surprise: a peaceful, New Age oasis amid the Red Light District. Stock up on crystals, incense and oils, ambient CDs and books on the healing arts, then visit the lovely tearoom.

KOKOPELLI Map pp286-7   Smart Drugs

☎ 421 70 00; Warmoesstraat 12

Were it not for its main trade, you might swear this large, beautiful space was a fashionable clothing or home-wares store. In addition to mushrooms and smart drugs, there's an art gallery, Internet facilities, books and a chill-out lounge area overlooking Damrak.

MR B Map pp286-7   Erotica/Gay

☎ 422 00 03; www.misterb.com; Warmoesstraat 89

Kinkeeee. This renowned shop for leather and rubber goods for gay men is right in the heart of Warmoesstraat. Some of the tamer wares include rubber suits, hoods and bondage equipment, and you can use your imagination for some of the rest.

RED LIGHT DISTRICT

ABSOLUTE DANNY Map pp286-7   Sex Shop

☎ 421 09 15; Oudezijds Achterburgwal 78

Named by Dutch *Playboy* as Amsterdam's classiest sex shop, Absolute Danny specialises in fetish clothing, lingerie and leather, plus hard-core videos and dildos just for fun.

ANTIQUARIAAT KOK Map pp286-7   Books

☎ 623 11 91; Oude Hoogstraat 14-18

A wide and engaging range of used and antiquarian stock (literature, coffee-table books, old prints etc) is sold here, including biology, art and architecture titles.

DAM SQUARE & NIEUWE ZIJDE

AU BOUT DU MONDE Map pp286-7   Books

☎ 625 13 97; Singel 313; ☾ Mon-Sat

From angels to Zen, this tranquil two-storey shop stocks books on Eastern and Western philosophy, Tibet, Freud, alternative medicine and pretty much anything else you'll need for your religious, psychological or spiritual needs.

BAM BAM Map pp286-7   Children

☎ 624 52 15; Magna Plaza, Nieuwezijds Voorburgwal 182

Head here for luxurious clothes and handmade furniture for pampered little princes and princesses: everything from bureaus and beds to mosquito nets to cover them (we hope you won't need one).

TOP FIVE SHOPPING STRIPS

- Soak up the local atmosphere at the **Albert Cuypmarkt** (p107).
- If you've got dubloons to spare, **PC Hooftstraat** (p95) has the city's most high-end fashions.
- Head west to up-and-coming **Haarlemmerstraat** (p192) for the newest and coolest.
- Lose yourself in the **Negen Straatjes** (Nine Alleys; p84), where boutiques specialise in everything from clothing to art to tempting chocolates.
- Hunt for antiques in the **Spiegel Quarter** (p198) in the Southern Canal Belt.

BLUE NOTE Map pp286-7   Music

☎ 428 10 29; Gravenstraat 12

This is *the* place for jazz (Dutch, European and American), Japanese pressings, lounge music, jazz and a few listening decks.

CHILLS & THRILLS Map pp286-7   Smart Drugs

☎ 638 00 15; Nieuwendijk 17

Always packed with tourists straining to hear each other over thumping techno music, this busy shop sells herbal trips, mushrooms, psychoactive cacti, amino-acid and vitamin drinks, novelty bongs and life-size alien sculptures. Check out the minivaporiser, a smoke-free way to consume grass.

DE BIERKONING Map pp286-7   Food & Drink

☎ 625 23 36; Paleisstraat 125

Beer. Just beer. Some 950 varieties including hundreds from Belgium, Germany, Britain and, of course, Holland – plus glasses, mugs and books on home brewing. It's centrally located right near the Royal Palace, so you have no excuse not to go.

DE BIJENKORF Map pp286-7   Department Store

☎ 621 80 80; Dam 1

The city's most fashionable department store in the highest-profile location, facing the Royal Palace, it has a small restaurant or snack bar on each floor. Design-conscious shoppers will enjoy the well-chosen clothing, toys, household accessories and books.

DUO SPORTS

Map pp286-7   Camping, Outdoor & Sport

☎ 330 02 94; Nieuwendijk 156B

The city centre's exclusive outlet for official merchandise of Ajax, Amsterdam's football club. Don't expect bargains; jerseys sell for €60-plus and almost never go on sale. The only other official store is at the stadium.

FAME MUSIC Map pp286-7 — Music
☎ 638 25 25; Kalverstraat 2-4, at Dam
This megastore has an enormous number of titles with broad (and mainstream) collections of pop, jazz and classical CDs, DVDs and videos. It also sells tickets to big concerts. Sale prices can be quite reasonable.

FEMALE & PARTNERS
Map pp286-7 — Erotica/Clothing
☎ 620 91 52; femaleandpartners.nl; Spuistraat 100
Everything you need for your inner dominatrix…or the one who's waiting for you at home. Female & Partners is filled with clothing, undies, leather and toys for women and those who love them. Thank goodness men aren't the only ones who get to have fun!

HEMA Map pp286-7 — Department Store
☎ 638 99 63; Nieuwendijk 174
What used to be the nation's equivalent of Marks & Spencer or Woolworths has undergone a facelift and now attracts as many design aficionados as bargain hunters. Expect low prices, reliable quality and a wide range of products including good-value wines and delicatessen goods.

INNERSPACE Map pp286-7 — Smart Drugs
☎ 624 33 38; Spuistraat 108
Known for good service and information, this large shop started as a supplier to large parties, and now the shop sells herbal ecstasy, mushrooms, psychoactive plants and cactus. True to its origins, it's also a good place for party info and tickets.

Hema, one of the largest department stores in Amsterdam

INTERMALE Map pp286-7 — Books
☎ 625 00 09; www.intermale.nl; Spuistraat 251
One of Amsterdam's leading gay bookstores, it has 1½ floors of photo books, sexy mags, videos and pornographic postcards. As the name suggests, it's intended for men only.

MAGIC MUSHROOM GALLERY
Map pp286-7 — Smart Drugs
☎ 427 57 65; Spuistraat 249
There are fresh and dried magic mushrooms on sale (it's recommended that first-timers try the Mexican ones for a relaxed, happy trip) as well as mushroom-growing kits, herbal ecstasy and smart drinks.

MAGNA PLAZA Map pp286-7 — Shopping Centre
☎ 626 91 99; Nieuwezijds Voorburgwal 182
This grand 19th-century landmark building, once the main post office, is now home to some 40 upmarket fashion, gift and jewellery stores, including Bam Bam, Laundry Industry and Pinokkio.

PINOKKIO Map pp286-7 — Children
☎ 622 89 14; Magna Plaza, Nieuwezijds Voorburgwal 182
This pleasant shop stocks wooden and educational toys, rocking horses, wooden vehicles, replica canal houses, mobiles and, of course, lots of Pinocchio dolls. Since this is Holland, there's also a Miffy section.

VROLIJK Map pp286-7 — Books
☎ 623 51 42; www.vrolijk.nu; Paleisstraat 135;
☽ 11am-6pm Mon, 10am-6pm Tue, Wed & Fri, 10am-7pm Thu, 10am-5pm Sat, 1-5pm Sun, closed Sun Oct-Dec
Said to be the Netherlands' largest gay and lesbian bookstore, it carries most of the world's major gay and lesbian magazines, as well as novels, guidebooks and postcards. Head upstairs for art, poetry and DVDs.

AROUND THE SPUI
AMERICAN BOOK CENTER
Map pp292-3 — Books
☎ 625 55 37; www.abc.nl; Kalverstraat 185
Always jam-packed, this large store specialises in English-language books, holds interesting sales, has a good travel-guidebook section and stocks many US periodicals (eg the Sunday New York Times). It's often cheaper than its competitors.

ATHENAEUM BOOKSHOP & NEWSAGENCY Map pp292-3 Books
☎ 622 62 48; Spui 14-16

This multilevel store on the square has a vast array of both usual and unusual books and cheerful, helpful staff. The separate news-agency on the corner is your best choice for international newspapers and magazines.

BLOND Map pp292-3 Speciality Shop
☎ 06 2468 4086; Singel 369; ☺ Tue-Sat

Actual blondes Femque and Janneke glaze plates and dishes in designs that are hilarious, adorable and very colourful: ladies lunching, beach scenes, chocolates, cheeses etc. You can custom order as well.

FAIR TRADE SHOP
Map pp292-3 Speciality Shop
☎ 625 22 45; Heiligeweg 45

This charity shop features quality, stylish products from developing countries includ-ing clothes, toys, CDs and ceramics. The company works directly with producers and provides ongoing business training.

H&M Map pp292-3 Clothing
☎ 624 06 24; Kalverstraat 125

This fashion chain store has up-to-the-minute clothes for all ages at several locations. You may find higher quality elsewhere, but prices are remarkably low.

HERMAN BROOD GALERIE
Map pp292-3 Art & Antiques
☎ 623 37 66; Spuistraat 320

This gallery is dedicated to Herman Brood (see boxed text, p34), Amsterdam's legend-ary club promoter (1946–2001) who shone briefly but brightly before being undone by drugs and alcohol. His oil paintings are upstairs from the busy Café Dante.

KALVERTOREN SHOPPING CENTRE
Map pp292-3 Shopping Centre
Singel 457

This popular, modern shopping centre contains Vroom & Dreesmann, a small Hema, and big-brand fashion stores like Replay, Quiksilver, Levi's, Timberland and DKNY.

MARKETS

No visit to Amsterdam is complete if you haven't experienced one or more of its lively markets. The following are merely a selection. Watch out for pickpockets.

- **Albert Cuypmarkt** (p107)
- **Antiques markets** Nieuwmarkt (Map pp286-7; ☺ 9am-5pm Sun May-Sep) Amstelveld (Map pp292-3; ☺ 9am-6pm last Fri of the month in warmer months) There are many genuine articles here and lots of books and bric-a-brac.
- **Art markets** (Maps pp292-3; Thorbeckeplein & Spui Square; ☺ 10.30am-6pm Sun Mar-Oct) These quiet markets, dealing in mostly modern pictorial art, are a bit too modest in scope to yield real finds.
- **Boerenmarkt** (Farmers' Market; Map pp286-7; Noordermarkt & Nieuwmarkt Square; ☺ 10am-3pm Sat) Pick up home-grown produce, organic foods and picnic provisions.
- **Book markets** (Map pp286-7; Oudemanhuispoort; ☺ 11am-4pm Mon-Fri) In the old arcade between Oude-zijds Achterburgwal and Kloveniersburgwal (blink and you'll miss either entrance), this is the place to find that 19th-century copy of *Das Kapital* or a semantic analysis of Icelandic sagas, and some newer books and art prints. Another book market takes place on Spui Square (Map pp292-3; ☺ 8am-6pm Fri).
- **De Looier antiques market** (Map pp292-3; ☎ 624 90 38; Elandsgracht 109, Jordaan; ☺ 11am-5pm Sat-Thu) Indoor stalls selling jewellery, furniture, art and collectibles.
- **Lindengracht market** (Map p285; Lindengracht, Jordaan; ☺ 11am-4pm Sat) General market, very much a local affair.
- **Noordermarkt** (Map pp286-7; Noorderstraat, Jordaan; ☺ 9am-1pm Mon, 10am-3pm Sat) This Jordaan market is good for antiques, fabrics and second-hand bric-a-brac.
- **Plant market** (Map pp292-3; Amstelveld; ☺ 3-6pm Mon Easter-Christmas) All sorts of plants, pots and vases are sold here.
- **Stamp & coin market** (Map pp286-7; Nieuwezijds Voorburgwal 276; ☺ 10am-4pm Wed & Sat) This little street-side market, just south of Wijdesteeg, sells stamps, coins and medals.
- **Waterlooplein flea market** (Map pp292-3; Waterlooplein; ☺ 9am-5pm Mon-Fri, 8.30am-5.30pm Sat) Amster-dam's most famous flea market is full of curios, second-hand clothing, music, electronic stuff slightly on the blink, hardware and cheap New Age gifts.
- **Westermarkt** (Map p285; Westerstraat, Jordaan; ☺ 9am-1pm Mon) Cheapish clothes and textiles, some real bargains.

LAUNDRY INDUSTRY

Map pp292-3 — Clothing

☎ 420 25 54; Spui 1

Hip, urban types head here for well-cut, well-designed clothes by this Dutch design house. Watch glamorous couples coveting soft leather coats and perfectly fitted suits. There's another branch at Magna Plaza, but the Spui location is the main store.

MAISON DE BONNETERIE

Map pp292-3 — Department Store

☎ 531 34 00; Rokin 140

Exclusive and classic clothes for the whole family are featured here. Men are particularly well catered for with labels like Ralph Lauren and Armani, best purchased during the brilliant 50%-off sales, but there is still plenty for the ladies. Note the amazing chandeliers and beautiful glass cupola.

PIED À TERRE Map pp292-3 — Books

☎ 627 44 55; Singel 393

This shop specialises in pretty much any book you'll need for outdoor pursuits: hiking and cycling books, topographical maps and travel guidebooks.

UNIVERSITY SHOP Map pp292-3 — Clothing

☎ 525 36 55; Spui 23

The University of Amsterdam has a lovely logo, and you can wear it on your lovely person with T-shirts, sweatshirts and the like, or carry it around on book bags or even bottle openers.

VROOM & DREESMANN

Map pp292-3 — Department Store

☎ 622 01 71; Kalverstraat 201

Slightly more upmarket than Hema, this national chain is popular for its clothing and cosmetics. Its fabulous caféteria, La Place, serves well-priced, freshly prepared salads, hot dishes and pastries.

WATERSTONE'S Map pp292-3 — Books

☎ 638 38 21; Kalverstraat 152

Four storeys and a central location near Spui Square make Waterstone's a great resource for English-language books (often discounted). There's an emphasis on travel guidebooks, magazines, newspapers and novels.

NIEUWMARKT

A good deal of the commerce in this area takes place at the Waterlooplein flea market (opposite), but veer away and you'll discover home-grown shops that are much sweeter and more low key.

BIBA Map pp286-7 — Jewellery

☎ 330 57 21; Nieuwe Hoogstaat 26

This chichi little boutique near the Museum Het Rembrandthuis keeps them coming back for more: Vivienne Westwood, Jean Paul Gaultier, Erickson Beamon and Buddha to Buddha.

DE BEESTENWINKEL Map pp292-3 — Children

☎ 623 18 05; Staalstraat 11; ☷ Tue-Sun

From teeny tiny teddy bears to pink plastic pig snouts, this pleasantly crowded shop sells *de best* (best) of *de beesten* (animals). Other bests: plush toys from great toymakers, lamps in animal shapes, and lots of plastic reptiles.

DE KLOMPENBOER Map pp286-7 — Souvenirs

☎ 623 06 32; St Antoniesbreestraat 39-51; ☷ hours vary

Bruno, the eccentric owner of this cute clog shop, works downstairs from Knuffels toy shop. Come at the right time, and you can see shoes being made and painted (the cow print ones are pretty funky). There are also samples of miniature wooden shoes and a 700-year-old pair.

DROOG DESIGN Map pp292-3 — Furniture

☎ 523 50 59; www.droogdesign.nl; Staalstraat 7B; ☷ noon-6pm Tue-Sun

This design firm has been around for only about a decade, yet it's already become a leader with inventions like the 85-lamp chandelier, the cow chair and curtains with dress patterns. There are over 180 products by 100-plus designers.

JACOB HOOY & CO

Map pp286-7 — Alternative Medicine

☎ 624 30 41; Kloveniersburgwal 12; ☷ Mon-Sat

This charming chemist's shop – with its walls of massive, wooden drawers – has been selling medicinal herbs, homeopathic remedies and natural cosmetics since 1743. You can also get teas and seasonings for chicken or fish.

KNUFFELS Map pp286-7 Children
☎ 623 06 32; St Antoniesbreestraat 39-51
Avert the kids' eyes or they will be drawn by the irresistible force of bobbing mobiles from the ceiling of this busy corner shop. Adults, too, may be drawn in by the soft toys, puppets, beautiful mobiles, teddies and jigsaw puzzles.

NIJHOF & LEE Map pp292-3 Books
☎ 620 39 80; www.nijhoflee.nl; Staalstraat 13A; ⏳ Tue-Sat
Design fans will want to head here for a swell selection of international architecture, art and typography books and posters in an intimate but contemporary setting. One wall boasts a substantial selection of well-priced remainders.

PO CHAI TONG
Map pp292-3 Alternative Medicine
☎ 428 49 56; Waterlooplein 13; ⏳ Mon-Sat
If nothing seems to take away your stress, fatigue or jet lag, pay a visit to Dr Kai Zhang's kindly Chinese herbal-medicine and acupuncture shop. It's far from fancy, but clients have included opera singers and conductors from the nearby Stopera.

PUCCINI BOMBONI Map pp292-3 Food
☎ 626 54 74; Staalstraat 17
We're not the only ones who go gaga over Puccini's large, handmade chocolate bonbons with rich fillings. Unforgettable chocolates include plum, marzipan or the calvados cup. There is another branch at Singel 184 (☎ 427 83 41). Note: shops have been known to close in warm weather – for the sake of the chocolates, of course.

RIELE Map pp286-7 Clothing & Accessories
☎ 623 34 08; St Antoniebreestraat 128; ⏳ daily
Fancy and edgy at the same time, this minimalist space lets the clothes do the talking. Designers include Ines Raspoort (Dutch), E Play (Italian), Tone Barker (Danish) and Ghost (British). Accent them with accessories from the Dutch designers Chick on a Mission.

SEVENTYFIVE Map pp286-7 Clothing
☎ 626 46 11; Nieuwe Hoogstraat 24
At this true temple to trainers, stimulate your sports-shoe obsession with brands like Gola, Diesel, Everlast, Nike, Adidas. Naturally, Von Dutch makes an appearance too.

A SHOPPER'S GLOSSARY
Virtually any sales clerk you meet in Amsterdam will speak English, but to make things quick, here's a short list of words you're likely to encounter on signage:

korting – discount, as in '25% korting'

vanaf – or v.a. (literally, 'and up'), as in '€20 v.a.', '€20 and up'. Note that this can be a clever ploy in which, for example, a clothing rack marked '€10 v.a.' includes just a few items at that price – the rest can be much higher.

kassa – cashier

kassakorting – discount taken at register

laatste dagen – final days

opruiming, uitverkoop – clearance sale

sale – sale, also known as soldes

tot – (aka t/m) up to, as in 'tot 50% korting'

TYPO GALLERY Map pp292-3 Art
☎ 623 85 52; www.ewaldspieker.nl; Groenburgwal 63; ⏳ ring for hr
A peek inside the artistic mind of Ewald Spieker, who creates graphic art out of typography. He's been exhibited all over and published books of his work. Just a few of his works are for sale; the red 'YES' made of stacks of cardboard (€95) had our name written all over it.

WONDERWOOD Map pp286-7 Furniture
☎ 625 37 38; www.wonderwood.nl; Rusland 3; ⏳ noon-6pm Wed-Sat & by appt
Head here for originals or reproductions of '40s and '50s Dutch furniture design. Classics include the T46 coffee table by Hein Stolle, works by Gijs Bakker and Han Pieck, and the box chair, which folds up into its own box – you can actually ship it with your luggage!

JORDAAN & WESTERN ISLANDS

Shops here have an artsy, eclectic, homemade feel. The area around Elandsgracht is the place for art, particularly photography, and speciality shops from hats to cats. On Haarlemmerstraat and its extension Haarlemmerdijk, lots of new shops have opened to pick up the overflow of shoppers.

ARCHITECTURA & NATURA

Map pp286-7   Books

☎ 623 61 86; www.architectura.nl; Leliegracht 22; ☺ Mon-Sat

This charming canalside shop has art, architecture, design, landscape and coffee-table books. Upstairs, **Architectuurantiquariat Opbouw** (Architecture Antique Shop; ☎ 638 70 18) has a selection of its namesake.

ARNOLD CORNELIS Map p285   Food & Drink

☎ 625 85 85; Elandsgracht 78; ☺ Mon-Sat

Your dinner hosts will think you're in the know if you present them with something from this long-standing shop. Just a sample: marzipan fruits, chocolate bonbons with wasabi (it creeps up on you) and blue spheres made with Malaga wine. At lunch, grab a flaky pastry filled with cheese, meat or vegetables. There is another branch at **Van Baerlestraat 93** (☎ 662 12 28).

ARTIMO A-Z Map p285   Art books

☎ 320 46 30; Elandsgracht 6; ☺ Mon-Sat

Artimo, the Dutch publisher, has opened this artfully designed shop. About half of the books (with authors like Bruce Mau and Alexander Payne) are from their own catalogue, and periodicals take you to the cutting edge of the art world.

BROER & ZUS Map p285   Children

☎ 422 90 02; www.broerenzus.nl; Rosengracht 94; ☺ Mon-Sat

Cosy little 'bro and sis' specialises in Dutch designers and fabrics for kids from birth to six years. You can get brands like Kidscase, tiny tops emblazoned with slogans like 'Mr Charming' and 'ladykiller', and wild prints (think Hawaiian shirts).

CATS & THINGS Map p285   Speciality Shop

☎ 428 30 28; Hazenstraat 26

Head here when the cat (or cat-lover) back home deserves a souvenir. There's the expected assortment of kitty toys, sculptures, grooming needs, beds and climbers, but this shop proves that feline-themed merchandise need not be kitschy and can even be cool.

CHRISTODOULOU & LAMÉ

Map p285   Speciality Shop

☎ 320 22 69; Rozengracht 42

Handwoven Tibetan silk pillows, velvet throws and hand-beaded saris from this treasure-trove of sumptuous soft furnishings will transform your home into a plush sanctuary. It's a real festival of colours.

CLAIRE V Map p285   Accessories

☎ 421 90 00; Prinsengracht 234F; ☺ Mon-Sat

The silk handbags, wraps and accessories embroidered with patterns and floral designs are gorgeous, but that's not the only reason they're worthy. Claire's wares are made at a training centre for Cambodian landmine victims, so by shopping here you'll look good and do good.

DE BELLY Map p285   Food

☎ 330 94 83; Nieuwe Leliestraat 174

This organic supermarket, in the Jordaan for over three decades, has a great bakery and a small but smart selection of prepared foods, even organic tarts and chocolates.

DE LACH Map p285   Speciality Shop

☎ 626 66 25; Eerste Bloemdwarsstraat 14; ☺ Tue, Thu-Sat

This eccentric corner shop sells vintage movie posters from all over the world (eg the Italian version of *Some Like it Hot*) from €12 to €1000. There's a mini Walk of Fame, signed by Dutch stars, on the path outside.

DISCOSTARS Map pp286-7   Music

☎ 626 11 77; Haarlemmerdijk 86

Both the disco generation and the 'disco sucks' generation will enjoy this repository of music of yesteryear. If any of the names Olivia Newton-John, Engelbert Humperdinck, Paul Young, Celia Cruz, Candy Dulfer, Buddy Holly, Yves Montand, Doris Day or Roy Rogers mean anything to you, you'll find lots more to like.

ENGLISH BOOKSHOP Map p285   Books

☎ 626 42 30; Lauriergracht 71; ☺ Tue-Sun

This attractive, canalside shop has a well-chosen selection of English-language biographies, novels and translations of the works of Dutch writers.

FOTOGRAFIA Map p285   Books

☎ 639 39 39; Tweede Laurierdwarsstraat 60-64; ☺ Tue-Sat

This classy new shop is as simple as a photo lab, stocked full of publications featuring the likes of Alfred Stieglitz, Charlotte Dumas, Rineke Dijkstra and Magritte.

FRONTIER Map p285   Books
☎ 330 91 51; Eerste Bloemdwarsstraat 15
For anything to do with conspiracies, aliens, UFOs, lost civilisations, crop circles and the like, this is the flagship bookshop of the Dutch magazine of the same name. It specialises in both common and hard-to-find books – some overseas bookshops use it as a supplier!

GALLERIA D'ARTE RINASCIMENTO
Map p285   Traditional Souvenirs
☎ 622 75 09; Prinsengracht 170
This pretty shop sells Royal Delftware ceramics (both antique and new), all manner of vases, platters, brooches, Christmas ornaments and interesting 19th-century wall tiles and plaques.

GOLDSTRASSE Map pp292-3   Jewellery
☎ 420 20 95; Elandsgracht 89; ☺ Wed-Sat
Some 14 designers from the Netherlands, Germany, Norway, Austria and more exhibit here. One example is Amsterdam-based Marina Alexandre, a jewellery designer and teacher. You'll see rings (in gold, silver and silicone). Fittingly since many of the artists graduated from the Rietveld Academy, works here are more like wearable art.

HET OUD-HOLLANDSCHE
SNOEPWINKELTJE Map p285   Food & Candy
☎ 420 73 90; Egelantiersdwarsstraat 2
This corner shop is lined with jar after apothecary jar of Dutch penny candies with flavours from chocolate to coffee, all manner of fruit and the inscrutable, salty Dutch liquorice known as *drop*.

HUG GALLERY FOR INTERNATIONAL
PHOTOGRAPHY Map p285   Art Gallery
☎ 489 42 40; www.hughug.info;
Eerste Tuindwarsstraat 16
Small but important gallery that attracts some of the top names, especially from Britain. It's one of the few galleries that partners with photography museums like Huis Marseille (p87) and FOAM (p92).

INTERNATIONAAL DESIGN CENTRUM
Map p285   Speciality Shop
☎ 521 87 10; Rozengracht 215-217; ☺ Tue-Sat
Begun over a century ago, this shop has repped the forefront of Dutch design ever

since – Gispen, Edra and Artifoort – and some foreign designers as well. Its affiliate, De Kasstoor (across the street) applies the same design concept to kitchens and lighting (towel hooks are simultaneously slick and cute).

JOSINE BOKHOVEN Map p285   Art & Antiques
☎ 623 65 98; Prinsengracht 154
Across the canal from the Anne Frank Huis, this friendly gallery features contemporary art and the work of emerging young artists, including German artist, Ralph Fleck.

KITSCH KITCHEN Map p285   Speciality Shop
☎ 622 82 61; Rozengracht 8-12
You want it flowered, frilly, colourful, over the top or just made from plastic? Chances are you'll find it here – everything from handbags to home wares to kiddie toys and doll gowns. Plus lamps, Mexican tablecloths, pink plastic chandeliers from India and, of course, bouquets of plastic flowers.

KLEURGAMMA Map p285   Art Gallery
☎ 423 05 03; Hazenstraat 51-55; ☺ Mon-Sat
In this minimalist space you may find the work of some nearby photographers on the walls, or have your own prints processed. You'll feel better knowing that the Rijks and Van Gogh Museums get theirs done here too.

Kitsch Kitchen – anything you want in bright colours

LA DIABLITA Map pp286-7   Speciality Shop

☎ 06 1085 7333; Binnen Oranjestraat 11;
☼ Mon & Wed-Sat

You've got a night on the town and need sparkly, spangly jewellery, gold sandals, yellow shoes or pink high tops? This tiny storefront off the Haarlemmerstraat can help you. You say you need the same for your young daughter? They have a small selection of those too.

MEEUWIG & ZN Map pp286-7   Food

☎ 626 52 86; Haarlemmerstraat 70; ☼ Mon-Sat

Fill your own bottle from metal crocks containing over 50 types of olive oil from around the world. You'll also find bottles of gourmet vinegar, mustard, chutney and fresh olives.

NOU MOE STRIPWINKEL

Map pp286-7   Speciality Shop

☎ 693 63 45; Lindenstraat 1

This tiny corner shop features Asterix to Garfield, Tintin to 24 (yes, that 24). More importantly, it sells the merchandise: soft toys, notebooks, stickers, games, coffee mugs and bedroom slippers.

PETSALON Map p285   Speciality Shop

☎ 624 73 85; Hazenstraat 3; ☼ Wed-Sat

In Dutch a pet is a cap, and lifelong milliner Ans Wesseling has been designing hats from this shop since around 1990 – you can see the actual workshop. One perennial favourite has an elaborately woven net down the back. It gives new meaning to letting your hair down.

'T ZONNETJE Map pp286-7   Food

☎ 623 00 58; Haarlemmerdijk 45; ☼ Tue-Sat

In a space that's been a teashop since 1642, you can find teas from all over the world, coffees and implements, and be waited on by a commendably cheerful owner. High tea is served upstairs (reserve for large groups).

TORCH GALLERY Map p285   Art Gallery

☎ 626 02 84; Lauriergracht 94; ☼ Thu-Sat

Torch, one of Amsterdam's most cutting-edge galleries, is proud of its diverse selection. Around a dozen shows per year include photography and new media from many countries, and occasional painting and sculpture from artists like Anton

SMART-DRUG SHOPS

Generally funky but sometimes quite swanky, 'smart-drug' shops began popping up all over the city in the mid-1990s and are now an established addition to the coffeeshop scene. They sell legal, organic hallucinogens like magic mushrooms, herbal joints, seeds (poppy, marijuana, psychoactive), mood enhancers and aphrodisiacs. Note that while it's legal to buy these items over the counter in Amsterdam, some of these products are probably illegal to take back home.

In addition to mood- and mind-enhancers, these shops sell books (on shamanism, psychedelia, spiritualism and the like), jewellery, trancey videos and bongs.

One thing we beg you: before you buy, ask the staff to explain exactly what dosage to consume and what to expect from your trip. If you happen to find a shop that has a problem with that, take your business elsewhere.

Corbijn (whose coverage of U2 was famous) and Annie Sprinkle.

UNLIMITED DELICIOUS Map pp286-7   Food

☎ 622 48 29; Haarlemmerstraat 122

Is it ever! It's tempting to dive into the gorgeous, sculptural cakes and tarts, but – if you can – walk past them to the dozens of varieties of chocolates made in-house. Some of the more outlandish combinations (that somehow work) are rosemary sea salt, caramel cayenne and Laphroaig whisky. More standard choices include coffee, nougat and our favourite: Ceylon cinnamon.

VOLKSBOND SHOP Map pp286-7   Clothing

☎ 428 30 72; Haarlemmerstraat 146-148

A relic from the days when Haarlemmerstraat was not so chic. Proceeds from sales of used clothing (most items €0.50 to €10) help finance facilities for the homeless: halfway houses, counselling services and the like.

WESTERN CANAL BELT

You could easily spend all of your shopping time in Amsterdam – indeed all your time in Amsterdam, period – in the Negen Straatjes (Nine Alleys; Map p84) in the Canal Belt just east of the Jordaan. The selection is arty, worthwhile and constantly changing, and lots of cafés mean plenty of break time.

AMSTERDAM WATCH COMPANY

Map pp286-7   Speciality Shop

☎ 389 27 89; www.amsterdamwatchcompany.nl; Hartenstraat 4; ☺ Tue-Sat

A husband and wife team of watchmakers and enthusiasts restore old watches (postwar to mid-1970s) and are the exclusive Amsterdam dealers of such brands as Germany's D Dornblüth and the Dutch Christiaan van der Klaauw, who makes fewer than 200 watches a year.

ANALIK Map pp286-7   Clothing

☎ 422 05 61; Hartenstraat 34-36; ☺ Mon-Sat

Although most Dutch fashion designers end up in Paris, Analik is one who has kept a strong presence at home. She's still one of the city's pre-eminent; if you don't catch her fashion shows around town, you can just browse here.

ANTONIA BY YVETTE

Map pp286-7   Shoes

☎ 627 24 33; Gasthuismolensteeg 12

If Sex in the City was shot in Amsterdam, we bet that the girls would spend half their time in this shop. Shoes, boots, sandals and espadrilles run from supremely classy to just plain fun. There's also a small section for guys.

BOEKIE WOEKIE Map p285   Books

☎ 639 05 07; Berenstraat 16; ☺ noon-6pm Tue-Fri, noon-5pm Sat

While other shops handle art books, here they sell books as art, created by artists specifically for this medium. Some tell stories (elegantly illustrated, naturally), others are riffs on graphic motifs; you may want to browse for a long time.

BRILMUSEUM Map pp286-7   Speciality Shop

☎ 421 24 14; Gasthuismolensteeg 7; ☺ Wed-Sat

This long-standing shop is an institution, both for its wares and its presentation. You can take in the 700-year history of eyeglasses, as well as a very 21st-century collection, some of them pretty outlandish.

DE KAASKAMER Map pp292-3   Food

☎ 623 34 83; Runstraat 7

A small shop full of hundreds of cheeses from around Europe and Holland, and deli items like pâté, cured meats and baguettes, this does a roaring sandwich trade at lunch-time.

DE NIEUWE KLEREN VAN DE KEIZER

Map pp292-3   Clothing

☎ 422 68 95; Runstraat 29

'The Emperor's New Clothes' sells clingy clubwear and tight-fitting shirts that seem to fit gay men to a T (and any other men who are reasonably fit). You'll need a little money to shop here, but you may catch a sale.

DE WITTE TANDEN WINKEL

Map pp292-3   Speciality Shop

☎ 623 34 43; Runstraat 5

We love shops that are obsessed, and The White-Teeth Shop certainly is – with dental hygiene. There's a huge selection of toothbrushes, toothpastes from around the world, brushing accessories you never knew you needed and friendly advice.

GAMEKEEPER Map pp286-7   Games

☎ 638 15 79; Hartenstraat 14

The selection of board games is dizzying, as is the imagination that went into making them. Start with checkers, chess and mah jong, or move on to Cathedral (build a city in styles like the Great Wall of China or the souk in Marrakech), or Rush Hour (help a car get out of traffic). 'Cooperative' games encourage players to play with, not against, each other.

KLEIN ANTIEK Map pp286-7   Antiques

☎ 622 82 61; Gasthuismolensteeg 11; ☺ 11am-6pm Tue-Sat

Tiles from tip to toe, including Delft blue, as well as Dutch pottery, some going back to medieval times. Don't expect great bargains (broken pieces sell from €25), but it's a lovely place to shop.

LADY DAY Map pp286-7   Clothing

☎ 623 58 20; Hartenstraat 9

This is the premier location for unearthing spotless vintage clothes from Holland and elsewhere. The leather jackets, swingin' 1960s and '70s wear, and woollen sailors' coats are well-priced winners. There are also some men's suits and new shoes.

LAURA DOLS Map pp286-7   Clothing

☎ 624 90 66; www.lauradols.nl; Wolvenstraat 7

Compulsive style-watchers head to this vintage-clothing store for fur coats, 1920s beaded dresses, lace blouses and '40s movie-star accessories like hand-stitched leather gloves.

LOCAL SERVICE Map pp292-3 — Clothing

☎ 620 86 38; Keizersgracht 400-402
Media types (male at 400, and female at 402) hunt here for the latest Paul Smith (Amsterdam's exclusive dealer for his main line), and the Ghost, Stone Island and Dreikorn collections.

MECHANISCH SPEELGOED
Map p285 — Children

☎ 638 16 80; Westerstraat 67; ⊗ Mon, Tue, Thu-Sat
This fun shop is crammed full of nostalgic toys including snow-domes, glow-lamps, masks, finger puppets and wind-up toys. And who doesn't need a good rubber chicken every once in a while?

MENDO Map p285 — Art & Antiques

☎ 612 12 15; Berenstraat 11; ⊗ Wed-Sun
The Mendo ad agency has opened this smart, black-walled gallery specialising in young Dutch painters – works range from the bright to the disturbing but alluring. It also sells an intriguing selection of art, design, architecture and photography books.

NIC NIC Map pp286-7 — Antiques & Kitsch

☎ 622 85 23; Gasthuismolensteeg 5
A trip here is like a visit to a gallery of 20th-century design. Cramped shelves take you from Art Deco to Bauhaus, googie, the '70s, *The Simpsons* and heaven knows what else.

PAUL ANDRIESSE GALLERY
Map p285 — Art & Antiques

☎ 623 62 37; Prinsengracht 116
Contemporary art's the go here – think video installations, avant-garde sculpture and works by international and Dutch artists like painter Marlene Dumas, photographer Thomas Struth and Keith Edmier, who works in several media.

RAZZMATAZZ Map pp286-7 — Clothing

☎ 420 04 83; Wolvenstraat 19
These flamboyant and expensive designer outfits and avant-garde club clothes include the Westwood, Frankie Morello and Andrew Mackenzie labels.

SANTA JET Map pp286-7 — Speciality Shop

☎ 427 20 70; Prinsenstraat 7
The interior's vivid colours alone are worth a visit, as are the Mexican shrines, religious icons, Day of the Dead paraphernalia, candles and love potions.

SKINS COSMETICS Map pp292-3 — Cosmetics

☎ 528 69 22; www.skins.nl; Runstraat 9
The Netherlands' exclusive importer of special brands of fragrances, cosmetics and skin-care and beauty products: think Aesop, Dyptique, Etro, Laura Mercier and the Art of Shaving. They also do makeup sessions and facials.

URBAN PICNIC Map pp286-7 — Food & Drink

☎ 320 88 66; www.urbanpicnic.net; Oude Spiegelstraat 4
Everything you need for a picnic in the park or a snack for the train: baskets, plastic ware, paper goods, nifty biodegradable wooden utensil and, oh yes, the food, like sandwiches of smoked Irish salmon with horseradish cream, or lamb sausage with mustard mayo.

VAN RAVENSTEIN Map pp292-3 — Clothing

☎ 639 00 67; Keizersgracht 359
Chic men and women shop here for up-market Dutch and Belgian designers including Dries Van Noten, Ann Demeulemeester, Dirk Bikkembergs, Martin Margiela and Viktor & Rolf.

VROUWEN IN DRUK Map p285 — Books

Women in Print; ☎ 624 50 03; Westermarkt 5; ⊗ Tue-Sat
Across from the Homomonument and Pink Point, this second-hand bookshop specialises in women's titles (with a reasonable English section): history, lesbian, biographies and fiction.

WHERE TO GET YOUR GROOVE ON

If your thing is club music, you can swing, sway and swap notes with knowledgeable locals at these shops. The chill cat next to you at the listening booth may be spinning for you that night. They're also supreme for the latest club- and dance-fest info.

- **Groove Connection** (Map pp286–7; ☎ 624 72 34; Sint Nicolaasstraat 41)
- **Kids Love Wax** (Map pp286–7; ☎ 528 68 80; Gasthuismolensteeg 6A)
- **Killa Cutz** (Map pp286–7; ☎ 428 40 40; Nieuwe Nieuwstraat 19D)
- **Massive Soul Food** (Map pp286–7; ☎ 428 61 30; Nieuwe Nieuwstraat 27C)
- **Rhythm Imports** (Map pp286–7; ☎ 622 28 67; Nieuwendijk 159)
- **Rush Hour Records** (Map pp286–7; ☎ 427 45 05; Spuistraat 98)

SOUTHERN CANAL BELT

ART MULTIPLES Map pp292-3   Art & Antiques
☎ 624 84 19; Keizersgracht 510; ☺ Mon-Sat
You could spend hours here flipping through thousands of postcards with unusual subject matter; take a peek at the raunchy ones in 3-D viewers. It also sells beautiful art posters and museum-shop gifts.

AURORA KONTAKT
Map pp292-3   Speciality Shop
☎ 623 40 62; Vijzelstraat 27-35
If your favourite electronic or computer gizmo has stopped working, this no-nonsense store can sell you a replacement at competitive prices.

BEVER ZWERFSPORT
Map pp292-3   Camping, Outdoor & Sport
☎ 689 46 39; Stadhouderskade 4; ☺ Mon-Sat
Everything you need for a local hike or a Himalayan expedition: camping equipment, mountaineering gear, clothes and shoes.

BLOEMENMARKT Map pp292-3   Souvenirs
Singel; ☺ closed Sun winter
The traders at the floating flower market, near Muntplein, should be able to tell you if you can take the flower bulbs back home: Ireland and the UK allow an unlimited number of bulbs to be brought back in, as do Canada and the USA (accompanied by a certificate, which will be provided). Japan permits up to 100 certified bulbs, while Australia and New Zealand have banned the importation of bulbs altogether.

Flower pots from the Bloemenmarkt make fun souvenirs

CARL DENIG
Map pp292-3   Camping, Outdoor & Sport
☎ 626 24 36; Weteringschans 113-115; ☺ closed Sun & most Mon
Opened in 1912, this is Amsterdam's oldest and best outdoor retailer, though you pay for the quality. There are five floors of packs, tents, hiking and camping accessories, snowboards and skis.

CITYBOEK Map pp292-3   Art & Antiques
☎ 627 03 49; www.cityboek.nl; Kerkstraat 211; ☺ by appt
We normally don't write up shops selling souvenir posters, but this small publishing house is an exception, with precisely drawn, multicoloured, architecturally faithful prints, books and postcards of Amsterdam's canalscapes (eg images of the entire Herengracht or Singel).

CONCERTO Map pp292-3   Music
☎ 623 52 28; Utrechtsestraat 52-60
Most excellent. This rambling shop, spread over several buildings, has Amsterdam's best selection of new and second-hand CDs and records; you could spend hours on end browsing in here. It's often cheap, always interesting and has good listening facilities.

CORA KEMPERMAN Map pp292-3   Clothing
☎ 625 12 84; Leidsestraat 72
Kemperman was a designer with larger Dutch fashion houses, but since 1995 she's been working on her own empire – now nine stores. Her creations feature floaty, layered separates and dresses in linen, cotton and wool.

DECORATIVA Map pp292-3   Art & Antiques
☎ 320 10 93; Nieuwe Spiegelstraat 9a
An amazing jumble of European antiques, collectables and weird vintage gifts fills this large space. Look up and you'll even see paintings on the ceilings.

DESHIMA Map pp292-3   Food & Drink
☎ 625 75 13; Weteringschans 65; ☺ Mon-Sat
Downstairs, Deshima is a health-food store with all sorts of macrobiotic products, but upstairs there's a lovely selection of prepared foods (plates from €8.50 to €10.50) and a few seats for eating in. Try the salads and cooked veggies, cakes and tarts.

DREAM LOUNGE Map pp292-3 — Smart Drugs
☎ 626 69 07; Kerkstraat 93

Enhance whatever needs enhancing at Amsterdam's original smart shop; the enthusiastic staff can explain everything about magic mushrooms, trippy herbs and cacti. There are books, club information and Internet facilities.

EDUARD KRAMER
Map pp292-3 — Art & Antiques

☎ 623 08 32; Nieuwe Spiegelstraat 64

Specialising in antique Dutch wall and floor tiles, glass and silver, Eduard Kramer is bursting with vintage home wares.

EH ARIËNS KAPPERS
Map pp292-3 — Art & Antiques

☎ 623 53 56; Nieuwe Spiegelstraat 32

This pretty gallery stocks original prints, etchings, engravings, lithographs, maps from the 15th to 20th centuries, and Japanese woodblock prints.

EICHHOLTZ Map pp292-3 — Food & Drink
☎ 622 03 05; Leidsestraat 48

This small deli is bursting with everything homesick Brits and Americans yearn for, such as Oreo cookies, Betty Crocker cake mix, Heinz baked beans, peanut butter (Skippy, Jif or Peter Pan!), HP sauce and Bird's custard.

FROZEN FOUNTAIN Map pp292-3 — Furniture
☎ 622 93 75; Prinsengracht 629; Mon-Sat

The city's best-known showcase of furniture and interior design. Prices are not cheap, but wares are offbeat and very memorable (designer pen-knives, kitchen gadgets).

GALERIE LAMBIEK Map pp292-3 — Books
☎ 626 75 43; www.lambiek.nl; Kerkstraat 78; ☽ daily

Serious collectors of comics will lose themselves amid tens of thousands of titles of Dutch and worldwide comic-book art. Crumb, Avril and Herriman are just the tip of the 4000-plus author iceberg.

GET RECORDS Map pp292-3 — Music
☎ 622 34 41; Utrechtsestraat 105

This deceptively large store has an eclectic and wide range of rock, folk, country and blues CDs. It's a decent break from the club music scene.

HART'S WIJNHANDEL
Map pp292-3 — Food & Drink

☎ 623 83 50; Vijzelgracht 27; ☽ Tue-Sat

Listen to classical music as you peruse the large selection of *genevers* and French and Italian wines at this peaceful shop. It's been around since 1880.

HEINEN Map pp292-3 — Traditional Souvenirs
☎ 627 82 99; Prinsengracht 440

With four floors of delftware, all the major factories are represented and all budgets catered for (spend about €4 for a spoon, €2600-plus for a replica 17th-century tulip vase).

INTERNATIONAL THEATRE & FILM BOOKS Map pp292-3 — Books
☎ 622 64 89; Leidseplein 26; ☽ Mon-Sat

In the Stadsschouwburg building, this excellent shop is crammed with books on its namesake subjects, as well as speciality sections on, for example, musicals and famous directors. A majority of titles are in English.

JASKI Map pp292-3 — Art & Antiques
☎ 620 39 39; Nieuwe Spiegelstraat 27-29

This large, commercial gallery sells paintings, prints, ceramics and sculptures by some of the most famous members of the CoBrA movement (p30).

LIEVE HEMEL Map pp292-3 — Art & Antiques
☎ 623 00 60; Nieuwe Spiegelstraat 3

You will find magnificent contemporary Dutch realist painting and sculpture at this smart gallery. It handles Dutch painters, Ben Snijders and Theo Voorzaat, and astounding, lifelike representations of clothing – hewn from wood! – by Italian Livio de Marchi.

MARAÑON HANGMATTEN
Map pp292-3 — Speciality Shop

☎ 622 59 38; www.maranon.com; Singel 488

Anyone who loves hanging around should come here and explore Europe's largest selection of hammocks. The colourful creations, made of everything from cotton to pineapple fibres, are for everyone from adults to babies, and are made by many producers from indigenous weavers to large manufacturers.

Shopping

SOUTHERN CANAL BELT

PRESTIGE ART GALLERY

Map pp292-3   Art & Antiques

☎ 624 01 04; www.prestige-art-amsterdam.com; Reguliersbreestraat 46; ☽ Mon-Fri & by appt

This gallery, located just off Rembrandtplein, has been in operation since 1935, specialising in 17th- to 20th-century oil paintings and bronzes. Many artists displayed here have been in museum exhibitions or art books.

REFLEX MODERN ART GALLERY

Map pp292-3   Art & Antiques

☎ 627 28 32; Weteringschans 79A; ☽ Tue-Sat

This prominent gallery, opposite the Rijksmuseum, is filled with contemporary art and photography, including works by CoBrA members and members of the Nouveau Réaliste movement.

REFLEX NEW ART GALLERY

Map pp292-3   Art & Antiques

☎ 423 54 23; Weteringschans 83; ☽ Tue-Sat

This new branch specialising in new art is across the street from the original Reflex. There's an emphasis on photography, and artists include young up-and-comers like David La Chapelle, Robin Lowe, Roger Ballen, Larry Sultan and Nobuyoshi Araki.

ROB

Map pp292-3   Erotica/Gay

☎ 625 46 86; www.rob.nl; Weteringschans 253

RoB has been keeping it up since the 1970s, selling anything and everything to enhance one's bondage and rough-sex fantasy life: army gear, leather and rubber are just the start. Oh my!

SCHELTEMA

Map pp292-3   Books

☎ 523 14 11; Koningsplein 20

The largest bookshop in town is a true department store with many foreign titles, and New Age and multimedia sections. It can be dizzying.

SHIRT SHOP

Map pp292-3   Clothing

☎ 423 20 88; Reguliersdwarsstraat 64

On gay Amsterdam's main street, this funky, two-storey shop sells tight-fitting men's shirts to make you look fabulous. Some go on sale from about €25.

TINKERBELL

Map pp292-3   Children

☎ 625 88 30; Spiegelgracht 10; ☽ Mon-Sat

The mechanical bear blowing bubbles outside this shop fascinates kids, as do the intriguing technical and scientific toys inside. You'll also find historical costumes, plush toys and an entire section for babies.

VLIEGER

Map pp292-3   Speciality Shop

☎ 623 58 34; Amstel 34

Since 1869 this two-storey shop has been supplying paper to Amsterdam, and not just any paper: Egyptian papyrus; lush handmade papers from Japan, India, Nepal and Guatemala; papers inlaid with flower petals or bamboo; and paper textured to look like snakes.

WALLS

Map pp292-3   Art & Antiques

☎ 616 95 97; Prinsengracht 737; ☽ Tue-Sat

If you're looking for paintings by the next generation, this long, cheerful warehouse-

---

DIAMONDS

Amsterdam has been a diamond centre since Sephardic Jews introduced the cutting industry in the 1580s. The 'Cullinan', the largest diamond ever found (3106 carats), was split into more than 100 stones here in 1908, after which the master cutter spent three months recovering from stress. The Kohinoor (Mountain of Light) – a very large, oval diamond (108.8 carats), acquired by Queen Victoria and now forming part of the British crown jewels – was cut here too.

Five diamond factories in the city offer guided tours – the Gassan tour is probably the most enlightening, but Coster is centrally located and has a great history. Tours are free and usually run 9am to 5pm daily.

Diamonds aren't necessarily cheaper in Amsterdam than elsewhere, but between the tours and extensive descriptions a factory offers, you know what you're buying.

Amsterdam Diamond Center (Map pp286-7; ☎ 624 57 87; Rokin 1)

Coster Diamonds (Map pp292-3; ☎ 305 55 55; Paulus Potterstraat 2-6)

Gassan Diamonds (Map pp290-1; ☎ 622 53 33; Nieuwe Uilenburgerstraat 173-175)

Stoeltie Diamonds (Map pp292-3; ☎ 623 76 01; Wagenstraat 13-17)

Van Moppes & Zoon (Map p297; ☎ 676 12 42; Albert Cuypstraat 2-6)

type space leases its walls to some 20 artists working in abstract, realism, photography, oils and more. Shows change about every two months.

OLD SOUTH

The real concentration of shops is around the PC Hooftstraat, which teems with brands that need no introduction: Hugo Boss, Chanel, Dolce & Gabbana, J.A. Henckels, Louis Vuitton, Mont Blanc, Zegna and more. Across the Vondelpark, Overtoom has furniture and home-design stores as well as second-hand shops.

BROEKMANS & VAN POPPEL

Map p296   Music

☎ 679 65 75; Van Baerlestraat 92-94; ✆ Mon-Sat
Near the Concertgebouw (surprise!), it's the city's top choice for classical and popular sheet music, as well as music books. Head to the 1st floor for a comprehensive selection from the Middle Ages through classical to today.

DE WATERWINKEL Map p296   Food & Drink

☎ 675 59 32; Roelof Hartstraat 10
Thirsty? With over 100 types of bottled water (mineral, sparkling, still and flavoured), this calm and pretty store will quench your thirst.

DE WINKEL VAN NIJNTJE

Map p296   Children

Miffy Shop; ☎ 671 97 07; Beethovenstraat 71;
✆ Mon-Sat
Dutch illustrator Dick Bruna's most famous character, Miffy ('Nijntje' in Dutch), is celebrated in toys and kids' merchandise. Items range from pencils and soap bubbles to note pads, mouse pads, books, plush toys, clothing and playhouses, to Royal Delftware plates.

JACOB VAN WIJNGAARDEN

Map pp282-3   Books

☎ 612 19 01; www.jvw.nl; Overtoom 97;
✆ closed Sun
This shop is just minutes away from Leidseplein, away from the fray. It has an extensive selection of travel books, and gift items for the traveller of your choice.

TOP FIVE SHOPS FOR DUTCH DESIGN

- **Droog Design** (p191)
- **Frozen Fountain** (p199)
- **Internationaal Design Centrum** (p194)
- **Post Amsterdam** (p202)
- **Wonderwood** (p192)

LAIRESSE APOTHEEK Map p296   Pharmacy

☎ 662 10 22; De Lairessestraat 40hs; ✆ Mon-Sat
Both pharmacy and installation art, with graphics of the periodic table filling the entrance and a rotunda of green backlit cases inside.

MEVIUS & ITALIAANDER

Map pp292-3   Speciality shop

☎ 618 02 56; Overtoom 21-25
This shop doesn't have a lot of street presence, but it's cavernous where it counts (in the back) and loaded with the unexpected: old posters and dishes from faraway lands, new espresso pots and used LPs, furniture and lamps. Prices start at €0.50.

REFLECTIONS Map pp292-3   Clothing

☎ 664 00 40; Pieter Cornelisz Hooftstraat 66-68;
✆ daily
This surprisingly unintimidating store attracts the haute-couture crowd with its men's and women's collections by Issey Miyake, Dolce & Gabbana, Comme des Garçons, Junaba Watanabe and John Galliano.

SHOEBALOO Map pp292-3   Clothing

☎ 626 79 93; Leidsestraat 10
We like the chic shoes here: imports like Fendi, Helmut Lang, Miu Miu and Prada Sport, and the less expensive, but just as wearable, house label. The branch at PC Hooftstraat (☎ 671 33 10; Pieter Cornelisz Hooftstraat 80) has one of our favourite interiors in town: imagine a giant spaceship-green tanning bed lined with shoe shelves and eggs for you to sit on.

WOMEN'S OUTDOOR WORLD

Map pp292-3   Camping, Outdoor & Sport

☎ 412 28 79; Overtoom 51-53
Owned by Bever, one of the city's leading sporting-equipment shops, the WOW

Shoebaloo (p201) on Leidsestraat, for all your foot needs

had to open a separate shop due to overwhelming demand. They also sell equipment that you don't need to be female to buy (eg tents).

XSMALL Map p296 — Children
☎ 470 26 00; Van Baerlestraat 108; ☾ Mon-Sat
Outfitting the moppets of the Old South with toys and extra-cute clothes for kids aged 0 to 10. They can also create digital portraits in Andy Warhol style, from your own digital photo of your little darling (from €45).

DE PIJP

Most shoppers in De Pijp seem to be at the Albert Cuypmarkt, and with a good reason. It's block after block of clothing food, and home wares, reasonably priced. More than that, it's where the city comes together: from the most recent immigrant to the Queen (locals are still talking about how she shopped here for the market's 100th birthday in 2005 – and ran out of money).

DE EMAILLEKEIZER Map p297 — Home Wares
☎ 664 18 47; Eerste Sweelinckstraat 15;
☾ noon-6pm Tue-Sat
Email sounds like something you want to send, but in Dutch it means 'enamel', so it's something you'll want to keep. This colourful store brims with it: metal tableware and more coated in interesting designs from China, Ghana, Poland etc.

FRAME FIETS GALLERY
Map pp292-3 — Art Gallery
☎ 672 75 88; Frans Halsstraat 26A; ☾ Tue-Sun
Wessel van den Bosch trained as an architect, and now he makes custom bicycles from this gallery space on a busy corner. It will make sense when you see it. Some people come in for the art, some come in for a custom-made bike, and often they end up with the other – or both.

STADSBOEKWINKEL Map pp282-3 — Books
☎ 572 02 29; Amsteldijk 67
Run by the city printer, this is the best source for books about Amsterdam's history, urban development, ecology and politics. Most titles are in Dutch (but you can always look at the pictures) – you'll also find some in English. It's in the City Archives building.

STENELUX Map pp292-3 — Speciality Shop
☎ 662 14 90; Eerste Jacob van Campenstraat 2;
☾ Thu-Sat
Buy an old fossil for that old fossil you left back home. Stenelux has a smart collection from this world and beyond (including meteorites).

EASTERN ISLANDS

POST AMSTERDAM Map pp290-1 — Furniture
☎ 421 19 33; www.postamsterdam.nl; 5th, 9th & 10th fl, Oosterdokskade
Above the temporary quarters of the Stedelijk Museum is this unexpectedly cool furniture showroom. See, feel and sit in the pieces on display, and staff will direct you to the nearest retailer. This is only a temporary location, so check the website for any changes.

EASTERN DOCKLANDS

DE ODE Map pp282-3 — Speciality Shop
☎ 419 08 82; Levantkade 51, KNSM Island;
☾ by appt only
Here you can find a final resting place with a difference: a bookcase that converts to a coffin when you join the library in the sky, or a coffin on wheels with bicycle towbar – perfect for pedalling friends to their last bike rack.

1 *Tuschinskitheater (p44), Southern Canal Belt* **2** *Amsterdam ArenA (p184), Greater Amsterdam, a hi-tech complex that seats 52,000 people* **3** *Performer at Paradiso (p170), Southern Canal Belt* **4** *Queen's Day celebrations (p9) in front of the Royal Palace (p70), Medieval Centre*

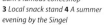

1 *'t Blauwe Theehuis (p146) in the Vondelpark, Old South* **2** *Barney's (p166), Western Islands, Amsterdam's famous coffeeshop* **3** *Local snack stand* **4** *A summer evening by the Singel*

1 *Clubbing at mega-venue Paradiso (p170), Southern Canal Belt* 2 *Vegetarian restaurant De Bolhoed (p140), Western Canal Belt* 3 *Brown café Hoppe (p156), Medieval Centre* 4 *Lokaal 't Loosje (p156), Nieuwmarkt*

1 *Miniature souvenir gabled buildings* **2** *Amsterdam window display* **3** *Chic boutique of the Negen Straatjes (p84), Western Canal Belt* **4** *Laundry Industry design shop (p191), Medieval Centre*

1 *Amsterdam Centrum* 2 *Antique shop Decorativa (p198), Southern Canal Belt* 3 *Window display celebrating Amsterdam's shipping history* 4 *Flowers for sale at Westermarkt (p190), Western Canal Belt*

1 Display at the Verzetsmuseum (p110-11), Plantage **2** Tropen-museum (p111), Oosterpark **3** Van Gogh Museum (p97), Old South **4** Museum Amstelkring (p67), Red Light District

1 *Rijksmuseum (p96), Old South*
2 *Painting at the CoBrA Museum (p116), Greater Amsterdam*
3 *Exhibit at FOAM (Fotografie Museum Amsterdam (p92), Southern Canal Belt* 4 *Creatively painted truck*

Intimate Strangers
Susan Meiselas

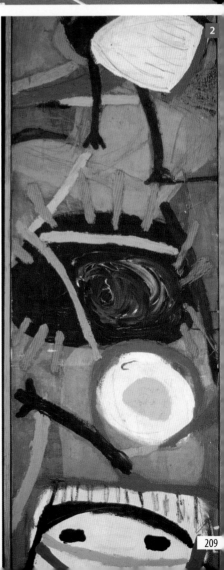

1 *Police Station, Den Haag (p233)*
2 *Cheese market, Alkmaar (p245)*
3 *Leiden (p240) has almost as many canals as Amsterdam*
4 *Keukenhof Flower Gardens (p240), Haarlem, the largest gardens in the world*

Sleeping ■

Sleeping

In its typically charming way, Amsterdam has loads of hotels in creative spaces: old buildings have been repurposed, and canal houses have been joined together to create wholes much greater than the sum of their parts. Some of these lodgings overlook gorgeous canals or courtyards, others are filled with art that's historic or modern, still others are triumphs of design.

However, charm doesn't come cheap. There are 37,750-plus hotel rooms in Amsterdam, and at peak times it can seem that all of them are full. If you're looking to 'do' Amsterdam on the cheap, you might find yourself in a tiny, threadbare room and pay more for it than you thought possible. Leave the budget options to the college kids, take a deep breath, swipe that card and sally forth. Or look on the Internet for substantial discounts even at the top hotels.

If you're driving, inquire about parking in advance. In almost all cases parking is a major problem and the most you'll get is a (payable) parking permit out on the street – with all the attendant headaches and security risks – or a referral to the nearest parking garage (up to €35 a day), which may be a fair distance away. Top-end hotels have their own parking arrangements but prefer prior notification. See Parking (p250) for other important info.

Styles of Accommodation

Amsterdam's lodgings run the gamut from large multinational hotel chains and splendid boutique properties, to little 'mum and dad' B&Bs, youth hostels and some sprawling budget hotels. Amsterdam lodgings are small compared with those in other capitals – any hotel with more than 20 rooms is considered large.

This is because a lot of hotels have their origins as houses lining the canals. Some of the more interesting, unique and very agreeable hotels string two or more such homes together; the Hotel Pulitzer (p220) is composed of 25 houses!

You'll see a 'star' plaque on the front of every hotel, indicating its rating according to the Benelux Hotel Classification. The stars (from one to five) have to do with the existence of certain facilities, rather than quality.

This means that a two-star hotel, for example, may be in better condition than a hotel of higher rank, though admittedly with fewer facilities. Accommodation that rates less than one star cannot call itself a hotel, but a pension, guesthouse or B&B. If a room has both *en-suite* toilet and shower (or bath) we've used the term 'private facilities'; if the bathroom and toilet are in the corridor we've used 'shared facilities'.

> ### TOP FIVE GAY & LESBIAN LODGINGS
>
> While most hotels in town are lesbian- and gay-friendly (by law as well as by nature), some hotels cater specifically to a lesbian or gay clientele.
> - Aero Hotel (p220)
> - Amistad Hotel (p220)
> - Black Tulip Hotel (p218)
> - Liliane's Home (p226)
> - Orfeo Hotel (p223)

If you have a special need (wheelchair access, elevator, bathtub as opposed to shower, triple or family-size room), be sure to inquire.

BED & BREAKFASTS

By law, an inn with four rooms or fewer cannot be called a hotel, but a number of interesting B&Bs have sprung up in recent years. Most don't have exterior signage and access is by reservation only, but many visitors enjoy the intimate settings and the ability to feel more like a local in a home, an experience that's difficult to get in a larger lodging. Styles range from classic to kitsch to contemporary.

TOP FIVE MIDRANGE HOTELS

- **Hotel Arena** (p227)
- **Hotel Brouwer** (p215)
- **Hotel de Filosoof** (p225)
- **'t Hotel** (p220)
- **Seven Bridges** (p222)

'STONER' HOTELS

This being Amsterdam, there is a number of hotels in the budget category where pot smoking is welcome. By and large they're pretty shabby affairs, but we've included a few for those who can't resist the temptation.

If in doubt whether smoking is permitted, be sure to ask when you make your reservation. At many hotels, smoking of any kind is prohibited in rooms, and others have strict no-drugs policies. Don't be embarrassed about asking ahead of time – you'll hardly be the first.

YOUTH HOSTELS

The Netherlands youth-hostel association goes by the name **Stay Okay** (☎ 010-264 60 64, in Rotterdam; www.stayokay.com) and is affiliated with Hostelling International (HI). There are two Stay Okay hostels in Amsterdam.

A youth-hostel card entitles you to receive €2.50 a night discount. Prices include breakfast and clean linen upon arrival. Be sure to book well ahead, especially in busy periods (spring, summer and autumn holidays).

There are also a number of non–Stay Okay/HI hostels in town.

Price Ranges

Once you get used to the idea of cramped rooms at high rates, in general you'll find you get what you pay for. Lodgings in the lowest price bracket (below €70 for a double) can be run-down with mouldy smells (due to the damp climate and the Dutch aversion to decent ventilation). But the more you spend, the grander you get.

We list rates for single/double/triple rooms where available. Some hotels offer family rates.

The rates in this book are the nondiscounted 'rack' rates; treat them as a guide only. Prices at many hotels drop in the low season (roughly October to April excluding Christmas/New Year and Easter). Even in high season it's worth asking for 'special' rates, especially for longer stays. Top-end hotels often rely on business travellers and tend to lower rates in the summer months and on weekends. Many hotels also offer discounts via their websites, especially for last-minute bookings.

Sleeping

Seven Bridges boutique hotel (p222) on the Southern Canal Belt

Most of the quoted rates include a 5% city-hotel tax; at the most expensive hotels, however, this is added separately to the bill. Also, if you're paying by credit card, some hotels add a surcharge of up to 5%.

MIDRANGE (DOUBLES €70 TO €140)

Most hotels in this category are big on comfort, low on formality and small enough to offer personal attention. All rooms have a toilet and shower (and/or bath) and, unless stated, come with TV, phone and breakfast.

TOP END (DOUBLES €140 TO €270)

For a bit of luxury, loads of privacy and lashings of personal service, these hotels will put a smile on your dial. Expect lifts, in-room Internet access, minibars and room service. Unless stated, rates include breakfast.

DELUXE (DOUBLES OVER €270)

Facilities like air-conditioning, fitness centres (some with pocket-sized swimming pools), conference and banquet rooms, and business services are par for the course. Breakfast is rarely included (and can cost €20 and up).

Reservations

Offices of the VVV (p259) and GWK (p257) have last-minute hotel-booking services, though expect queues during peak season. The VVV charges €14 commission per booking, the GWK office €9.75.

If you're targeting a particular hotel, check its website or phone directly to inquire. Otherwise, try a travel agent or discount travel websites (see boxed text, opposite), where you may be able to get last-minute bookings even at tippity-top hotels.

Some smaller hotels won't accept credit-card details over the phone (if they accept cards at all) and may insist on a deposit by cheque or money order before they'll confirm the booking.

When booking for two people, make it clear whether you want a twin (two single beds) or double (a bed for two). It usually makes no difference to the price, but the wrong bed configuration could be impossible to fix on the spot if the hotel is fully booked.

Always get a confirmation in writing.

Long-term Stays

If you'll be in town for a while, it may make sense to rent a flat. Get yourself a bike and you'll practically be a local. Prices for furnished apartments start at about €700 per month but can easily be triple that. Houseboats are another option. Many agencies have a minimum rental period (eg six months).

FLAT CHAT

- **Amsterdam Apartment** (☎ 668 26 54; www.amsterdamapartment.nl; Oude Nieuwstraat 1)
- **Apartment Services** (☎ 672 18 40; www.apartmentservices.nl; Waalstraat 58)
- **Citymundo** (☎ 676 52 70; www.citymundo.com; Schinkelkade 47)
- **Goudsmit Estate Agents** (☎ 644 19 71; www.goudsmit.com; AJ Ernststraat 735)
- **IDA Housing Services** (☎ 624 83 01; www.idahousing.com; Den Texstraat 30)

Some visitors (and this author) have achieved excellent results via local message boards. Among them:
- **www.craigslist.com** Worldwide resource for just about anything. Its Amsterdam presence is small but effective.
- **www.expatica.com** An excellent resource for the expat community. Go directly to the classified ads.
- **www.viavia.nl** For this one you'll need to read Dutch (click 'Woon & Bedrijfsruimte' to start, then click 'Tijdelijk' (temporary) under 'Woningen' (housing).

ACCOMMODATION ONLINE

- www.amsterdam-hotels-guide.com
- www.bookings.nl
- www.hotelres.nl
- www.lastminute.com
- http://amsterdam.ratestogo.com

MEDIEVAL CENTRE

BELLEVUE HOTEL

Map pp286-7   International Hotel

☎ 530 95 30; www.bellevuehotel.nl;
Martelaarsgracht 10; s/tw/tr/q from
€80/110/150/180; ⊠ 🖵

Of the small hotels around Centraal Station, this is the only one we'd stay at. Opened spring 2005, rooms are small, white and tidy and feature mod loos and themes of sand, water and grass. If you're sensitive to noise, get a room in the back. American-style breakfast costs €10.

GRAND AMSTERDAM SOFITEL

DEMEURE Map pp286-7   Luxury Hotel

☎ 555 31 11; www.thegrand.nl; Oudezijds
Voorburgwal 197; r from €420; ⊠ 🖵 🔊

…and grand it is. Amsterdam's former city hall (1808–1987) was the scene of Queen Beatrix's civil wedding in 1966. You may feel royal yourself as you wander through the cavernous lobby, grandiose stairwells and spacious inner courtyard. Linger in your black-and-white bathroom or lounge in your bathrobe. All rooms are meticulously kept in Old World style, and there's an indoor pool with fitness and steam rooms. One incongruity: it's on the edge of the Red Light District, but if it was good enough for the Queen…

HOTEL BROUWER

Map pp286-7   Boutique Hotel

☎ 624 63 58; www.hotelbrouwer.nl; Singel 83;
s/d €50/85; ⊠

Our favourite hotel in this price range, just eight rooms in a house dating back to 1652. Its rooms, named for Dutch painters, are furnished with simplicity, but all have canal views and private facilities. There's a mix of Delft-blue tiles and early-20th-century furniture, and, get this, a tiny elevator. Staff dispense friendly advice. Reserve well in advance. No credit cards accepted.

HOTEL DE L'EUROPE

Map pp292-3   Luxury Hotel

☎ 531 17 77; www.leurope.nl; Nieuwe
Doelenstraat 2-8; s/d €295/365; ⊠ 🔊

Oozing Victorian elegance, L'Europe welcomes you with a glam chandelier, marble lobby, 100 gloriously large rooms (some have terraces and all have handsome marble bathrooms), and smart extras like shoeshine service and boats for canal cruises. The attached Excelsior restaurant and chichi gym (said to be admired by no less than Governor Schwarzenegger) are equally impressive.

HOTEL HOKSBERGEN

Map pp286-7   Boutique Hotel

☎ 626 60 43; www.hotelhoksbergen.nl; Singel 301;
s & d €72-104, tr €130, apt €150-200

You sure can't beat Hoksbergen's fantastic canalside location, and there's a new breakfast buffet, but be warned: even sardines would have trouble squishing into the microscopically small rooms (with TV, phone, private facilities, and clean but plain furnishings). If you feel claustrophobic, self-contained apartments (up to 5 people) may be a better option.

HOTEL RÉSIDENCE LE COIN

Map pp292-3   Boutique Hotel

☎ 524 68 00; www.lecoin.nl; Nieuwe Doelenstraat 5;
s €110, d €130-145, q €248

This shiny new inn owned by the University of Amsterdam offers 42 high-class small apartments spread over seven historical buildings, all equipped with designer furniture, wood floors, wireless Internet and kitchenettes – and all reachable by lift. Staff are pleasant, and breakfast costs €9 per person.

HOTEL THE CROWN

Map pp286-7   Party Hotel

☎ 626 96 64; www.hotelthecrown.com; Oudezijds
Voorburgwal 21; with/without private showers
€50/45, d €100/90; ⊠

Rooms at this Brit-run, Red Light District hotel are pretty Spartan (shared toilet, no TV or phone), and don't even bother asking for breakfast. Although it is priced in our upper-middle bracket, quality is firmly lower-middle. So what's the draw? Fun. The 1930s Art Deco bar has sports on TV, pool

TOP FIVE DELUXE HOTELS

- **Amstel Intercontinental Hotel** (p221)
- **Hilton Amsterdam** (boxed text, p227)
- **Hotel Okura** (boxed text, p227)
- **Seven One Seven** (p223)
- **Dylan** (p219)

table, dartboard and hordes of celebrating stag-nighters. Spliff-smoking is permitted (some would say encouraged) in the bar, but no smoking in rooms.

HOTEL WINSTON   Map pp286-7   Party Hotel
☎ 623 13 80; www.winston.nl; Warmoesstraat 123; s/d from €65/89

Party central for touring bands and up-for-anything tourists, with rock'n'roll rooms and a busy club downstairs. Most rooms are 'art' rooms: local artists were given free rein, with results from super-edgy (entirely stainless steel) to playful to questionably raunchy. Group rooms sleep up to eight. Look for mid-week and off-season discounts. Staff can be less than warm, but hey, it's rock'n'roll, man. Deal with it.

NH BARBIZON PALACE
Map pp286-7   International Hotel
☎ 556 45 64; www.nh-hotels.com; Prins Hendrikkade 59-72; standard d €150-280; 🖳

Spread over 19 houses (some 17th-century) and incorporating the 15th-century St Olof Chapel, the Barbizon Palace seamlessly blends Old World charm with modern amenities, especially visible in top-floor rooms. Both traditional and contemporary rooms are a decent size for the price, and the health club (with Turkish bath, solarium and massage) is large for a hotel gym. Plus, it's just across the canal from Centraal Station.

NH GRAND HOTEL KRASNAPOLSKY
Map pp286-7   International Hotel
☎ 554 91 11; www.nh-hotels.com; Dam 9; d €270; 🖳

Pride of place belongs to this gargantuan, 468-room edifice across from the Royal Palace, one of the city's first grand hotels (1866). It has elegant if compact rooms and spectacular public spaces. The 19th-century 'winter garden' dining room, with its soaring steel-and-glass roof, is a national monument (splendid breakfast buffet €22 extra), and there are fitness and business centres. Note: rates can vary widely.

NH HOTEL DOELEN
Map pp292-3   International Hotel
☎ 554 06 00, toll free ☎ 00800-0115 0116; www.nh-hotels.com; Nieuwe Doelenstraat 24; s/d from €139/169; ✕ 🔁 🖳

Art-history buffs will want to stay here, where you'll find a portion of the wall where Rembrandt painted the *Nightwatch*. Its location at the confluence of the inner Amstel and Kloveniersburgwal means grand views, especially from the breakfast room (buffet €16). Rooms were being renovated as we went to press.

Hotel Winston rooms were decorated by an assortment of artists

RADISSON SAS

Map pp286-7   International Hotel

☎ 623 12 31; www.radissonsas.com; Rusland 17; d €260; ✗ 💻

The Radisson's row-home façade is very much in keeping with the style of its old-city surrounds, yet once you enter the skylit, soaring, post-industrial cool lobby you know you're somewhere else. Rooms are not enormous but are well kept, recently redesigned in themes including Scandinavian and maritime. There's a fitness centre, sauna, the 18th-century Pastorie bar and friendly, professional staff. Breakfast is €21.50.

SWISSÔTEL AMSTERDAM

Map pp286-7   International Hotel

☎ 522 30 00; www.swissotel-amsterdam.com; Damrak 96; d €295; ✗ 🐾 💻

An understated escape from the madness that is Damrak. Standard rooms are typically Amsterdam-cramped (bigger rooms available), but they make up for it with a smart remodel of hardwood, very comfy beds, contemporary design, Internet hookups and complimentary espresso machines. Good discounts are often available.

Cheap Sleeps

AIVENGO YOUTH HOSTEL

Map pp286-7   Hostel

☎ 620 11 55, 421 36 70; www.aivengoyouthhostel .com; Spuistraat 6; dm weekday/weekend €18/20; 💻

Funky Aivengo's, with two rooms (18 and 19 beds respectively), is a real winner. It's got a quiet, respectful vibe and wonderful, cheery, modern–Middle Eastern interior. Rates include clean bed linen, towels and safety deposit box, but no breakfast or common rooms. Note: there's a 1pm to 5pm lockout and a 4am curfew.

CHRISTIAN YOUTH HOSTEL
'THE SHELTER CITY' Map pp286-7   Hostel

☎ 625 32 30; www.shelter.nl; Barndesteeg 21; dm €16, Jul & Aug €19, incl breakfast; ✗ 💻

The price is right at this rambling hostel just off the Red Light District, but *only* if you can handle Christian rock music piped through the PA system and enormous 'Jesus loves you' signs. The pros of staying

TOP FIVE HOTELS TO SEE & BE SEEN

- **College Hotel** (p224) A hip addition to the Old South.
- **Flying Pig Downtown Hostel** (below) Proof that a young-person's scene doesn't have to cost a fortune. Put that in your pipe and smoke it.
- **Hotel Winston** (opposite) Snag a room individually decorated by an artist at Amsterdam's most rocking lodging.
- **Lloyd Hotel** (p228) Both hotel and cultural centre, and a hub of the Eastern Docklands.
- **Quentin Hotel** (p222) Steps from the theatres of the Leidseplein, for star-spotting.

here include large, airy, single-sex dorms (and bathrooms, frequently cleaned), filling breakfasts, a quiet garden courtyard, eternal salvation and a tough no-drugs or alcohol policy. The cons include a 2am curfew – and a tough no-drugs or alcohol policy. Its partner hostel in the Jordaan (p218) has somewhat less missionary zeal.

FLYING PIG DOWNTOWN HOSTEL

Map pp286-7   Stoner Hostel

☎ 420 68 22; www.flyingpig.nl; Nieuwendijk 100; dm €22-30; 💻

Hang out with hundreds of dope-smoking, young backpackers at this very relaxed, very central, 30-room hostel; rates vary by time of year and number of beds per room (the smallest has four). It's pretty grungy, but no-one seems to mind, especially when there's so much fun to be had in the throbbing lobby bar with pool table, DJs some nights and a chilled-out, cushion-lined basement nicknamed the 'happy room'.

HOTEL BRIAN Map pp286-7   Stoner Hostel

☎ 624 46 61; www.hotelbrian.com; Singel 69; s/d with shared facilities €37/54; 💻

This ardently shabby and relaxed joint ('joint' being the operative word) was recently renovated, but to be honest it's hard to tell. Anyway, it's churlish to quibble when the rates include a good breakfast buffet, advice from fun, knowledgeable staff, and the odd chance of scoring a room with skylights and canal views. Kitchen facilities are available, but no phones or TVs in rooms.

Sleeping   MEDIEVAL CENTRE

NIEUWMARKT
BLACK TULIP HOTEL

Map pp286-7 — Boutique Hotel

☎ 427 09 33; www.blacktulip.nl; Geldersekade 16; s €115, d €145-190; 💻

The nine rooms of this exclusively gay male hotel are fitted out with a mind-boggling array of bondage equipment: slings, cages, hooks, chairs, masses of black leather and latex etc. Lest you think that it's somehow sleazy, the Tulip is well tended, fashionable, bright and (pardon the expression) spanking clean. Rates include buffet breakfast and wireless Internet access; all rooms have private facilities, fridge and minibar.

MISC EAT DRINK SLEEP

Map pp286-7 — Boutique Hotel

Previously known as Hotel Zosa; ☎ 330 62 41; www.hotelmisc.com; Kloveniersburgwal 20; s/d/tr €120/145/167; 💻

Steps from Nieuwmarkt Square, the Misc's six rooms make up in visuals what they lack in size. Feeling romantic? Book the lovely 'baroque' room. The 'Africa' room is an escape, while the 'room of wonders' is a modern Moroccan escapade. It's so relaxed that a fresh-cooked breakfast (included in rate) is served until noon, and they will arrange for massage services.

Cheap Sleep
STADSDOELEN YOUTH HOSTEL

Map pp292-3 — Hostel

☎ 624 68 32; www.stayokay.com; Kloveniersburgwal 97; dm €24-26, d €61; 🍴 💻

Efficient Stadsdoelen is always bustling with backpackers and we can understand why. The staff is friendly and the mix of 11 ultraclean, single-sex and mixed rooms (each with up to 17 beds and free lockers) offer a modicum of privacy. There's a big TV room, a great smoke-free bar, pool table and laundry facilities.

JORDAAN & WESTERN ISLANDS

HOTEL VAN ONNA Map p285 — Inn

☎ 626 58 01; Bloemgracht 102-108; r per person €45; 🍴

Even if the 41 rooms here won't win any design awards, they're reasonably priced

with private facilities and breakfast included, and you're in a gorgeous section of the Jordaan, within earshot of the bells of the Westerkerk (get a room in the back if you're sensitive to noise). Rooms sleep up to four people. Try to book the attic room with its old wooden roof beams and panoramic views over the Jordaan. No phone, TV or credit cards.

Cheap Sleep
CHRISTIAN YOUTH HOSTEL
'THE SHELTER JORDAN' Map p285 — Hostel

☎ 624 47 17; www.shelter.nl; Bloemstraat 179; dm €16-22; 🍴 💻

OK, we'll put up with the 'no-everything' (smokin', drinkin', spliffin') policy and curfew at this small hostel because it's such a gem, on a quiet block yet steps from the tram line. Single-sex dorms are quiet and clean, breakfasts – especially the fluffy pancakes – are beaut and the garden patio is a relaxing retreat. The café serves cheap, cheap, cheap meals the rest of the day.

WESTERN CANAL BELT
AMBASSADE HOTEL

Map pp286-7 — Boutique Hotel

☎ 555 02 22; www.ambassade-hotel.nl; Herengracht 341; s/d/tr from €165/185/195

Flick through the books in Ambassade's spiffy little library and you'll spy signed copies by Salman Rushdie and Umberto Eco. Literary luminaries and well-heeled tourists alike love this tastefully appointed hotel, spread over 10 canal houses. The antique furniture and fixtures are traditional without being overbearing, service is kind, and the sparkling lounge (with fresh flowers and chandeliers) is ideal for business meetings or afternoon tea. Breakfast costs €16.

BUDGET HOTEL CLEMENS
AMSTERDAM Map pp286-7 — Inn

☎ 624 60 89; www.clemenshotel.nl; Raadhuisstraat 39; d/tr €120/150, s/d/tr with shared facilities €60/75/80; 💻

Tidy, renovated, steep-staired Clemens gears itself to all budgets. Take your pick of the chic, themed rooms (one with a sexy red-gold interior, another with delicate French antiques) all with TV, phone, safe

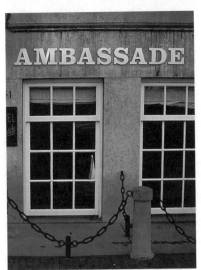

Ambassade Hotel (opposite) on Herengracht

where world beats don't so much play as fizz. Its 41 sophisticated, individually decorated rooms might have Japanese or Indonesian motifs; fluffy towels, silk pillows piled high and spacious bathrooms make them serene and sumptuous. Plus, there's free health club access, and a lounge *par excellence*.

HAMPSHIRE CLASSIC HOTEL TOREN

Map pp286-7   Boutique Hotel

☎ 622 60 33; www.toren.nl; Keizersgracht 164; s/d from €125/145; ✕ ✕ ▢

A title-holder for price, room size and personal service. The Toren's communal areas are pure 17th century with gilded mirrors, fireplaces and magnificent chandeliers, while its guest rooms are elegantly furnished with modern facilities. Treat yourself and book the room with the two-person Jacuzzi and the garden patio (from €270). Breakfast costs €12.

HOTEL AMSTERDAM WIECHMANN

Map pp292-3   Inn

☎ 626 33 21; www.hotelwiechmann.nl; Prinsengracht 328; s/d/tr/q from €75/125/175/190; ▢

This family-run hotel occupies three houses. It has a marvellous canalside location, cosy but lovingly cared-for rooms furnished like an antique shop with country quilts and chintz, and lobby *tchotchkes* (knick-knacks) that have been there for some 50 years (eg suit of armour, potbellied stove). It's very *Ghost & Mrs Muir* and very friendly.

HOTEL NEW AMSTERDAM

Map pp286-7   Boutique Hotel

☎ 522 23 45; www.hotelnewamsterdam.nl; Herengracht 13-19; s €80-95, d €90-160; ✕ ▢

This building, a one-time brothel, sailors' hostel and the basic Hotel New York, received a makeover in 2004 and has become a quick favourite among the cultural crowd, as well as establishing quite a considerable gay following. Perhaps it's because of the fresh-painted murals in guest rooms and common rooms (some peppered with naughty bits), fresh-pressed OJ for breakfast, and fresh-faced, friendly staff. Phone calls and drinks won't break the bank.

and fridge. Your gregarious hostess will lend PCs for in-house wireless Internetting (€8 per night). Breakfast is €7 extra.

CANAL HOUSE HOTEL

Map pp286-7   Boutique Hotel

☎ 622 51 82; www.canalhouse.nl; Keizersgracht 148; r €140-190

Where to spend your time in this splendid 26-room hotel dating from MDCCLXXX (as it says on the façade)? In the ornately furnished, high-ceilinged, 17th-century dining room resplendent with chandeliers, grand piano and garden views? The plush, burgundy-hued bar? Or the small but inviting, antique-filled guest rooms? Staff are agreeable, and rooms have phones and computer connections.

DYLAN Map p285   Boutique Hotel

☎ 530 20 10; www.dylanamsterdam.com; Keizersgracht 384; s/d from €255/405

London hotelier Anouska Hempel was behind the design of this hotel, known as Blakes until recently. Although Hempel has parted company and the name has changed, the Dylan remains a true temple of style. Slink through the 17th-century canal house's courtyard entrance, past the gorgeous staff, to ensconce yourself in the restaurant or black-and-white lobby

Canal House Hotel (p219) is even lovelier on the inside

and understated spot. Its eight comfort-able, individual rooms all have canal or (upscale) neighbourhood views, and top-floor rooms have loads of light. The staff is very accommodating. Significant off-season discounts are available.

Cheap Sleeps

HOTEL PAX Map pp286-7   Inn
☎ 624 97 35; Raadhuisstraat 37; s €25-40, d €35-60, with private facilities from €55
This budget choice in hotel-lined Raadhuis-straat – run by two friendly, funky brothers – has an artsy-student vibe. All eight rooms have a TV and each is individually decorated. The larger rooms face the street, which has noisy trams, so bring earplugs. Breakfast is not included.

SOUTHERN CANAL BELT

AERO HOTEL Map pp292-3   Boutique Hotel
☎ 622 77 28; www.aerohotel.nl; Kerkstraat 45-49; d €70, with private facilities €85-100
Mere steps away from some of gay Am-sterdam's favourite places, the Aero Hotel features cosy, if not particularly glamor-ous, rooms. The renovated rooms are more spacious and have wood laminate floors and modern bathrooms. All rooms come with TV and DVD player, phone and break-fast. Rooms facing the back are quieter. Guests (and others) can greet the world at Camp Café downstairs – try the perenni-ally popular Sunday champagne brunch. Extra bonus: a TV in the corner streaming *Ab Fab* 24/7.

AMISTAD HOTEL
Map pp292-3   Boutique Hotel
☎ 624 80 74; www.amistad.nl; Kerkstraat 42; s/d €69/85, with private facilities €107/138
Rooms at this bijou hotel in the middle of the gay action are dotted with hip designer flourishes like Philippe Starck chairs, CD players and chic soft furnishings (in addition to TV, phone, safe and fridge). Highlights include breakfasting in the kitchen/dining room – with ruby-red walls and make-a-friend communal tables – while chatting with the two super-spunky owners. In the afternoon, the breakfast room becomes an Internet café for the gay community.

HOTEL PULITZER Map p285   Luxury Hotel
☎ 523 52 35; www.luxurycollection.com/pulitzer; Prinsengracht 315-331; d €250; ⊠ ⊠ 💻 ⌨
Spread over 25 17th-century canal houses, the Pulitzer manages to combine big-hotel efficiency with boutique-hotel charm. Beautifully restored rooms vary from house to house, but all have mod cons galore, including sweet and cosy bathrooms. There are loads of extras too: choose from a cigar bar, art gallery, private 75-minute canal cruises, garden courtyards and a wonderful restaurant, all high on elegance and low on pomposity.

MAES B&B Map pp286-7   B&B
☎ 427 51 65; www.bedandbreakfastamsterdam .com; Herenstraat 26hs; s €70, d €95-115; ⌨ ⊠
If you were designing your own home in the western canals and wanted it to have lots of traditional character, it would prob-ably turn out a lot like this four-bedroom property: oriental carpets, wood floors, exposed brick and it's actually fairly spa-cious for such an old building. The kitchen (open all day for guests to use) is definitely *gezellig*. Rooms have TVs but no phones.

'T HOTEL Map pp286-7   Boutique Hotel
☎ 422 27 41; www.thotel.nl; Leliegracht 18; d €145-165; ⌨
Dutch modern furnishing meets 17th-century canal-house setting at this quiet

AMSTEL INTERCONTINENTAL HOTEL

Map pp290-1   International Hotel

☎ 622 60 60; www.amsterdam.intercontinental .com; Professor Tulpplein 1; r from €575; ✂ 🔊 💻 Everything about this five-star edifice is spectacular, from its imposing location overlooking the Amstel, to its magnificent colonnaded lobby and, of course, its wallet-walloping room prices. Lavishly decorated rooms, reverential service and luxe extras such as La Rive restaurant (two Michelin stars, p142), chauffeured limousines, heated indoor pool and fitness centre with all sorts of steam options delight even the fussiest trans-Atlantic celebrities and Euro-royalty.

AMSTERDAM AMERICAN HOTEL

Map pp292-3   International Hotel

☎ 556 30 00; www.amsterdamamerican.com; Leidsekade 97; r €265; ✂ ✂ 💻 You can't get much closer to the action than this, right off Leidseplein and a quick walk to the Museum Quarter. Its grand Art Deco shell is filled with a mixture of Deco and '90s contemporary furnishings; new owners took over in 2005, so expect changes. Guests have use of a gym with sauna. Thankfully you don't need to be staying at the hotel to dine in the stunning Café Americain.

BANKS MANSION

Map pp292-3   International Hotel

☎ 420 00 55; www.banksmansion.nl; Herengracht 519-525; s/d from €255/285; ✂ 💻 One of our favourite new hotels in town. There's no nickel-and-diming over incidentals like the lobby bar, breakfast, coffee, Internet and snacks. It was recently renovated, meaning that rooms feature contemporary décor, plasma-screen TV, DVD player, wet bar (free gin, whisky etc), terry-cloth robe and enormous showerhead.

CITY HOTEL Map pp292-3   Inn

☎ 627 23 23; www.city-hotel.nl; Utrechtsestraat 2; d with shared/private facilities €70/90; 💻 Above the Old Bell pub practically on Rembrandtplein is this unexpectedly fabulous choice: it's clean, neat, well run by a proud, warm family, and a good value. The rooms are decorated with crisp linens and each comes with TV. Rooms sleep two to eight people (from €25 per person).

EUPHEMIA HOTEL Map pp292-3   Stoner Hotel

☎ 622 90 45; www.euphemiahotel.com; Fokke Simonszstraat 1; dm €25-40, s €40-75, d €65-100; ✂ 💻 Euphemia's institutional layout falls short of glamorous, but the rooms are neat and many are quite large. Other pluses? It's gay-friendly, on a quiet block (with even less traffic during Metro construction on nearby Vijzelstraat), and there's a sharp, funny manager (though maybe too sharp for some). Smoking is prohibited in the rooms, but even spliffing is OK in common areas. Check the website for specials.

HEMP HOTEL Map pp292-3   Stoner Hotel

☎ 625 44 25; www.hemp-hotel.com; Frederiksplein 15; s with shared facilities €50, d with shared/private facilities €65/70; 💻 Proof positive that Amsterdam is the capital of the northern 'hempisphere', this chilled-out hotel serves hemp-flour rolls (tetrahydrocannabinol or THC-free) with your breakfast, the café sells hemp teas and beers, and all five colourful and individually decorated rooms (hemp soap and fabrics included) exude a 'just back from Goa' vibe. Dope-smokers reserve now (though you can't buy pot here – you gotta draw the line somewhere).

HOTEL AGORA Map pp292-3   Inn

☎ 627 22 00; www.hotelagora.nl; Singel 462; s & d €103-120, tr from €158, q €175; 💻 Fifteen minutes by foot from everything, the well-run Agora offers smallish rooms with understated décor, up-to-date bathrooms, and a cheerful garden off the breakfast room. All rooms have phone, TV and computer hookups. Rooms without private facilities cost about one-third less.

HOTEL DE ADMIRAAL Map pp292-3   Inn

☎ 626 21 50; de-admiraal-hotel@planet.nl; Herengracht 563; d with shared/private facilities €70/98 Near bustling Rembrandtplein, the Admiraal is sweet, homely and blessed with an interesting history. Nine clean and bright canalside rooms (all with safes and TV, no phone) are outfitted with seriously mismatched furniture. There's also a large 'family room'. The hotel attic was a hideout for Jews during WWII, while Nazi soldiers lodged and dined below. Breakfast is not available.

HOTEL DE MUNCK Map pp292-3 Inn

☎ 623 62 83; www.hoteldemunck.com; Achtergracht 3; s/d/tr/q from €75/95/145/185

De Munck is a sane choice in a quiet neighbourhood. All 16 rooms are bright, on the large side, well kept, and come with TV and phone. Its breakfast room is a slice of rock'n'roll heaven, like a 1960s diner with a working jukebox and record covers lining the walls. Add in a flower-filled courtyard and whip-smart, witty staff. Subtract €10 for rooms with shared facilities.

HOTEL KAP Map pp292-3 Inn

☎ 624 59 08; www.kaphotel.nl; Den Texstraat 5B; s/d/tw €57/95/80;

Wilhelmina Kap ran a pension here before the war, and some of the features seem that historic: mid-century wood panelling, no phones or non-smoking rooms. Still, some bright rooms have French windows, wicker furniture and up-to-date bathrooms. A buffet breakfast is served in an attractive dining room and courtyard garden, and courteous, gay-friendly owners round out the experience. Most rooms have private showers but shared toilets.

HOTEL MERCURE AMSTERDAM ARTHUR FROMMER

Map pp292-3 International Hotel

☎ 622 03 28; www.mercure.com; Noorderstraat 46; s/d/tr €135/155/175;

This French chain offers something few other Southern Canal Belt hotels do: genuinely quiet surrounds. Though rooms in one-time weavers' houses are a bit cookie-cutter and can be on the narrow side, all are well equipped with cable TV, minibar, hairdryer and wi-fi access. Breakfast is available for €14.

HOTEL ORLANDO

Map pp292-3 Boutique Hotel

☎ 638 69 15; www.hotelorlando.nl; Prinsengracht 1099; s/d from €85/100, tr €160;

Oh Orlando, how do we love thee? Let us count the ways. One: five biggish, high-ceilinged, canalside rooms at smallish rates. Two: hospitable, gay-friendly host. Three: breakfast in bed. Four: impeccably chic, boutique style with custom-made cabinetry and satin curtains. We could go on, but we'll leave you more to discover.

HOTEL PRINSENHOF Map pp292-3 Inn

☎ 623 17 72; www.hotelprinsenhof.com; Prinsengracht 810; s/d €45/65, d with shower €85

An honest value, this 18th-century house features ahh-lovely canal views, a breakfast room with some Delft-blue tiles, and 'Captain Hook', the electric luggage hoist in the central stairwell (gets around the no-lift issue). Staff are affable and the rooms spacious with antique and, well, not-antique furnishings. The attic quarters with diagonal beams are most popular.

NH SCHILLER HOTEL

Map pp292-3 International Hotel

☎ 554 07 00, toll free ☎ 00800-0115 0116; www.nh-hotels.com; Rembrandtplein 26-36; s/d €190/230;

Although it's been restored to its original (1912) Art Deco splendour, this hotel has blandly corporate rooms (scheduled for renovation). You'd best lap up the atmosphere in the attached Brasserie Schiller (the stained-glass windows are magnificent) or out on bustling Rembrandtplein. Breakfast is not included.

QUENTIN HOTEL Map pp292-3 Party Hotel

☎ 626 21 87; www.quentinhotels.com; Leidsekade 89; s with shared facilities €40, d with/without private facilities €90/65

The Quentin, decorated with colourful murals, rock-star art and contemporary handmade furniture, offers a variety of rooms for the weary traveller from cramped to well sized, some with balconies, canal views, phone and TV. It's popular with the gay community and international actors and musicians performing at nearby Theatre Bellevue, Melkweg and Paradiso. There's an elevator, and breakfast costs €7.

SEVEN BRIDGES Map pp292-3 Boutique Hotel

☎ 623 13 29; Reguliersgracht 31; s €80-170, d €100-190

Private, sophisticated and intimate, the Seven Bridges is one of the city's loveliest little hotels on one of its loveliest canals. It has eight tastefully decorated rooms (all incorporating lush oriental rugs and elegant antiques). Morning sightseeing will seem superfluous once breakfast, served on fine china, is delivered to your room.

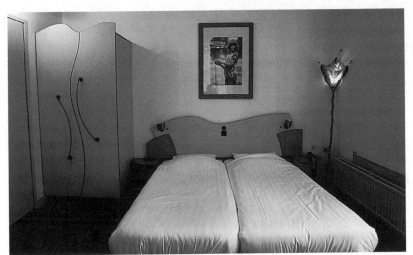

Modern decoration and contemporary furniture at the Quentin Hotel (opposite)

SEVEN ONE SEVEN

Map pp292-3   Boutique Hotel

☎ 427 07 17; www.717hotel.nl; Prinsengracht 717;
r €405-660; 🎬 🖳

Without a doubt, the most wonderful hotel
in Amsterdam – designed, boutiqued and
simply breathtaking. Its eight hyper-plush,
deliciously appointed rooms come with
that rare luxury: space. Step into the splashy
Picasso suite – with its soaring ceiling, pro-
digiously long sofa, gorgeous contemporary
and antique decorations, and bathroom as
big as some European principalities – and
you may never, *ever* want to leave. Rates
include breakfast, afternoon tea, house wine
and oodles of one-on-one service.

Cheap Sleeps
HANS BRINKER BUDGET HOTEL

Map pp292-3   Party Hostel

☎ 622 06 87; www.hans-brinker.com; Kerkstraat
136; dm €21, tw/tr/q per person €35/30/24; 🖳

When a hotel promotes itself with the
slogan 'Improve your immune system' next
to a close-up of bacteria, you're bound to
be pleasantly surprised. The lobby is may-
hem, Spartan rooms have all the ambience
of a public hospital, and its 538 beds are
almost always filled to capacity with school
groups and boisterous backpackers. But the
bar is bright and happy, the disco pulsates,

the restaurant serves cheap meals, rooms
have shower and toilet, and rates include
breakfast and bed linen. Drug-use equals
automatic expulsion.

INTERNATIONAL BUDGET HOSTEL

Map pp292-3   Stoner Hostel

☎ 624 27 84; www.internationalbudgethostel.com;
Leidsegracht 76; dm/tw €28/70; 🖳 ✗

Reasons to stay: canalside location in a
former warehouse; really close to nightlife; four-person limit in rooms; cool mix
of backpackers from around the world
smoking in the lounge (though smoking
is strictly prohibited in rooms, as are hard
drugs); clean rooms with lockers; staff
who're more pleasant than they need to
be; lower off-season rates. Reasons not:
your money will go further elsewhere as
breakfast isn't included.

ORFEO HOTEL Map pp292-3   Hostel

☎ 623 13 47; www.hotelorfeo.com; Leidsekruisstraat 14; s with private facilities €50, d with/without
private facilities €115/75, tr €140; 🖳

A cheap option for gay fellas, opened
in 1969, central Orfeo has simple, small,
wood-panelled rooms (with TV, phone,
minibar), sexy staff (they told us so themselves) and the flirtiest breakfast room in
town. It turns into a reasonably priced bar-
restaurant for dinner.

OLD SOUTH

BILDERBERG HOTEL JAN LUYKEN
Map pp292-3   Luxury Hotel

☎ 573 07 30; www.janluyken.nl; Jan Luijkenstraat 58; s/d from €195/210; ✕ ⬚ ⬚

This Art Nouveau delight is in top form, with a crisp white and caramel colour scheme and sleek designer furniture. Other pleasures: solarium, steam bath and whirlpool, a menu of books, pillows and CDs, alluring bar with garden views, and staff who take their time with you. Buffet breakfast is €17 per person.

COLLEGE HOTEL
Map p296   Boutique Hotel

☎ 571 15 11; www.thesteingroup.com/college; Roelof Hartstraat 1; s/d from €175/200; ✕ ⬚

One of the city's newest hotels is also one of its oldest, originally a 19th-century school, updated with tremendous style: flat-screen TVs, silk-throw pillows, cordless phones, the occasional stained-glass window and exposed beams on the top floor. Here's the difference, though: it's staffed by hotel-school students. Continental breakfast costs a steep €17.50, but if the dining hall was this cool where we went to college, we'd have figured out a way not to graduate.

FLYNT B&B
Map pp292-3   B&B

☎ 618 46 14; www.flynt.nl; Eerste Helmersstraat 34; r €70-120; ⬚

Flynt's building, on a quiet block off the Overtoom, is almost a century old, but the look is contemporary, bright and spotless. Frank, the easy-going owner, will purchase breakfast food for you, and the kitchen is yours 24/7. The owners have cats and dogs, and your pets are welcome too. Rooms are non-smoking, though hallways are not.

HESTIA HOTEL
Map pp292-3   Inn

☎ 618 08 01; www.hotel-hestia.nl; Roemer Visscherstraat 7; s €70-84, d €93-135, tr/q €158/188

Friendly, family-run Hestia, with 18 rooms decorated in fresh blue and white, offers a quiet retreat after a day of sightseeing. Scrupulously neat rooms vary in size and height – some have balconies overlooking the Vondelpark. The stair-phobic can rejoice: there's an elevator too.

HOTEL AALDERS
Map pp292-3   Inn

☎ 662 01 16; www.hotelaalders.nl; Jan Luijkenstraat 13-15; s/tw/tr from €75/87/143; ✕ ⬚

There are fancier hotels in town, but the family-owned Aalders is homely and well situated on a quiet street near the Museum-

Bilderberg Hotel Jan Luyken provides lots of little extras

plein. Each room in its two row homes is different (the old-style room has wood panelling and leaded windows), but all have TV, phone, shower and wireless Internet access. The breakfast room has a Venetian-glass chandelier. Huge rooms are available for large groups.

HOTEL ACRO Map pp292-3 Party Hotel
☎ 662 55 38; www.acrohotel.nl; Jan Luijkenstraat 44; s €65-110, d €75-165, tr €90-165, q €105-185; 🖳
So it's a bit austere and its '80s-décor rooms could use an update, but that aside it's a great place. Rates are reasonable for the quiet location (near Museumplein), the bar is welcoming (it's just had a makeover from its big-hair club to more of a brown café), and the staff are warm and helpful. Maybe that's why so many British guests return year after year.

HOTEL BEMA Map p296 Inn
☎ 679 13 96; www.bemahotel.com; Concertgebouwplein 19B; s from €45, d with/without private facilities €85/65; 🖳
Climb the stairs to this seven-room hotel in a higgledy-piggledy mansion house across from the Concertgebouw and filled with African art. Expect extra-big doubles and breakfast in bed but no phone in the room. Staff can also arrange private apartments for up to four people.

HOTEL DE FILOSOOF
Map pp282-3 Boutique Hotel
☎ 683 30 13; www.hotelfilosoof.nl; Anna van den Vondelstraat 6; s/d from €111/125
A hotel owned by two sisters, with 38 rooms themed after philosophers. Sounds quaint, no? But it's also a professional, warm and well-run operation near the Vondelpark. There are larger rooms in town, but few more thoughtfully decorated: from lush furniture and over-the-top wallpaper to minimalist paeans to serenity. The variety of breakfast rooms may remind you of museums you've visited.

HOTEL FITA Map pp292-3 Boutique Hotel
☎ 679 09 76; www.hotelfita.com; Jan Luijkenstraat 37; s €90, d €120-145; 🗶 🖳
This tiny, family-owned hotel on a quiet street off Museumplein and PC Hooftstraat was renovated a few years ago and is now one of the best in the Old South. It's got 16

handsome rooms, nicely appointed bathrooms, an English-style breakfast buffet and an elevator. Plus, rates include free telephone calls to Europe and the USA.

HOTEL VONDEL Map pp292-3 Boutique Hotel
☎ 612 01 20; www.hotelvondel.nl; Vondelstraat 28-30; r from 129; 🗶 🖳
It's finally the year of the Hotel Vondel. Its seven houses used to be disconnected such that you needed to go outside to get from one to the next, but a 2005 renovation has changed that. They upgraded the rooms too, with minimalist yet stylish décor. Discounts are available in low season.

MARRIOTT HOTEL
Map pp292-3 International Hotel
☎ 607 55 55; www.marriotthotels.com/amsnt; Stadhouderskade 12; d from €169; 🗶 📞 🖳
American visitors will feel right at home in the Marriott's spacious rooms and décor that could be in the Midwest. 'Executive' suites (from €219) allow access to the private lounges and are especially nice for business travellers. Extras include a fitness centre, shops and a Pizza Hut. American-style breakfast buffet (steak and eggs, waffles and more) costs €24.

NH AMSTERDAM CENTRE
Map pp292-3 International Hotel
☎ 685 13 51; www.nh-hotels.com; Stadhouderskade 7; r from €145; 🗶 📞 🖳
In an Amsterdam School building that dates back to around the Amsterdam Olympics, this hotel was recently renovated, with striking results. Rooms have all mod cons, darkwood floor beneath a pale tan-and-white colour palette (and your choice of pillow), plus there's a fitness centre with a spa and sauna.

OWL HOTEL Map pp292-3 Inn
☎ 618 94 84; www.owl-hotel.nl; Roemer Visscherstraat 1; s €75-92, d €98-125; 🖳
Some guests love this place so much that they send in owl figurines from all over the world. Staff are warm and welcoming, and the dapper, bright and quiet rooms come with lots of facilities (hairdryers, laptop plug-ins). Best of all, buffet breakfast (included in the price) is served in a serene, light-filled room overlooking a gorgeous garden.

COLLECTOR Map p296   B&B
☎ 673 67 79; www.the-collector.nl;
de Lairessestraat 46 hs; r €80-115; 🖵
This B&B is a real find: just three rooms near the Concertgebouw. The 1914 building is spotless with contemporary renovations and furnished with museum-style displays of clocks, Amsterdam School furnishings, wooden shoes etc. Each room has a balcony and TV, and the owner will buy food for you to prepare breakfast at your leisure; the kitchen is open all day.

Cheap Sleeps
STAY OKAY VONDELPARK
Map pp292-3   Hostel
☎ 589 89 96; www.stayokay.com; Zandpad 5;
dm €24-30, tw €74; 🖵 ⊠
A blink away from the Vondelpark, this 535-bed hostel attracts over 75,000 guests a year – no wonder the lobby feels like a mini-UN. All bedrooms are non-smoking, have lockers, a shower, toilet and well-spaced bunks. There are lifts, a café, two restaurants and bike-hire opportunities. There's no curfew but the no-visitors-at-night, no-drugs policy is strictly enforced. From March to October and during public holidays the maximum stay is three nights. Discounts are offered in low season.

DE PIJP
BETWEEN ART & KITSCH B&B
Map p297   B&B
☎ 679 04 85; www.between-art-and-kitsch.com;
Ruysdaelkade 75-2; d €80-110, tr €120; 🖵
Mondriaan once lived here – that's part of the art – and the kitsch is bits like a crystal chandelier in the baroque room and the smiling brass Buddha nearby. The Art Deco room, meanwhile, has seriously gorgeous tile work and views of the Rijksmuseum. Husband and wife Ebo and Irene (and Ruysdael the Jack Russell terrier) are your hosts, 3½ storeys up on a quiet canalbank at the edge of De Pijp. Rooms are non-smoking, though common areas are not.

LILIANE'S HOME Map pp290-1   Inn
☎ 627 40 06; l.meisen@zonnet.nl;
Sarphatistraat 119; d €80-110
Once Amsterdam's sole women-only inn, this seven-bedroom private home recently began to allow male visitors, and that's a nice thing for you gents. It has loads of personality, rooms with huge windows (some with balconies), and amenities including TV (no phone), fridge and books to read. Reservations are required, since there is no bell desk.

You'll feel safe at Hotel Arena (opposite) with this dog guarding your sleep

WORTH THE TRIP

Although it's an old-school hotel with lots of business guests, the **Hilton Amsterdam** (Map p296; ☎ 710 60 00; www.hilton.com; Apollolaan 138-140; r from €202; 🖳 ❎) grabs the spotlight every once in a while. It was 'flower power' central in 1969 when John Lennon and Yoko Ono staged their 'bed-in' for world peace (you can rent the room), and Herman Brood, Holland's most famous junkie-artist-musician, committed suicide here in 2001 by jumping off the roof – he used to frequent the hotel's popular bar (carrying a parrot on his head). This tower fronts a grassy park with a marina out back; rooms are international business standard; the health club features sauna and Turkish bath; and service is crisp and professional.

Hotel Okura (Map p297; ☎ 678 71 11; www.okura.nl; Ferdinand Bolstraat 333; s/d from €240/275; ❎ 🖳 ❎ 🔊) is the business traveller's choice, with close proximity to the RAI exhibition centre, private in-room fax lines, wi-fi for computers, and professional staff. Plus, it's got Holland's largest hotel pool, an amazing health club, several fine restaurants (including two with Michelin stars, Yamazato and Ciel Bleu) and delicious, panoramic views of Amsterdam.

PLANTAGE & OOSTERPARK

BEST WESTERN LANCASTER HOTEL

Map pp290-1   International Hotel

☎ 535 68 88; www.edenhotelgroup.com; Plantage Middenlaan 48; s/d/tr/q from €120/130/150/170; ❎ 🖳

This 93-room place next to a park is bigger than it looks, and a tip-to-toe renovation in 2003 has made it one of the smartest lodgings in the Plantage. Rooms all have TV, phone, free wi-fi and motifs of blond-wood, brick red, cream, and the stylised St Andrew's crosses of the city seal. Breakfast costs €14 and includes hot dishes.

HOTEL ARENA Map pp290-1   Party Hotel

☎ 850 24 00; www.hotelarena.nl; 's Gravesandestraat 51; d/tr from €110/165; 🖳

With more facelifts than a Hollywood star, this building, bordering lush Oosterpark, has morphed from chapel to orphanage to backpackers' hostel and, now, a modern, 121-room hotel with trendy restaurant, café and nightclub. Minimalist rooms – 'designer industrial hospital' chic – are more Ikea than *Wallpaper** magazine, but the large, split-level double rooms are a sun-drenched delight. Rooms in sections A, B, E and F tend to be quieter. Breakfast costs €12.50.

HOTEL PARKLANE Map pp290-1   Inn

☎ 622 48 04; www.hotel-parklane.nl; Plantage Park-laan 16; s/d Sun-Thu €65/95, Fri & Sat €75/105; 🖳

This 12-room, one-time dressmaker's shop is being renovated room by room by kindly owners who care about doing things right. Unrenovated rooms are…well, stay in the renovated rooms. Quad rooms are available.

HOTEL REMBRANDT Map pp290-1   Inn

☎ 627 27 14; www.hotelrembrandt.nl; Plantage Middenlaan 17; s €73, d €85-112.50, tr/q €135/155; 🖳

Although the hallways could stand a touch-up, the Rembrandt shines where it matters: rooms are spotless and have TV, phone, coffee-maker and some hardwood floors and bathtubs. And the wood-panelled breakfast room is a beaut, with chandeliers and 17th-century paintings on linen-covered walls. Rooms 2 (large double with a balcony overlooking a small garden) and 21 (four-person, split-level, sunny and modern) offer plenty of bang for your buck.

Cheap Sleeps

HOTEL HORTUS Map pp290-1   Stoner Hotel

☎ 625 99 96; www.hotelhortus.com; Plantage Parklaan 8; dm €25, s/d €35/50; 🖳

Facing the Botanical Garden, this old-shoe comfy, 20-room hotel has small doubles with or without showers (luck of the draw); all have safe and sink. It's run by the same crew as Hotel Brian, so it's no surprise that the lounge is chock-full of young, happy stoners transfixed by the large-screen TV. Large rooms sleep up to eight people. Rates include a cooked breakfast.

HOTEL PENSION KITTY Map pp290-1   Inn

☎ 622 68 19; Plantage Middenlaan 40; s/d with shared facilities €45/55

We love Kitty, and how could you not? She's 80-something and speaks halting English, and a night in her creaky, antique-filled, ruby-red-carpeted mansion is like a stay at grandma's. Its 10 rooms are big, comfortable and very lived-in. No wonder she has so many loyal guests. Breakfast is not included and there are no phones in rooms.

EASTERN ISLANDS

AMSTEL BOTEL Map pp290-1   Party Hotel
☎ 626 42 47; www.amstelbotel.com; Oosterdokskade 2-4; s & d with land/water view €87/92, tr with land/water view €117/122; 🖳
Five minutes' walk from Centraal Station, this floating hotel is packed with dazed, Europe-in-four-days bus groups and packs of Brit boys/girls celebrating bucks'/hens' nights. Rooms are sterile (in both senses) and have TV, phone and itty-bitty bathrooms. Breakfast is €10 per person, and note occasional two- and three-night stay requirements (eg on weekends).

EASTERN DOCKLANDS

LLOYD HOTEL Map pp290-1   Party Hotel
☎ 561 36 36; www.lloydhotel.com; Oostelijke Handelskade 34; d €80-300; 🖳
Like your artiest friend, the Lloyd is always fabulous and occasionally exasperating. In 1921 the building was a hotel for migrants, and many of the original fixtures still exist (tiles, cabinetry etc) combined with triumphs of more contemporary Dutch design. The result is a combination hotel, cultural centre and local gathering place. Rooms span one-star (facilities down the hall) to five-star (plush and racquetball-court sized). Yet many are also so quirky and individualistic (teeny tiny doubles, bathtub in the centre, giant bed for eight) that some guests may be turned off. Accept it on its terms and you'll love it.

Excursions

Excursions

If you're like us, you have trouble tearing yourself away from Amsterdam. But venture out and you'll find a slower pace and tremendous history, beauty and tradition, in the Randstad (rim-city), a circular urban agglomeration formed by Amsterdam, Den Haag (The Hague), Rotterdam, Utrecht and smaller towns such as Haarlem, Leiden and Delft. It's all within an hour of Amsterdam Centraal, easily accessible by train or bus.

Note: lodging rates quoted in this chapter are for high season. Discounts may be available.

CITIES
Lovely Haarlem (p232) and its central Grote Markt are within easy reach. Leiden (p240) is an easy-going university town, Utrecht (p235) is historic and gorgeous, while Den Haag (p233) is known for its stately atmosphere. For cutting-edge architecture, make sure you don't miss Rotterdam (p236).

WINDMILLS
They're atmospheric, they're beautiful, they're Holland. See them in Zaanse Schans (p246) and Leiden (p240).

CHEESE & FLOWERS
Only in the Netherlands will you see events such as the Alkmaar cheese market (p245), and the world's biggest flower auction in Alsmeer (p245). 'Amazing' is the only way to describe the gardens of the 32-hectare Keukenhof (boxed text, p240), when it explodes in colour between March and May.

ART
Explore Dutch art, from the masters to modern, at museums in Den Haag, Haarlem and Rotterdam. East of the city, the Kröller-Müller Museum (p244) gets special mention for a fantastic collection of Van Goghs in a gorgeous national park.

Windmills in the mist, Zaanse Schans (p246)

HAARLEM

It's hard not to be enthusiastic about Haarlem, which has retained more of its 17th-century layout than any other Randstad city. Its wealth of historic buildings, courtyards and posh antique shops lends a refined elegance.

The main square is Grote Markt, flanked with restaurants and cafés and a clutch of historical buildings. Its florid, 14th-century **Stadhuis** (Town Hall) has many extensions including a balcony where high-court judgments were pronounced. The Counts' hall contains 15th-century panel paintings, and is occasionally open during office hours for a discreet peek.

Across from the Stadhuis looms the **Grote Kerk** (of St Bavo), the Gothic cathedral with a 50m-high steeple. It contains some fine Renaissance artworks, but the star attraction is its **Müller organ** – one of the most magnificent in the world, standing 30m high with about 5000 pipes; try to catch a recital. It was played by Handel and Mozart.

In the centre of Grote Markt stand **De Hallen**, halls including the 17th-century **Vleeshal**, a former meat market, and the **Verweyhal** – today they are annexes of the Frans Hals Museum. The Verweyhal contains the museum's collection of modern art, including Dutch Impressionists and CoBrA artists. On the square north of the Grote Kerk is a **statue of Laurens Coster**, whom Haarlemmers claim, along with Gutenberg, as the inventor of moveable type.

The **Frans Hals Museum** is a must for anyone interested in the Dutch masters. In an almshouse where Hals spent his final, impoverished years, the collection focuses on the 17th-century Haarlem School, the pinnacle of Dutch Mannerist art. The museum's pride, eight group portraits by Hals detailing the companies of the Civic Guard, reveal the painter's exceptional attention to mood and psychological tone.

The **Teylers Museum** is the oldest museum in the country (1778), named after the philanthropist-merchant Pieter Teyler van der Hulst. Its collection includes an array of whizz-bang inventions, drawings by Michelangelo and Raphael, and paintings from the Dutch and French schools. The interiors are as good as the displays.

Haarlem has several lovely **hofjes** (courtyards and gardens) – usually open 10am to 5pm Monday to Saturday. The tourist office has walking guides to monuments.

TRANSPORT

Direction 20km west.

Travel time 15 to 20 minutes.

Train Services to Haarlem are frequent (€3.10, up to six per hour). Grote Markt is a 500m walk to the south.

Car From the ring road west of the city, take the N200 which becomes the A200.

Information

Tourist Office (☎ 0900-616 16 00, per min €0.50; www.vvvzk.nl; Stationsplein 1; ⊗ 9am-5.30pm Mon-Fri, 10am-4pm Sat Apr-Sep, 9.30am-5pm Mon-Fri, 10am-3pm Sat Oct-Mar)

Sights

Canal-boat tours (☎ 023-535 77 23; adult/child €6.50/3; ⊗ first tour noon) Tours leave from opposite the Teylers Museum. Available in English. Six times most days March to October; ring for schedules.

De Hallen (☎ 023-511 57 75; adult/child €5/free; ⊗ 11am-5pm Tue-Sat, noon-5pm Sun)

Frans Hals Museum (☎ 023-511 57 75; www.franshalsmuseum.nl; Groot Heiligland 62; adult/child €7/free; ⊗ 11am-5pm Tue-Sat, noon-5pm Sun)

Grote Kerk of St Bavo (adult/child €1.50/1; ⊗ 10am-4pm Mon-Sat; organ recitals 3pm Thu Jul-early Sep & 8.15pm Tue mid-May–mid-Oct)

Teylers Museum (☎ 023-531 90 10; Spaarne 16; adult/child €5.50/1; ⊗ 10am-5pm Tue-Sat, noon-5pm Sun)

Eating

Café Studio (☎ 023-531 00 33; Grote Markt 25) Café and former cinema, sometimes hosts arts events.

De Haerlemsche Vlaamse (☎ 023-532 59 91; Spekstraat 3; regular French fries €1.70) Frites house and local institution.

Sleeping

Hotel Amadeus (☎ 023-532 45 30; www.amadeushotel.com; Grote Markt 10; s/d incl breakfast €60/85; ⌨) Nestled in a row of old gabled houses on the main square.

Hotel Carillon (☎ 023-531 05 91; www.hotelcarillon.com; Grote Markt 27; s without/with private facilities €33/55, d €58/76, incl breakfast) Great deal on the Grote Markt – primo location.

DEN HAAG (THE HAGUE)

The Netherlands' third-largest city has a refined air, thanks to the stately mansions and palatial embassies lining its green boulevards. It's known for its prestigious art galleries and one of the world's best jazz festivals (North Sea Jazz), held annually near the seaside suburb of Scheveningen.

Confusingly, although the parliament and royal family are based here, Den Haag is not the national capital. It *was* the capital until 1806, when Louis Napoleon installed his government in Amsterdam. Eight years later, the French were kicked out and the government returned to Den Haag, but Amsterdam retained the title of capital.

In the 20th century, Den Haag became the home of several international legal entities including the UN's International Court of Justice and the Academy of International Law. These genteel organisations and their attendant legions of diplomats give the town its rather sedate and urbane air today.

TRANSPORT

Direction 56km southwest.

Travel time 45 minutes.

Trains Run from Amsterdam Centraal Station four times per hour, and cost €9.40. While there are some non-stop trains, most run via Den Haag Hollands Spoor (hs) Station, a short distance away.

Car From the southwest point of the A10 ring road, take the A4, from where Den Haag will be clearly signposted.

The **Mauritshuis** is a small but grand museum, housing some of the world's best-loved Dutch and Flemish works. Almost every piece is a masterpiece, including Rembrandt's *Anatomy Lesson of Dr Tulp*, Vermeer's *Girl with a Pearl Earring* and a touch of the contemporary with Andy Warhol's portrait of Queen Beatrix.

The parliamentary buildings around the adjoining **Binnenhof** (Inner Court) have long been the heart of Dutch politics, though parliament now meets in a modern building (1992) on the south side. The buildings are best seen on a tour.

Admirers of De Stijl, and in particular of Piet Mondriaan, should not miss the HP Berlage–designed **Gemeentemuseum**. Mondriaan's unfinished *Victory Boogie Woogie* takes pride of place (it should; the museum paid €30 million for it), and there are also a few Picassos and other works by some famous 20th-century names. It's also home to a fabulous **Photography Museum.**

Admirers of the work of MC Escher will not want to miss the **Escher in het Paleis** exhibition. His woodcuts and etchings (including *Waterfall* and *Drawing Hands*) appear in a historic building once home to Queen Beatrix's great-grandmother.

You can take a tour of the Binnenhof (p235)

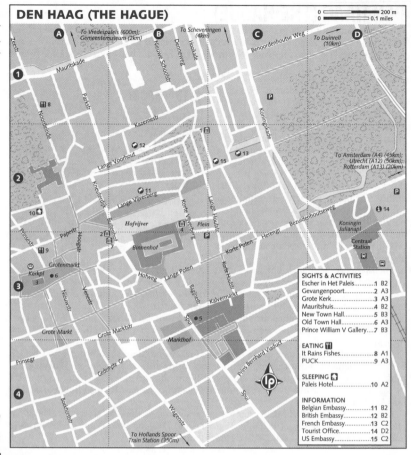

DEN HAAG (THE HAGUE)

SIGHTS & ACTIVITIES

Escher in Het Paleis	1 B2
Gevangenpoort	2 A3
Grote Kerk	3 A3
Mauritshuis	4 B2
New Town Hall	5 B3
Old Town Hall	6 A3
Prince William V Gallery	7 B3

EATING 🍴

It Rains Fishes	8 A1
PUCK	9 A3

SLEEPING 🏠

Paleis Hotel	10 A2

INFORMATION

Belgian Embassy	11 B2
British Embassy	12 B2
French Embassy	13 C2
Tourist Office	14 D2
US Embassy	15 C2

The **Gevangenpoort** (prison gate) is a surviving remnant of the 13th-century city fortifications. It has hourly tours showing how justice was dispensed back then (painfully). Next door, the **Prince William V Gallery** was the first public museum in the Netherlands (1773). It's being restored to its original appearance and at the time of writing was expected to reopen very soon.

The **Grote Kerk** (1450) has a fine pulpit, which was constructed 100 years after the church itself. The neighbouring 1565 **old town hall** is a splendid example of Dutch Renaissance architecture.

The huge **new town hall** at the corner of Grote Marktstraat, is the hotly debated work by US architect Richard Meier (who also designed Los Angeles' Getty Center). The 'official' nickname of the building is the 'white swan', but locals prefer the 'ice palace'.

It stands in contrast to the **Vredespaleis** (Peace Palace), housing the UN's International Court of Justice. The grand building was donated by American steel-maker Andrew Carnegie for use by the International Court of Arbitration, an early international body whose goal was the prevention of war. Sadly, WWI broke out soon after it opened in 1913. There are hourly guided tours, though these might be cancelled when courts are in session. You will need to book ahead (security is strict). Take tram 10 or bus 24 from Centraal Station.

Information

Tourist Office (☎ 0900-340 35 05, per min €0.45; info@vvvdenhaag.nl; Koningin Julianaplein 30; ⏱ 10am-6pm Mon, 9am-6pm Tue-Fri, 10am-5pm Sat, 10am-2pm Sun Jul & Aug)

Sights

Binnenhof tour (☎ 070-364 61 44; adult/child €3.50/1.50; ⏱ 10am-3.45pm Mon-Sat) One-hour tours.

Escher in het Paleis (☎ 070-427 77 30; Lange Voorhout 74; adult/child €7.50/5; ⏱ 11am-5pm Tue-Sun)

DETOUR: MADURODAM

Madurodam (☎ 070-416 24 00; www.madurodam .nl; George Maduroplein 1; adult/child 4-11yr/senior €12/8.75/11; ⏱ 9am-10pm Jul & Aug, 9am-8pm late Mar-Jun, 9am-6pm Sep-late Mar) contains everything quintessentially Dutch in 1/25th-scale: little buildings, people, aeroplanes and more. Not surprisingly, it's big with children, as well as adults.

It was started by JML Maduro as a memorial to his son, who fought the Nazi invasion and later died at Dachau.

Madurodam's a little overpriced and slightly tacky, but also, curiously, one of those very Dutch reference points: even most Dutch who decry it as touristy will admit to having been.

Take tram 9 or bus 22 from Den Haag Centraal Station.

Gemeentemuseum (☎ 070-338 11 20; Stadhouderslaan 41; adult/concession/child under 18 yr €7.50/5/free; ⏱ 11am-5pm Tue-Sat)

Gevangenpoort (☎ 070-346 08 61; Buitenhof 33; tour adult/child €4/3; ⏱ by tour only, 11am-4pm Tue-Fri, noon-4pm Sat & Sun)

Mauritshuis (☎ 070-302 34 56; Korte Vijverberg 8; adult/child €7/3.50; ⏱ 10am-5pm Mon-Sat, 11am-5pm Sun)

New Town Hall (Spui 170)

Prince William V Gallery (☎ 070-362 44 44; Buitenhof 35; adult/child €1.50/1; ⏱ 11am-4pm Tue-Sun)

Vredespalais (☎ 070-302 41 37; Carnegieplein 2; adult/child €2.50/1.50; tours ⏱ 10am-4pm Mon-Fri) Hour tours.

Eating

It Rains Fishes (☎ 070-365 25 98; Noordeinde 123; lunch mains €9.50-16.50, dinner mains €20-36; ⏱ lunch Mon-Fri, dinner nightly) Top seafood place with a delightfully bizarre name.

PUCK (Pure Unique Californian Kitchen; ☎ 070-427 76 49; www.puckfoodandwines.nl; Prinsestraat 33; mains €18 -25; ⏱ lunch & dinner Tue-Sat) Perhaps the most innovative menu in the Netherlands, also including small 'tastes' and large 'bites'.

Sleeping

Paleis Hotel (☎ 070-362 46 21; www.paleishotel.nl; Molenstraat 26; r from €135) The location, on a quiet sidestreet, feels very 'Hague' and rooms are suitably 'paleis'-tial.

UTRECHT

This lovely, historic city is an antique frame surrounding an increasingly modern interior. Its 14th-century canals, once bustling wharves and cellars, are now full of chic shops, restaurants and cafés.

Utrecht is dominated by the **Domtoren** (Cathedral tower), the country's tallest church tower; you can climb its 465 steps for a magnificent view. Another key point of interest is the undeniably photogenic **Oudegracht**.

Of over a dozen museums, the **Catharijneconvent** is the leader, with the finest collection of medieval religious art in the Netherlands. Others include the **Centraal Museum** (covering applied arts and Utrecht School paintings), quirky offerings like the **Museum voor het Kruideniersbedrijf** and the **National Museum van Speelklok tot Pierement**. Canal-boat trips are also available.

In summer, Utrecht is festival central, with offerings such as jazz (with musicians seemingly on every corner) and the Netherlands Film Festival (September).

The area around Utrecht is known as place to commune with nature. Surrounding woods are perfect for a walk or bike ride and the Vecht lake area is great for water sports as well as the scenery.

TRANSPORT

Direction 40km southeast.

Travel time 30 minutes.

Train NS runs about five services per hour (€6.10).

Car From the Amsterdam ringroad, take the A2.

Information

Tourist Office (VVV Utrecht; ☎ 0900-128 87 32, per min €0.50; www2.holland.com/utrechtstad/gb; Vinkenburgstraat 19; ☺ 9.30am-6.30pm Mon-Wed & Fri, 9.30am-9pm Thu, 9.30am-5pm Sat, 10am-2pm Sun Apr-Sep)

Sights

Catharijneconvent (☎ 030-231 72 96; Nieuwegracht 63; adult/child/senior €7/5/6; ☺ 10am-5pm Tue-Fri, 11am-5pm Sat & Sun)

Centraal Museum (☎ 030-236 23 62; Nicolaaskerkhof 10; adult/concession €8/5; ☺ 11am-5pm Tue-Sun)

Domtoren (☎ 030-233 30 06; Domplein 9-10; adult/child/concession €7.50/4/6; ☺ 10am-5pm Mon-Sat, noon-5pm Sun late Mar-Sep, noon-5pm Sun-Fri, 10am-5pm Sat Oct-late Mar)

Museum voor het Kruideniersbedrijf (Grocery Museum; ☎ 030-231 66 28; Hoogt 6; adult/child €3/2; ☺ 10am-5pm Tue-Sat, noon-5pm Sat & Sun)

National Museum van Speelklok tot Pierement (National Museum from Musical Clock to Street Organ; ☎ 030-231 27 89; Steenweg 6; adult/child €7/4.75; ☺ 10am-5pm Tue-Sat, noon-5pm Sun)

Eating

De Winkel van Sinkel (☎ 030-230 30 36; Oudegracht 158; dishes €3-17.50; ☺ lunch & dinner daily) Marvellously located historic building with grand café, restaurant and night spots.

Deeg (☎ 030-233 11 04; Lange Nieuwstraat 71; 3-course menu €30; ☺ dinner) New but already acclaimed for fresh, organic, creative cooking.

Sleeping

Grand Hotel Karel V (☎ 030-233 75 55; www.karelv.nl; Geerteblowerk 1; r from €225) Lavishly converted 14th-century building, with flawless service.

Hostel Strowis (☎ 030-238 02 80; www.strowis.nl; Boothstraat 8; s & d €53, dm €13.50-16.50) 17th-century building and former squat that's been lovingly restored as a hostel.

ROTTERDAM

Europe's busiest port, Rotterdam has a history as a shipping nexus dating back to the 16th century. However, modern Rotterdam's genesis began on 14 May 1940, when the invading Germans issued an ultimatum to the Dutch: surrender, or Rotterdam would be destroyed. The government capitulated, but the raid was carried out anyway (Amsterdam was spared).

As a result, Rotterdam spent most of the 20th century rebuilding. The results are unique in Europe: by turns vibrant, ugly, impressive and astonishing. Today's Rotterdam (the Netherlands' second-largest city) has a dynamic, Berlin-like postmodern-metropolis aesthetic and a crackling energy that seems to feed off the 'anything goes' attitude for reconstruction.

Rotterdam is split by the Nieuwe Maas, a vast shipping channel crossed by a series of tunnels and bridges. The mostly reconstructed centre is north of the water. From Centraal Station, a 20-minute walk along the canal-like ponds leads to the waterfront. The commercial centre is to the east, with most of the museums to the west.

The recently expanded **Museum Boijmans van Beuningen** is one of the best in the Netherlands, if not Europe. The collection includes superb Old Masters, works from Renaissance Italy, French Impressionists, and 'the other surrealists': Dali, Duchamp, Magritte and Man Ray.

At the south end of Museum Park, the **Kunsthal** hosts temporary exhibitions. The building is a sight in itself.

In nearby De Heuvel park on the Nieuwe Maas is the needle-like (185m) **Euromast**. It's one of the less successful – yet most recognisable – examples of modern architecture in the city. If the sky is clear, you can go to the top and see great views of the city that *don't* include it.

Highlights of maritime Rotterdam include the **Maritiem Museum Rotterdam**, right near the landmark Erasmus Bridge, with

TRANSPORT

Direction 77km southwest.

Travel time One hour.

Train NS runs four services per hour (€12.40); look for the intercity service to save a lot of time.

Bus Rotterdam is a hub for **Eurolines bus services** (☎ 412 44 44; Conradstraat 20; ☺ 9.30am-5.30pm Mon-Fri, 9.30am-3pm Sat). Long-distance bus stops are southwest of Centraal Station.

Car From the Amsterdam ring road, take the A4, and then the A13 from Den Haag.

ROTTERDAM ARCHITECTURE

A brief tour of Rotterdam's stunning architecture can begin at the north end of Ben van Berkel's 800m-long **Erasmus-brug** (Erasmus Bridge, 1996), spanning the Nieuwe Maas near the Leuvehaven metro station or via tram 5. Walk part of the way across and you'll see the **KPN Telecom** building (2000) – the Renzo Piano–designed building looks like it's about to fall over but for a long pole giving it support.

Retrace your steps and walk northeast alongside the water, past the three **Boompjestoren** (1988) apartment blocks, and continue on until you see the striking **Willemswerf** (1988), headquarters of the huge Nedlloyd shipping company. Note the dramatic lines casting shadows on its sleek, white surface.

Another 100m will bring you close to Rotterdam's other signature bridge, the **Willemsbrug** (1981), with its red pylons. When you reach the Maas Theater, turn north at Oude Haven on Geldersekade. The regal 11-storey building on the corner is the **Witte Huis** (White House; 1897), a rare survivor of the prewar period.

Walk north for about three minutes to Blaak and the metro/bus station of the same name. The surprising **Overblaak** (1978–84) is to your right, marked by the cube-shaped apartments and pencil-shaped tower. Designed by Piet Blom, the project has graced a thousand postcards.

The **Netherlands Architecture Institute** is in a fittingly stunning building on Museum Park. The institute stages ambitious special exhibitions through the year, and building tours are available.

Ask at the VVV and Architecture Institute about architectural tours of the city.

the usual array of models that any youngster would love to take into the tub. The **Oude Haven** area preserves bits of the oldest part of the harbour, some of which date from the 14th century. It's a decent place for a stroll, especially for the large collection of historic boats, and you can learn about them at the **Havenmuseum**.

The city's history is preserved at one of the few surviving 17th-century buildings in the centre at the **Historisch Museum Het Schielandhuis**. Exhibits focus on items from everyday life through the ages, such as the (purportedly) oldest-surviving wooden shoe.

The **Nederlands Fotomuseum** has recently amalgamated with other photographic institutions, and offers interesting exhibits, as well as a shop and a library.

Information

Use-it Rotterdam (☎ 010-240 91 58; www.use-it.nl; Schaatsbaan 41-45; ☼ 9am-5pm Tue-Sat mid-Sep–mid-May, 9am-6pm Tue-Sun mid-May–mid-Sep, plus 9am-6pm Mon Jul & Aug) Information for independent travellers.

CAUTION!

The area about 1km west of Centraal Station is the scene of many hard-drug deals.

Maritiem Museum Rotterdam (p239)

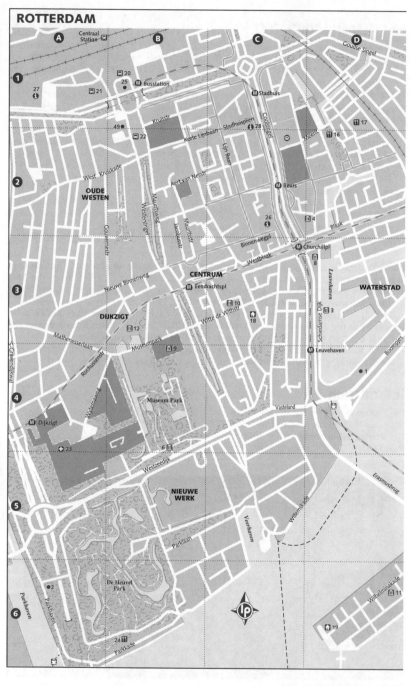

VVV (☎ 010-413 31 24; www.vvv.rotterdam.nl; Coolsingel 67; ⊙ 9am-6pm Mon-Fri year round, 9am-5pm Sat & Sun in midsummer)

Sights

Euromast (☎ 010-436 48 11; Parkhaven 20; adult/child €8/5.20; ⊙ 10am-5pm Oct-Mar, 10am-9pm Apr-Sep, hrs vary btwn 9.30am & 11pm Jul & Aug)

Havenmuseum (☎ 010-404 80 72; Leuvehaven 50-72; admission free; ⊙ 10am-5pm Tue-Fri, 11am-5pm Sat & Sun)

Historisch Museum Het Schielandhuis (☎ 010-217 67 67; Korte Hoogstraat 31; adult/child €3/1.50; ⊙ 10am-5pm Tue-Fri, 11am-5pm Sat & Sun)

Kunsthal (☎ 010-440 03 00; Westzeedijk 341; adult/child under 12yr/13-18yr €8.50/free/2.50; ⊙ 10am-5pm Tue-Sat, 11am-5pm Sun)

Maritiem Museum Rotterdam (☎ 010-413 26 80; Leuvehaven 1; adult/child 4-15yr €5/3; ⊙ 10am-5pm Tue-Sat, 11am-5pm Sun, plus 10am-5pm Mon Jul & Aug)

Museum Boijmans van Beuningen (☎ 010-441 94 00; www.boijmans.rotterdam.nl; Museumpark 18-20; adult/child under 18yr €7/free; ⊙ 10am-5pm Tue-Sat, 11am-5pm Sun)

Nederlands Fotomuseum (☎ 010-213 2011; Witte de Withstraat 63; adult/child €3.50/1.60; ⊙ 11am-5pm Tue-Sun)

Netherlands Architecture Institute (☎ 010-440 12 00; Museumpark 25; adult/child 4-16yr €6.50/4; ⊙ 10am-5pm Tue-Sat, 11am-5pm Sun)

Eating

Dudok (☎ 010-433 31 02; Meent 88; mains €10-16, smaller dishes €2.90-6.70) Contempo café-brasserie in an oh-so-Rotterdam building.

Toaster (☎ 010-413 70 81; Pannekoekstraat 38B; most dishes €3-9.50; ⊙ lunch & dinner Tue-Sun) Cosy, funky café in a low-slung neighbourhood. Snacks, shakes, salads and occasional DJ nights.

Sleeping

Hotel Bazar (☎ 010-206 51 51; www.hotelbazar.nl; Witte de Withstraat 16; s/d from €60/75) This is what Rotterdam's all about: polyethnic vibe, air of tolerance and fantastic ground-floor bar and restaurant (3-course menu €15).

Hotel New York (☎ 010-439 05 00; www.hotelnewyork.nl; Koninginnenhoofd 1; r €91-208; ⊠ ⧆ 🖳 🖵) The city's favourite hotel, in the former headquarters of the Holland-America passenger-ship line.

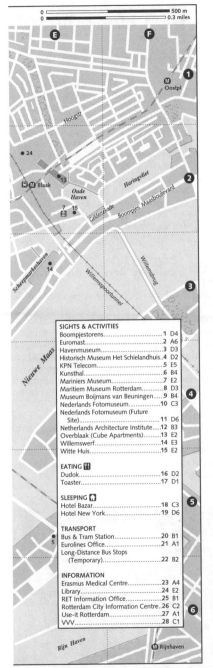

LEIDEN

This easy-going, pretty town is home to the country's oldest **university**. Its 20,000 students make up one-sixth of the population and lend an effervescent, intellectual aura. The university was a gift from William the Silent for withstanding two Spanish sieges in 1574; a third of the residents starved before the Spaniards retreated on 3 October (the town's big festival day).

Wealth from the linen industry buttressed Leiden's growing prosperity, and during the 17th century the town produced several brilliant artists, most famously Rembrandt van Rijn – he was born here in 1606 and remained here for 26 years, before achieving greater fame in Amsterdam.

Leiden may not look traditional in the super-modern Centraal Station, but the five-minute walk to the old city is a trip back in time. Leiden is divided by many waterways, the most notable being the Oude Rijn and also the Nieuwe Rijn, which meet at Hoogstraat to form a canal called simply the Rijn.

De Burcht, an 11th-century citadel on an artificial hill, lost its protective functions as the city grew around it. Now it's a park with lovely places to view the steeples and rooftops.

The **Rijksmuseum van Oudheden** (National Museum of Antiquities) has a world-class collection, particularly from Egypt, including human and animal mummies and the Temple of Taffeh.

The 17th-century **Lakenhal** (Cloth Hall) houses the Municipal Museum, with an assortment of works by Old Masters, as well as period rooms and temporary exhibits. The 1st floor has been restored to the way it would have looked when Leiden was at the peak of its prosperity.

Leiden's landmark windmill museum, **De Valk** (the Falcon), has been carefully restored; many consider it the best example of its kind. It spins 'whenever possible' and even occasionally grinds grain.

Leiden University was an early centre for Dutch medical research, and you can see the often-grisly results (five centuries of pickled organs, surgical tools and skeletons) at the **Museum Boerhaave**.

A stuffed elephant greets you at **Naturalis – Nationaal Natuurhistorisch Museum** (National Museum of Natural History), a large, well-funded collection of all the usual dead critters and, notably, the million-year-old Java Man discovered by Dutch anthropologist Eugene Dubois in 1891.

DETOUR: KEUKENHOF FLOWER GARDENS

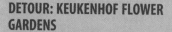

Covering some 32 hectares, **Keukenhof** (☎ 0252-46 55 55; www.keukenhof.nl; Stationsweg 166, Lisse; adult/child/senior €12.50/5.50/11.50; ☾ 8am-7.30pm late March–late May, last entry 6pm) is the world's largest bulb-flower garden, attracting a staggering 750,000 visitors during a mere eight weeks every year. Nature's talents are combined with artificial precision to create a wonder of landscaping where seven million tulips and daffodils bloom, perfectly in place and exactly on time. You can easily spend half a day here.

Opening dates vary slightly from year to year, so check before setting out. During opening season, Connexxion runs Keukenhof Express buses from Leiden Centraal Station (€4 or five 'strips' on the *strippenkaart*, 20 minutes, three times hourly).

Keukenhof Flower Gardens, Leiden

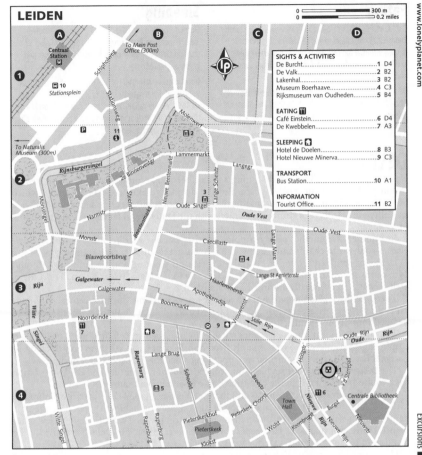

LEIDEN

SIGHTS & ACTIVITIES
De Burcht................................1 D4
De Valk..................................2 B2
Lakenhal................................3 B2
Museum Boerhaave...............4 C3
Rijksmuseum van Oudheden...5 B4

EATING
Café Einstein..........................6 D4
De Kwebbelen........................7 A3

SLEEPING
Hotel de Doelen......................8 B3
Hotel Nieuwe Minerva............9 C3

TRANSPORT
Bus Station.............................10 A1

INFORMATION
Tourist Office..........................11 B2

Information

Tourist Office (☎ 0900-222 23 33, per min €0.70; www .hollandrijnland.nl; Stationsweg 2D; ⏱ 11am-5.30pm Mon, 9.30am-5.30pm Tue-Fri, 10am-4.30pm Sat year round, 11am-3pm Sun mid-Apr–Aug)

Sights

De Burcht (admission free; ⏱ sunrise-sunset)

De Valk (☎ 071-516 53 53; Tweede Binnenvestgracht 1; adult/child €2.50/1.50; ⏱ 10am-5pm Tue-Sat, 1-5pm Sun)

Lakenhal (☎ 071-516 53 60; Oude Singel 28-32; adult/under 18yr €4/free; ⏱ 10am-5pm Tue-Fri, noon-5pm Sat & Sun)

Museum Boerhaave (☎ 071-521 42 24; Lange St Agnietenstraat 10; adult/concession €6/3; ⏱ 10am-5pm Tue-Sat, noon-5pm Sun)

Naturalis – Nationaal Natuurhistorisch Museum (☎ 071-568 76 00; Darwinweg 2; adult/child €9/5; ⏱ 10am-6pm Tue-Sun)

Rijksmuseum van Oudheden (National Museum of Antiquities; ☎ 071-516 31 63; Rapenburg 28; adult/child 4-17yr €7.50/5.50; ⏱ 10am-5pm Tue-Fri, noon-5pm Sat & Sun)

TRANSPORT

Direction 45km southwest.

Travel time 35 minutes.

Train NS runs services from Amsterdam six times per hour (€7.30).

Car From the southwest point of the A10 ring road, take the A4.

Eating

Café Einstein (☎ 071-512 53 70; Nieuwe Rijn 19; lunch mains €2.75-10, dinner mains €11.50-14; ☺ lunch & dinner) Informal fun café with student vibe, river views and lovely waterside setting. Expect Thai dinner Sunday and Monday.

De Kwebbelen (☎ 071-512 61 90; Noordeinde 19; mains €12-17, 3-course menu €17.50; ☺ dinner) The most fun restaurant in Leiden, with kitschy menu ('Joe Formaggio' cheese fondue) but fantastic cooking.

Sleeping

Hotel de Doelen (☎ 071-512 05 27; www.dedoelen .com; Rapenburg 2; s/d €70/90; ☐) Slightly faded air of classical elegance; some canalside rooms are larger and better appointed.

Hotel Nieuwe Minerva (☎ 071-512 63 58; www.nieuw minerva.nl; Boommarkt 23; s/d €75/100; ☐) Located in six 16th-century canalside houses, this central hotel has themed rooms, including a room with a bed in which King Lodewijk Bonaparte slept.

DELFT

Had the potters who lived in Delft long ago not been so accomplished, today's townsfolk would probably live in relative peace. But the distinctive blue-and-white pottery, which the 17th-century artisans duplicated from Chinese porcelain, became famous worldwide as 'delftware'. Delft has a strong association with the Dutch royal family and was the home of Vermeer.

In summer, the number of day-tripping tourists can be overwhelming; in winter, however, its old-world charm and narrow, canal-lined streets make a pleasant day trip.

Delft was founded around 1100 and grew rich off weaving and trade in the 13th and 14th centuries. In the 15th century a canal was dug to the Maas River; the small port there, Delfshaven, was eventually absorbed by Rotterdam.

There are three places where you can see the artists working; the most central and modest is the **Aardewerkatelier de Candelaer**, just off the Markt. When it's quiet you can usually get a detailed tour of the manufacturing process.

The other two locations are factories outside the town centre. **De Delftse Pauw** is the smaller, employing 35 painters who work mainly from home – you won't see them on weekends. **De Porceleyne Fles** is the only original factory operating since the 1650s; it's slick and pricey.

The **Museum Lambert van Meerten** has a fine collection of porcelain tiles and delftware dating back to the 16th century, in the one-time home of a merchant family.

One of the greatest Dutch masters, Johannes Vermeer (1632–75), lived his entire life in Delft, fathering 11 children and dying at age 43, leaving behind a mere 35 incredible paintings. His works have rich and meticulous colouring and he captures light as few other painters have ever managed. His scenes come from everyday life in Delft. You can visit the location of his most-famous exterior work, *View of Delft*, at Hooikade.

Unfortunately, none of Vermeer's works remain in Delft. *View of Delft* can be seen at the Mauritshuis in Den Haag.

The 14th-century **Nieuwe Kerk** houses the crypt of the Dutch royal family and the mausoleum of William the Silent. The same ticket admits you to the Gothic **Oude Kerk**; it looks every one of its 800 years, with its tower leaning 2m from the vertical. Among the tombs inside is Vermeer's.

Opposite the Oude Kerk is the **Prinsenhof**. This collection of buildings is a former convent and is where William the Silent held court until he was assassinated in 1584. The bullet hole in the wall has been enlarged by visitors' fingers and is now covered. The buildings host displays of historical and contemporary art.

In old Delft, the **Beestenmarkt** is a large open space surrounded by fine buildings where much of Tracy Chevalier's novel *Girl with a Pearl Earring* was set. Further east, **Oostpoort** is the sole surviving piece of the town's walls. **Koornmarkt**, leading south from the **Waag**, is a quiet and tree-lined canal.

TRANSPORT

Direction 62km southwest.

Travel Time 50 minutes.

Train Two trains per hour run from Amsterdam Centraal Station (€10.60).

Car From the Amsterdam ring road, take the A4 to Den Haag and turn onto the A13, from which Delft will be clearly signposted.

Information

Tourist Office (☎ 015-215 40 51; www.delft.nl;
Hippolytusbuurt 4; ⏰ 10am-4pm Mon, 9am-6pm Tue-Fri,
10am-5pm Sat, 10am-4pm Sun Apr-Oct, 11am-4pm Mon,
10am-4pm Tue-Sat, 11am-3pm Sun Nov-Mar)

Sights

Aardewerkatelier de Candelaer (☎ 015-213 18 48; Kerkstraat 14; ⏰ 9am-5pm Mon-Sat, 9am-5pm Sun Mar-Oct)

De Delftse Pauw (☎ 015-212 49 20; Delftweg 133;
⏰ 9am-4.30pm Mon-Fri, 11am-1pm Sat & Sun Nov-Mar)
Take tram 1 to Pasgeld, walk up Broekmolenweg to the
canal, and turn left.

De Porceleyne Fles (☎ 015-251 20 30; Rotterdamseweg
196; tour €3; ⏰ 9.30am-5pm Mon-Sat Nov-Mar) Bus 63
from the train station, which stops nearby at Jaffalaan.

Museum Lambert van Meerten (☎ 015-260 23 58;
Oude Delft 199; adult/child €2/1; ⏰ 10am-5pm Tue-Sat,
1-5pm Sun)

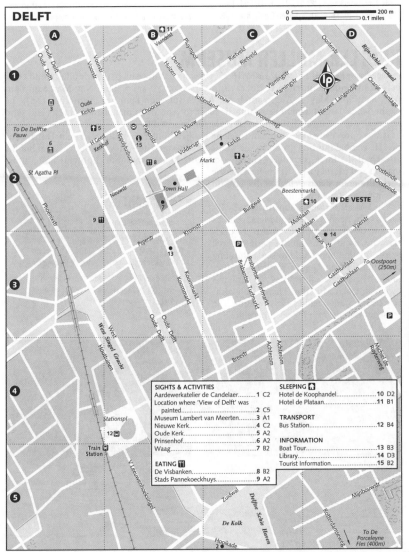

DELFT

0   200 m
0   0.1 miles

SIGHTS & ACTIVITIES
Aardewerkatelier de Candelaer	1 C2
Location where 'View of Delft' was painted	2 C5
Museum Lambert van Meerten	3 A1
Nieuwe Kerk	4 C2
Oude Kerk	5 A2
Prinsenhof	6 A2
Waag	7 B2

EATING 🍴
De Visbanken	8 B2
Stads Pannekoeckhuys	9 A2

SLEEPING 🏠
Hotel de Koophandel	10 D2
Hotel de Plataan	11 B1

TRANSPORT
Bus Station	12 B4

INFORMATION
Boat Tour	13 B3
Library	14 D3
Tourist Information	15 B2

Nieuwe Kerk (☎ 015-212 30 25; adult/child €2/1; ⏰ 9am-6pm Mon-Sat, till 4pm Nov-Mar)

Prinsenhof (☎ 015-260 23 58; St Agathaplein 1; adult/child €2.20/1; ⏰ 10am-5pm Tue-Sat, 1-5pm Sun)

Eating

De Visbanken (☎ 015-212 38 31; Cameretten 2) Historic corner stand where just about everyone grabs a snack of fresh or fried fish.

Stads Pannekoeckhuys (☎ 015-213 01 93; Oude Delft 113; mains €3-10; ⏰ lunch & dinner) Eighty-five kinds of pancakes, classic Dutch pea soup, and indoor and canalside seating.

Sleeping

Hotel de Koophandel (☎ 015-214 23 02; www.hotelde koophandel.nl; Beestenmarkt 30; s/d from €75/90; 🖥) A little generic but well kept, fans of *Girl with a Pearl Earring* may be able to look out their window and see locations from the book (though not the movie).

Hotel de Plataan (☎ 015-212 60 46; www.hotelde plataan.nl; Doelenplein 10; s/d €85/98) Delft's nicest accommodation is on a delightful square, with hospitality to match.

KRÖLLER-MÜLLER MUSEUM

De Hoge Veluwe National Park (☎ 0318-59 16 27; www.hogeveluwe.nl; park only adult/child €6/3, park & museum adult/child €12/6, car surcharge €6; ⏰ 9am-5.30pm Nov-Mar, 8am-8pm Apr, 8am-9pm May & Aug, 8am-10pm Jun & Jul, 9am-8pm Sep, 9am-7pm Oct), the Netherlands' largest, would be a fantastic place to visit for its marshlands, forests and sand dunes alone, but its brilliant museum makes it unmissable.

It was once owned by Anton and Helene Kröller-Müller, a wealthy German-Dutch couple. He wanted hunting grounds, she wanted a museum site – they got both. Ticket booths at each of the three entrances (Hoenderloo, Otterlo and Rijzenburg) provide basic information and useful maps. In the heart of the park, the main **visitors centre** has displays on the flora and fauna within.

The **Kröller-Müller Museum** shows works by Picasso, Gris, Renoir, Sisley and Manet, but it's the Van Gogh collection that makes it world-class. It's about 10km into the park, but well worth the one-hour cycle to see a stunning collection of Van Gogh's work (and other modern masterpieces) rivalling Amsterdam's own Van Gogh Museum. There's an evocative **sculpture garden** behind the museum. The museum is 1km from the visitors centre.

TRANSPORT

Travel time One hour.

Train Take the train from Amsterdam to Apeldoorn (€12.70) from where public buses depart for the park. Inquire for the latest schedule information.

Car Take the A10 ring road to the A1 towards Amersfoort and Apeldoorn. Exit at Exit 19 (N304) and follow the signs.

Excursions

KRÖLLER-MÜLLER MUSEUM

The sculpture park, Kröller-Müller Museum

ALKMAAR

Most visitors come to this picturesque ringed town for the traditional **cheese market**, dating back to the 17th century.

On Friday mornings, rounds of *kaas* (cheese) are ceremoniously stacked on the square. Porters appear in colourful hats (denoting the cheese guild), and dealers (in white smocks) insert a hollow rod to extract a cheese sample, and sniff and crumble to check fat and moisture content. Once deals are struck, the porters whisk the cheeses on wooden sledges to the old cheese scale, accompanied by a zillion camera clicks. It's primarily for show – nowadays the dairy combines have a lock on the cheese trade. Still, as living relics go it's quite a spectacle.

The **Waaggebouw** (weigh house, 1390) has tourist information and the **Hollands Kaasmuseum**, a display of cheese-making utensils, photos and a stock of paintings by 16th-century female artists. The building's mechanical tower **carillon** with jousting knights still springs to life.

Across the square, the **Nationaal Biermuseum** has a decent collection of beer-making equipment and wax dummies showing how the suds were made. Cool off in the friendly bar.

TRANSPORT

Direction 35km northwest.

Travel time 30 to 40 minutes.

Train Services run at least twice per hour from Amsterdam (€6.10, 40 minutes). The canal-bound centre is 500m southeast of the train station; allow 20 minutes to the cheese market.

Car Take the A9 to the west of Amsterdam which goes directly to Alkmaar.

Information

Tourist Office (☎ 072-511 42 84; www.vvvalkmaar.nl; Waagplein 2; ☺ 10am-5.30pm)

Sights

Carillon (☺ 6.30pm & 7.30pm Thu, noon & 1pm Sat, 11am & noon Fri mid-Apr–mid-Sep)

Cheese Market (Waagplein; ☺ 10am-12.30pm Fri Apr-early Sep)

Hollands Kaasmuseum (Dutch Cheese Museum; ☎ 072-511 42 84; adult/concession €2.50/1.50; ☺ 10am-4pm Mon-Sat year round, from 9am Fri Apr-Oct)

Nationaal Biermuseum (☎ 072-511 38 01; Houttil 1; adult/child €3/1.50; ☺ 10am-4pm Tue-Fri, 1-4pm Sat & Sun)

Eating

De Tromp Kaaswinkel (☎ 072-511 34 22; Magdalenenstraat 11) If you're looking to grab some cheese after seeing so much of it, check out this quality certified shop with Dutch and French cheeses stacked everywhere you look.

Het Hof van Alkmaar (☎ 072-512 12 12; Hof van Sonoy 1; lunch €3.50-12.50, dinner mains €15-19; ☺ lunch & dinner Tue-Sun) Contempo-creative cooking in a former 15th-century monastery.

AALSMEER

This town hosts the world's biggest **flower auction** (☎ 029-739 21 85; www.aalsmeer.com; adult/child €4/2; ☺ 7-11am Mon-Fri), in Europe's largest commercial complex (one million sq metres). The experience may blow you away: about 90 million flowers and two million plants worth €6 million change hands here every single day. Arrive by 9am to catch the spectacle from the viewing gallery. Selling is conducted – surprise! – by Dutch auction, with a huge projection clock showing the starting price dropping until someone takes up the offer. There's a self-guided tour of the site with audio boxes at strategic points – allow about one hour.

Mondays are busiest, Thursdays quietest.

TRANSPORT

Direction 22km southwest.

Travel time 50 minutes.

Bus Connexxion bus 172 from Amsterdam Centraal Station to Aalsmeer VBA stop (four times hourly).

Car Take the A4 a short way to Haarlemmermeer then left (southeast) onto the N201.

ZAANSE SCHANS

Zaanse Schans is a good stab at recreating a local village from the 17th and 18th centuries. The most striking structures are the six working **windmills** along the riverbanks. One mill sells its freshly ground mustard; others turn out pigments, oils, meal and timber. Most are open for inspection, and it's a treat to clamber about the creaking works while the mills shake in the North Sea breeze.

This open-air museum also stands out because its 'residents' actually live here, in historic structures brought from around the country. The workshops, shops and homes sit on a sweet little tract complete with canals and gardens. In sunny weather, it's a grand day out despite the inevitable crowds. Admission is free to the site, but some buildings charge admission (about €2.50/1.40 per adult/child) and there are shops where you can spend: an early Albert Heijn market, a cheese maker and a popular **clog factory**. The clog maker will demonstrate a device that grinds out wooden shoes in tandem. The engaging pewter smith will explain the story behind dozens of tiny figures in several languages while the soft metal sets in the moulds.

The shiny new **Zaans Museum**, by the parking lot, runs temporary exhibitions about the Zaan river communities, and has an information centre that sells area maps for €1.

Sights & Information

Boat Tours (adult/child €5/2.50, ☻ Tue-Sun Apr-Sep)

Zaans Museum & Information Centre (☎ 075-616 28 62; adult/child €4.50/2.70; ☻ 10am-5pm Tue-Sat, noon-5pm Sun)

TRANSPORT

Direction 10km northwest.

Travel time 15 minutes.

Train Take the 'Sprinter' train towards Alkmaar; get off at Koog Zaandijk (€2.60, 20 minutes, four times hourly). It's a 1km walk to Zaanse Schans.

Car Travel to the northwestern side of the city on the A10 ring road, and take the A8 turn-off. Exit at Zaandijk.

Directory

Directory

TRANSPORT

Amsterdam has copious air links worldwide, including many on low-cost European airlines. Train links are especially good from France, Belgium and Germany, and most journeys within the Netherlands are so short that you can reach your destination before your next meal.

Once you arrive, you'll find that Amsterdam is very much a walking city; you can traverse the city centre in 30 minutes, and reach the outer areas in an hour. To save time, ride a bike like the locals do. The tram system is also reliable, though not necessarily faster than a bike.

AIR
Airport

A mere 18km from central Amsterdam, Schiphol airport is the Netherlands' main international airport and the fourth-busiest passenger terminal in Europe. It's the hub of Dutch passenger carrier KLM, and over 100 airlines have direct flights and connections to all continents. Its shopping arcades, both in public areas and the See Buy Fly duty free areas, are renowned. We also love it because its name is unpronounceable (say 'S-*khip*-hol' fast).

Meet arrivals in the large lobby known as Schiphol Plaza. For airport and flight information call ☎ 0900-01 41 (per minute €0.10) or see www.schiphol.nl.

The airport is in the same telephone area code as Amsterdam proper (☎ 020).

LEFT LUGGAGE

Luggage may be deposited at the left luggage office (☎ 601 24 43) in the basement between arrival areas One and Two. Cost is €5 for the first 24 hours, €3.50 for each subsequent 24 hours (days two to five), and €3 per day thereafter.

TO/FROM THE AIRPORT

Trains run on the Nederlandse Spoorwegen (NS; national railway) to Centraal Station (one way/return €3.10/5.50, 15 to 20 minutes, every 10 to 15 minutes) from right beneath Schiphol Plaza. Train-ticket counters and vending machines are in Schiphol Plaza's central court; buy your ticket before taking the escalator down to the platforms (see instructions for domestic tickets on p251). If you need a *strippenkaart* (a ticket for local transport within Amsterdam), purchase it at the Ako newsstand near the ticket windows.

Note: if you're flying with KLM and you bought your ticket in the Netherlands, your ticket gives free train transport within the country to/from the airport on your day of departure/arrival.

Taxi services between Amsterdam and Schiphol airport take 20 to 45 minutes (maybe longer in rush hour) and cost from about €32. Aficionados swear by **Amsterdam Airport Business Taxi** (☎ 06 5376 9753; www.aabt.info), who have Mercedes cars and professional drivers and cost about €32 to €40 depending on your destination or origin in town.

Some of the international hotel chains have free shuttle services for their guests. Public services such as Connexxion bus Interliner 370 also run regular services to/from central Amsterdam. Connexxion also runs a paid hotel shuttle (around €11/17.50 one-way/return). When making your hotel reservation, ask whether it is on the route.

Another way to get to the airport is by the minivan service **Schiphol Travel Taxi** (☎ 0900-88 76, per minute €0.10, from outside the Netherlands ☎ 31-38-339 47 68; www.schiphol.nl). Figure on about €20 per person.

AIRPORT PARKING

The airport's P1 and P2 short-term (under cover) parking garages charge €1.90 per half-hour for the first three hours, then €2.70 per hour. Daily charges are €24 a day for the first three days, €12.50 a day thereafter. The long-term (open air) parking area is a fair distance from the terminal but is linked by a 24-hour shuttle bus. The charge is €50 for up to three days and €5 for each day thereafter.

By car, take the A4 freeway to/from the A10 ring road around Amsterdam. A short stretch of A9 connects to the A4 close to Schiphol. Car-rental offices at the airport are in the right corner near the central exits of Schiphol Plaza.

Travel Agents

One of the more conveniently located travel agents in the city is **Kilroy Travels** (Map pp292–3; ☎ 524 51 00; www.kilroytravels.com; Singel 413-415; ☺ noon-6pm Mon, 10am-6pm Tue-Fri, 11.30am-4.30pm Sat). For more listings, look in the telephone book under 'Reisbureaus'.

Also try **lastminute.com** (☎ 0900-405 06 07, per minute €0.15; www.nl.lastminute.com).

Gay and lesbian travellers might want to try **Mantrav** (Map pp286–7; ☎ 638 83 63; Kloveniersburgwal 40). It specialises in gay resort and tour travel.

BICYCLE & SCOOTER

With 750,000 Amsterdammers and an estimated 600,000 bikes, you *know* how most of the population gets around. Many visitors rent a bike towards the end of their stay and wish they had done so sooner, although the chaotic traffic can be challenging. Please see the cycling rules (boxed text, p124) before setting out.

Electric-powered scooters have recently come on the scene, with speeds of 25km/h and a range of 40-plus km on one charge. Helmets are not required.

Bicycle Rental

All the companies listed below require ID plus a credit-card imprint or a cash deposit with a passport. Many rental agencies require that you bring your passport as proof of ID. Prices are for basic 'coaster-brake' bikes; gears and handbrakes, and especially insurance, usually cost more

Bike City (Map p285; ☎ 626 37 21; Bloemgracht 68-70; per day/week €8.50/41, deposit: credit card imprint) There's no advertising on the bikes, so you can pretend you're a local.

Damstraat Rent-a-Bike (Map pp286–7; ☎ 625 50 29; Damstraat 20-2; per day/week, €7/31, deposit: credit-card imprint)

Holland Rent-a-Bike (Map pp286–7; ☎ 622 32 07; Damrak 247 (Beurs van Berlage); per day/week €6.50/34.50, deposit €150, credit card OK)

MacBike (www.macbike.nl; per day/week €8.50/29.75, plus deposit ID & €50 or credit card); **Centraal Station** (Map pp286–7; ☎ 624 83 91); **Visserplein** (Map pp290–1; ☎ 620 09 85; Mr Visserplein 2); **Weteringschans** (Map pp292–3; ☎ 528 76 88, Weteringschans 2) The most expensive (and the bikes are equipped with big placards that say 'LOOK OUT!' to locals), but they have the most locations.

Mike's Bike Tours (Map pp292–3; ☎ 622 79 70; www.mikesbiketours.com; Kerkstraat 134; half day/full day/additional day €5/7/5, must leave passport or other ID or deposit €200)

To carry a bike aboard a train, you'll need to purchase a bike day pass (€6), valid throughout the country, and carriage is subject to availability of space. Many train stations also have bike rental facilities on the spot. Collapsible bikes can be carried for free.

An alternative to renting a bike is to buy one. Figure on about €80 for a used bike and at least that much again for the locks.

Scooter Rental

The best bet is to try **Nieuws Rent a Scooter** (Map p285; ☎ 423 43 39; www.rentascooter.nl; Prinsengracht 297-BG; half day/full day/week €20/36/150).

BOAT
Ferries

There are free ferries from behind Centraal Station to destinations around the IJ, notably Amsterdam Noord. Ferries to the Eastern Docklands cost €1.

Canal Boat, Bus & Bike

Canal Bus (Map pp286–7; ☎ 623 98 86; www.canalbus.nl; day pass per adult/child €16/11) Does several circuits between Centraal Station and the Rijksmuseum between 9.50am and 8pm. The day pass is valid until noon the next day. The same company rents canal bikes (pedal boats) for €8 per person per hour (€7 if more than 2 people per canal bike). Docks are by Leidseplein and near the Anne Frank Huis.

Lovers Museum Boat (Map pp286–7; ☎ 622 21 81; www.lovers.nl; day pass per adult/child €14.25/9.50) Leaves every 30 or 45 minutes from the Lovers terminal in front of Centraal Station. Discounts after 1pm.

CAR & MOTORCYCLE

We absolutely don't recommend having a car in Amsterdam, but if you must...

Driver's Licence

Visitors are entitled to drive in the Netherlands on their foreign licenses for a period of up to 185 days. If you stay in the Netherlands over 185 days per calendar year, under Dutch law you must get a Dutch licence (with some exceptions).

For all queries, ring the **National Transport Authority** (☎ 0900-07 39, per min €0.10).

Parking

Parking in the city hits you where it hurts. Pay-and-display applies in the central zone from 9am to midnight from Monday to Saturday, and noon to midnight on Sunday, and costs €3/18/12 per hour/day/evening; prices ease as you move further away from the centre. Day passes are available.

Parking police are merciless. Nonpayers in the Centrum district will find a bright yellow *wielklem* (wheel clamp) attached to their car and have to pay €90.80 to get it removed; visit the closest **Stadstoezicht office** (City Surveillance; ☎ 553 01 82) to pay the fine. Otherwise, within 24 hours the vehicle will be towed and the fine skyrockets to €300.

Parking garages in the city centre include locations at Damrak, near Leidseplein and under Museumplein and the Stopera, but they're often full and cost more than a parking permit. Other options for parking:

Amsterdam North Park for free and take the ferry across.

Car Hotel (☎ 493 12 78; www.carhotel.nl; per 24 hr €20) Collects and delivers your car from and to your hotel.

Stadionplein Park and ride in the southwestern outskirts.

Transferium parking garage (☎ 400 17 21; Bijlmer; per day incl 2 return tickets for public transport to Centraal Station €5.50) Under the Amsterdam Arena.

Rental

Local companies are usually cheaper than the big multinationals, but don't offer as much backup or flexibility. Rates start at about €38/42 per day for a two/four-person car, but they do change frequently, so call around. Rentals at Schiphol airport incur a €40 surcharge.

Look for local car-rental firms in telephone directories under the heading *Autoverhuur*. This is a list of some of the better-known car-rental companies:

Avis Autoverhuur (Map pp292–3; ☎ 683 60 61; www.avis.nl; Nassaukade 380)

Budget Rent a Car (Map pp282–3; ☎ 0900-15 76, per min €0.15; www.budget.nl; Overtoom 121; ☒ 8am-8pm Mon-Fri, 8am-5pm Sat)

easyCar (www.easycar.nl)

Europcar (Map pp282–3; ☎ 683 21 23; www.europcar.nl; Overtoom 197)

Hertz (Map pp282–3; ☎ 612 24 41; www.hertz.nl; Overtoom 333)

Sixt (☎ 023-569 86 56; www.e-sixt.nl; Smaragdlaan 3, Hoofddorp)

Road Rules

Traffic in Amsterdam travels on the right and is generally quite busy. The minimum driving age is 18 years for cars and 16 years for motorcycles. Seat belts are required for everyone in a vehicle. Children under 12 must ride in the back if there's room.

Be alert for bicycles, and if you are trying to turn right, bikes have priority. Trams always have the right of way. In traffic circles (roundabouts), approaching vehicles technically have right of way, but in practice they yield to vehicles already on the circle.

The blood-alcohol limit when driving is 0.05%, and the speed limits are 50km/h in built-up areas, 80km/h in the country, 100km/h on major rural through-roads and 120km/h on freeways (sometimes this is reduced to 100km/h, but is generally clearly indicated).

TAXI

Amsterdam taxis are among Europe's most expensive. Worse, drivers tend not to know the streets; you often have to tell them how to get there. This is complicated because as a group taxi drivers are among the few people you meet in town who may not speak English well. A notable exception is **Taxicentrale Amsterdam** (TCA; ☎ 677 77 77).

You're not meant to hail taxis on the street, but many cars will stop if you do. You can also usually find them at taxi stands at hotels and, especially at night, on Leidseplein.

Flag fall is €3.20 and the rate is €1.90 per kilometre, plus a 5% to 10% tip. Some independent cabs charge lower fares; many will charge more – best play it safe. There's also the informal strategy of setting a price with the driver before you get in – figure about two thirds of the metered price. Some haggling is usually involved. If a driver's been waiting long enough, he may agree.

TRAIN

Trains are frequent and serve domestic destinations at regular intervals, sometimes five or six times an hour. However, the network has been plagued by poor punctuality in recent years, particularly at rush hour.

Amsterdam's main train station is Centraal Station (CS).

Domestic Tickets

Tickets can be bought at the window or ticketing machines. Buying a ticket on board means you'll pay almost double the normal fare.

To use ticketing machines, generally in Dutch only, find your destination on the list of place names, enter the code into the machine, then choose: 1st or 2nd class (there's often little difference in comfort, but if the train is crowded there are usually more seats in 1st class); zonder/met korting (without/with discount – discount card required, see p254); and vandaag geldig/zonder datum (valid today/without date). The machine will indicate how much it wants to be fed (coins or PIN cards only). Change is given. For zonder datum, validate the ticket in a yellow punch gadget near the platform.

With a valid ticket you can break your journey along the direct route. Day return tickets are 10% to 15% cheaper than two one-ways.

Children under four travel free if they don't take up a seat. Ages four to 11 pay a 'Railrunner' fare of €2 as long as an adult comes along.

If you plan to do a lot of travelling, a one-day travel card costs €39.80. For longer stays, the €55 Voordeel-Urenkaart is valid for one year and gives a 40% discount on train travel weekdays after 9am, as well as weekends, public holidays and the whole months of July and August. The discount also applies to up to three people travelling with you on the same trip. Seniors (60-plus) can receive an additional seven days free travel a year.

International Tickets

For international train information and reservations, visit the NS international office (Centraal Station; www.ns.nl; ☿ 6.30am-10.30pm) facing Track 2 and see Dutch inefficiency at its worst. At peak times (eg summer) the queues can be up to two hours.

Upon entering, pick up a numbered ticket based on the kind of train ticket you need: advance, pick-up of a reservation, or departing within an hour. Pick-ups and immediate departures get higher priority. Don't take a number for other than what you're planning to buy, smartypants – you will be dismissed and sent back to start all over.

You may also purchase tickets over the telephone (☎ 0900-92 96, per min €0.35; ☿ 8am-midnight), but you will still have to pick them up here.

There's a left-luggage desk downstairs from Track 2, near the southeastern corner of the station.

Schedules

In stations, schedules are posted by route, though trip duration and arrival time information aren't. Outside of the station, contact the NS directly (☎ 0900-92 92, per min €0.70; www.ns.nl; ☿ 8am-midnight).

TRAM, BUS & METRO

Most public transport within the city is by tram; buses and Amsterdam's metro (subway) serve some outer reaches. Services are run by the local transit authority, the GVB; national railway (NS) tickets are not valid on local transport.

The GVB has an information office (Map pp286–7; ☎ 0900-80 11, per min €0.10; www.gvb.nl; Stationsplein 10; ☿ 7am-9pm Mon-Fri, 8am-9pm Sat & Sun) across the tram tracks from the Centraal Station main entrance. Here you can get tickets, maps and the like. The website has lots of useful information including details of how to reach key sights.

You must either purchase a ticket on board or validate it when you board. If you get caught without a ticket or properly stamped strip, playing the ignorant foreigner (the 'dufus' strategy) will guarantee that you get fined €37.40. Some trams have conductors responsible for ticketing (usually towards the rear of the tram), while others do not. Drivers can also handle tickets but prefer not to as it slows things down. If you are transferring from another line, show your ticket to the conductor or driver as you board. Buses are more conventional, with drivers stamping the tickets as you board.

There are also a few *sneltram* ('fast tram', or light rail) to the southern and south-eastern suburbs. Tickets are validated in the same way as ordinary trams except where the *sneltram* shares the metro line, in which case you use the yellow machines at the stairways to the platforms.

Always assume that pickpockets are active on busy trams.

GVB Fares

Tickets on trams and buses are calculated by zone and are valid for one hour from the time they're stamped. Within the city centre you are in Zone 1. When in doubt, consult the maps at bus and tram stops, or ask the driver or conductor. Single-trip fares for one/two zones are €1.60/2.40.

GVB passes are valid in all zones, and fares for one/two/three days are €6.20/10/13. Children (aged four to 11) and seniors can obtain a day pass for €4.20 per day, but multiple day passes are not available.

Strippenkaart

Depending on how much you intend to travel, consider a *strippenkaart* ('strip card'; 15-/45-strip cards €6.50/19.20) available at train and bus stations, post offices, many VVV (tourist information) offices, super-markets and tobacconists.

Each strip is numbered, but there's a trick; you need to stamp for the number of zones you're travelling *plus one,* and you stamp one strip only. In other words, if you're trav-elling in Zone 1, stamp the second available strip but not the first (this would invali-date the second stamp). You should begin stamping from the lowest number available. You can also use a strip card if you're travel-ling with a companion, so if both of you are travelling within Zone 1, you stamp only the fourth strip (two strips plus two strips).

If you're taking transport with a conduc-tor, simply state where you're going and the conductor will stamp your card for you. If you need to validate it yourself, fold the card so that the strip you want to stamp is first on the top, and insert it into the machine.

Strippenkaart are valid on local public transport throughout the country; however, under a plan announced recently, they are due to be phased out during 2007 in favour of a chip-card system. Check with the GVB for the latest.

PRACTICALITIES

ACCOMMODATION

This book breaks accommodation down by district, and within that we list midrange lodgings and up, with a separate category for cheap sleeps. Refer to the Sleeping chap-ter for a rundown on types of accommoda-tion, price ranges and reservations, and a list of websites that you can use for book-ings. Within the district listings, lodgings are listed alphabetically.

BUSINESS HOURS

Business hours are similar to that of most European countries:

Banks Open from 9am to 4pm Monday to Friday.

Cafés Open 10am to 1am Sunday to Thursday, till 3am Friday and Saturday

General Office Hours 8.30am to 5pm Monday to Friday.

Museums Often closed on Monday.

Pubs and Clubs Opening hours vary. Closing hours 1am Sunday to Thursday, 3am Friday and Saturday.

Restaurants Lunch 11am to 2.30pm, dinner 6pm to 10pm.

Shops Open from 9am to 5.30pm Monday to Friday, although some shops only open from noon on Mondays. *Koopavond* (late-night shopping) is on Thursday nights, with shops staying open until 8pm or 9pm. Within the canal belt, shops are allowed to open from noon until 5pm on Sunday, although not all choose to do so.

Supermarkets Stay open until 8pm.

CHILDREN

There is much to keep kids occupied in Am-sterdam, but be careful of all the open water (Dutch kids all learn to swim at school). Lonely Planet's *Travel with Children* is worth reading.

In general, attitudes to children are very positive, apart from some hotels with a no-children policy – check when you book. Most restaurants have high chairs and children's menus. Facilities for changing nappies, however, are limited to the big de-partment stores, major museums and train stations and you'll pay to use them. Breast-feeding is generally OK in public if done dis-creetly. Kids are allowed in pubs but aren't supposed to drink until they're 16.

See listings in the Sights and Entertain-ment chapters, or check local listings for special events (under *jeugd* for 'youth').

Babysitting

Babysitters charge range between €5 and €6 per hour depending on the time of day, sometimes with weekend and/or hotel supplements and service fee for the agency, and you might have to pay for their taxi home if it gets late. Agencies use male and female students and you may not always be able to specify which gender you prefer. Agencies may be booked out on weekends, so book ahead. Ask at hotels about babysitting services or try **Oppascentrale Kriterion** (Map pp290–1; ☎ 624 58 48; Valckenierstraat 45hs; ❍ 4.30-8pm daily, 9-11am Mon & Wed).

CLIMATE

Amsterdam has a temperate maritime climate with cool winters and mild summers. Precipitation is spread evenly over the year, often in periods of endless drizzle, though between March and May it tends to fall in short, sharp bursts. May is a pleasant time to visit; the elms along the canals are in bloom, and everything is nice and fresh.

The warmest months are June to September, though it's best to bring a jacket in case of the occasional cold snap or rainstorm. Very few hotels have air conditioning. Indian summers are common in September and into early October, which is usually an excellent time to visit. Blustery autumn storms occur in October and November.

December to February is the coldest time of the year, with occasional slushy snow and temperatures around freezing. Frosts usually aren't severe enough to allow skating on the canals, but when they are, the city comes alive with colourfully clad skaters. And you couldn't wish for better photo material than Amsterdam after a snowfall.

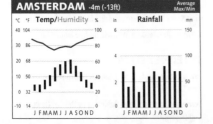

COURSES

Here are some options if you're interested in studying the Dutch language:

Amsterdam Maastricht Summer University (☎ 620 02 25; www.amsu.edu; Keizersgracht 324) Based in the Felix Meritis Building.

British Language Training Centre (☎ 622 36 34; www.bltc.nl; Nieuwezijds Voorburgwal 328E) Offers Dutch and English courses and has a good reputation.

Tropeninstituut (Royal Institute for the Tropics, Language Training Department; ☎ 568 85 59; www.kit.nl) Intensive language courses with a large component of cultural training, aimed specifically at foreigners moving to the Netherlands.

Volksuniversiteit Amsterdam (☎ 626 16 26; www.volksuniversiteitamsterdam.nl in Dutch; Rapenburgerstraat 73) Well-regarded day and evening courses that don't cost a fortune.

CUSTOMS

Each person may bring up to the following quantities of each item tax free into the Netherlands:

Coffee 500g of coffee or 200g of coffee extracts or coffee essences.

Perfume 50g of perfume and 0.25L of eau de toilette.

Tea 100g of tea or 40g of tea extracts or tea essences.

Tobacco 200 cigarettes or 250g of tobacco (shag or pipe tobacco) or 100 cigarillos or 50 cigars.

Wine 1L of strong liqueur or 2L of sparkling wine or fortified wine such as sherry or port; 2L of non-sparkling wine.

DISABLED TRAVELLERS

Travellers with reduced mobility will find Amsterdam only moderately well equipped to meet their needs. A large number of government offices and museums have lifts (elevators) or ramps. Many hotels, however, are in old buildings with steep stairs and no lifts; restaurants tend to be on ground floors, though 'ground' sometimes includes a few steps. The metro stations have lifts, many trains have wheelchair access, and most train stations and public buildings have toilets for the disabled.

People with a disability get discounts on public transport and, with some limitations, can park in the city free of charge. There are train timetables published in Braille.

Residents can make use of the *stadsmobiel* (citymobile), which is a fabulous taxi service for people with limited mobility, but foreigners will have to use one of the commercial wheelchair-taxi services:

Connexxion Jonkcars (☎ 606 22 00; per hour €35; ◷ 6.30am-5.30pm).

Garskamp (☎ 633 39 43; ◷ 7am-1am)

Ring a couple of days in advance to ensure a booking at a time that suits you. Fares are similar to taxi fares. If you're travelling by rail on the NS, ring ☎ 030-235 78 22 a day in advance to arrange assistance.

The helpful Utrecht-based **Nederlands Instituut voor Zorg & Welzijn** (NIZW; ☎ 030-230 63 11; www.nizw.nl) has extensive information and can refer you to other organisations for more specific requests. The Amsterdam Uitburo and the VVV (see Tourist Information, p259) provide information regarding accessible entertainment venues and museums.

DISCOUNT CARDS

Artists, journalists, museum conservators, students and teachers should bring professional accreditation for discounts at (some) venues. There are also other options:

Cultureel Jongeren Paspoort (Cultural Youth Passport; www.cjp.nl; €12.50) Big discounts to museums and cultural events nationwide for people under 27.

Hostelling International Card Provides €2.50-per-night discounts at associated youth hostels.

I Amsterdam Card (per 24/36/72 hr €33/43/53) Available at VVV offices and some hotels. Admission to most museums, canal boat trips, and discounts and freebies at shops, attractions and restaurants. Also includes a GVB transit pass.

Museumkaart (Museum Card; over/under 26yr €25/12.50, plus €4.95 for first-time registrants) Free entry to some 400 museums all over the country for one year.

Senior discounts For people over 65 (60 for partner) covering certain public transport, museum admissions, concerts etc. Proof of age may be required (passport is best).

ELECTRICITY

The standard voltage throughout the Netherlands is 220V, 50Hz. Plugs are of the Continental two-round-pin variety. If you need an adapter, get it before you leave home because most of the ones available in the Netherlands are for locals going abroad.

EMBASSIES & CONSULATES

Amsterdam is the country's capital, but confusingly Den Haag is the seat of government – so that's where all the embassies are. The following countries have consulates in Amsterdam:

France (Map pp292–3; ☎ 530 69 69; Vijzelgracht 2)

Germany (Map pp292–3; ☎ 574 77 00; Honthorststraat 36-8)

Italy (Map pp292–3; ☎ 550 20 50; Vijzelstraat 79)

Spain (Map pp292–3; ☎ 620 38 11; Frederiksplein 34)

UK (Map pp282–3; ☎ 676 43 43; Koningslaan 44)

USA (Map pp296; ☎ 575 53 09; Museumplein 19)

These countries have embassies in Den Haag:

Australia (☎ 070-310 82 00; Carnegielaan 4)

Canada (☎ 070-311 16 00; Sophialaan 7)

Denmark (☎ 070-302 59 59; Koninginnegracht 30)

India (☎ 070-346 97 71; Buitenrustweg 2)

Ireland (☎ 070-363 09 93; Dr Kuyperstraat 9)

Israel (☎ 070-376 05 00; Buitenhof 47)

Japan (☎ 070-346 95 44; Tobias Asserlaan 2)

New Zealand (☎ 070-346 93 24; Carnegielaan10-IV)

Norway (Map pp292–3; ☎ 070-311 76 11; Lange Vijverberg 11)

EMERGENCIES

In a life-threatening emergency, the national telephone number for ambulance, police and fire brigade is ☎ 112.

GAY & LESBIAN TRAVELLERS

Without a doubt, Amsterdam is one of the gay capitals of Europe (see p14), so as you would expect there's no shortage of information and support organisations. See also Safety (p258).

Information
GUIDES & MAPS

Bent Guide (Pink Point) Published in English, updated at least annually, full of insider info on all facets of gay life.

Gay News Amsterdam Available for free around town.

Gaymap Amsterdam Available for free around town.

INTERNET SITES

www.cocamsterdam.nl Organises club nights and other events.

www.gayamsterdam.nl Published by the Gay News. Comprehensive.

www.gay.nl Directory to pretty much anything in town. It's only in Dutch but you can figure it out.

www.pinkpoint.org With referrals to just about anything else you could need.

BOOKSTORES & INFORMATION POINTS

Intermale (p189)

Pink Point (p87)

Vrolijk (p189)

Vrouwen in Druk (p197)

The local gay radio station MVS broadcasts 7pm to 8pm nightly on 106.8 FM (cable 88.1 FM), with an English program on Sunday.

Organisations

COC Amsterdam (Map p285; ☎ 623 40 79; www.coc amsterdam.nl; Rozenstraat 14) Amsterdam branch of the national gay and lesbian organisation. It also offers club nights and other events.

Gay & Lesbian Switchboard (☎ 623 65 65; www.switch board.nl; ☺ noon-10pm Mon-Fri, 4-10pm Sat & Sun) The best source to start for gay and lesbian information. Also provides advice on an anonymous basis.

IHLIA (Internationaal Homo/Lesbisch Informatiecentrum & Archief; Map pp282–3; ☎ 606 07 12; www.ihlia.nl; Nieuwpoortkade 2A; ☺ 10am-4pm Mon-Fri, telephone inquiries 9am-5pm) The largest international gay and lesbian library collection in the Netherlands.

Safe Sex

The government and organisations such as the Schorer Foundation, HIV Vereniging and COC all do their bit to prevent the spread of STDs and HIV. Most bars, bookshops and saunas that cater for gays provide safe-sex leaflets; many also sell condoms.

HOLIDAYS
Public Holidays

People take public holidays seriously and you won't get much done on them. Most museums adopt Sunday hours on the days below (except Christmas and New Year) even if they fall on a day when the place would otherwise be closed.

Nieuwjaarsdag New Year's Day. Parties and fireworks galore.

Pasen (Easter) Goede Vrijdag (Good Friday); Eerste and Tweede Paasdag (Easter Sunday and Easter Monday).

Koninginnedag Queen's Day, 30 April.

Bevrijdingsdag Liberation Day, 5 May. This isn't a universal holiday; government workers have the day off but almost everyone else has to work.

Hemelvaartsdag Ascension Day.

Eerste and Tweede Pinksterdag Whit Sunday (Pentecost) and Whit Monday. Depending on Easter, Ascension Day and the Whit holidays usually fall between mid-May and mid-June.

Eerste and Tweede Kerstdag Christmas Day and Boxing Day.

Many people also treat **Remembrance Day** (4 May) as a day off.

INTERNET ACCESS

Amsterdam led the digital revolution in Europe, so the city is as wired as many of its visitors are.

Most hotels offer Internet access, from business centres and in-room wi-fi to a simple computer behind the front desk.

There are Internet cafés around town; costs are roughly €1.50 to €2 per hour, via snappy high-speed lines.

easyInternetcafé (Map pp292–3; www.easyeverything .co.uk; Reguliersbreestraat 22; ☺ 9am-10pm). There are smaller outlets at Damrak 33 (Map pp286–7; ☺ 9am-10pm) and at Leidsestraat 24 (Free Record Shop; Map pp292–3; ☺ 11am-7pm Mon, 9.30am-7pm Tue-Sat, 11am-6pm Sun).

Internet City (Map pp286–7; ☎ 620 12 92; Nieuwendijk 76; ☺ 9am-midnight) Over 100 terminals in a bland office not far from the main coffee-shop drag. Draws backpackers and bleary-eyed party animals.

Many coffeeshops double as Internet cafés. You can also surf the Web for free at public libraries (Openbare Bibliotheek).

Centrale Bibliotheek (Map pp292–3; ☎ 523 09 00; Prinsengracht 587; ☺ 1pm-9pm Mon, 10am-9pm Tue-Thu, 10am-5pm Fri & Sat, 1pm-5pm Sun)

Roelof Hartplein (Map p296; ☎ 662 00 94; Roelof Hartplein 430; ☺ 2-8pm Mon & Wed, 10am-5pm Tue & Fri, 11am-5pm Sat)

LEGAL MATTERS

The Amsterdam *politie* (police) are pretty relaxed and helpful unless you do something instinctively wrong like chucking litter or smoking a joint right under their noses. They can hold offenders for up to six hours for questioning (plus another six hours if they can't establish your identity, or 24 hours if they consider the matter serious) and do not have to grant a phone call, though they'll ring your consulate. You're presumed innocent until proven guilty.

In principle there's a 'limited' requirement for anyone over 12 years of age to carry ID. Roughly speaking this means on public transport, at soccer games, in the workplace or when opening a bank account. Foreigners should carry a passport or a photocopy of the relevant data pages; a driver's licence isn't sufficient.

MAPS

The maps in this book will probably suffice for casual touring. Lonely Planet's handy *Amsterdam City Map* is plastic-coated against the elements, and has a street index that covers the most popular parts of the city.

Otherwise you'll find a wide variety of maps for sale at any VVV office, as well as at bookstores and newsstands.

MEDICAL SERVICES

The Netherlands has reciprocal health arrangements with other EU countries and Australia – check with your public health insurer which form to include in your luggage (E111 for British and Irish residents, available at post offices). You still might have to pay on the spot but you'll be able to claim it back again at home. Citizens of other countries are advised to take out travel insurance; medical or dental treatment is less expensive than in North America but still costs enough.

There are no compulsory vaccinations, but if you've just travelled through an area with yellow-fever, you could be asked for proof that you're covered. Up-to-date tetanus, polio and diphtheria immunisations are always recommended whether you're travelling or not.

For minor health concerns, see a local *drogist* (chemist) or *apotheek* (pharmacy, to fill prescriptions). For more serious problems, go to the casualty ward of a *ziekenhuis* (hospital) or try the **Centrale Doktersdienst** (☎ 0900-503 20 42), the 24-hour central medical service that will refer you to an appropriate doctor, dentist or pharmacy.

Forget about buying flu tablets and antacids at supermarkets; for anything more medicinal than toothpaste you'll have to go to a *drogist* or *apotheek*.

A number of hospitals have 24-hour emergency facilities:

Academisch Ziekenhuis der VU (Map pp282–3; ☎ 444 44 44; De Boelelaan 1117, Amsterdam Buitenveldert) Hospital of the VU (Vrije Universiteit; Free University).

Boven-IJ Ziekenhuis (Map pp282–3; ☎ 634 63 46; Statenjachtstraat 1, Amsterdam North) Take bus No 34 from Centraal Station.

Onze Lieve Vrouwe Gasthuis (Map pp282–3; ☎ 599 91 11; Eerste Oosterparkstraat 1) At Oosterpark near the Tropenmuseum. The closest public hospital to the centre of town.

St Lucas Andreas Ziekenhuis (Map pp282–3; ☎ 510 89 11; Jan Tooropstraat 164) In the western suburbs.

Slotervaart Ziekenhuis (Map pp282–3; ☎ 512 93 33; Louwesweg 6) In the southwestern suburbs.

STDs & HIV/AIDS

HIV/AIDS is a problem in the Netherlands but it has been contained to some extent by practical education campaigns and free needle-exchange programs.

Free testing for sexually transmitted diseases is available at the **GG&GD STD Clinic** (Municipal Medical & Health Service; Map pp292–3; ☎ 555 58 22; www .ggd.amsterdam.nl; Groenburgwal 44; ⏰ 8.30-10.30am & 1.30-3.30pm Mon-Fri, 7-8.30pm Tue & Thu). You must arrive early in the morning for same-day testing. If a problem is diagnosed they'll provide free treatment immediately, but blood-test results take a week (they'll give you the results over the phone if you aren't returning to Amsterdam). The HIV Vereiniging offers HIV testing on Friday nights (€15; ring for an appointment), with results in 15 minutes.

There are bilingual telephone help lines available for those seeking information or a friendly ear:

HIV Vereiniging (Map pp292–3; ☎ 616 01 60, help line ☎ 689 25 77; Eerste Helmersstraat 17; ⏰ 2-10pm Mon-Fri) National organisation for the HIV positive; provides personal assistance.

Schorer Foundation (Map pp290–1; ☎ 573 94 44; www.schorer.nl; Sarphatistraat 35; ⏰ 9am-5pm Mon-Fri) NGO offering lesbian and gay health-care services; HIV prevention, buddy care.

MONEY

The Netherlands is one of the European nations to use the euro. There are €5, €10, €20, €50, €100, €200 and €500 notes, and €0.01, €0.02, €0.05, €0.10, €0.20, €0.50, €1 and €2 coins (amounts under €1 are called cents). Euro notes are the same in all participating countries: coins have a 'European' side and a 'national' side (in the Netherlands, with an image of Queen Beatrix). All are legal tender throughout the euro area, although many businesses will not accept larger notes.

To check the latest exchange rates, visit www.oanda.com.

ATMs

Automatic teller machines can be found outside most banks, at the airport and at Centraal Station. Most will accept credit cards like Visa and MasterCard or Eurocard, as well as cash cards that access the Cirrus and Plus network systems. Check with your home bank for service charges before leaving.

Changing Money

Avoid the private exchange booths dotted around tourist areas. They're convenient and open late, but rates and commissions tend to be lousy. Banks and the Postbank (at post offices) stick to official exchange rates and charge a sensible commission, as does the GWK (Grenswisselkantoren), accessible at two branches: **Centraal Station** (☎ 627 27 31; 🕑 8am-10pm Mon-Sat, 9am-10pm Sun); **Schiphol airport** (☎ 627 27 31; 🕑 7am-10pm).

Credit Cards

All the major international cards are recognised, and most hotels, restaurants and major stores accept them – but always check first to avoid disappointment. Some establishments levy a 5% surcharge (or more) on credit cards to offset the commissions charged by card providers.

To withdraw money at a bank counter instead of through an ATM, go to a GWK branch (see above). You'll need to show your passport.

Report all lost or stolen cards to the appropriate 24-hour number. For American Express and Visa, phoning the emergency contact number for your home country will speed things up.

American Express (☎ 504 80 00, 504 86 66)

Diners Club (☎ 654 55 11)

Eurocard and **MasterCard** (Utrecht; ☎ 030-283 55 55)

Visa (☎ 660 06 11)

PIN Cards

While in Amsterdam you'll notice folks gleefully using 'PIN' cards everywhere, from shops to public telephones and cigarette vending machines. The cards look like credit or bank cards with little gold-printed circuit chips on them, and they link directly to the owner's bank account. However, they won't be of much use to visitors without a Dutch bank account.

Travellers Cheques

Banks charge a commission to cash travellers cheques (and require ID such as a passport). American Express and Thomas Cook don't charge commission on their own cheques but their rates might be less favourable. Shops, restaurants and hotels always prefer cash; a few might accept travellers cheques but rates will be anybody's guess.

The use of Eurocheques is on the decline, although you can still cash them at banks and GWKs with a guarantee card. Few shops accept them.

NEWSPAPERS & MAGAZINES

Amsterdam-based *De Telegraaf* is the Netherlands' biggest newspaper: an untidy, right-wing daily with sensationalist news but good finance coverage. Many Amsterdammers swear by *Het Parool* for the low-down on the capital's culture and politics. The highly regarded *NRC Handelsblad*, a merger of two elitist papers from Rotterdam and Amsterdam, sets the country's journalistic standards, while the populist *Volkskrant* has leftish leanings. The *Financieële Dagblad* is the country's leading daily for financial and business news. Many commuters pick up copies of the free *Metro* from train-station racks.

The English-language *Amsterdam Weekly* comes out each Thursday and has both cultural articles and useful listings. See the boxed text on p174 for Dutch listings papers.

English-speakers can easily find European editions of the *Economist, Newsweek* and *Time*, as well as many major international newspapers, at major book stores. The main British newspapers are available (same day), as is the *International Herald Tribune*.

POST

Post offices are generally open 9am to 5pm weekdays. The main **post office** (Map pp286–7; Singel 250; ⏰ 9am-7pm Mon-Fri, 9am-noon Sat) is large and well equipped, and there's also a branch in the **Stopera complex** (Map pp292–3; Waterlooplein 10; ⏰ 9am-6pm Mon-Fri, 10am-1.30pm Sat). For queries about postal services ring ☎ 058-233 33 33 between 8am and 8pm Monday to Friday, or 9am to 4pm Saturday.

The standard rate for letters under 20g is €0.39 within the Netherlands, €0.61 within Europe, and €0.76 outside Europe. Unless you're sending mail within the Amsterdam region, use the slot marked Overige Postcodes (Other Postal Codes) on the red letterboxes.

RADIO

Radio stations include Noordzee FM (100.7 FM), Radio 538 (102 FM) and Sky Radio (101.2 FM), plus offerings from RTL and NOS (Nederlandse Omroep Stichting). All broadcast half-hourly news reports (in Dutch), with Europop and chat sandwiched in between.

SAFETY

Theft is rare in normal hotel rooms, but it's always wise to deposit valuables for safekeeping at the reception desk or, where available, in your in-room safe. Theft is more common at hostels; bring your own lock for your locker.

Watch out for pickpockets in crowded markets and trams. Violent crime is rare, especially involving foreigners, although there have been a small number of high-profile gay-bashing incidents recently.

Cars with foreign registration are popular targets for smash-and-grab theft. Don't leave valuable items in the car; remove registration and ID papers and the radio/stereo if possible.

If something is stolen, get a police report for insurance purposes, but don't expect the police to retrieve your property or apprehend the thief.

There are occasionally some junkie-types around the Zeedijk and Gelderskade, and also on the Nieuwendijk near Centraal Station. Generally they won't bother you if you don't bother them.

Bicycles are numerous and can be dangerous for pedestrians. When crossing the street look for speeding bikes as well as cars; *please* don't stray into a bike lane without looking both ways. Cyclists, meanwhile, should take care to watch out for unwitting foreign tourists, and to lock up their bikes.

Finally, two words: dog dirt.

TELEPHONE

The Dutch phone network, KPN, is efficient, and prices are reasonable by European standards. Phone booths are scattered around town.

Collect call *(collect gesprek;* domestic ☎ 0800-01 01, free call; international ☎ 0800-04 10, free call).

International directory inquiries (☎ 0900-84 18, per number €1.15).

National directory inquiries (☎ 118, per number €0.60, voice-activated; ☎ 0900-8008, per number €1.15, human operator).

Operator assistance (☎ 0800-04 10, free call, though if you could have rung directly you'll be charged €4).

Costs

All calls are time-based. KPN Telecom public phones charge €0.10 per 20 seconds for national calls, around the clock (minimum charge €0.20), and you may need a phone card or pump coins in repeatedly to avoid disconnection. Phones in cafés, supermarkets and hotel lobbies often charge more.

Calling from private phones is considerably cheaper. Typically, calls within the metropolitan area cost €0.028 a minute from 8am to 7pm weekdays, €0.0155 a minute in the evenings, and €0.01 a minute from midnight to 8am and from 7pm Friday to 8am Monday. There's a €0.048 connection charge. Calls outside the metropolitan area cost €0.0439 a minute between 8am and 7pm weekdays, about half that at other times.

The cost of international calls varies with the destination, and changes frequently due to competition. At the time of writing, calls to Britain and the USA cost €0.056 to €0.071 per minute respectively, and

Australia €0.19. The connection charge is about €0.10. To all three countries, rates jump to €0.10 every 13 seconds when ringing from a KPN phone box.

Ringing a mobile number costs about €0.55 per minute from a public phone and around €0.20 from a private line. Incoming calls to mobile phones are generally free to the recipient (assuming it's a Dutch mobile phone used in the Netherlands).

See right if you plan to use public phones with phonecards rather than carrying around kilos of change. Many public phones accept credit cards, although cards issued outside of the Netherlands or Europe may require extra steps during dialling or may not work at all.

Mobile Phones

The Netherlands uses GSM 900/1800, compatible with the rest of Europe and Australia but not with the North American GSM 1900 (some convertible phones work in both places).

Prepaid mobile phones, which run on chips that store call credits, are available at mobile-phone shops starting from around €40 on special. Look for KPN, Telfort, Orange, T-Mobile and Vodafone shops in major shopping areas including along Rokin, Kalverstraat and Leidsestraat. Some stores, such as T for Telecom and Bel Company, handle many brands.

New prepaid phones generally come with a small amount of call time already stored. To top it up, purchase more minutes at one of the branded stores, news dealers or supermarkets, and follow the instructions.

Phone Codes

To ring abroad, dial ☎ 00 followed by the country code for your target country, the area code (you usually drop the leading 0 if there is one) and the subscriber number. The country code for calling the Netherlands is ☎ 31 and the area code for Amsterdam is ☎ 020; again, drop the leading 0 if you're calling from outside the Netherlands. Do not dial the city code if you are in the area covered by it.

Free information calls ☎ 0800

Mobile or pager numbers ☎ 06

Paid information calls ☎ 0900 Cost varies between €0.10 and €1.15 per minute.

Phonecards

For public telephones, cards are available at post offices, train station counters, VVV and GWK offices and tobacco shops for €5, €10 and €20. KPN's Hi card is the most common but other brands are muscling in – T-Mobile, Orange, Vodaphone, Belnet etc – with superior rates. Railway stations have Telfort phone booths that require a Telfort card (available at GWK offices or ticket counters), although there should be KPN booths nearby.

TELEVISION

Leading TV channels are the national broadcaster **NOS** (www.nos.nl), RTL4 and RTL5, and the local AT5, as well as Dutch-language MTV. Foreign channels – BBC, CNN, Belgium's Canvas and Germany's ARD are widely available. Foreign programs are usually broadcast in their original language with subtitles.

TIME

The Central European time zone (same as Berlin and Paris) is one hour ahead of the UK, six hours ahead of New York, nine hours ahead of Los Angeles and eight hours behind Sydney. For Daylight Savings Time, clocks are put forward one hour at 2am on the last Sunday in March and back again at 3am on the last Sunday in October.

When telling the time, be aware that Dutch uses 'half' to indicate 'half before' the hour. If you say 'half eight' (8.30 in some dialects of English), a Dutch person will take this to mean 7.30.

TIPPING

Restaurant bills usually include a service charge and taxes, but a little extra is always welcome as tip. It could be something as simple as rounding up to the next euro – or up 10% (considered quite generous).

For porters, figure €1 per bag. Figure also €1 for taxi drivers unless it's a long trip (then add more). The standard for toilet attendants is €0.50.

TOURIST INFORMATION

Tourist information is supplied by the VVV's **Amsterdam Tourist Office** (Vereniging voor Vreemdelingenverkeer, Netherlands

Tourism Board; www.holland.com). Information is extensive, even if the offices can be quite busy. Note: most VVV publications cost money and there are commissions for services like hotel bookings (eg €2 to €3).

The **VVV information number** (☎ 0900-400 40 40; ☺ 9am-5pm Mon-Fri) costs €0.40 a minute; from abroad call ☎ 020-551 25 25 (no extra charge). Offices are inside **Centraal Station** (Map pp286–7; ☺ 8am-8pm Mon-Sat, 9am-5pm Sun) by platform 2; in front of **Centraal Station** (Map pp286–7; Stationsplein 10; ☺ 9am-5pm Mon-Fri); and just off **Leidseplein** (Map pp292–3; cnr Leidsestraat; ☺ 9.15am-5pm Sun-Thu, 9.15am-7pm Fri & Sat) as well as at the **Holland Tourist Information** (☺ 7am-10pm daily) at Schiphol airport.

Amsterdam's **Uitburo** (Map pp292–3; ☎ 0900-01 91, per minute €0.40; www .aub.nl in Dutch; cnr Leidseplein & Marnixstraat) can provide information on anything entertainment-related and sells tickets.

VISAS

Tourists from nearly 60 countries – including Australia, Canada, Israel, South Korea, New Zealand, Japan, Singapore, the USA and most of Europe – need only a valid passport to visit the Netherlands for up to three months. EU nationals can enter for three months with just their national identity card.

Nationals of most other countries need a so-called Schengen visa, valid within the EU member states (except the UK and Ireland), plus Norway and Iceland, for 90 days within a six-month period.

Schengen visas are issued by Dutch embassies or consulates and can take a while to process (up to two months). You'll need a passport that will remain valid until at least three months after your visit, and to be able to prove you have sufficient funds for your stay. Fees vary depending on your nationality – the embassy or consulate can tell you more.

Visa extensions are handled by the **Immigratie en Naturalisatiedienst** (Immigration & Naturalisation Service; ☎ 0900-123 45 61, per minute €0.10; www.ind.nl; Postbus 30125, 2500 GC Den Haag). Study visas must be

applied for via your college or university in the Netherlands. For working visas, see below. Also check www.lonelyplanet.com/ destinations/europe/netherlands for up-to-date visa information.

WOMEN TRAVELLERS

Equality has long been taken for granted, although far fewer women than men are employed full-time, and fewer still hold positions in senior management.

In terms of safety, Amsterdam is probably as secure as it gets in the major cities of Europe. There's little street harassment, even in the Red Light District, although it's best to walk with a friend to minimise unwelcome attention.

Rutgershuis Amsterdam (Map pp290–1; ☎ 616 62 22; Sarphatistraat 618; ☺ 9am-5pm Mon-Fri) is a clinic offering information and help with sexual problems and birth control, including morning-after pills.

WORK

Work permits must be applied for by your employer in the Netherlands; in general, the employer must prove that the position cannot be filled by someone from within the EU before offering it to a non-EU citizen. Nationals from many countries must apply for a Temporary Entry Permit (MVV or Machtiging tot Voorlopig Verblijf). Citizens of EU countries, Japan, Australia, Canada, Iceland, Monaco, New Zealand, Norway, Switzerland and the USA are exempt.

You'll need to apply for temporary residence before an employer can ask for your work permit. The process should take five weeks; contact the Dutch embassy or consulate in your home country.

In the Netherlands, residence permits are issued by the **Immigratie en Naturalisatiedienst** (☎ 0900-123 45 61, per minute €0.10; www.ind.nl; Postbus 30125, 2500 GC Den Haag). For details of work permits, contact the **CWI** (Employment Services Authority; ☎ 079-371 29 03; www.cwinet.nl; Box 195, 2700 AD Zoetermeer). The CWI also runs a bilingual **website** (www.werk.nl) with up-to-date job offers.

Language

Language

It's true – anyone can speak another language. Don't worry if you haven't studied languages before or that you studied a language at school for years and can't remember any of it. It doesn't even matter if you failed English grammar. After all, that's never affected your ability to speak English! And this is the key to picking up a language in another country. You just need to start speaking.

Learn a few key phrases before you go. Write them on pieces of paper and stick them on the fridge, by the bed or even on the computer – anywhere that you'll see them often.

You'll find that locals appreciate travellers trying their language, no matter how muddled you may think you sound. So don't just stand there, say something! If you want to learn more Dutch than we've included here, pick up a copy of Lonely Planet's user-friendly *Europe Phrasebook*, which also includes many of Europe's other languages.

SOCIAL
Meeting People
Hello.
Dag/Hallo.
Goodbye.
Dag.
Please.
Alstublieft/Alsjeblieft. (pol/inf)
Thank you.
Dank u/je (wel). (pol/inf)
Thank you very much.
Hartelijk bedankt.
Yes/No.
Ja/Nee.
Do you speak English?
Spreekt u/Spreek je Engels? (pol/inf)
Do you understand (me)?
Begrijpt u/Begrijp je (me)? (pol/inf)
Yes, I understand.
Ja, ik begrijp het.
No, I don't understand.
Nee, ik begrijp het niet.

Could you please ...?
Kunt u ... alstublieft?

repeat that	dat herhalen
speak more slowly	trager spreken
write it down	dat opschrijven

Going Out
What's on ...?
Wat is er ... te doen?

locally	hier
this weekend	dit weekend

today	vandaag
tonight	vanavond

Where are the ...?
Waar zijn de ...

clubs	(nacht)clubs
gay venues	gay clubs en cafés
places to eat	eetgelegenheden/ restaurants
pubs	cafés/kroegen

Is there a local entertainment guide?
Heeft u een plaatselijke uitgaansgids?

PRACTICAL
Question Words

Who?	Wie?
What?	Wat?
When?	Wanneer?
Where?	Waar?
How?	Hoe?

Numbers & Amounts

1	één
2	twee
3	drie
4	vier
5	vijf
6	zes
7	zeven
8	acht
9	negen
10	tien
11	elf

12	twaalf
13	dertien
14	veertien
15	vijftien
16	zestien
17	zeventien
18	achttien
19	negentien
20	twintig
21	eenentwintig
22	tweeëntwintig
30	dertig
40	veertig
50	vijftig
60	zestig
70	zeventig
80	tachtig
90	negentig
100	honderd
1000	duizend
2000	tweeduizend

Days

Monday	maandag
Tuesday	dinsdag
Wednesday	woensdag
Thursday	donderdag
Friday	vrijdag
Saturday	zaterdag
Sunday	zondag

Banking

I'd like to ...
Ik wil graag ...

cash a cheque	een cheque wisselen
change money	geld/cash wisselen
change some travellers cheques	(een paar) reischeques wisselen

Where's the nearest ...?
Waar is ...?

automatic teller machine	de dichtsbijzijnde geldautomaat
foreign exchange office	het dichtsbijzijnde wisselkantoor

Post

Where is the post office?
Waar is het postkantoor?

I want to send a ...
Ik wil een ... versturen.

fax	fax
parcel	pakket
postcard	briefkaart

I want to buy ...
Ik wil een ... kopen.

an aerogram	luchtpostblad/ aerogram
an envelope	envelop
a stamp	postzegel

Phone & Mobile Phones

I want to buy a phone card.
Ik wil een telefoonkaart kopen.

I want to make ...
Ik wil ...

a call (to ...)	telefoneren (naar ...)
reverse-charge/ collect call	voor rekening van de opgeroepene telefoneren

Where can I find a/an ...?
Waar vind ik een ...?
I'd like a/an ...
Ik wil graag een ...

adaptor plug	adaptor plug
charger for my phone	lader voor mijn telefoon
(rechargeable) battery for my phone	(herlaadbare) batterij voor mijn telefoon
mobile/cell phone for hire	GSM (telefoon) huren
prepaid mobile/ cell phone	voorafbetaalde GSM (telefoon)
SIM card for your network	SIM-kaart voor uw netwerk

Internet

Where's the local Internet café?
Waar is het plaatselijke internetcafé?

I'd like to ...
Ik wil graag ...

check my email	mijn email checken
get online	op het net gaan

Transport

What time does the ... leave?
Hoe laat vertrekt ...?

bus	de bus
ferry	de veerboot/ferry
train	de trein

What time's the ... bus?
Hoe laat is de ... bus?

first	eerste
last	laatste
next	volgende

Are you free? (taxi)
Bent u vrij?
Please put the meter on.
Gebruik de meter alstublieft.
How much is it to ...?
Hoeveel kost het naar ...?
Please take me to (this address).
Breng mij alstublieft naar (dit address).

FOOD

For more detailed information on food and dining out, see the Eating chapter, pp129-52.

breakfast	ontbijt
lunch	lunch/middageten
dinner	diner/avondeten
snack	snack
eat	eten
drink	drinken

Can you recommend a ...
Kunt u een ... aanbevelen? (pol)
Kan je een ... aanbevelen? (inf)

bar/pub	bar/café
café	café/koffiehuis
coffeeshop	koffieshop (note: a café where legal soft drugs are sold)
restaurant	restaurant

EMERGENCIES

It's an emergency!
Dit is een noodgeval!
Could you please help me/us?
Kunt u me/ons alstublieft helpen?
Call the police/a doctor/an ambulance!
Haal de politie/een dokter/een ziekenwagen!
Where's the police station?
Waar is het politiebureau?

HEALTH

Where's the nearest ...?
Waar is de dichtsbijzijnde ...?

chemist (night)	apotheek (met nacht-dienst)
doctor	dokter
hospital	ziekenhuis

I need a doctor (who speaks English).
Ik heb een dokter nodig (die Engels spreekt).

Symptoms

I have (a) ...
Ik heb ...

fever	koorts
headache	hoofdpijn
pain	pijn

GLOSSARY

amsterdammertje – phallic-shaped posts, about knee-high, lining streets of inner Amsterdam
apotheek – chemist/pharmacy
aub – abbreviation of *alstublieft* (please)

bibliotheek – library
bier – beer
boot – boat
bos – woods, forest
brood – bread
broodje – breadroll (with filling)
bruin café – brown café; traditional Dutch pub
burgwal – fortified embankment

café – pub, bar; also known as *kroeg*
coffeeshop (also spelt *koffieshop* in Dutch) – café authorised to sell cannabis
CS – Centraal Station

dagschotel – daily special in restaurants
drop – salted or sweet liquorice
dwarsstraat – street connecting two (former) canals

eetcafé – cafés serving meals

fiets – bicycle
fietsenstalling – secure bicycle storage
fietspad – bicycle path

gasthuis – hospice, hospital (old)
geen fietsen plaatsen – no bicycle parking
gemeente – municipal, municipality
genever – Dutch gin; also spelled *jenever*
gezellig – convivial, cosy
GG&GD – Municipal Medical & Health Service
gracht – canal
grachtengordel – canal belt
GVB – Gemeentevervoerbedrijf; Amsterdam municipal transport authority
GWK – Grenswisselkantoor; official currency exchanges

hal – hall, entrance hall
haven – port
hof – courtyard
hofje – almshouse or series of buildings around a small courtyard, such as the Begijnhof

jacht – yacht

kaas – cheese
kade – quay

kamer – room
kassa – cashier, check-out
kerk – church
koffiehuis – espresso bar (as distinct from a *coffeeshop*)
koningin – queen
koninklijk – royal
korfball – a cross between netball, volleyball and basketball
kunst – art

markt – town square
meer – lake
merguez – type of spicy sausage

NS – Nederlandse Spoorwegen; national railway company

openbare – public

paleis – palace
plage – beach
plein – square
polder – area of drained land
postbus – post office box

Randstad – literally 'rim-city'; the urban agglomeration including Amsterdam, Utrecht, Rotterdam and Den Haag
Rijk, het – State, the
rondvaart – boat tour

sneltram – light rail
spionnetje – outside mirror allowing a house occupant to see who's at the door downstairs

spoor – platform (in train station)
stadhouder – stadholder, or chief magistrate
stadhuis – town hall
stedelijk – civic, municipal
stichting – foundation, institute
straat – street
strand – beach
strippenkaart – stampable multi-use ticket used on public transport

toren – tower
tuin – garden
tulp – tulip

veer/veerboot – ferry
vis – fish
Vlaams – Flemish
VVV – tourist office

waag – old weigh house
wallen – Red Light District
wasserette/wassalon – laundrette
wielklem – wheel clamp attached to illegally parked vehicles
winkel – shop

zaal – hall
zee – sea
ziekenhuis – hospital

Behind the Scenes

THE LONELY PLANET STORY

The story begins with a classic travel adventure: Tony and Maureen Wheeler's 1972 journey across Europe and Asia to Australia. There was no useful information about the overland trail then, so Tony and Maureen published the first Lonely Planet guidebook to meet a growing need.

From a kitchen table, Lonely Planet has grown to become the largest independent travel publisher in the world, with offices in Melbourne (Australia), Oakland (USA) and London (UK). Today Lonely Planet guidebooks cover the globe. There is an ever-growing list of books and information in a variety of media. Some things haven't changed. The main aim is still to make it possible for adventurous travellers to get out there – to explore and better understand the world.

At Lonely Planet we believe travellers can make a positive contribution to the countries they visit – if they respect their host communities and spend their money wisely. Every year 5% of company profit is donated to charities around the world.

THIS BOOK

This 5th edition of Amsterdam was researched and written by Andrew Bender, who also wrote the previous (4th) edition. The 2nd and 3rd editions were written by Rob van Driesum and Nikki Hall. The 1st edition was written by Rob van Driesum. The guide was commissioned in Lonely Planet's London office and produced by the following:

Commissioning Editor Judith Bamber

Coordinating Editor Helen Koehne

Coordinating Cartographer Diana Duggan

Coordinating Layout Designer Laura Jane

Assisting Editors & Proofreaders Miriam Cannell, Nigel Chin, Simone Egger, Laura Gibb

Assisting Cartographers Hunor Csutoros, Kusnandar, Chris Thomas

Cover Designer Wendy Wright

Managing Cartographers Corinne Waddell, Mark Griffiths

Managing Editor Bruce Evans

Project Managers Glenn van der Knijff, Fabrice Rocher

Language Content Coordinator Quentin Frayne

Thanks to Glenn Beanland, Ryan Evans, Gerard Walker, Wayne Murphy, Sally Darmody, Celia Wood, Adriana Mammarella

Cover photographs: Row of parked bicycles, Helen King/APL/Corbis (top); Keukenhof Flower Gardens, Leiden, Roy Rainford/Getty (bottom); café culture of Amsterdam, Juliet Coombe/Lonely Planet Images (back).

Internal photographs by Lonely Planet Images and Richard Nebeský except for the following: 2 (#4), 17, 20, 24, 27, 41, 58, 65, 69, 75, 79, 87, 94, 99, 101 (#2, 4), 103 (#2, 3, 4), 104 (#2), 105 (#2, 4), 106 (#2, 3), 111, 118, 126, 137, 143, 145, 148, 155, 159, 171, 179, 184, 189, 194, 203 (#2, 3), 204 (#1, 2), 205 (#2, 4), 206 (#3), 207 (#2, 3, 4), 208 (#1, 4), 209 (#1, 2, 4), 219, 223, 224 Martin Moos; p11 Paul Beinssen; p100 (#1), p237 Thomas Winz; p100 (#3) Anthony Pidgeon; p101 (#4) Juliet Coombe; p102 (#2), p244 Chris Mellor; p102 (#4), p210 (#3), p233, p240 John Elk III; p104 (#1) Jon Davison; p104 (#4) Lou Jones; p105 (#1), p167 Christian Aslund; p204 (#4) Wayne Walton; p206 (#1) Amerens Hedwich; p207 (#1), p210 (#1) Zaw Min Yu; p210 (#4) Leanne Logan; p210 (#2) Rick Gerharter; p231 Adina Tovy Amsel. All images are the copyright of the photographers unless otherwise indicated. Many of the images in this guide are available for licensing from Lonely Planet Images: www.lonelyplanetimages.com.

THANKS
ANDREW BENDER

First thanks go to Constant Broeren, Els Wamsteeker and their colleagues at the Amsterdam Tourism & Convention Board, for their unflagging help and *gezelligheid*. Thanks also to Dirk Baalman and Thea Mollink, Suzanne Blonk, Camille Boyer, Valentino Borghesi, George Dean, Jennifer Dempsey, Dennis Edeler, Gary Feingold, Erik Kouwenhoven, Maarten Kloos, Nelson Lee, Todd Savage, Andrea Zanardi, anyone else who lavished me with more time and energy than I deserved, and the trusty, rusty Union bicycle.

In-house thanks go to Judith Bamber and Imogen Hall, Mark Griffiths for being open to new ideas, and Helen Koehne and Diana Duggan for their patience and good cheer.

OUR READERS

Many thanks to the hundreds of travellers who used the last edition and wrote to us with helpful hints, useful advice and interesting anecdotes:

Jaap Abrahams, Catherine Allnutt, Ivan Bartal, Kaitlin Beare, Natasha Cabrera, Robert Caden, Kim Cerrone, Matt

Colonell, Rita Colonell, Nathan Coombs, Anne Core, Susan Cross, Peter Dahlstrand, Martijn de Langen, Katrijn de Ronde, Steve Dougherty, Sam Durkin, Bronwyn Edwards, Sam Ehrenreich, Marco Estrafallaces, Paige Foltermann, Agnes Frank, Angel Gambrel, Sjoerd Gehring, Anne Goldgar, John Graven, Edward Haughney, Susan Herman, Robert Holmes, Peter Hopcroft, David Hopkinson, Lewis Hulatt, Nina Innocenti, Vero Isaia, Marco Jacobs, R Jacques, Eric Johnson, Minte Kamphuis, Jason Kaufman, Maureen Kelly, Kim King, Sven Lanser, Andrew Larcos, Carol Lawless, Morar Lucas, Antti Maattanen, Yve Macartney, Lis Maurer, Debra McBride, Kev McCready, Guillaume Morelli, Stephen Nau, Roisin Neylon, William Noble, Chris Noke, Lauren Norwood, Brian Perrett, Gemma Phillips, Tony & Jill Porco, Mark Quandt, Jonathan Rebholz, Kurt Rebry, Maurits Renes, Nancy Roberts, Jeffrey Ross, Danny Ruddock, Niels Sadler, Andrew Saunders, Valerie Schofield, Maureen Sheehan, Olga Sicars, Chantal Sire, Raymond Smith, Benny Snepvangers, Bonnie Spoales, Susen Sprenger, Michael Staff, Anouchka-Virginie Thouvenot, Ivan Valencic, Wouter van Weijden, Antonia Walckiers, Vera Wellner, E Wheale, Kylie Williamson, Andrea Willis, Alethea Wood

SEND US YOUR FEEDBACK

We love to hear from travellers – your comments keep us on our toes and help make our books better. Our well-travelled team reads every word on what you loved or loathed about this book. Although we cannot reply individually to postal submissions, we always guarantee that your feedback goes straight to the appropriate authors, in time for the next edition. Each person who sends us information is thanked in the next edition – and the most useful submissions are rewarded with a free book.

To send us your updates – and find out about Lonely Planet events, newsletters and travel news – visit our award-winning website: www.lonelyplanet.com /feedback.

Note: We may edit, reproduce and incorporate your comments in Lonely Planet products such as guide-books, websites and digital products, so let us know if you don't want your comments reproduced or your name acknowledged. For a copy of our privacy policy visit www.lonelyplanet.com/privacy.

Notes

Notes

Notes

Index

See also separate indexes for Eating (p278), Shopping (p279) and Sleeping (p280).

Index

Index

000 map pages
000 photographs

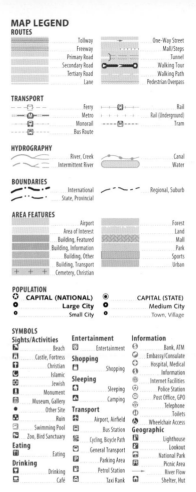

MAP LEGEND

ROUTES

Tollway
Freeway
Primary Road
Secondary Road
Tertiary Road
Lane
One-Way Street
Mall/Steps
Tunnel
Walking Tour
Walking Path
Pedestrian Overpass

TRANSPORT

Ferry
Metro
Monorail
Bus Route
Rail
Rail (Underground)
Tram

HYDROGRAPHY

River, Creek
Intermittent River
Canal
Water

BOUNDARIES

International
State, Provincial
Regional, Suburb

AREA FEATURES

Airport
Area of Interest
Building, Featured
Building, Information
Building, Other
Building, Transport
Cemetery, Christian
Forest
Land
Mall
Park
Sports
Urban

POPULATION

CAPITAL (NATIONAL)
Large City
Small City
CAPITAL (STATE)
Medium City
Town, Village

SYMBOLS

Sights/Activities
Beach
Castle, Fortress
Christian
Islamic
Jewish
Monument
Museum, Gallery
Other Site
Ruin
Swimming Pool
Zoo, Bird Sanctuary

Eating
Eating

Drinking
Drinking
Café

Entertainment
Entertainment

Shopping
Shopping

Sleeping
Sleeping
Camping

Transport
Airport, Airfield
Bus Station
Cycling, Bicycle Path
General Transport
Parking Area
Petrol Station
Taxi Rank

Information
Bank, ATM
Embassy/Consulate
Hospital, Medical
Information
Internet Facilities
Police Station
Post Office, GPO
Telephone
Toilets
Wheelchair Access

Geographic
Lighthouse
Lookout
National Park
Picnic Area
River Flow
Shelter, Hut

Maps

A B WESTPOORT C D

1

Enlargement 0 200 m
29
OUD WEST
39
1e Helmersstr
37 54
Vondelkerk 52
42 55 14 8
Overtoom 53 40
57
36 Vondelpark
48

Noordzeeweg

To Haarlem (18km)

Einsteinweg Nieuwe Hemweg

Isolatorweg

Spaarndammerstr 25

Transformatorweg 13 12

Basisweg

Station Sloterdijk

WESTERGASFABRIEK 38 Westerpark
50 46
SLOTERDIJK Volkstuinenpark
Sloterdijkermeer 31 Haarlemmerpoort 47

Haarlemmerweg Windmill
17 See Jordaan Map (p285)

2

Abraham Kuyperlaan
Eendrachtspark
Burgemeester de Vlugtlaan BOS EN LOMMER STAATSLIEDEN/FREDERIK
HENDRIKBUURT
GEUZENVELD De Vlugtlaan
Gerbrandy Park JORDAAN
SLOTERMEER Erasmuspark Jan van Galenstr Nassaukade
Burgemeester Roëllstr Rozengr
Jachthaven Sloterplas M Jan van Galenstr De Clercqstr
24 62 OUD WEST
Sloterpark DE BAARSJES 35 45
Sloterplas Hoofdweg OUD WEST
3
Sloterpark Rembrandtpark Kinkerstr See Southern
Canal Belt Map
President Allendelaan OVERTOOMSE VELD (pp292-3)

M Postjesweg See Enlargement

OSDORP SLOTERVAART Rembrandtpark Overtoom Vondelpark See Old South Map (p296)
Meer en Vaart Cornelis Lelylaan M Station Lelylaan 64 De Lairessestr OUD ZUID
4 Amstelveenseweg
OVERTOOMSE VELD Stadionweg
Einsteinweg Cornelis Krusemanstr Beatrixpark
Plesmanlaan M Aalsmeerweg NIEUW ZUID
Heemstedestraat Haarlemmermeer
63 Station
SLOTEN Johan Huizingalaan 20 65
Henk Sneevlietweg Stadionweg
BADHOEVEDORP Sportpark Amstelveenseweg
5 21 Parnassusweg
Nieuwe Haagseweg Ringweg-Zuid Station Zuid WTC
Oude Haagseweg 59
Amstelveenseweg 27 VU
Museum Tram Line A J Ernststr
To Haarlem (19km)
26 Van Nijenrodeweg
Het Nieuwe Meer BUITENVELDERT
NIEUWEMEER Van Boshuizenstr
To Leiden (45km);
Den Haag (55km) 4 Uilenstede
6 44 Amsterdamse Bos 15
Schiphol Airport 22 AMSTELVEEN

JORDAAN

0 ———— 200 m
0 ———— 0.1 miles

To Blender (250m)

JORDAAN

OUD WEST

See City Centre Map (pp286–7)
See Southern Canal Belt Map (pp292–3)

See Jordaan Map (p285)

A **B** **C** **D**

Oosterdokskade

🏠 54
🏛 28
🏛 46

1

🏛 27

Prins Hendrikkade

Oosterdok

Binnenkant

49
🏛 36
Nieuwe Jonkerstr
Oude Waal
Oude Schans

Korte Koningstr
● 20
Oude Schans

2

🏛 25
● 65

Dijksgracht

IJ-Tunnel

Naval Dockyards

🏛 23

Kattenburgergr

42

Oude Schans

Peperstr

Rapenburg

22, 42, 43

🏛 1

🏛 13
Nieuwe Uilenburgerstr
Uilenburgergracht

● 64
🏛 24

Kattenburgerstr

Kadijkspl
Nieuwe Vaart
🏛 33
🏛 38
Hoogte Kadijk

Oosterkerk

3

🏛 53
Jodenbreestr
🏛 35
44 🏛 12
● 66
21
37

Jodenbr Houttuinen

🏛 41

Valkenburgerstr
Anne Frankstr
Rapenburgerstr
Nieuwe Herengracht

Plantage Kade
Plantage Doklaan
6

🏛 39
🏛 11
Tussenkadijken
Laagte Kadijk
Binnenkadijk
Entrepotdok

Mätrozenhof
Buitenkadijken
Overhaalsgang

Entrepotdok
32 🏛

Mr Visserplein
30
🏛 26
15
Muiderstr
9, 14
Auschwitz
Monument
6

🏛 18
JD Meijerplein
M Waterlooplein

● 17

Wertheimpark
🏠 59
🏛 22
Plantage Parklaan
Plantage Middenlaan
61
58
PLANTAGE
Plantage Padlaan

Henri Polaklaan
🏛 31
45 🏛
40 🏛
19
47
🏛 16
🏛 3
60
56 🏛

🏠 34
Plantage Muidergr

P
● 5
🏛 6

Artis Zoo

Artis Zoo

7 🏛

Entrepotdok

4

Nieuwe Herengr
🏛 14
Nieuwe Herengr
Hortusplantsoen
Plantage Muidergr

Nieuwe Keizersgr
Plantage Kerklaan

Nieuwe Keizersgr

Weesperstr

Nieuwe Kerkstr

Manegestr
Nieuwe Prinsengr
Korte Lepelstr

Nieuwe Kerkstr
Roetersstr

Plantage Muidergracht
Westermanlaan
9, 14 ● 4
● 2

Plantage Badlaan
Plantage Lepellaan

Plantage Muidergr

Alexanderplein

5

Magere
Brug

Amstel

Lepelstr
Nieuwe Prinsengracht
Nieuwe Achtergr

Weesperstr

Universiteit van Amsterdam

Nieuwe Achtergr
Universiteit van Amsterdam

Valckenierstr
7, 10
Sarphatistr

Singelgracht

🏛 50

Amstelsluizen

Korte Amstelstr

Lepelstr

Voormalige Stadstimmertuin

Weesperplein

Kriterion
🏛 51
67
62

Roetersstr

Sarphatistr
7, 10
Spinozahof

Spinozastr

6

69

Pr. J Tulppl

🏛 55

Huddestr
Weesperstr
51, 53, 54
M Weesperplein

Spinozastr
Singelgracht

Rhijnspoorplein
Mauritskade

OOST

🏛 57

Sajetplein
M Zeldenruststr
's Gravesandestr

Oosterpark

0 ————————— 200 m
0 ————————— 0.1 miles

ZEEBURG

SIGHTS & ACTIVITIES	(pp57–116)
ARCAM	**1** C2
Artis Aquarium	**2** D5
Artis Geological Museum	**3** C4
Artis Library	**4** C4
Artis Planetarium	**5** C4
Artis Zoo Entrance	**6** C4
Artis Zoological Museum	**7** D4
Bierbrouwerij 't IJ	**8** F4
Dockworker Statue	**9** A4
EnergeticA	**10** E4
Entrepotdok	**11** C3
Garden Gym	**12** A3
Gassan Diamonds	**13** A3
Hermitage Amsterdam	**14** A4
Het Vrouwenhuis	**15** B4
Hollandsche Schouwburg	**16** C4
Hortus Botanicus	**17** B4
Joods Historisch Museum	**18** A4
Moederhuis	**19** C4
Montelbaanstoren	**20** A2
Mozes en Aäronkerk	**21** A3
Nationaal Vakbondsmuseum	**22** B4
Naval Officers' Residences	**23** C1
Nederlands Scheepvaartmuseum	**24** C2
NEMO	**25** C1
Portuguese-Israelite Synagogue	**26** A4
Scheepvaarthuis	**27** A1
Stedelijk Museum (Temporary Location)	**28** B1
Tropenmuseum	**29** E5
TunFun	**30** A4
Verzetsmuseum	**31** C4
Werfmuseum 't Kromhout	**32** D4

EATING 🍴	(pp129–52)
11	(see 28)
A Tavola	**33** C3
Abe Veneto	**34** C4
Albert Heijn Supermarket	**35** A3
Gall & Gall	(see 35)
Hemelse Modder	**36** A2
King Solomon	**37** A4
Koffiehuis van den Volksbond	**38** C3
Kromhout	**39** C3
La Rive	(see 55)
La Sala	**40** C4
Mediamatic Supermarket	**41** B3
Odessa	**42** H1
Panama	**43** G1
Pinto	**44** A3
Plancius	**45** C4
Sea Palace	**46** B1
Soeterijn Café-Restaurant	(see 52)
To Dine	(see 57)

DRINKING 🍷	(pp153–84)
Amstel Bar & Brasserie	(see 55)
Café Koosje	**47** C4
KHL	**48** H1

ENTERTAINMENT 🎭	(pp153–84)
Amsterdams Marionetten Theater	**49** A2
Koninklijk Theater Carré	**50** A6
Kriterion	**51** B5
To Night	(see 57)
Tropeninstituut Theater	**52** E5

SHOPPING 🛍	(pp185–210)
Blokker	**53** A3
Post Amsterdam	(see 28)

SLEEPING 🛏	(pp211–28)
Amstel Botel	**54** B1
Amstel Inter-Continental Hotel	**55** A6
Best Western Lancaster Hotel	**56** C4
Hotel Arena	**57** D6
Hotel Hortus	**58** B4
Hotel Parklane	**59** B4
Hotel Pension Kitty	**60** C4
Hotel Rembrandt	**61** B4
Liliane's Home	**62** B6
Lloyd Hotel	**63** H1

TRANSPORT	(pp248–52)
Canal Bus Stop	**64** C2
Canal Bus Stop	**65** C2
MacBike	**66** A3

INFORMATION	
Oppascentrale Kriterion	**67** B6
Rutgershuis Amsterdam	**68** E5
Schorer Foundation	**69** A6

See Jordaan Map (p285)

To Gary's Muffins (600m)

Kinkerstr

Elandsgr
3e Looiersdwarsstr
2e Looiersdwarsstr
Oude Looiersstr
Looiersgr
Looiersgracht
Circus Elleboog
Passeerdersgracht
Passeerdersstr
Nwe Passeerdersstr
Raamplein
Raamstr
Leidsekade
Leidsegracht
Leidsegr
De Genestetstr
3e Helmersstr
2e Helmersstr
Eerste Helmersstr
Nassaukade
Marnixstr
Overtoom
Stadhouderskade
Vondelstr
Tesselschadestr
Zandpad
Vondelpark
Roemer Visscherstr
Vossiusstr
Pieter Cornelisz Hooftstr
Van de Veldestr
Jan Luijkenstr
OUD ZUID
Paulus Potterstr
Huijgensstr
Willem Sandentodr
Van Baerlestr
Willemsparkweg
Museumplein
Honthorststr

Prinsengr
Runstr
Huidenstr
Herengr
Keizersgr
Wijde Heist
Heist
Old Lutheran Church
Beulingstr
Koningplein
Leidsegracht
Keizersgracht
Leidsestr
Molenpad
Leidsegr
Langbaamsgr
Leidsekruisstr
Lange Leidsedwarsstr
Leidseplein
Kleine Gartmanplantsoen
Hirschpassage
Max Euweplein
Weteringschans
Lijnbaansgr
Ziezeniskade
Nieuwe Spiegelstr
Spiegelgr
Keizersgr
Keizersgrachtkerk
Kerkstr
Prinsengr
Lange Leidsekruisstr
Derde Weteringdwarsstr
Stadhouderskade
Canal Bike
Weteringschans
Singelgracht
Boerenwetering
Frans Halsstr
Te Jacob Van Campenstr

Paleis van Justitie
Kleine Gartmanplantsoen
Max Euweplein
Canal Bike

SOUTHERN CANAL BELT (pp292–3)

OLD SOUTH

0 ——————————— 200 m
0 ——————————— 0.1 miles

DE PIJP

SIGHTS & ACTIVITIES (pp57–116)
Cooperatiehof.................................1 C3
Heineken Experience.........................2 A1
Henriëtte Ronnerplein.......................3 D4

EATING (pp129–52)
Albert Cuyp 67...............................4 A2
Albert Heijn Supermarket....................5 D2
Albert Heijn Supermarket, Gall & Gall..6 C1
Bagels & Beans..............................7 A1
Bakken met Passie...........................8 A2
Bakkerij Bart..............................(see 14)
Balti House.................................9 A2
Bazar Amsterdam............................10 C1
Café de Pijp...............................11 A1
Cambodja City..............................12 A2
De Soepwinkel..............................13 C1
Dirk van den Broek.........................14 B1
Gelateria Italiana Peppino.................15 C1
Mamouche...................................16 B1
Más Tapas..................................17 A1
Nieuw Albina...............................18 A2
Puyck......................................19 B2
Sal Meijer.................................20 A5
Turkiye....................................21 A1
Volendamer Vishandel......................(see 14)
Zagros.....................................22 A1
Zen..23 A1

DRINKING (pp153–84)
18 Twintig.................................24 A1
Bar Ça.....................................25 B1
Pilsvogel..................................26 B1
Sarphaat...................................27 C2
The Coffee Company.........................28 A1

ENTERTAINMENT (pp153–84)
De Badcuyp.................................29 C1
Rialto Cinema..............................30 B2

SHOPPING (pp185–210)
Albert Cuypmarkt...........................31 B1
De Emaillekeizer...........................32 C1
Van Moppes & Zoon..........................33 A2

SLEEPING (pp211–28)
Between Art & Kitsch.......................34 A1
Hotel Okura................................35 B4

INFORMATION
Clean Center Laundry.......................36 A1

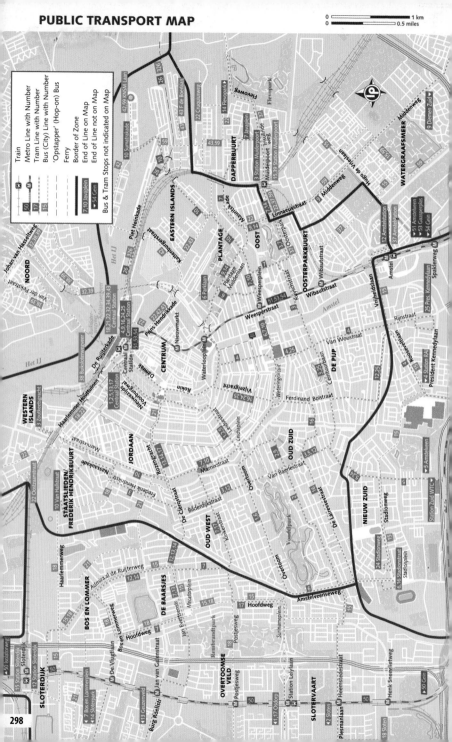

PUBLIC TRANSPORT MAP